RENEWALS 458-4574
DATE DUE

WITHDRAWN
UTSA Libraries

Tax Compliance and Tax Morale

Tax Compliance and Tax Morale

A Theoretical and Empirical Analysis

Benno Torgler

Associate Professor, School of Economics and Finance, Queensland University of Technology, Australia, Research Fellow, Center for Research in Economics, Management and the Arts (CREMA), Switzerland and Research Affiliate, CESifo Research Network, Munich, Germany

Edward Elgar

Cheltenham, UK • Northampton, MA, USA

© Benno Torgler 2007

All rights reserved. No part of this publication may be reproduced, stored in a retrieval system or transmitted in any form or by any means, electronic, mechanical or photocopying, recording, or otherwise without the prior permission of the publisher.

Published by
Edward Elgar Publishing Limited
Glensanda House
Montpellier Parade
Cheltenham
Glos GL50 1UA
UK

Edward Elgar Publishing, Inc.
William Pratt House
9 Dewey Court
Northampton
Massachusetts 01060
USA

Library
University of Texas
at San Antonio

A catalogue record for this book
is available from the British Library

Library of Congress Cataloguing in Publication Data

Torgler, Benno, 1972–
  Tax compliance and tax morale : a theoretical and empirical analysis / by Benno Torgler.
    p. cm.
  Includes bibliographical references and index.
  1. Taxpayer compliance—Cross-cultural studies. 2. Taxation—Public opinion—Cross-cultural studies. I. Title.
  HJ2305 T1624 2007
  336.2'91—dc22

2006037091

ISBN 978 1 84542 720 7

Printed and bound in Great Britain by MPG Books Ltd, Bodmin, Cornwall

Contents

Preface vi
Acknowledgements x

PART I BACKGROUND AND RESEARCH OVERVIEWS

1 Introduction 3
2 What do we know about tax morale and tax compliance? 64
3 Speaking to theorists and searching for facts: tax morale and tax compliance in experiments 85

PART II WHAT SHAPES TAX MORALE?

4 The importance of faith: tax morale and religiosity 113
5 Tax morale and institutions 152
6 Tax morale in Latin America 189
7 Does culture matter? A comparison of tax morale in the former East and West Germany 215

PART III TAX POLICY STRATEGIES

8 Moral suasion: an alternative tax policy strategy? Evidence from a controlled field experiment in Switzerland 239
9 Tax amnesties and political participation 264

Index 297

Preface

Taxation is an issue that has been relevant in the past 5000 years of human history and will continue to be relevant in the future. Tax compliance and tax morale are interesting topics, as they allow us to check the extent to which it makes sense to extend economics using aspects of other social sciences, such as, for example, social psychology or sociology. The literature is a good example of the fruitful interdisciplinary dialogue between the different social sciences. Furthermore, an attraction for a young scientist is the fact that that this topic allows to learn how to deal with different instruments such as surveys, experiments or even field experiments.

All of the chapters draw on some of the material contained in, or are thoroughly revised and updated versions of, my dissertation. Many people have contributed a great deal to this book. I would like to start the acknowledgements with two short stories that are connected with both dissertation advisors. Undecided about what to study at the University of Zurich, my brother Andreas, who at that time was just finishing his studies in business administration, said to me: 'I see you as a typical economics student. Take this book about economics to see whether you know what to do with it.' Interestingly, it was the book *Wirtschaft, Staat und Wohlfahrt* written by René L. Frey, which I started to read immediately and which attracted my attention and helped in my decision to study economics. Thus, René L. Frey influenced me many years before I became an assistant at his department. At that time, I never thought about the possibility of working with him in the future. I will never be able properly to express the thanks I owe him. He always enthusiastically supported and encouraged my work, reading and commenting on all first drafts of papers and reducing all possible research restrictions (e.g. buying data sets and statistical programs, paying submission fees, stressing the relevance of participating at international conferences and so on). I am deeply impressed by his ability always to see the major limitations and strengths of a paper. His comments significantly improved the quality of the original papers. Furthermore, I was strongly influenced by his philosophy to make papers 'understandable', avoiding complex structures that affect the readability, to see the relevance of an applied research focus, and to expose the research thoughts not only in academia but also to a broader audience. His friendly character helped to create an excellent working atmosphere in our department. Furthermore, he offered me the possibility of independently managing parts of *KYKLOS*, which I appreciated very much. His dedication as an academic teacher is impressive and I hope I will be able to follow his example.

One of the first lectures that I attended at the University of Zurich was given by Bruno S. Frey, and showed how the economic way of thinking and analysing can be fruitfully used to analyse social problems that go beyond the traditional topics of economics. As a consequence, from that day on there was often a divergence between those books and papers that I had to read in some classes, which were based on the traditional economic approach, and the ones that I preferred to read, which focused on the expansion of economics to other spheres, and on the reorientation of economics to include aspects of other social sciences. Bruno S. Frey has been an enormous source of inspiration. His work attitude as a researcher, over the years publishing continually in top journals and always having fascinating new ideas, is exemplary, and his dedication to helping young economists to become good researchers is remarkable. He always stimulated me and thus it is not surprising that many parts of this book have been strongly influenced by his research activities. He has supported my work since the beginning and his comments helped to increase the quality of the original papers now presented in this book.

A key figure in this book has been Doris Aebi. She went patiently through several chapters and her skilful editorial work and profound suggestions were invaluable. She has advanced to being an expert in tax compliance. I remember, for example, that three times she found a mistake in the interpretation of multiple regression results. Furthermore, it was a pleasure to work with her for *KYKLOS*, where we made a good team.

In addition, I would like to acknowledge the contribution of my working colleagues. The department was an extremely congenial and intellectually stimulating environment. It was an interesting experience to work together with Christoph A. Schaltegger. He is also co-author of one of the chapters that appear in this book. I especially admire his professionalism as an economist and look forward to co-operating with him on future projects.

Christoph Kilchenmann and Markus Gmünder always offered sound advice, also in situations when they had a lot of work to do. Their remarkable general knowledge was a great help and their kindness was the basis for enjoyable days in the office. People from other departments are also acknowledged. I would like to mention the analytical help from Oliver Serfling and Balthasar Freuler when searching for solutions regarding statistical problems.

Special thanks go to Markus Schaffner, who has done the experimental programming with z-Tree and has assisted all experiments. I will never forget his flexibility and efforts to implement my ideas in the programming of the experimental designs, as well as his spontaneous assent to accompanying me to Costa Rica to assist in the experiments.

I wish to express my gratitude to Edwin Alberto Chacón Villegas, Natalia Chacón Villegas, Alberto Pérez Vindas, Gabriela Pérez Vindas, Maria Isabel Pérez Vindas, Andreas Torgler, Ester Viviana Villegas Pérez, Jenny Patricia Villegas Pérez and Ramón Librado Villegas Brenes, who have helped to organize and to conduct some of the experiments in Costa Rica. Furthermore, thanks are due to Alberto Trejos (INCAE), Roderick Macgregor (INCAE) and Jesus Merino Serna (Universidad Fidélitas), who made it possible for me to conduct the laboratory experiments in Costa Rica; and to Alonso Arroyo, who gave me specific information about tax reforms in Costa Rica.

It is a pleasure to pay tribute to the indispensable and careful cooperation of the tax administration in Trimbach. I would like to mention Adolf Müller and Gary Bitterli, who offered me the opportunity to collect the data and assisted in the field experiment.

Several of the original papers have been presented at Frey–Frey seminars. I thank the participants, in particular Matthias Benz, Simon Lüchinger, Stephan Meier, Reto Jegen and Alois Stutzer, for their comments and suggestions. Chapters in this book have also been presented at the Summer School on Advanced Methods in the Social Sciences in Lugano (August–September 2001), the Public Choice Society and Economic Science Association Meetings in San Diego (March 2002), the European Public Choice Society Meeting in Belgirate (March 2002), the National Tax Association Conference in Orlando (November 2002), the Public Choice Society and Economic Science Association Meeting in Nashville (March, 2003, by Christoph A. Schaltegger) and the Annual Meeting of the Swiss Society of Economics and Statistics 2003 in Berne. I thank those participants who gave me their comments and suggestions.

For advice and suggestions offered in a specific paper thanks are due to James Alm, Magdalena Bunikowska, Mark Bühlmann, Eleanor D. Craig, Martin Daepp, Reiner Eichenberger, Lars P. Feld, Gebhard Kirchgässner, Bruno Jeitziner, Caroline Le Bourdonnec, Simon Lüchinger, Rudi Peters, Friedrich Schneider, William F. Shughart II and Alois Stutzer.

Also, I would like to thank the WWZ Forum. The funds I received from them made it possible for me to dedicate more time to completing the task when I was working on my dissertation. Furthermore, I would like to acknowledge the financial support of the Swiss National Science Foundation, which allowed me to finish the book during my stays at Yale

University and the University of California at Berkeley. I greatly benefited from these two extended and stimulating stays, and I am grateful to Susan Rose-Ackerman, Frances Rosenbluth and Bob Cooter for arranging and supporting my visits.

Thanks are due to several anonymous referees and journal editors who, with their critical comments, helped to improve the chapters and thus contributed to the quality of this book.

In addition, I would like to express to my gratitude and indebtedness to my wife, Manuela, for her support and understanding. She had the patience to prevent me from overemphasizing work in my life. Furthermore, I am deeply indebted to my mother Lisbeth Torgler and her partner André Sörensen for their enormous support, their valuable advice and their inspiring discussions. And last but not least, I want to acknowledge the contribution of my two daughters, Jessica and Vanessa. Both were sitting or sleeping next to me for many hours while I was working on the book.

Acknowledgements

Almost all of the chapters (except Chapter 1) draw on material contained in, or are thoroughly revised and updated versions of, articles published in various scientific journals. The last chapter is co-authored with Christoph A. Schaltegger. I am grateful for permission to use this material.

Chapter 2 draws on an article entitled 'What do we know about tax morale and tax compliance?' published in *RISEC: International Review of Economics and Business*, **48** (2001), 395–419, and used by permission of CEDAM.

Chapter 3 uses material contained in article entitled 'Speaking to theorists and searching for facts: tax morale and tax compliance in experiments', published in the *Journal of Economic Surveys*, **16** (2002), 657–84, and used by permission of Blackwell Publishing.

Chapter 4 is based on the paper 'The importance of faith: tax morale and religiosity' which appeared in the *Journal of Economic Behavior and Organization*, **61** (2006), 81–109, and is used by permission of Elsevier.

Chapter 5 is an extended version of the paper 'Tax morale and direct democracy', published in the *European Journal of Political Economy*, **21** (2005), 525–31, and is used by permission of Elsevier.

Chapter 6 draws on material contained in 'Tax morale in Latin America', which appeared in *Public Choice*, **122** (2005), 133–57, and is used by permission of Springer Netherlands.

Chapter 7 uses material contained in the article 'Does culture matter? tax morale in an East–West-German comparison', published in *FinanzArchiv*, **59** (2003), 504–28, and is used by permission of Mohr Siebeck.

Chapter 8 is based on a paper 'Moral suasion: an alternative tax policy strategy? Evidence from a controlled field experiment in Switzerland', published in *Economics of Governance*, **5** (2004), 235–53, and is used by permission of Springer Verlag.

Chapter 9 uses material contained in 'Tax amnesties and political participation', jointly written with Christoph A. Schaltegger and published in *Public Finance Review*, **33**, 403–31, and is used by permission of Sage Publications.

PART I
Background and research overviews

> Though tax records are generally looked upon as a nuisance, the day may come when historians will realize that tax records tell the real story behind civilized life. How people were taxed, who was taxed, and what was taxed tell more about a society than anything else (p. 21).
>
> Charles Adams (1994), *For Good and Evil: the Impact of Taxes on the Course of Civilization*, London: Madison Books.

1. Introduction

TAX MORALE

Today, just as in the past, taxation is an important issue, and it can be expected to remain important in the future. The first detailed information about taxation can be found in Ancient Egypt.[1] Countries were confronted with problems similar to those that we face today. For example, the pharaohs searched for ways to reduce corruption amongst their tax collectors (called *scribes*). The scribes were paid high salaries to reduce their incentive to enrich themselves by cheating taxpayers. Furthermore, scribes working in the field were controlled by a group of special scribes from the head office. Today, corruption of the tax agency is still a problem, especially in developing countries. The famous Rosetta Stone, inscribed around 200 BC during the reign of Ptolemy, did not only help to maintain the hieroglyphic knowledge, but it is also the first 'tax-oriented' documentation that reports a tax amnesty, in which tax rebels were released from prison, remitting them also the tax debts. The success of the tax amnesty increased the incentive to use this instrument as a regular medicine to check civil disorder (see Adams, 1994). Even today, there is still a huge political interest in tax amnesty programs all around the world. The pharaohs were also confronted with the question of how taxpayers should be treated. The tomb of Khiti describes a scene in which taxpayers were roughly treated by tax scribes – for example, being clubbed with evident ferocity (Adams, 1994, p. 8). However, Adams (1994) collected inscriptions showing that tax collectors were taught to be kindly: 'If a poor farmer is in arrears with his taxes, remit two-thirds of them' and 'cheer up everyone and put them in good humour', or 'if anyone is suffering under pressure of taxation or is at the end of his means, you must let the case go unchecked'. As we will see, questions about the effects of the tax administration's behaviour towards taxpayers have gained increasing attention in the present tax compliance literature.

However, despite their crucial importance in citizens' life, many issues had rarely been studied. This book is designed to bring new light into the tax compliance literature, focusing on tax morale. Why is it important to analyse tax morale? Why do people pay taxes? This question has gained increasing attention in the tax compliance literature in the past few years. It can be supposed that no one likes to pay taxes. One possibility is to 'enforce' people to pay their taxes following a deterrence policy. In line with the economics-of-crime approach based on the expected utility-maximization calculus, Allingham and Sandmo (1972) presented a formal model with the insight that the extent of tax evasion is negatively correlated with the probability of detection and the degree of punishment. However, this pathbreaking model has been criticized by many authors (see, e.g., Graetz and Wilde, 1985; Alm et al., 1992; Frey and Feld, 2002). A main point that is connected to the empirical and experimental findings is that these deterrence models predict too little compliance and far too much tax evasion. In many countries, the level of deterrence is too low to explain the high degree of tax compliance. Furthermore, there is a big gap between the amount of risk aversion that would grant such a compliance and the effectively reported degree of risk aversion. For the United States, the estimated Arrow–Pratt measure of risk aversion is between 1 and 2, but only a value of 30 would explain the observed compliance rate (see Graetz and Wilde, 1985; Alm et al., 1992). Similarly, in Switzerland the relative risk aversion varies between 1 and 2, but a value of 30.75 would be necessary to reach the observed level of tax compliance of 76.52 per cent (see Frey and Feld, 2002). Furthermore, tax compliance experiments mostly report a higher level of income declaration than the expected utility model would predict (for a survey, see Torgler, 2002). Elffers (2000) pointed out that 'the gloomy picture of massive tax evasion is a phantom' (p. 185). Pyle (1991) criticized the assumption that individuals are amoral utility maximizers: 'Casual observation suggests that not all individuals think quite like that. Indeed, it seems that whilst the odds are heavily in favour of evaders getting away with it, the vast majority of taxpayers behave honestly' (p. 173).

To resolve this puzzle of tax compliance, many researchers have argued that tax morale, seen as the intrinsic motivation to pay taxes, can help to explain the high degree of tax compliance (see, e.g., Schwartz and Orleans, 1967; Lewis, 1982; Roth et al., 1989; Alm et al., 1992, 1999; Pommerehne et al., 1994; Frey, 1997, 2003; Frey and Feld, 2002; Feld and Tyran, 2002: for a survey, see also Frey and Torgler, 2002).

The first important findings in the tax morale literature date from the 1960s and 1970s by German scholars centred around Günter Schmölders (1951/1952, 1960, 1962, 1970a, b) known as the 'Cologne school of tax psychology'. They emphasized that economic phenomena should not only be analysed from the traditional point of view. They saw tax morale as an attitude regarding tax (non-) compliance (see, e.g., Schmölders, 1960). In their surveys, they used the subjective tax burden as an indicator of the level of tax morale and found that self-employed people had a lower tax morale than employees. Strümpel (1969), for example, analysed tax morale and the tax systems on the basis of an international comparative survey in Europe. He points out that treating taxpayers with great caution helps to cultivate tax morale and reduce tax compliance costs.

In the 1990s, aspects of tax morale increasingly attracted attention. Why so many people pay their taxes although fines and the probability of an audit are low has become a central question in the tax compliance literature. Erard and Feinstein (1994) stressed the relevance of integrating moral sentiments into the models to provide a reasonable explanation of actual compliance behaviour. And Andreoni et al. (1998) pointed out that 'adding moral and social dynamics to models of tax compliance is as yet a largely undeveloped area of research' (p. 852).

Many researchers have stressed that a considerable proportion of taxpayers are always honest. Some taxpayers are 'simply predisposed not to evade' (Long and Swingen, 1991, p. 130) and thus do not even search for ways to cheat on taxes (see Frey, 1999). Furthermore, Elffers (2000) has pointed out that not everyone with 'an inclination to dodge his taxes is able to translate his intention into action' (p. 187). Many individuals do not have the opportunity or the knowledge and resources to evade.

Weck (1983) found, in an empirical analysis, that there is a negative correlation between tax morale and the size of the shadow economy. Compared to other variables, tax morale had the most significant impact on the size of the shadow economy. However, in such an analysis, tax morale is treated as an exogenous residual. One of the main purposes of this book is to identify which factors have an impact on tax morale.

The analysis of tax morale as a dependent variable is rather novel in the tax compliance literature. Recently, Orviska and Hudson (2002) found, with the British Social Attitudes Survey, that law abidance has a positive effect on tax morale.

METHODOLOGY

Similar to Leijonhufvud's (1973) classic paper 'Life among the Econ', we observe the tendency that, from a methodological point of view, economists behave like two isolated tribes. The intention of this book is to use a broad variety of different methodological instruments to analyse tax morale and tax compliance, as each instrument has advantages and shortcomings. Dependent on the research question, the adequate instrument of analysis has been taken into account. Thus, this book tries to bridge the gap between the two methodologies or research communities, working either with surveys or experiments, and each criticizing the other 'tribe'. Starmer (1999), for example, focusing on the enthusiasm and the scepticism regarding experiments, points out 'One might be forgiven for wondering whether these writers are talking about the same discipline!' (p. 2).

Robustness can also be analysed using different methodologies for the same question. If both instruments show the same tendencies we can suppose that the results are quite robust.

Surveys

The most frequently used instrument in this book is the survey. One reason is that there is a lack of empirical evidence in the analysis of tax morale. New survey data sources allow us to measure tax morale as a dependent variable and to search for factors that shape tax morale. Thus, this part of the investigation offers a novel perspective in the tax compliance literature. First of all, in the next two subsections the advantages and disadvantages of surveys are treated before the way tax morale has been measured is introduced and information is given about the econometric estimation methods.

Advantages
Surveys provide a good source of information about tax morale. A main advantage is that they include many socio-economic, demographic and attitudinal variables. This helps us to investigate and test a rich set of (new) theories on tax morale. In a multivariate analysis, what shapes tax morale can be analysed. Furthermore, surveys help us to compare different countries and to gain insights into the development of tax morale over time. In recent years, economists have increasingly focused on surveys (see, for example, the happiness research done by Frey and Stutzer, 2002). One reason might be that survey research uses more sophisticated statistical techniques and designs compared to earlier times. Jackson and Milliron (1986) point out that compliance variables appear to be highly correlated, which makes multivariate rather than univariate testing appropriate.

Disadvantages and problems
A critical aspect of surveys is the fact that studies can be biased if they do not cover a representative share of the population. A high response rate is therefore essential. We will work with well-known data sets such as the *World Values Survey, the International Social Survey Programme* (ISSP) and the *Latinobarómetro*, which cover many countries and are conducted on a regular basis. These surveys pay especial attention to the representativeness of the data set. The sensitive nature of compliance information might create an incentive not to participate in such a survey. To reduce this problem, this book focuses on data sets that cover a broad variety of questions on different topics. Furthermore, as we will see, the way in which we define

tax morale is less sensitive compared to a question asking whether or not a person has evaded taxes. Thus, it can be supposed that we observe a higher degree of honesty in the answers to these questions.

Measurement of tax morale and data sources

Many empirical studies have used data from the Taxpayer Compliance Measurement Program (TCMP) (see, e.g., Clotfelter, 1983; Witte and Woodbury, 1985; Dubin and Wilde, 1988). The TCMP is a program of audits conducted on a stratified random sample of returns (the last one in 1988). Forty per cent of US households underpaid their taxes in 1988, 53 per cent paid correctly and 7 per cent overpaid. The main advantage of this data is the possibility to estimate the impact of policy parameters such as, for example, audit rates, penalty rates and marginal tax rates upon measures of tax evasion. However, although the TCMP seems to be among the best data sources, the data have some deficiencies: for instance, tax administrations cannot detect all of the under-reported income, as tax evaders are often not caught. Furthermore, there is the difficulty of separating 'honest' errors and intentional errors (see Alm, 1991). Finally, the TCMP is based on data from the United States and has a lack of socio-economic variables. It might be important to analyse European data empirically to get a broader picture. Compared to TCMP data, surveys of taxpayers' attitudes have the advantage that they include many socio-economic, demographic and attitudinal variables that are not available in tax return and audit data. In general, empirical evidence is rare in the tax compliance literature. Pyle (1993) points out in a survey that 'The solution should lie in the results of empirical studies. Alas, the current harvest of such studies is remarkably thin' (p. 73). Similarly, Andreoni et al. (1998) stress that 'Although many empirical studies of noncompliance have been conducted during the past decade, we believe that the empirical literature is still in its youth, with many of the most important behavioural hypotheses and policy questions yet to be adequately investigated' (pp. 835–6).

In general, evidence on tax compliance and tax morale in countries outside the United States is rare. Little is therefore known about general tendencies of tax compliance in Europe, Asia or Latin America. One of the aims of this book is to fill this gap, working with different kinds of data sets.

We will work intensively with the World Values Survey (WVS). It is a worldwide investigation of sociocultural and political change, which collects comparative data on values and belief systems among people around the world. WVS builds on the European Values Surveys, first carried out in 1981–1984. A second wave of surveys was completed in 1990–1993, a third one in 1995–1997 and a fourth has been done jointly by the EVS and WVS groups, in 1999–2001. We will analyse the first three waves. This huge data set permits cross-country comparison of people's tax morale in more than 40 societies around the world, representing about 70 per cent of the world population, and is based on representative national samples. Thus, the WVS has the advantage of covering a wide variety of religious and cultural traditions and helps to analyse value changes over time. The WVS has been broadly used by political scientists (see, e.g., Inglehart, 1997, 2000), and also economists such as, for example, Knack and Keefer (1997), Slemrod (2002) and Torgler (2003a) have started to analyse the WVS data.[2]

To assess the level of tax morale in the WVS, we use the following question throughout the whole book:

> Please tell me for the following statement whether you think it can always be justified, never be justified, or something in between: ... 'Cheating on tax if you have the chance'. The question leads to a ten-scale index of tax morale with the two extreme points 'never justified' and 'always justified'.

The ten-point scale has been recoded into a four-point scale (0, 1, 2, 3), with the value 3 standing for 'never justifiable'. Values 4–10 have been integrated into value 0 due to a lack of variance.

A second important data set in this work is the Latinobarómetro. It is an annual public opinion survey carried out in 17 Latin American countries (since 1996). It reports the opinions, attitudes and behaviours of the roughly 400 million inhabitants of the region. The survey started with eight countries in 1995 and was extended to 17 countries in 1996. It covers most of Latin America, with the exception of Cuba, the Dominican Republic and Puerto Rico. This data set is not as well known as the WVS. However, economists have also recently discovered this data source (see, e.g., Graham and Pettinato, 2002, who contributed to happiness research). We will analyse the 1998 Latinobarómetro, which considered tax morale and tax evasion questions. This data set has integrated a similar question that allows us to measure tax morale:

> On a scale of 1 to 10, where 1 means not at all justifiable and 10 means totally justifiable, how justifiable do you believe it is to: A taxpayer does not report all of his or her income in order to pay less income taxes?

To compare both data sets (WVS and Latinobarómetro), tax morale has been coded as previously (3 = highest tax morale, 0 = lowest tax morale). Furthermore, the Latinobarómetro has the advantage of covering additional tax compliance questions. Tax avoidance and tax evasion are often not distinguished in economic studies. We have the possibility of analysing both components. Whereas the World Values Survey focuses on evasion, the Latinobarómetro takes tax avoidance into account. Tax evasion might produce higher moral costs than tax avoidance, as the latter is more broadly accepted being a rather legal strategy to escape from tax payments.

In one chapter, we will work with the International Social Survey Programme (ISSP). Similar to the previous data sets, it is a continuing annual program of cross-national collaboration. It started in 1983 and has grown to cover more than 30 nations (mostly European countries). We will analyse the data set RELIGION II (ISSP 1998). The following question was asked:

> Do you feel it is wrong or not wrong if a taxpayer does not report all of his or her income in order to pay less income taxes? (1 = not wrong, 2 = a bit wrong, 3 = wrong, 4 = seriously wrong).

These three data sets have the advantage that they are designed as a wide-ranging survey, which reduces the probability of being suspicious and of creating framing effects by other tax context questions.

The way in which tax morale is measured in this book is not free of bias. It can be argued that a taxpayer who has taken part in some illegal behaviour in the past will tend to excuse this kind of behaviour, declaring a high tax morale. However, our results indicate that in general there is a negative correlation between the degree of tax morale and the size of that shadow economy. Moreover, our results in Switzerland are in line with those of other studies that use the degree of tax evasion as a dependent variable. Certainly, it is possible to develop a tax morale variable using more than a single question to capture taxpayers' willingness to pay taxes, and thus increasing the reliability and validity of a variable. On the other hand, it might be important to focus on a specific tax compliance question to constitute a reliable measure of tax morale. Using a single question also has the advantage that problems associated with the construction of an index, such as complexity, especially regarding the measurement procedure or a low correlation between the items, can be reduced. However, in cross-cultural comparisons, single-item measures should be treated with some caution. In countries where tax revenues are collected to finance a dictator's war machine, for example, tax evasion might be justifiable. There could even be a moral duty not to pay taxes. Similarly, in authoritarian political systems people will search for 'voice' or 'exit' mechanisms such as, for example, tax resistance to express their preferences (see Torgler, 2001).

Econometric estimation methods

In the analysis of partial correlations, we will use weighted ordered probit models. We have used *weighted* ordered probit estimations to correct the samples and thus to get a reflection of the national distribution. In the estimations where we have pooled several countries, we have integrated an additional weighting variable. To get an equal number of weighted observations (around 1500) for each survey, the original weight variable was multiplied by a constant for each country.

The ordered probit models are relevant in such an analysis insofar as they help to analyse the ranking information of the scaled dependent variable tax morale. However, as in the ordered probit estimation, the equation has a non-linear form, and only the sign of the coefficient can be directly interpreted and not its size. Calculation of the marginal effects is therefore a method for finding the quantitative effect that a variable has on tax morale (see, e.g., Frey and Stutzer, 2002). The marginal effect indicates the change in the share of taxpayers (or the probability of) belonging to a specific tax morale level, when the independent variable increases by one unit. In all survey evaluations, the marginal effects are presented only for the highest tax morale value. To check the robustness of the results, in some estimations weighted least-squares models are presented, using tax morale as a cardinal variable. Furthermore, it should be noted that answers such as 'don't know' and missing values have been eliminated in all estimations.

In general, to avoid bias and inconsistency we are not going to knock out variables that are not statistically significant (see McCloskey and Ziliak, 1996). Furthermore, much weight has been given to doing sensitivity tests; for example, trying to evaluate whether the main variables are fragile, and making minor changes to the number of variables, in order to see whether the main variables change and thus the conclusions would alter fundamentally.

Experiments

During the past 20 years, economists have increasingly used experiments to analyse various topics (for a survey, see, e.g., Roth, 1995). Before this period, it could be argued that economics was a non-experimental science. Now, experimental papers have been published in the leading international economic journals. The recent Nobel Prize award to Vernon Smith indicates that experiments are an important instrument in economics and have acquired a significant degree of recognition and legitimation. The experiments that are going to be presented in this book are interactive, considering the problem of public goods. The general design of all experiments was that the taxes paid were multiplied by a factor and then redistributed in equal shares to the members, independent of how much tax someone had paid.

Advantages

Measuring tax evasion and tax compliance involves some problems. It is difficult to obtain information about tax compliance behaviour. Even if data about tax evaders could be obtained, tax evaders' behaviour could be affected by specific circumstances, which are difficult to control. An experimental approach circumvents the problem of getting honest answers on illegal behaviour. Researchers can use their own data obtained from experiments. The strength of this approach is the possibility of controlling for and manipulating the variables of interest. This allows us to reduce causality problems and thus gives good information not only about the relationship between two variables but also about the direction of the effect. Fehr et al. (2003) point out that 'The exogenous variation of variables in controlled environments is the only truly reliable way to make causal inferences' (p. 1).

In general, the experiments carried out in this book intend to replicate the structure of voluntary income reporting. Subjects receive income and pay taxes on the reported income. The tax administration is simulated by defining, for example, the probability of audit and the tax penalty on tax evasion. As we hold tax administration parameters constant, we check the relevance of other parameters such as tax amnesties, or voting on tax compliance.

Disadvantages
The laboratory experiment has been criticized as a method that lacks realism. Choices in the laboratory may not accurately reflect the choices in the 'outside world', as the setting is too artificial. In our experiments, we tried to increase their external validity by making them more realistic. Important factors in the tax compliance experiments, such as audit probability, fine rate, tax rate and so on, have been adapted to real values. Furthermore, implementing *incentives* as money might further realism, increasing subjects' motivation to act in a realistic manner. However, it is still difficult to find out how big incentives have to be. We worked with pay-off levels that were common in the newest tax compliance experiments published in leading journals such as, for example, the *American Economic Review* or the *Journal of Public Economics*.

An experiment should not replicate a real-world decision setting in every detail, but it should create an appropriate abstract setting that isolates the key elements. Certainly, it is still questionable whether the design of the experiment provides appropriate abstraction, but if a simplified experiment driven by theory fails to predict the theory, then it is also questionable whether a more complex environment can predict more (see Wilde, 1980).

One problem cannot be solved completely using experiments. Heavy punishments, such as jail, cannot possibly be implemented in tax compliance games. The absence of social pressures could inhibit the same psychological processes, which are important in the real world. However, recent experiments aim to capture social stigma as a factor (see, e.g., Bosco and Mittone, 1997).

Furthermore, an experimenter effect might be observable that reduces the validity of the experiment, influencing participants' views of what to do or creating an incentive to outwit the experimenter, seeing the whole situation as a 'gamelike' atmosphere (see, e.g., Cross, 1980; Starmer, 1999). To reduce such a problem, we have designed experiments where subjects have been randomly allocated to either an experimental group or a control group. This allows us to single out the treatment effect. Thus, we analyse whether a behaviour varies, making *one* systematic change in the design of the experiment. It can then be assumed that changes in the behaviour are due to changes in the experimental conditions (Starmer, 1999). Furthermore, we have avoided instructing the participants to maximize their net income, as done in earlier studies (see, e.g., Friedland et al., 1978).

Many tax compliance games are done with students as participants. Do students have enough experience of filling in tax forms? Are students a satisfactory sample for studies of tax behaviour? It can be argued that students are not useless, but that the results should be interpreted carefully (see Webley et al., 1991). They correspond to a subject pool with a higher education and a higher IQ than an average citizen. They often come from families with a higher income than the average and their age ranges are limited (Fehr et al., 2003). However, there is evidence that students' responses are no different from those of other subjects in tax compliance experiments (see, e.g., Baldry, 1987).[3] Alm (1998) states that 'There is also no reason to believe that the cognitive processes of students are different from those of "real" people' (p. 43). On the other hand, Gërxhani and Schram (2001), in their cross-country experiments in the Netherlands and Albania, have shown the importance of subject pools. Thus, there isn't much that speaks against conducting the experiments with a broader population set. Certainly, the big advantage of working with students is their ability easily to understand abstract problems and experimental conditions. Working with the broader subject pool, it is important that the experiments are not too long or complicated. The instructions should be understandable; otherwise, strong biases could make the experiments useless. In all experiments, we paid attention to whether the subjects had understood the design well enough. In our laboratory experiments, three rounds were conducted before starting the main evaluations.

The experiments covered several periods. This should take into account the fact that real-world behaviour may be, contrary to experiments, a product of learning and adapting (see Starmer, 1999). Allowing subjects sufficient time in the experiments gives them the possibility of developing an analogous mechanism. Furthermore, we gave them the opportunity to adjust their behaviour in each round. Feedback was generated and circulated before each decision. Subjects were informed in each round on the audit probability, the penalty, the accumulated income (fortune) and the individual tax redistribution.

Certainly, experiments in the social sciences will never have the robustness of experiments done using physical objects. Human subjects are less predictable and the system that they interact with is much more open and variable. They might react more sensitively to the rules defined or to the context of an experiment in general. Thus, it is important to replicate the experiments to check the robustness of the results. Fehr et al. (2003) argue as follows:

> If somebody believes that an important factor has been left unspecified or uncontrolled, or that this factor could not play a role in the experiment although in the external world it is likely to play a role, it is often possible to change the experimental conditions such that the factor that had initially been left out can now play a role (p. 1).

Similarly Starmer (1999) points out the following:

> For example if the hypothesis is that 'the free-rider theory failed because the incentives were too small', then run a new experiment with bigger incentives. If it is suspected that communication between subjects enabled them to 'beat' the free-rider problem, design a new experiment which makes communication more difficult (p. 12).

Thus, the tax compliance literature can profit from experiments if researchers try to check the robustness of the design. In general, such a research procedure can be seen as a learning process: the more experiments are conducted, the clearer is the obtained picture to be explained. You will never see the picture absolutely clearly – or, in other words, you will never have the possibility of completing the jigsaw – but the more pieces you have, the better you can identify some tendencies.

Econometric estimation methods and experimental designs
Contrary to many experimental evaluations in the literature, in most cases we will use models that allow us to evaluate temporal dynamic processes. This is important, as longitudinal data are available from experiments of 25 rounds. We use, for example, Tobit maximum likelihood estimations, as the compliance rate varies between 0 and 1 and there were many observations with the values 0 and 1. To consider the panel structure of the data, we include a random-effect function. The experiments were accompanied by a post-experiment questionnaire. For many years, experimentalists have

ignored combining surveys with experiments. Certainly, the questionnaires should be designed so that questions with a strong relation to the previous experiment should be avoided, because of possible biases. But nothing speaks against the use of surveys that allow us to develop control variables such as gender, marital status, age, education and so on if not all of the participants were students. Interestingly, researchers such as Fehr et al. (2003), who did not combine surveys with experiments for many years, have now started to work with both instruments.

All of the laboratory experiments had some similar structural elements. The experiments were conducted on computers programmed with z-Tree (*Zurich Toolbox for Readymade Economic Experiments*; Fischbacher, 1998). The experimental software was quite interactive. Subjects were informed in each round about the audit probability, penalties, the accumulated income (fortune) and the individual tax redistribution. The use of a computer allowed for minimal experimenter–subject interaction during experimental sessions, which reduced possible framing effects. Furthermore, a computer system facilitates the accounting process (income distribution, tax redistribution and the accumulation of the income). Subjects were informed that their performance in the practice periods did not affect their payments. They were told that all the accumulated earnings during the experiment would be redeemed for cash at the end of the experiment at a fixed conversion rate. The only 'veil of uncertainty' was on the number of rounds. This helps to prevent strategic behaviour in the final round. All of the fiscal parameters, such as the tax rate, the fine rate and the probability of detection, were known.

As people were well informed about the different tax parameters, they were confronted with a tax-context language. We used tax terms such as income to declare, tax rate, audit probability and fine rate, to integrate contextual factors that are important in determining tax reporting behaviour. This helps the experiment to be perceived as more than a mere gamble.

Many tax compliance experiments assume that tax agencies randomly select tax returns for audit and do not use information from the returns to determine audits. Contrary to such experiments, we introduced an endogenous audit selection rule in our experiment. Thus, the probability of audit is endogenous, depending on the behaviour of the taxpayers. Subjects were told that they faced a 5 per cent random probability of audit in each period. If a subject was audited and found to be evading taxes, then the previous four periods were controlled. All the unpaid taxes plus a penalty on unpaid taxes of the same amount (fine rate = 2) had to be paid. If the audited subject had reported all income, the previous periods were not examined. Furthermore, in all experiments the audit probability increased from 5 per cent to 10 per cent depending on the amount of non-declared income between this year and last year's declaration. In such an experimental design the probability of audit is endogenous, depending on the behaviour of the taxpayers throughout the experiment.

For this book, cross-cultural experiments were conducted in Switzerland and Costa Rica. We paid attention to reducing the problems that arise in conducting a cross-cultural experiment (see Roth, 1995, pp. 282–4). Experiments were carried out with the same experimenters, to eliminate possible variations arising from uncontrolled procedural differences or uncontrolled personal differences between the experimenters. All instructions were presented in the same language (English) in both countries, because otherwise systematic differences between countries might arise due to the way in which the instructions were translated. Furthermore, payments given to the subjects are adapted to the situation in the country. The sum paid in the experiment was calculated in relation to the price of cross-cultural homogenous goods (Coca Cola, a hamburger (Big Mac) and the price of a cinema ticket). Thus, differences in the degree of compliance are not caused by differences related to the experimental payments.

Field Experiments

Advantages

The use of controlled field experiments has many advantages. Compared to laboratory experiments, one of the main advantages is the implementation of tax authorities rather than experimenters, which evokes real processes in the normal environment outside the laboratory setting. It helps better to test the effects of different instruments on taxpayers in the real situation of 'filling out the tax form' and 'paying the taxes'. This helps to formulate practical advice on tax policy, based on scientific testing. Certainly, compared to laboratory experiments, this kind of experiment allows social and economic interactions and is thus less controlled, but causality can be better determined than in non-experimental studies (for the advantages and problems of randomized field trials, see Burtless, 1995).

There is no observable experimental effect, as subjects are completely unaware of having taken part in the field experiment. The experiments are thus conducted in the normal environment, where social and economic interactions occur (see Burtless, 1995). This has the advantage that the subject pool is more representative than in laboratory experiments.

I had the possibility of working together with a local tax administration in Switzerland and thus of generating data that are rarely available to researchers. The study is presented in Chapter 8. Individuals were randomly assigned, to avoid systematic correlation between treatment status and (un)observed characteristics of participants (Burtless, 1995). Field experiments in tax compliance allow us to test specific policy alternatives such as, for example, the effects of a higher perceived audit probability or the effects of moral suasion on tax compliance. Thus, the results have a strong policy implication and might be relevant for policymakers. However, it is surprising that we hardly find any field experiments in the tax compliance literature. Higher transaction costs in organizing co-operation between the tax administration and the researchers, compared to laboratory experiments, and the sensitivity of the tax filling data might be reasons why field experiments are less frequently used.

Disadvantages
Field experiments consume a great deal of real resources. First, co-operation between the tax authorities must be established. It is difficult to develop and implement a treatment, as it has to be approved by the tax administration and other government authorities. Thus, it can be supposed that sensitive or unorthodox treatments cannot be developed. Second, compared to laboratory experiments, such experiments are costly in terms of time. The experiment has to be prepared before individuals receive their tax forms. It takes almost a year until all tax forms are returned to the tax administration and are thus ready to evaluate. Thus, field experiments are limited in duration. While experiments can analyse intertemporal aspects, field experiments are mostly conducted once. For some questions it might be interesting to analyse to what extent a policy instrument works over time. A short-duration intervention might have an immediate effect, but the long-term effects are unknown. Furthermore, questions concerning what would happen if a policy instrument such as, for example, moral suasion were used regularly remain unanswered.

Econometric estimation method
First, we will check whether there is a significant difference between the control group and the treatment group. We will use an independent-samples t-test to compare the mean values for the reference and the treatment group in the year 2001. However, the findings of the paired sample t-statistics alone cannot determine whether there is a significant treatment effect. To get a real picture of the extent to which such behaviour is the consequence of a treatment effect, a control and treatment group are compared with values from the previous years. As assignments to treatment and control groups have been made at random, one can simply compare the change in compliance across the treatment and control groups to estimate the treatment effect. To calculate the difference-in-differences, we also take

the averages of two time periods before the experiment. We are also going to include a multivariate analysis using one of the compliance variables as the dependent variable. A dummy variable 'MORAL SUASION' has been constructed to compare the control group with the treatment group.

OVERVIEW

Part I: Background and Research Overviews

Part I, which covers three chapters, aims to set the stage, not only giving an overview of the actual research status in the tax compliance literature, but also looking at possible shortcomings and open questions.

Chapter 2, entitled 'What do we know about tax morale and tax compliance?', discusses three key factors that seem to be important for understanding tax morale: moral rules and sentiments, fairness, and the relationship between taxpayer and government. These three key elements in this survey will be important determinants in the empirical part of this book. The first part focuses on social norms and discusses the four sentiments guilt, shame, duty and fear. A false declaration will generate anxiety, guilt or, if caught, shame, and will thus prejudice the taxpayer's self-image. It is assumed that a taxpayer feels these moral costs, which act as a restriction of the possibility set. On the other hand, if someone believes that the tax system is unfair – for example, that the tax burden is too high – the moral costs to behave honestly decrease and tax evasion can be seen as a sort of self-defence. The analysis of social norms in general will be one of the most demanding challenges in the future research agenda. One of the main shortcomings is the limited amount of empirical evidence.

The shared conviction of how people ought to behave is part of a society's social norms (see, e.g., Elster, 1989). Adapting to the tax compliance literature, it means that individuals will comply and pay taxes as long as they believe that compliance is a social norm (see Alm et al., 1999).

The second section of Chapter 2 presents two interesting economic theories that intend to explain tax morale and tax compliance by showing the limits of traditional economics. The approach of both theories is characterized by partially including a specific psychological effect to detect the relative importance of an effect without losing the spirit of the economic foundations (see Frey, 1997, 1999).

In general, this book can be seen as an attempt to extend the traditional neoclassical assumption, enriching theory with conceptions from other sciences such as psychology without losing the economic foundation and testing them empirically. A neutral concept of taxpayers' utility or preferences is considered, which includes different sorts of human motivation. Such a basis allows for a multi-faceted approach which goes beyond the traditional emphasis on enforcement strategies to understand why individuals pay taxes. Investigations in recent years have uncovered systematic deviations from the traditional *Homo economicus* (for a survey, see Torgler, 2003b). In many experiments, subjects appear to care about aspects as fairness, reciprocity and distribution. Henrich et al. (2001) undertook a large cross-cultural study of behaviour using ultimatum, public good and dictator games. They found a large variation across the different cultural groups and they argue that preferences and/or expectations are affected by group-specific conditions such as institutions or cultural fairness norms. Thus, it makes sense to work with the concept of *Homo Oeconomicus Maturus* (HOM) proposed by Frey (1997), endowed with a more refined motivation structure. This model implicates a stronger psychological orientation, not only taking into account the price effect but also a crowding-out effect. As Frey (1997) pointed out, the crowding-out effect is compatible with economic reasoning, overcoming the limits of traditional economics and moving towards a homogeneous social science, but ensuring comparability with the traditional economic model, maintaining its simplicity and robustness.

The third section of Chapter 2 analyses two important factors in the tax compliance literature: fairness and the interaction between taxpayers and the government. For a long time, fairness has been considered irrelevant for economic analysis. However, the tax compliance literature has successfully demonstrated that a taxpayer's perception of fairness has an impact on the willingness to pay taxes. An unfair tax system could enhance the incentives to rationalize cheating. On the basis of equity theory, it can be argued that taxpayers perceive their relationship with the state not only as a relationship of coercion, but also as one of exchange. Taxpayers are more inclined to comply with the law if the exchange between the paid tax and the performed government services is found to be equitable. The second aspect, the interaction between taxpayers and the government, is also an important determinant. The hypothesis is that positive actions by the state are intended to increase taxpayers' positive attitudes and commitment to the tax system and tax payment, and thus to enhance compliant behaviour. More trust in the government, the tax administration and the legal system tends to increase tax morale and thus taxpayers' willingness to contribute with their taxes. This idea is strongly linked to the effects of institutions on tax morale. As the tax compliance literature has often disregarded whether *institutions matter*, we will present empirical evidence that they have a strong impact on tax morale.

After this general survey chapter, the next contribution in Part I, entitled 'Speaking to theorists and searching for facts: tax morale and tax compliance in experiments', surveys experimental findings in the tax compliance literature. As we have seen in the methodological part of this introduction, each instrument has its own advantages and shortcomings. A special survey on the evidence from experiments is presented because this instrument has convincingly shown that tax compliance is higher than traditional theories, based on the expected utility concept, would predict. Such findings have increased incentives to search for new factors that affect tax compliance. Furthermore, experimental findings show that the direction of the change in the degree of tax compliance, as a response to different deterrence policies, is not always consistent. The results tend to suggest that a higher audit rate leads to more compliance, and that tax compliance is an increasing function of income and a decreasing function of the tax rate. However, mixed results indicate that it is important to let deterrence parameters remain constant and to analyse the relevance of social and institutional factors. Chapter 3 surveys such alternative factors. Experiments tried to evaluate the effects of social norms on tax compliance, including aspects such as collective blame, moral constraints or communication. Recently, cross-cultural experiments have gained increasing attention. The idea is to isolate cultural effects by conducting the same experiments in different countries. In general, the findings indicate that social norms affect the individual reporting decision. Furthermore, while most studies focus on *punishment*, experiments have started to analyse the effects of *rewards* on tax compliance. The results indicate that rewards help to increase tax compliance. However, as the analysis of positive rewards in tax compliance research is still in its infancy, it is difficult to get a clear picture. For example, the long-term effects of rewards are still not known.

Equity considerations, on the other hand, merit a lot of attention in the tax compliance literature. It is interesting to note that experimental findings are in line with survey findings, indicating that a higher equity leads to a higher compliance and a lower perceived equity to a lower tax compliance. However, most experiments have focused on the effect of horizontal equity, without analysing the perceived fairness of a taxpayer's exchange with the government. As some experiments have made efforts to design treatments to evaluate such an exchange mechanism, the chapter surveys these findings. These experiments implemented treatments in which a public good is provided. Taxes paid in a round were multiplied by a specific factor, and the resulting amount was then redistributed in equal shares to the members of the group, independently of the paid amount (see, e.g., Alm et al., 1992, 1993). The results show that taxpayers are more inclined to comply with the law if the exchange between the paid tax and the performed government services is found to be equitable. Furthermore, if taxpayers can vote for the way in which taxes will be spent, they may feel more inclined to pay their taxes. A few experiments have shown that voting has a positive effect on tax compliance (Alm et al., 1993, 1999).

In general, the survey in Chapter 3 presents evidence of the extent to which alternative variables have enriched tax compliance research. A key 'evolution' has been to expand the experiments based on a game between taxpayers and the tax authority to situations in which taxpayers' interactions are considered; for example, by including a public good structure. Chapter 3 ends with an analysis of the limits and possibilities of tax compliance experiments and mentions some topics for future research endeavours.

Part II: What Shapes Tax Morale?

The first chapter in Part II, entitled 'The importance of faith: tax morale and religiosity', analyses religiosity as a potential factor that affects tax morale. The starting point is a theoretical section, where the link between religiosity and tax morale/compliance has been developed. Religiosity might act as a kind of internal moral enforcement mechanism that prevents individuals from behaving in a certain way. Religiosity settles thought patterns and might inhibit illegal behaviour, acting as a sanctioning system that legitimizes and reinforces social values (see, e.g., Hirschi and Stark, 1969). Therefore, it restricts the possibility set of individuals. Bringing religiosity into the analysis introduces agents other than the state who pose a threat to violators (see Grasmick et al., 1991). Empirical studies report that states and countries with higher rates of religious memberships have significantly lower violent and non-violent crime (see, e.g., Hull and Bold 1989; Lipford et al., 1993; Hull 2000).

Arguing that religion encourages moral commitments and internal enforcement of social norms, the chapter investigates empirically the link between religiosity and tax morale/compliance. This is interesting and relevant, as to the author's knowledge there are only two papers that examine the effects of religiosity on tax morale (Tittle, 1980; Grasmick et al., 1991).

Religiosity has been analysed using different measurements such as church attendance, religious education, being an active member of a church or a religious organization, perceived religiosity, religious guidance and trust in the church, controlling for the specific religion of a person to check also whether some religions are more tax compliant than others. To the author's knowledge, there are only two previous papers that examine the effect of religiosity on tax cheating. Compared to the previous studies, our analysis has a higher sample size, covering more than 30 countries, more measurements of religiosity and more control variables. Since in some countries in our analysis corruption is quite high, it cannot be assumed that the obligation to pay taxes to the government is an accepted social norm. Thus, it is relevant to include a measurement of corruption in the analysis to check the robustness of the results.

Furthermore, we investigate whether trustworthiness, such as lying ('claiming government benefits to which someone is not entitled'), cheating ('avoiding a fare on public transport') and buying a stolen product ('buying something you knew was stolen') also explain tax morale.

As most empirical research on tax compliance has generally been done using US data, there is a lack of research within countries outside the United States. Thus, this chapter contributes to expanding the focus, as it includes a great number of countries to get a general idea of the effect of religiosity on tax morale. Before starting with the empirical section, the chapter introduces the economics of religiosity and argues that religiosity works as a constraint on individual behaviour.

The empirical findings indicate that religiosity has a significant positive effect on tax morale, even if other determinants such as corruption, trustworthiness, demographic and economic factors are controlled for. Thus, the empirical findings support the relevance of incorporating non-economic factors into the analysis of tax compliance. Tax morale and tax compliance are not just a function of the opportunity to evade taxes, tax rates and the probability of detection. It might therefore be fruitful to work with models that systematically integrate ideas borrowed from other social sciences. An extension of the economic model of man by integrating factors such as religiosity opens up a new working instrument, without loss of simplicity and robustness.

Chapter 5, 'Tax morale and institutions', goes a step further in the analysis, evaluating the impact of direct democracy, trust in government, the court and the legal system, as well as federalism, on tax morale in Switzerland, working with two different data sets: the World Values Survey 1995–1997 and the International Social Survey Programme 'Religion II' for the year 1999. This contribution might be interesting for the tax compliance literature, as it systematically analyses the influence of institutions such as direct democracy and federalism on tax morale, which has been strongly neglected in the literature. Furthermore, contrary to many survey studies, the empirical model presented in this chapter has integrated such traditional variables as audit probability, legal fines or individual tax rates.

The chapter starts with theoretical considerations regarding the effects of direct democracy, local autonomy and trust in institutions on tax morale. Direct democracy can be seen as a government precommitment, imposing restraints on its power and thus sending a signal that taxpayers are seen as responsible persons. Taxpayers are in the position better to monitor and control politicians via referenda, and can act as rule-setters via initiatives; for example, renegotiation of the tax contract. Such an active role of taxpayers enhances civic virtue and thus tax morale. Federalism is a second institution that has been analysed in this chapter. Small structures have the advantage that citizens' preferences are met better, as mechanisms of entry and exit and voice provide a strong incentive to produce public services in accordance with taxpayers' preferences (see Hirschman, 1970). Furthermore, if politicians are elected at the local level, they have an incentive to take citizens' preferences into account (see Frey and Eichenberger, 1999). The closeness between taxpayers, the tax administration and the local government may induce trust and thus enhance tax morale. A further advantage of a decentralized system is a better transparency of the input (taxes) – output (expenditures) relationship.

The empirical section of this chapter starts by analysing the effects of the traditional variables of an economics-of-crime approach on tax morale, considering three basic variables of this approach: the fine rate for tax evasion, the probability of detection and the individual tax rate. The results indicate that the basic tax evasion model does not perform in a satisfactory way. The coefficients of these main variables are mostly not significant in both data sets. Only in one estimation is the audit probability significant at the 10 per cent level, showing a positive sign. On the other hand, there is a negative correlation between the fine rate and the degree of tax morale, without this being statistically significant. Finally, the individual tax rate has a significant negative effect on tax morale in one equation. The interesting finding is that coercion does not play such an eminent role in determining the degree of tax morale. Thus, the 'basic evasion model' has to be extended with additional factors such as, for example, formal and informal institutions.

The degree of direct democratic participation rights is measured in different ways. First, the aggregated index of direct democratic rights developed by Stutzer (1999) is used. In a second step, the effects of all the single index components have been evaluated. Interestingly, in both data sets, the index with the strongest direct connection to taxes, the financial referendum index, has the highest coefficient value and the strongest marginal effects among the indexes. As including the single items into the equations separately disregards the fact that the instruments of initiative and referendum have different rationales, and as indexes do not tell us as much as single instruments, dummies on legislative referenda (mandatory) and the degree of signature requirements for legislative initiatives have been introduced. For both data sets, the instrument of legislative referendum has a positive effect on tax morale, while on the other hand higher signature requirements lead to a lower tax morale, but without being statistically significant. The results remain stable, controlling for cultural differences.

Trust is measured, as trust in the government and the legal system has a positive effect on tax morale. As democracy works as an institution that induces trust, the trust variables have been estimated first of all in separate estimations and then together with the variables direct democracy and federalism. In all estimations there is a highly significant positive correlation between trust and tax morale.

A higher local autonomy has also a statistically significant positive impact on tax morale in both data sets. Interestingly, introducing the variable of direct democracy, the coefficient for local autonomy loses its significance and its size in the WVS, while the direct democracy index remains robust. On the other hand, the ISSP data indicate that the variable for local autonomy remains highly significant, but with a lower significance level and with lower coefficient and marginal effect values for the direct democracy variable. These findings indicate that the two constitutional factors interact with each other, working as complements.

In general, Chapter 5 reports strong empirical evidence that formal and informal institutions significantly influence tax morale in a positive way, controlling for the probability of detection, the fine rate, the tax rate, socio-demographic and socio-economic factors and the carrying out of sensitivity tests.

Chapter 6 analyses 'Tax morale in Latin America'. Similar to the previous chapter, more than one data set has been used to get a robust picture of Latin America: the Latinobarómetro (1998) and the World Values Survey (1981–1997). The issue of tax compliance is important, as many problems are observed; for example, poor administration performance, inefficiency in the collection of tax revenues, lack of equity considerations in the tax structure and so on. Not surprisingly, the general level of tax revenues as a percentage of GDP are quite low. In the 1980s and 1990s, several tax reforms were made. The chapter gives a short overview of the main tax reforms in countries such as Peru, Bolivia, Chile, Guatemala, Colombia and Mexico. Mexico is a special case, as in this country the tax system has been reformed repeatedly, implementing very modern tax revenue structures. However, Mexico is a country with a high degree of tax evasion, a large shadow economy and, as this chapter shows, a low degree of tax morale. Martinez-Vazquez (2001) tried to find possible reasons for this phenomenon. He mentions that the modern tax system structure is undermined by factors such as *ad hoc* policy measures or the lack of an adequate ability on the part of the tax administrations to deal with a modern tax system. Bird et al. (2006) argue that countries may tend to achieve an equilibrium position with respect to the size and nature of their fiscal systems that largely reflects the balance of their political forces and institutions, and that they stay in this position until 'shocked' into a new equilibrium. The fundamental conclusion of their study is that a more legitimate and responsive state is probably an essential precondition for a more adequate level of tax effort in developing countries. They argue that improving social institutions, such as enhancing the rule of law and reducing corruption and increasing tax morale, may not take longer, nor be necessarily more difficult, than changing the opportunities for tax handles and the economic structure, such as the relative share of agriculture in the economy or the contribution of imports and exports to GDP.

The findings of this chapter indicate that there is a significant correlation between tax morale and the size of the shadow economy. Furthermore, people who said they knew, or had heard about, practised tax avoidance had a significantly lower tax morale than others. On the other hand, if people believe that others obey the law, their intrinsic motivation to pay taxes increases. Looking at individuals' perception of reasons for tax evasion, the results indicate that the tax burden (46.8 per cent), a lack of individual honesty (44.5 per cent) and corruption (44.2 per cent) are seen as the main factors. We observed a significantly lower tax morale in South America/Mexico than in the Central American/Caribbean area. Mexico in particular has a very low tax morale. Furthermore, trust in the president and the officials, and the belief that other individuals obey the law have a significant positive effect on tax morale. As political participation can be seen as a social innovation for Latin America, strengthening democracy in countries such as Chile, Mexico or Argentina, it is interesting to check whether a higher level of support for a democratic system has an impact on tax morale. The previous chapter in this book shows the relevance of political participation as an important factor in enhancing tax morale. The two proxies used show that people with a higher pro-democratic attitude have also a higher tax morale. Additionally, the chapter shows that pride, financial satisfaction, personal satisfaction and happiness affect tax morale in a positive way.

The last chapter in Part II, 'Does culture matter? A comparison of tax morale in the former East and West Germany', provides a comparison of tax morale between inhabitants of the former East and West Germany after the post-reunification periods, using World Values Survey data from 1990 and 1997. Such a comparison is interesting, due to the historical event of German reunification with the fall of the Berlin Wall on 9 November 1989. Eastern and Western taxpayers grew up in different social environments. German reunification allows us better to isolate so-called cultural factors from other factors and is close to a natural experiment. Many factors can be controlled for because they are similar – such as, for example, a common language, similar education systems and a shared cultural and political history prior to the separation after the Second World War. As a consequence, a comparison between the former East and West Germany has a methodological advantage compared to cross-country studies. Thus, Chapter 7 helps to provide important insights into the effects of social norms.

The chapter starts with the question of whether there is a cultural difference between the former East and West Germany. Culture can be seen as a kind of language that is based on rule systems, such as ideas, values, internal institutions as customs and conventions and external institutions. Thus it can be argued that cultural transmission mechanisms provide a means of solving the problem of co-operation, building a mechanism of conformism (see Henrich et al., 1999). Social norms are learned through daily experience. An important aim of the GDR regime was the adherence to norms enforcing, for example, trust in the authority. Ockenfels and Weimann (1999) report that there is the common belief that former East Germans are more co-operative and less selfish than former West Germans. Mummert and Schneider (2002) report a significantly lower share of black labour in the former East Germany than in the former West Germany. The Forschungsstelle für empirische Sozialökonomik (1997) found that eastern taxpayers had a higher tax morale than western taxpayers. Compared to this study, the chapter uses larger sample units for both regions and analyses tax morale as a dependent variable with multivariate regressions, also considering the development over time. It can be argued that if norms are learned, a decrease in tax morale in the East over time can be supposed. Furthermore, for older individuals who were exposed for a longer time to an environment in which adherence to social norms was important, a higher tax morale should be observed.

The descriptive section of this chapter shows that in 1990 and 1997, former East Germans reported a higher tax morale than former West Germans. However, a decay over time is observed for the former East Germany. Wilcoxon rank-sum tests show that the differences between east and west are significant. However, as such a difference can be explained in terms of differences in socio-demographic and socio-economic factors, multiple regressions are conducted. Analysing both regions independently shows a sizeably different impact of the age profile on tax morale. While not significant in the west, it exerts a hugely significant influence in the east. To check whether this significant difference persists, the two data sets have been pooled, adding a dummy variable. First, the difference just after reunification has been analysed. The results show that tax morale is significantly higher among Eastern taxpayers. In a next step, Chapter 7 analyses whether the significant difference observed can also be found for the year 1997. The results indicate that the east–west difference has strongly diminished. In seven years, around three-quarters of the east–west differential has disappeared. Thus, a strong convergence in the level of tax morale between the two populations can be observed. Finally, the development of tax morale over time has been analysed in the former East and West Germany separately. In the east, a significant decay in tax morale has been observed. On the other hand, there were no significant differences between 1990 and 1997 for the former West Germany. Thus, cultural background seems to have an effect on tax morale. However, it would be wrong to conclude that the communist system always had a positive effect on tax morale. The tax morale in the former East Germany is quite high compared to other former communist countries. Other factors, such as liberty, freedom or happiness, are essential. A lower tax morale can express taxpayers' dissent. Such behaviour restricts the government's possibilities to act as a Leviathan, maximizing its own preferences. Furthermore, there might be a bias in the analysis due to the transition process, which included extensive money transfers from the west to the east. Nevertheless, the findings indicate that it is fruitful to go beyond the standard economic model of tax compliance integrating the aspect of social norms.

Thus, this chapter closes Part II, showing – in line with the preceding chapters – the relevance of incorporating non-economic factors into the analysis of tax compliance.

Part III: Tax Policy Strategies

In the last part of this book, we will focus on tax policy strategies. The government has a variety of strategies for pursuing an increase of tax morale and tax compliance. Recognizing the importance of institutions and social norms raises the question of what alternative policies, beyond deterrence strategies, might have an effect on tax morale and tax compliance. Such strategies are interesting, as an increase in deterrence parameters is connected to higher government expenditure. However, enforcement is costly and it is not possible to reach complete compliance. Slemrod (1992) states that

> From the tax collection standpoint, it is extraordinarily expensive to arrange an enforcement regime so that, from a strict cost–benefit calculus, noncompliance does not appear attractive to many citizens. It follows that methods that reinforce and encourage taxpayers' devotion to their responsibilities as citizens play an important role in the tax collection process (p. 7).

An increased enforcement of the tax system might produce disincentive effects similar to higher tax rates and bases (see also Slemrod, 1992). Frey (1997) stresses that increasing monitoring and penalties might damage the intrinsic motivation to pay taxes.

As we have seen, a self-interest model does not fully account for the degree of compliance. In line with the whole book, this part follows a perspective that goes beyond analysing deterring policies only, moving towards strategies based on 'positive encouragement'. Thus, we will analyse in Part III to what extent it is helpful to provide a 'carrot for compliance' instead of a 'stick for non-compliance'. As there is a lack of empirical evidence about the effects of alternative policy strategies, both chapters present empirical and experimental evidence that helps to provide a better picture of the possibilities and limitations of such strategies.

Chapter 8, entitled 'Moral suasion: an alternative tax policy strategy? Evidence from a controlled field experiment in Switzerland', starts by analysing the effects of moral suasion on the timely paying (TP) and filling out of the tax form (TF). In co-operation with a local tax administration in Switzerland, a controlled field experiment with taxpayers has been carried out. It allows us to analyse taxpayers in their natural situation of filling out the tax form or paying their taxes. Similar to other chapters, this contribution starts with theoretical considerations about the effects of moral suasion on tax compliance and surveys the literature on that topic. Moral appeals might frame tax compliance as a positive act (see Hasseldine, 2000). However, the efficiency of moral suasion might depend on the circumstances (e.g. it works better in emergency situations: see De Alessi, 1975; Baumol and Oates, 1979). Furthermore, it is unclear whether moral suasion significantly influences behaviour over time.

There is hardly any empirical evidence about individuals' compliance behaviour regarding moral suasion. The empirical evaluation in this chapter tries to overcome these shortfalls, analysing the factors 'timely filling out of the tax form' and 'paying individual taxes on time' as dependent variables and searching for factors that influence those variables. Contrary to a previous controlled experiment done by Blumenthal et al. (2001), which found little or no evidence of a positive effect of normative appeals on tax compliance, we chose to co-operate with a *local* tax administration, because moral suasion efforts might be more effective at this lower level. After introducing the design of the field experiment, results are presented. To get a real picture of the extent to which such behaviour is the consequence of a moral suasion effect, TF and TP values for the years 1999 and 2000 are included. As assignments to treatment and control groups have been made at random, one can simply compare the change in compliance across the treatment and control groups to estimate the treatment effect. For time 1 (before) and 2 (after the experiment), groups A (treatment) and B (control), compliance (TC), $[TC(2,A) - TC(2,B)] - [TC(1,A) - TC(1,B)]$, or equivalently $[TC(2,A) - TC(1,A)] - [TC(2,B) - TC(1,B)]$, is the difference-in-difference. The change in compliance regarding the timely paying suggests a successful moral suasion effect, with mean increases of 0.048 and 0.046 respectively. We can observe the strongest increase in the highest compliance scale (2.1

and 2.3 per cent, respectively). On the other hand, a positive treatment effect regarding timely compliance is only observable taking the average of the years 1999 and 2000 into consideration. However, a regression framework using time and treatment dummy variables ($TC_{it} = \beta_0 + \beta_1 treatment_{it} + \beta_2 after_{it} + \beta_3 treatment_{it} * after_{it} + \varepsilon_{it}$) shows that the differences are not statistically significant.

In a next step, the chapter uses *TP* as a dependent variable, controlling in a multivariate analysis for additional factors working with the 2001 data. A dummy variable 'MORAL SUASION' has been constructed to compare the control group with the treatment group. The results indicate that being in the moral suasion group increases the probability of being in the most compliant group by around three percentage points, but the coefficients are not significant. In sum, our results indicate that moral suasion has hardly any effect on taxpayers' compliance behaviour. The strongest effect can be observed for the variable that measures the timely paying of the taxes.

Chapter 9, 'Tax amnesties and political participation', analyses in a laboratory experiment the acceptance of tax amnesties and the effects of having the possibility of voting on a tax amnesty. Tax amnesties are increasingly used by governments around the world. However, it is debatable whether in the long run tax amnesties undermine tax compliance. Honest taxpayers may feel upset by an amnesty. If most taxpayers voluntarily comply with the tax laws, the option of an amnesty given to a small group of tax evaders can be understood by a majority of taxpayers as a violation of equity. The issue has also a moral dimension, since it touches the sentiments of taxpayers. Thus, it is also possible that an amnesty ends up in a lower *ex-post* level of tax compliance.

When deciding whether or not to conduct an amnesty, it is crucial to take taxpayers' attitudes towards an amnesty into account. However, in hardly any country was an amnesty subject to approval. The aim of this chapter is to evaluate the impact of voter participation on tax amnesties by conducting laboratory experiments in several countries. Voters might interpret the remission given by the government as a signal that tax evasion must be high and that other taxpayers' tax morale is low. Thus, voters may not want to reward tax evaders with an amnesty. Nevertheless, the results of our experiments show that the mere possibility for taxpayers to decide on a tax amnesty increases future tax compliance. These results are consistent with the argument that voting procedure, namely public discussion prior to votes, brings about a sense of civic duty, as taxpayers become aware of the importance of contributing to public goods. Voting without discussion produces mixed findings. Thus, discussion before voting is an essential feature in increasing group co-operation: it enhances the moral costs of free-riding and thus increases the social norm of compliances, generating a higher tax compliance. In addition, tax compliance may increase after voting given the possibility of an increasing likelihood of stricter enforcement efforts.

Furthermore, in line with another study, amnesties tend to increase tax compliance in our experiments. However, contrary to previous findings, an amnesty with an increase in the post-amnesty enforcement parameters does not outperform an amnesty without changes in the enforcement factors. The results also indicate that the effect of a second amnesty does not improve tax compliance. The coefficient is mostly negative, but not statistically significant. Amnesty expectations reduce the positive effects of an amnesty. When the government does not keep its promise, tax compliance decreases. Such a result has a strong policy implication. If a government intends to increase the long-term effects of a tax amnesty, its commitment should be reliable, and only one amnesty should be conducted.

Generally, the results indicate that there are limitations to the economics-of-crime approach. The results show the importance of incorporating the role of societal institutions and social norms into tax compliance models to better understand why so many individuals comply.

WHAT SHAPES TAX MORALE: A SUMMARY

As many chapters in this book present empirical and experimental evidence, it helps to give an overview on the different variables that have been analysed as independent factors. We also present results reported in the original dissertation but not in the book.[4] It should be noted that not all of the variables will be summarized. Looking at marital and the employment status, only specific variables have been selected (married, self-employed and unemployed), comparing them with the reference group. As the overview has only focused on the main variables, this summary also gives insights into the effects of socio-demographic and socio-economic variables. To get a robust picture of the correlations between those variables and tax morale, we present in this section a couple of tables, with the findings for each variable.

We will see that some variables do not appear in all of the estimations. The variation in the number of variables can be mainly accounted for by many missing values, due to data not having been collected in specific countries or having been differently coded. However, I have tried as far as possible to use similar estimations for different countries. As in each country/region more than one estimation has been carried out, the tables presented in the following subsections will show tendencies. But in the cases where the coefficients were significant, the results remain mostly stable over a variety of estimations.

We start with socio-demographic and socio-economic variables, as they have not been treated in the previous section. After that, we present the evidence of our main variables. Having a general picture of results from different countries allows us better to develop policy strategies to enhance tax morale and tax compliance.

Socio-demographic and Socio-economic Variables

Socio-demographic variables appear to be important determinants of behaviour. However, as many empirical findings are based on the Taxpayer Compliance Measurement Program (TCMP), relatively little empirical evidence is available. With different methodological instruments (survey and (field) experiments), we can capture the extent to which there are clear tendencies.

Age, gender and education

We start with the variables age, gender and education (Tables 1.1–1.3). Instead of using age as a continuous variable, most of the survey estimations have formed four classes: 16–29, 30–49, 50–64 and 65+, with 16–29 as the reference group. Tables 1.1–1.3 indicate the sign of the coefficient values of the different groups compared to the reference group and whether the effect is statistically significant. In some studies, mostly experiments, age has been coded as a continuous variable. Similarly, gender has been coded as a dummy variable (being male in the reference group).

Most theories regarding the effects of socio-demographic factors on compliance have been developed by social psychologists. Tittle (1980) argues that older people are more sensitive to the threats of sanctions and over the years have acquired greater social stakes, such as material goods, status, and a stronger dependency on the reactions from others, so that the potential costs of sanctions increase. The results in Tables 1.1–1.3 show a clear picture of the effect of the age variables. In most estimations, a higher age is significantly correlated with a higher tax morale or tax compliance.

Similarly, social psychological research suggests that females are more compliant and less self-reliant than males (e.g. Tittle, 1980). However, if social psychology argues that the difference is based on the traditional female role, today's female generation, which is more independent, would have a lower tax morale or tax compliance. Another possibility could be that females are more risk averse than males. It is interesting to look at the results as different cultural regions have been analysed. The results reported in Tables 1.1–1.3 show that in many cases females report a significantly higher tax morale and tax compliance than males. No difference between developing and developed countries can be observed, which invalidates the argument that the position of the female in a society has an effect on tax morale.

Education is related to taxpayers' knowledge about tax law. Better-educated taxpayers are supposed to know more about tax law and fiscal connections: they are better aware of the benefits and services the state provides for its citizens from the revenues and thus are in a better position to assess the degree of compliance (see Lewis, 1982). On the other hand, highly educated taxpayers should also be more aware of possible government waste. Furthermore, they may be less compliant because they better understand the opportunities for evasion and avoidance, and they might be more critical about and better aware of how the state uses the tax revenues. However, this argumentation might be less relevant for the degree of tax morale. On the basis of these different arguments, it is interesting to check empirically the effects of education on tax morale and tax compliance. Not surprisingly, the results show an ambivalent picture. In many estimations, the effects of education on tax morale/tax compliance are not statistically significant. In the estimations where the coefficient indicates a significant influence, the signs are also mixed. These results might indicate that the current politico-economic situation (government spending, the input–output relation between paid taxes and obtained benefits) influences the education variable.

Marital status, employment, economic situation and religiosity
Marital status might influence legal or illegal behaviour, depending on the extent to which individuals are constrained by their social networks (see Tittle, 1980). Such a constraint might have an impact on tax morale. On the other hand, it should be noted that this variable might interact with the tax system. Differences in the degree of tax morale might be based on different tax treatments of married and non-married people. However, evidence from Switzerland and the United States shows a tendency for married people to have a higher tax morale than singles, which would not be in line with this argumentation. Such a tendency can be observed among different cultural settings, especially regarding the significant coefficient values.

Regarding occupational status, special attention has been paid to the question of whether self-employed taxpayers have a lower tax morale than full-time employees. Tables 1.4–1.6 present the findings. In many equations, the coefficient is not significant. However, it is interesting to notice that in the transition countries (see also the former East Germany) the coefficient is mostly significant, with a negative sign. In these countries, self-employed individuals might feel the financial restriction much more, as the compliance costs and taxes become more visible. The rapid collapse of institutional structures produced a vacuum in many countries, followed by large social costs, especially in terms of worsening income inequality

Table 1.1 The effects of age, gender and education on tax morale and tax compliance in Europe (dependent variables: tax compliance and tax morale)

	Sign and significance of the coefficient					
	Age (dummies compared to age 16–29)			Age	Gender FEMALE	Education
Countries	AGE 30–49	AGE 50–64	AGE 65+			
Countries pooled						
Europe, 1989–1990 (WVS)	+	+	+		+	
Specific countries						
Switzerland						
1989 (WVS)	+	+	+		+	(−)
1996 (WVS)	(+)	+	(+)		+	(+)
1999 (ISSP)	(±)	(±)	(±)		(±)	+
Experiment (public good)				+	(±)	
Experiment (public good)				−	+	+
Experiment (tax amnesty)				+	+	
Field experiment	(+)	(+)	+		+/(−)*	
Germany						
Western Germany, 1997 (WVS)	(−)	(+)	(+)		(+)	−
Eastern Germany, 1997 (WVS)	+	+	+		(+)	−
W. Germany, 1990 and 1997 (pooled)	(−)	+	+		+	
E. Germany, 1990 and 1997 (pooled)	+	+	+		+	

Spain					
1990 (WVS)	+	+	+	(+)	+
1995 (WVS)	(−)	(±)	(±)	+	(−)
Belgium					
1990 (WVS)	+	+	+	+	
United Kingdom					
1990 (WVS)	(+)	+	+	(+)	(±)

Notes: In the surveys the dependent variable is tax morale, in the experiments tax compliance. Gender: reference group MALE. +, Significant positive coefficient; (+) and (−), positive and negative coefficient signs, respectively without being significant; (±) positive and negative signs of the coefficient without being significant. * Females have a higher compliance regarding timely paying the taxes than couples; on the other hand, regarding timely filling out there is a lower compliance, but without being significant.

Table 1.2 The effects of age, gender and education on tax morale and tax compliance in North and Latin America (dependent variables: tax compliance and tax morale)

	Sign and significance of the coefficient					
	Age (dummies compared to age 16–29)			Age	Gender FEMALE	Education
Countries	AGE 30–49	AGE 50–64	AGE 65+			
Countries pooled						
Latin America (WVS 1995–1997)	+	+	+		+	(−)
Latin America (Latinobarómetro 1998)	+	+	+		(+)	(+)
Specific countries						
United States						
1995 (WVS)	(+)	(+)	(+)		+	(+)
1987 (Taxpayer Opinion Survey)				+	(±)	−
Canada						
1990 (WVS)	+	+	(+)		+	(+)
Costa Rica						
1998 (Latinobarómetro)	(+)	(+)	+		(±)	
Experiment (public good)				+	+	+
Experiment (alternative tax policy strategies)*				(+)	+	+

Notes: In the surveys the dependent variable is tax morale, in the experiments tax compliance. Gender: reference group MALE. +, Significant positive coefficient; (+) and (−), positive and negative coefficient signs, respectively, without being significant; (±) positive and negative signs of the coefficient without being significant. * Only descriptive statistics.

and poverty rates and bad institutional conditions, based on uncertainty and high transaction costs.

The effects of income on tax morale are difficult to assess theoretically. Depending on risk preferences and the progression of the income tax schedules, income may increase or reduce tax morale. Looking at tax evasion, it can be argued that in countries with a progressive income tax rate, taxpayers with a higher income realize a higher dollar return by evading, but with possibly less economic utility. On the other hand, lower-income taxpayers might have lower societal 'stakes' or restrictions but be less in a position to take these risks, because of a high marginal utility loss (wealth reduction) if they are caught and penalized (Jackson and Milliron, 1986). Thus, it does not come as a surprise that the empirical findings show a mixed picture. Looking at the statistically significant coefficient, there is a tendency for a higher income to lead to a lower tax morale. The positive results obtained in the experiments cannot be compared to the surveys, as individual income has not been integrated into the estimations but, instead, the income assigned during the experiments.

Finally, Tables 1.4–1.6 present evidence regarding the variable religiosity, measured as church attendance and the degree of religiosity. As the previous section has already introduced the variable, we proceed directly to the empirical findings. The results suggest a positive correlation between religiosity and tax morale.

Trust and national pride

The results of the trust variable imply a clear tax policy strategy: induce trust at the constitutional level as well as at the current politico-economic level. In all the different cultural settings, such a strategy has a positive effect on tax morale. If taxpayers trust the government, the courts and legal system and the tax administration, taxpayers are more willing to pay taxes. Therefore, all of these actors have to act trustworthily. The results show that the relationship between them and the taxpayers (relational contract) can be maintained by positive actions and well-functioning institutions, implementing a positive social capital atmosphere. Such a strategy will be honoured with a higher tax morale. In the light of the current politico-economic process, these findings are interesting and relevant. According to Frey (2003), it is possible that the European Union will levy its own taxes in the future. This would mean '*new* and additional taxes' (p. 20). It is questionable whether a deterrence strategy would help to maintain tax compliance under these circumstances. It even might enforce the disincentive effects of additional taxes. Thus, building trust might be an alternative strategy to guarantee that tax morale is not crowded out. Furthermore, as our results show that trust plays an essential role in increasing tax morale

Table 1.3 The effects of age, gender and education on tax morale and tax compliance in transition and Asian countries (development variable: tax morale)

	Sign and significance of the coefficient				
	Age (dummies compared to age 16–29)			Gender	Education
Countries	AGE 30–49	AGE 50–64	AGE 65+	FEMALE	
Countries pooled					
Transition countries (WVS 1989–1993)	+	+	+	+	
Transition countries (WVS 1995–1998)	+	+	+	+	
Asia (WVS 1995–1997)	+	+	+	(+)	+
Specific countries					
Transition countries					
Former Soviet countries					
Russia 1991 and 1995 (pooled)	+	+	+	(±)	
Estonia 1990 and 1996 (pooled)	+	+	+	+	
Latvia 1990 and 1996 (pooled)	+	+	+	+	
Lithuania 1990 and 1996 (pooled)	+	+	+	+	
Belarus 1990 and 1996 (pooled)	+	+	+	(−)	
Central/Eastern Europe					
Poland 1989 and 1997 (pooled)	+	+	+	+	+
Bulgaria 1990 and 1997 (pooled)	+	+	+	(+)	
Slovenia 1992 and 1995 (pooled)	+	+	+	+	

Asia
India
1995/1996   +   +   +   (+)   (+)
1990 and 1995/1996 (pooled)   +   +   +   −   +

Japan
1995   +   +   +   (+)   (±)
1981, 1990 and 1995 (pooled)   +   +   +   +   +

Notes: Dependent variable: tax morale. Gender: reference group MALE. +, Significant positive coefficient; (+) and (−), positive and negative coefficient signs, respectively, without being significant; (±) positive and negative signs of the coefficient without being significant.

Table 1.4 The effects of marital and employment status, economic situation and religiosity on tax morale and tax compliance in Europe (dependent variables: tax compliance and tax morale)

	Sign and significance of the coefficients					
	Marital status	Employment	Economic situation		Religiosity	
Countries	MARRIED	SELF-EMPLOYED	INCOME	FINANCIAL SATISFACTION	CHURCH ATTENDANCE	RELIGIOUS
Countries pooled						
Europe 1989–1990 (WVS)	+	−	−	+	+	
Specific countries						
Switzerland						
1989 (WVS)	(±)	(−)	−	(+)	+	
1996 (WVS)	+	(+)	(+)	+	+	
1999 (ISSP)	(±)*		(+)		+	
Experiment (public good)	+		+			
Experiment (public good)			(−)			
Experiment (tax amnesty)			(+)	+	+	
Field experiment	−	(+)			(+)	(+)
Germany						
Western Germany 1997 (WVS)	+	(−)	−	+	+	
Eastern Germany 1997 (WVS)	(+)		(−)			
W. Germany 1990 and 1997 (pooled)	+	(+)	−			
E. Germany 1990 and 1997 (pooled)	(+)	(−)	−			+

Spain					
1990 (WVS)	+				
1995 (WVS)	(+)	−	(+)	+	+
					(+)
Belgium					
1990 (WVS)	+	−		+	+
United Kingdom					
1990 (WVS)	(+)	(−)	(+)	+	+

Notes: In the surveys the dependent variable is tax morale, in the experiments tax compliance. Marital status: reference group SINGLE, employment status: FULL TIME EMPLOYED. +, Significant positive coefficient; (+) and (−), positive and negative coefficient signs, respectively, without being significant; (±) positive and negative signs of the coefficient without being significant. *Married and people living together are in one class.

39

Table 1.5 *The effects of marital and employment status, economic situation and religiosity on tax morale and tax compliance in North and Latin America (dependent variables: tax compliance and tax morale)*

| | Marital status | Employment | | Economic situation | | Religiosity | |
| | | | | | | | |
Countries	MARRIED	SELF-EMPLOYED	INCOME	FINANCIAL SATISFACTION	CHURCH ATTENDANCE	RELIGIOUS
Countries pooled						
Latin America (WVS 1995–1997)	+	(+)	+	+		+
Latin America (Latinobarómetro 1998)	+*	(+)	(±)			
Specific countries						
United States						
1995 (WVS)	+	(+)	−	+	+	+
1987 (Taxpayer Opinion Survey)	(−)		(−)			
Canada						
1990 (WVS)	+	(±)	−	+	+	+
Costa Rica						
1998 (Latinobarómetro)	(−)	(+)	−			+
Experiment (public good)			+			+
Experiment (alternative tax policy strategies)**	+		−			+

Notes: In the surveys the dependent variable is tax morale, in the experiments tax compliance. Marital status: reference group SINGLE, employment status: FULL TIME EMPLOYED. +, Significant positive coefficient; (+) and (−), positive and negative coefficient signs, respectively without being significant; (±) positive and negative signs of the coefficient without being significant. * Married and people living together are in one class. ** Only descriptive statistics.

in transition countries, the EU enlargement should be steered taking the effects of trust on tax morale into account. Also, taking the results for Latin America into consideration, we can argue that the observed tax reform efforts at the present time should not forget to enhance how to further the relational contract between taxpayers and the government. It seems that this component has been neglected in various reform efforts.

Tables 1.7–1.9 also show the empirical evidence of a further variable: national pride. Taking into account that, to the author's knowledge, this variable has been completely neglected in the tax compliance literature, the evidence shows that more attention should be paid to the effects of pride on tax morale and tax compliance. In almost all estimations, a higher level of pride leads to significantly better tax morale. Thus, independent of the cultural setting, this variable has a strong effect on tax morale.

Institutions

In the previous subsection, we have analysed the constitutional and current politico-economic levels, taking attitudinal questions into consideration. In a next step, empirical evidence will be presented about the effects of direct democracy and local autonomy, which set the rules between taxpayers and the state at the constitutional level. Both a higher level of direct democracy and a higher level of local autonomy lead to a significantly higher tax morale in Switzerland and in the United States. Giving individuals the possibility of deciding about the implementation of a tax amnesty or the degree of enforcement also has a significantly positive effect on tax compliance, as experiments in Switzerland and Costa Rica have shown. The policy implication for the countries analysed is clear: more direct democratic participation and greater local autonomy might be fruitful strategies to produce beneficial effects. The results emphasize the following argument by Frey (2003):

> The option of building up a closer relationship between citizens and the European Union is arduous and takes much time, but is desirable. It is laborious, because it requires fundamental changes in the EU constitution. The citizens must be involved in both fundamental and daily decisions. It also conforms to a Europe of the twenty-first century built on fundamental trust between citizens and government (p. 24).

Such results do not only hold for the EU. Table 1.10 shows that a higher pro-democratic attitude leads to a higher tax morale in Latin America and in transition countries as well. A move towards more democracy, as we observe in transition countries (see, e.g., Frey, 2002), might help to enhance tax morale and civic virtue over time.

Table 1.6 *The effects of marital and employment status, economic situation and religiosity on tax morale in transition and Asian countries (dependent variable: tax morale)*

Countries	Sign and significance of the coefficients					
	Marital status	Employment		Economic situation		Religiosity	
	MARRIED	SELF-EMPLOYED	INCOME	FINANCIAL SATISFACTION	CHURCH ATTENDANCE	RELIGIOUS
Countries pooled						
Transition countries (WVS 1989–1993)	+	–		+		
Transition countries (WVS 1995–1998)	+	–		(+)		
Asia (WVS 1995–1997)	+			+		
Specific countries						
Transition countries						
Former Soviet countries						
Russia 1991 and 1995 (pooled)	(+)	–				
Estonia 1990 and 1996 (pooled)	(±)	–				
Latvia 1990 and 1996 (pooled)	(+)	–				
Lithuania 1990 and 1996 (pooled)	(+)	–				
Belarus 1990 and 1996 (pooled)	+					
Central/Eastern Europe						
Poland 1989 and 1997 (pooled)	(±)					
Bulgaria 1990 and 1997 (pooled)	(+)	(–)				
Slovenia 1992 and 1995 (pooled)	(+)	–				

Asia
India

1995/1996	(+)	(−)	—
1990 and 1995/1996 (pooled)	(+)	—	—

Japan

1995	—	—	(+)	—*
1981, 1990 and 1995 (pooled)	+	—	—	+**

Notes: Dependent variable: tax morale. Marital status: reference group SINGLE. Employment status: FULL TIME EMPLOYED. +, Significant positive coefficient; (+) and (−), positive and negative coefficient signs, respectively, without being significant; (±), positive and negative sign of the coefficient without being significant. * Hindu compared to people without a religion denomination. ** Buddhist compared to people without a religion denomination.

Table 1.7 The effects of trust and national pride on tax morale in Europe (dependent variable: tax morale)

Countries	Sign and significance of the coefficients			
	Trust			PRIDE
	TRUST IN GOVERNMENT	TRUST IN LEGAL SYSTEM	TRUST IN COURT AND LEGAL SYSTEM	
Countries pooled				
Europe 1989–1990 (WVS)		+		+
Specific countries				
Switzerland				
1989 (WVS)				
1996 (WVS)	+	+		(+)
1999 (ISSP)			+	
Spain				
1990 (WVS)		+		+
1995 (WVS)	+	+		
Belgium				
1990 (WVS)		+		+

Notes: Dependent variable: tax morale. +. Significant positive coefficient; (+) and (−), positive and negative coefficient signs, respectively, without being significant; (±) positive and negative signs of the coefficient without being significant.

Table 1.8 The effects of trust and national pride on tax morale in North and Latin America (dependent variable: tax morale)

Countries	Sign and significance of the coefficients			
	Trust			PRIDE
	TRUST IN GOVERNMENT	TRUST IN PRESIDENT	TRUST IN PUBLIC OFFICIALS	
Countries pooled				
Latin America (WVS 1995–1997)		+	+	+
Latin America (Latinobarómetro 1998)				
Specific countries				
United States				
1987 (Taxpayer Opinion Survey)			+	
Canada				
1990 (WVS)	+			+
Costa Rica				
1998 (Latinobarómetro)		+		

Notes: Dependent variable: tax morale. +: Significant positive coefficient; (+) and (–), positive and negative coefficient signs, respectively, without being significant; (±) positive and negative signs of the coefficient without being significant.

Table 1.9 The effects of trust and national pride on tax morale in transition and Asian countries (dependent variable: tax morale)

Countries	Sign and significance of the coefficients			
	TRUST IN GOVERNMENT	Trust TRUST IN LEGAL SYSTEM	TRUST PUBLIC OFFICIALS	PRIDE
Countries pooled				
Transition countries (WVS 1989–1993)		+		+
Transition countries (WVS 1995–1998)	+	+	+	+
Asia (WVS 1995–1997)	+	+		
Specific countries				
Transition countries				
Former Soviet countries				
Russia 1991 and 1995 (pooled)	+	+		+
Estonia 1990 and 1996 (pooled)	+	+		+
Latvia 1990 and 1996 (pooled)	+	+		+
Lithuania 1990 and 1996 (pooled)	+	+		+
Belarus 1990 and 1996 (pooled)	+	+		
Central/Eastern Europe				
Poland 1989 and 1997 (pooled)	+	+		+

Bulgaria 1990 and 1997 (pooled)	+	+		+
Slovenia 1992 and 1995 (pooled)		+		+
Asia				
India				
1995/1996	+			+
1990 and 1995/1996 (pooled)	+	+		+
Japan				
1995		+	+	(+)
1981, 1990 and 1995 (pooled)		+		+

Notes: Dependent variable: tax morale. +, Significant positive coefficient; (+) and (−), positive and negative coefficient signs, respectively, without being significant; (±), positive and negative signs of the coefficient without being significant.

Table 1.10 The effects of direct democracy and federalism on tax morale and tax compliance (dependent variables: tax compliance and tax morale)

	Sign and significance of the coefficients			
		Democracy		Federalism
Countries	DIRECT DEMOCRACY	VOTING	PRO DEMOCR. ATTIT.	LOCAL AUTONOMY

Countries	DIRECT DEMOCRACY	VOTING	PRO DEMOCR. ATTIT.	LOCAL AUTONOMY
Countries pooled				
Latin America (WVS 1995–1997)			+	
Transition countries (WVS 1995–1998)			+	
Specific countries				
Switzerland				
1996 (WVS)	+			+
1999 (ISSP)	+			+
Experiment		+		
Switzerland and Costa Rica (pooled)				
Experiment		+		
Experiment		+		

United States
1995 (WVS) +
1987 (Taxpayer Opinion Survey) +

Spain
1990 (WVS) +

Japan
1995 (WVS) +

India
1995/1996 (WVS) +

Notes: Dependent variable: tax morale. +, Significant positive coefficient.

Deterrence and perceptions, the tax system and the tax administration

What about the traditional tax policy strategies? A generally interesting finding of this chapter is the fact that a deterrence strategy does not work well. This strongly reduces the significance of such an instrument for resolving the social dilemma of tax payments. The results seem to confirm that in modern democratic states, which are based on a high level of consent among the actors, deterrence factors do not work well (see Frey, 2003). Furthermore, the results show that, after having been audited, individuals cannot be supposed to find their way back to the legal path.

In general, Table 1.11 shows that a tax policy should maintain a high level of social capital. If people believe that others are honest, their willingness to pay taxes increases. Otherwise, the government and the tax administration get into hot water. If individuals notice that many others evade taxes, their intrinsic motivation to comply with taxes decreases. Evasion is a signal that intrinsic motivation is not recognized. Thus, taxpayers get the feeling that they can also be opportunistic and the moral costs of evading taxes decrease. On the other hand, Table 1.11 indicates that if the tax administration tries to be honest, fair, informative and helpful, acting as a *service* institution and thus treating taxpayers as partners, taxpayers' willingness to cooperate increases.

Connected to these findings on the determinants of tax morale, we observe that there has been a noticeable shift towards a more balanced set of strategies in tax administrations. In many countries there is an increased emphasis on quality, customer service and reasonable and fair treatment of taxpayers. However, studies that investigate the impact of such a shift are still hardly available – for exceptions, see Torgler (2004a) for Japan and Torgler and Murphy (2004) for Australia.

Japan, for example, offers a good example for a consequent strategy with the aim of intensifying interaction between the tax administration and the taxpayers based on trust. After the reorganization in 1949, the Japanese tax administration had a high rate of tax delinquency (around 40 per cent). A too fast implementation of the self-assessment system and high tax burdens frustrated Japanese taxpayers. The subsequent reforms, aimed at reducing the tax burden, simplifying the tax returns and improving taxpayers' assistance, helped to increase tax compliance. Today, Japan is known for a high degree of tax morale, which might be influenced by the intensive interaction between the tax administration and the taxpayers based on trust.

Another example is Australia. The 1980s saw public administration being faced with growing state and public demands to become more market-focused, service-oriented, open and efficient. In response to all this, the Australian Taxation Office (ATO) adopted a new, efficiency-oriented and

Table 1.11 Deterrence and perceptions, the tax system and the tax administration (dependent variable: tax morale)

	Countries					
	Switzerland (CH)		United States	Latin America		CH and CR (pooled)
	WVS (1996)	ISSP (1999)	TOS (1987)	Latin America (pooled) LB 98	Costa Rica (CR) LB 98	Exp. C. XVII Exp. C. XXII
Independent variable						
(a) Deterrence factors						
Fine rate	(−)	(−)				−
Audit probability	(+)	(±)				−
Having been audited			−			
(b) Tax system						
Individ. income tax rate	(−)	(−)				
Fairness of the tax system			+			
Complexity of the tax sys.			(−)			
(c) Tax administration (TA)						
Positive attit. towards ta			+			
(d) Taxpayers' perception						
Tax evasion/avoidance			−			
Probability of audit			−	(−)		
Fear of getting caught			+			
Trust people obey the law			+	+	+	

Notes: Dependent variable: tax morale. +, Significant positive coefficient; (+) and (−), positive and negative coefficient signs, respectively, without being significant; (±), positive and negative signs of the coefficient without being significant.

customer-focused organizational structure. Most interestingly, instead of focusing on compliance management, risk control or structuring the application of enforcement discretion, the ATO focused more on service, customer needs, quality, transparency and process improvement. In fact, the ATO was amongst the first tax administrations in the world to implement a new client-based organizational structure (the client-based model is where staff are assigned to units that focus on specific groups of customers; for example, salary and wage earners, small business income taxpayers and large business income taxpayers).[5] One of the advantages of such a client-based structure is that it allows tax administrations better to match their enforcement and educational programmes to the compliance patterns of different groups. This helps in the delivery of a higher-quality service to taxpayers (see Verhorn and Brondolo, 1999). If taxpayers recognize that such an approach is likely to achieve better compliance, it may also influence their own tax morale. Thus, a client-focused approach is likely to increase trust among taxpayers, as taxpayers' needs are being considered more thoroughly in the regulatory process.

WHAT THE FUTURE HOLDS

This section takes a brief look at future research possibilities. A first systematic analysis of what shapes tax morale has been carried out in this book. Empirical evidence has been found that informal and formal institutions have a significant impact on tax morale. However, this wide area still has many aspects, many important hypotheses and many policy questions that have scarcely been investigated up to the present time.

Methodology

As there is a lack of empirical evidence in the tax compliance literature, more empirical work is needed. One of the main purposes of this book is to remedy the lack of empirical evidence outside the United States. However, as the available databases show, it will be possible to intensify this work in the future. Moreover, we only observe a limited number of studies that use more than one methodology to investigate this question. Tax compliance is a complex behavioural issue, and investigation requires the use of a variety of methods and data sources, as each instrument has strength and weaknesses. An exception is, for example, the study by Cummings et al. (2005), which provides experimental and survey results from more than one country. Results from laboratory experiments conducted in different countries demonstrate that observed differences in tax compliance levels can be explained by differences in the fairness of the tax administration, in the perceived fiscal exchange and in the overall attitude towards the respective governments.

Surveys

In the past few years, economists have learned to work with survey data, thanks to more sophisticated statistical techniques and designs. This book has chiefly worked with the World Values Survey. The newest data wave (the fourth) was collected in 1999–2001 and covers a couple of new countries, especially developing countries where evidence is hardly available. Furthermore, as many European countries have participated in this wave, it will be possible to conduct a cross-sectional time-series analysis using European WVS data.

Africa has not been included in the analysis, although a new data set ('Afrobarometro') has recently collected data that will, in the future, allow us to analyse tax morale as a dependent variable (for a first study, see Cummings et al., 2005). In this book, I have worked with the ISSP data set to analyse Switzerland. However, this data set covers more than 30 countries though allowing to get deeper empirical insights going beyond investigating Switzerland. The greatest progress for the future research on tax morale and tax compliance might stem from sophisticated comparisons across societies. A comparative institution analysis among countries is especially important, as standard models of taxpayer behaviour do not pay enough attention to the influence of institutions on tax compliance. Are there differences in the level of tax morale due to differences in the degree of government stability and openness, in the tax system (self-assessment or not), equality and subjects' perception of the public sector and the degree of aggressiveness with which the system is enforced? Such questions merit further attention. They will help us better to understand the role of societal institutions for tax morale and tax compliance.

Another interesting data set is the British Social Attitudes Survey, a survey conducted on a regular basis that covers a wide range of questions. To the author's knowledge, only Orviska and Hudson (2002) have worked with this data set in the tax compliance literature, using the 1996 survey. As data for many years are available, a cross-sectional time-series analysis can be conducted.

More work can be done regarding the measurement of tax morale. In most cases in this book, a single question has been used to define tax morale as the dependent variable. The use of different data sets and countries will allow us to reduce possible biases due to one single question. Further research attempts could construct an index of tax morale using more than one question and check the robustness of the obtained results.

However, it should be noted that the use of an index is also associated with many problems. In some data sets, such an index can only be constructed considering questions about *morale*, rather than *tax* morale.

It general, it might be interesting to analyse further questions that measure trustworthiness, such as attitudes towards lying or returning money found in the street, claiming government benefits without entitlement, dodging fares on public transport, buying something known to have been stolen or accepting a bribe in the performance of one's duties. Such questions are interesting, as the empirical analysis of trustworthiness is just beginning in economics. However, in such an analysis it is also important to take the institutional conditions into account. For example, Leitzel (2003, p. 1) reported an interesting case from Bogota. As cars stopping at red lights late at night became favourite targets for robbery and carjacking, nocturnal drivers refused to respect the traffic rules, preferring the possibility of an accident to the possibility of being a victim of a violent crime. The authorities reacted to that situation by replacing the red and green lights with a flashing yellow light late at night. In general, civic disobedience always raises the question of whether the rules are fair and just, and the extent to which the disobedience has been intentional or unintentional.

In this book, we have analysed tax morale at the individual level. However, the WVS survey, for example, would also allow us to exploit the data at the aggregate level. It would therefore be possible to analyse whether the same relationships that explain attitudes towards tax compliance within a country also explain differences in average attitudes across countries. In investigating this question, it would be important to consider that in different countries individuals' exposure to the tax system is quite different. Furthermore, additional institutional variables such as corruption could be integrated (see Chapter 4 and Torgler, 2006a). This might be interesting as in countries where corruption is systemic and government budgets lack transparency, the obligation to pay taxes to the government might not be seen as an accepted social norm.

Experiments

It might be helpful to include experimental designs purposed by psychologists such as Webley et al. (1991) or Robben (1991), which emphasize more experimental reality. One point should merit special attention. In the experiments carried out in this book, tax compliance has only been measured by giving subjects the possibility of deciding how much income they were willing to declare. But tax compliance experiments should not only offer the possibility of under-declaring or not under-declaring. Subjects should have additional tasks to perform including, for example, deduction possibilities. Focusing only on income declaration might produce some biases. Subjects in the experiment could see what will happen when they under-declare. Furthermore, participants could be tempted to behave as clever gamblers, trying to check all possibilities, which would finally override the desire to behave as in real tax life. Finally, in all the experiments reported in this book, people were fully informed about all of the tax parameters. In real life, however, it can be supposed that people tend to overestimate the probability of audit.

The employment of students has often been criticized. Further experiments could intensify the work with real agents to check whether their behaviour is in line with that of students. Furthermore, it might be interesting to distribute real money from the outset. This might be important because it gives participants a clear notion of the situation, of the purchasing power of their income, an aspect that is often neglected in most experiments that take place in artificial settings.

Field experiments
I believe that field or social experiments, a strongly neglected instrument in the tax compliance literature, offer us one of the best instruments for the analysis of taxpayers' behaviour in the future. The main advantage is the implementation of tax authorities instead of experimenters, which evokes real processes in the normal environment outside the laboratory setting. It helps better to test the effects of different instruments on taxpayers in the real situation of 'filling out the tax form' and 'paying the taxes'. This helps to formulate practical advice on tax policy, based on scientific testing. In the future, researchers and the tax administration should co-operate more closely to remedy the lack of empirical findings and to gain innovative new insights.

Topics

As some aspects of this book are relatively novel in the tax compliance literature – for example, the empirical evaluation of what shapes tax morale – the work leaves many avenues open. As in many chapters of this book further research possibilities and open questions have been treated quite intensively, just a few ideas on aspects to consider in the future are presented here. The special focus is on three topics: institutions, complexity and business tax evasion.

Formal and informal institutions
Studies that analyse the impact of institutions on tax morale and tax compliance are relatively rare. In this book, we have analysed two elementary institutions at the constitutional level: direct democracy and federalism.

However, there are other formal institutions that might have an effect on tax morale and tax compliance. For example, audit courts have rarely been investigated (for exceptions, see Frey and Serna, 1990; Forte and Eusepi, 1994; Frey, 1994; Streim, 1994; Schelker and Eichenberger, 2003; Torgler, 2006b). As such an institution makes government activities more transparent, it can be hypothesized that a stronger audit court leads to a higher tax morale. Audit courts inform taxpayers about public finance aspects and control the activities of the government, thus reducing the asymmetry of information between taxpayers and the government, which might be honoured by a higher tax morale or tax compliance. Switzerland would be an idoneous country to analyse the effects of an audit court, as there is some variation in the degree of control at the local and the control level.

The tax compliance literature might be more closely connected to the social capital literature. In recent years many studies have investigated the effects of values, norms and attitudes on economic *behaviour* (see, e.g., Knack and Keefer, 1997). Thus, cultural studies seem to be in vogue in economics. The book has tried as far as possible to disentangle cultural effects from other aspects of the economic and institutional environment. However, further efforts are still needed better to control for the properties of the tax system and the way in which taxes are administered, and thus not to confound culture with features of the tax structure. In general, on the basis of the cultural diversity of Europe, economists can find a couple of excellent cases to analyse (Torgler and Schneider, 2007). This is particularly interesting, as most of the empirical evidence in the tax compliance literature has come from the United States. For example, it has been pointed out that southern Italy has a lower level of civic virtue than northern Italy (see, e.g., Putnam, 1993; Frey, 2003). Thus, it can be tested whether northern Italy has a higher tax morale than southern Italy, with the possibility of controlling for many aspects (e.g. language) that are more difficult to control in a cross-country analysis.

Regarding the analysis of culture, it might be fruitful to compare experimental findings with survey results to check whether there are similar tendencies. A higher level of tax compliance in experiments should be in line with a higher tax morale.

The complexity of the tax system

Can simplicity in the tax system induce a higher rate of tax compliance? Is complexity correlated with tax evasion? In general, simplicity is a major issue in tax reform concerns. A good tax system should be simple and easy to understand. Complexity may result in unintentional non-compliance if taxpayers have problems in filling out the tax form. It can reduce the moral costs of evading taxes and it might impose costs on the taxpayers. A simpler

Introduction 57

tax law would reduce taxpayers' expenditure in time and money to comply with the tax law. Up to now, only a little empirical evidence is available regarding the effects of simplification of the tax system on tax compliance and tax morale. This topic can be elucidated by surveys and experiments. These can help to provide insights into the direct causality in this complex area. As already mentioned, an experimental analysis might be innovative, as it would mean expanding the experimental designs from a single-choice decision to a multiple decision process, including, for example, deductions. Experiment participants must have the possibility of evading in many ways. Surveys, on the other hand, can give a better picture of whether a higher perceived complexity leads to a lower or a higher tax morale. Some evidence has been found with the Taxpayer Opinion Survey (see Torgler, 2003c). However, more empirical evidence outside the United States is necessary, especially in the light of many reforms that are conducted regularly all around the world.

Business tax evasion
In most of the studies on tax compliance, research has focused on personal income tax compliance. Business tax evasion in general, and VAT compliance in particular, have received very little attention. This is surprising, taking into account the economic importance of the business sector and the importance of business taxation for the tax administration. Work in this area is therefore highly relevant. Certainly, VAT has the advantage that it is more difficult to evade than a general retail sale taxes. However, there are possibilities for evading VAT, and Agha and Haughton (1996) provide a detailed list, including understatement of sales, inflation of claims for VAT paid inputs, claiming credit for tax paid on inputs used in producing goods that are exempt from VAT, non-registration for VAT, diversion of zero-rated exports to the domestic market or claiming that the transaction is not a taxable event. They report from audits in France in 1984 that two-thirds of those audited had understated the value of taxable sales, a quarter of them fraudulently. Two-fifths of those audited had overstated the value of taxable inputs. They also provide a summary of VAT evasion in different countries. For example, in the late 1970s, 40 per cent of the VAT revenues went uncollected in Italy, and in the Netherlands a third of all firms had evaded some VAT.

In general, Agha and Haughton's results indicate that VAT compliance improves with a lower VAT rate, fewer rates, a smaller population, more learning time and greater spending by the tax administration. They also conclude that a single rate on a broad base is the ideal form of VAT. It not only increases the degree of compliance but also lowers the costs of administration. Interestingly, there is evidence for a political trade-off between raising a smaller amount of revenue with an efficient broad-based, single and low-rated VAT and raising a higher amount of revenue with higher VAT rates, but on a narrow base with multiple rates. However, the authors state that this result must be treated with caution,

> because recommendations based on cross-country comparisons are apt to have a 'one size fits all' quality, which overlooks the history, traditions and special features of any given country and which are so important to the policy analyst. Nor are distributional effects treated here (p. 307).

All in all, knowledge on tax morale in the case of business taxes is very limited so far. For example, it could be important to have evidence on tax compliance for different business areas, covering topics such as deterrence, equity, competition, morality, attitudes towards VAT, the tax system, the administration, the tax burden (e.g. corporate taxes), other businesses, other businesses' compliance efforts, perceived seriousness to commit VAT fraud and so on. This research could be conducted using various methods.

NOTES

1. Adams (1994) and Webber and Wildavsky (1986) have provided good overviews on the history of taxation.
2. Torgler (2003a), for example, analysed the willingness to go to war in different OECD countries. The descriptive results indicate that the northern part of Europe, especially Scandinavian countries, has a high willingness to fight, contrary to countries such as Italy, Belgium, Japan and Germany. In general, a small increase in willingness over time is observed. In a second step, the paper evaluated the United States, Switzerland, Spain, Norway and West Germany separately to get a general picture about the robustness of the main variables. The study found evidence that factors such as national pride, and trust in the army, the government and the legal system, have a positive effect on individuals' willingness to go to war.
3. See Cooper et al. (1999) for another kind of experiment. They observed a convergence behaviour over time between students and managers.
4. See also Torgler (2003c–h, 2004a–c, 2005a–b, 2006a) and Alm and Torgler (2006).
5. Prior to this, a function-based structure was used by the ATO (e.g. a separate division for processing tax returns, another for auditing taxpayers and another for collecting arrears).

REFERENCES

Adams, C. (1994), *For Good and Evil: the Impact of Taxes on the Course of Civilization*, London: Madison Books.
Agha, A. and J. Haughton (1996), 'Designing VAT systems: some efficiency considerations', *Review of Economics and Statistics*, **78**: 303–8.
Allingham, M.G. and A. Sandmo (1972), 'Income tax evasion: a theoretical analysis', *Journal of Public Economics*, **1**, 323–38.

Alm, J. (1991), 'A perspective on the experimental analysis of taxpayer reporting', *The Accounting Review*, **66**, 577–93.

Alm, J. (1998), 'Tax compliance and administration', Working Paper, University of Colorado at Boulder.

Alm, J. and B. Torgler (2006), 'Culture differences and tax morale in the United States and Europe', *Journal of Economic Psychology*, **27**, 224–46.

Alm, J., B.R. Jackson and M. McKee (1993), 'Fiscal exchange, collective decision institutions, and tax compliance', *Journal of Economic Behavior and Organization*, **22**, 285–303.

Alm, J., G.H. McClelland and W.D. Schulze (1992), 'Why do people pay taxes?', *Journal of Public Economics*, **48**, 21–48.

Alm, J., G.H. McClelland and W.D. Schulze (1999), 'Changing the social norm of tax compliance by voting', *KYKLOS*, **52**, 141–71.

Andreoni, J., B. Erard and J. Feinstein (1998), 'Tax compliance', *Journal of Economic Literature*, **36**, 818–60.

Baldry, J.C. (1987), 'Income tax evasion and the tax schedule: some experimental results', *Public Finance*, **42**, 357–83.

Baumol, W.J. and W.E. Oates (1979), *Economics, Environmental Policy, and the Quality of Life*, Englewood Cliffs: Prentice-Hall.

Bird, R., J. Martinez-Vazquez and B. Torgler (2006), 'Societal institutions and tax effort in developing countries', in J. Alm, J. Martinez-Vazquez and M. Rider (eds), *The Challenges of Tax Reform in the Global Economy*. New York: Springer, pp. 283–338.

Blumenthal, M., C. Christian and J. Slemrod (2001), 'Do normative appeals affect tax compliance? Evidence from a controlled experiment in Minnesota', *National Tax Journal*, **54**, 125–38.

Bosco, L. and L. Mittone (1997), 'Tax evasion and moral constraints: some experimental evidence', *KYKLOS*, **50**, 297–324.

Burtless, G. (1995), 'The case for randomized field trials in economic and policy research', *Journal of Economic Perspectives*, **9**, 63–84.

Clotfelter, C.T. (1983), 'Tax evasion and tax rate: an analysis of individual return', *The Review of Economics and Statistics*, **65**, 363–73.

Cooper, D., J.H. Kagel, W. Lo and Qing Liang Gu (1999), 'Gaming against managers in incentive systems: experiments with Chinese managers and Chinese students', *American Economic Review*, **89**, 781–804.

Cross, J. (1980), 'Some comments on the papers by Kagel and Battalio and by Smith', in J. Kmenta and J. Ramsey (eds), *Evaluation of Econometric Models*, New York University Press.

Cummings, R.G., J. Martinez-Vazquez, M. McKee and B. Torgler (2005), 'Effects of tax morale on tax compliance: experimental and survey evidence', Working Paper No. 05-16. Atlanta: Georgia State University.

De Alessi, L. (1975), 'Toward an analysis of postdisaster cooperation', *American Economic Review*, **65**, 127–38.

Dubin, J.A. and L.L. Wilde (1988), 'An empirical analysis of federal income tax auditing and compliance', *National Tax Journal*, **41**, 61–74.

Elffers, H. (2000), 'But taxpayers do cooperate!', in: M. Van Vugt, M. Snyder, T.R. Tyler and A. Biel (eds), *Cooperation in Modern Society. Promoting the Welfare of Communities, States and Organizations*, London: Routledge, pp. 184–94.

Elster, J. (1989), *The Cement of Society: A Study of Social Order*, Cambridge: Cambridge University Press.

Erard, B. and J.S. Feinstein (1994), 'The role of moral sentiments and audit perceptions in tax compliance', *Public Finance*, **49**, 70–89.

Feld, L.P. and J.-R. Tyran (2002), 'Tax evasion and voting: an experimental analysis', *KYKLOS*, **55**, 197–222.

Fehr, E., U. Fischbacher, B. von Rosenbladt, J. Schupp and G.G. Wagner (2003), 'A nation-wide laboratory. Examining trust and trustworthiness by integrating behavioral experiments into representative surveys', CESifo Working Paper No. 866, February.

Fischbacher, U. (1998), *Zurich Toolbox for Readymade Economic Experiments*. Experimenter's Manual, University of Zurich.

Forschungsstelle für empirische Sozialökonomik (1997), 'Steuermentalität und Steuermoral der bundesdeutschen Bevölkerung und deren Einstellungen zur Steuerreform', Köln, Germany.

Forte, F. and G. Eusepi (1994), 'A profile of the Italian State Audit Court: an agent in search of a resolute principal', *European Journal of Law and Economics*, **1**, 151–60.

Frey, B.S. (1994), 'Supreme auditing institutions: a politico-economic analysis', *European Journal of Law and Economics*, **1**, 169–76.

Frey, B.S. (1997), *Not Just for the Money. An Economic Theory of Personal Motivation*, Cheltenham, UK and Lyme, USA: Edward Elgar.

Frey, B.S. (1999), *Economics as a Science of Human Behaviour*, Boston/Dordrecht/London: Kluwer.

Frey, B. S. (2002), 'Direct democracy for transition economies', paper for the Collegium Budapest, Institute for Advanced Study.

Frey, B.S. (2003), 'The role of deterrence and tax morale in taxation in the European Union', Jelle Zijlstra Lecture, Netherlands Institute for Advanced Study in the Humanities and Social Sciences (NIAS).

Frey, B.S. and R. Eichenberger (1999), *The New Democratic Federalism for Europe*, Cheltenham, UK and Northampton, MA, USA: Edward Elgar.

Frey, B.S. and L.P. Feld (2002), 'Deterrence and morale in taxation: an empirical analysis', CESifo Working Paper No. 760, August 2002.

Frey, B.S. and A. Serna (1990), 'Eine politisch-ökonomische Betrachtung des Rechnungshofs', *FinanzArchiv*, **48**, 244–70.

Frey, B.S. and A. Stutzer (2002), *Happiness and Economics*, Princeton: Princeton University Press.

Frey, L.R. and B. Torgler (2002), 'Entwicklung und Stand der Steuermoralforschung', *WiSt*, **3**, 130–35.

Friedland, N., S. Maital and A. Rutenberg (1978), 'A simulation study of income tax evasion', *Journal of Public Economics*, **10**, 107–16.

Gërxhani, K. and A. Schram (2001), 'Tax evasion and the source of income: an experimental study in Albania and the Netherlands', University of Amsterdam, CREED Working Paper.

Graetz, M.J. and L.L. Wilde (1985), 'The economics of tax compliance: facts and fantasy', *National Tax Journal*, **38**, 355–63.

Graham, C. and S. Pettinato (2002), *Happiness and Hardship: Opportunity and Insecurity in New Market Economies*, Washington, DC: The Brookings Institution.

Grasmick, H.G., R.J. Bursik and J.K. Cochran (1991), '"Render unto Caesar what is Caesar's": religiosity and taxpayers' inclinations to cheat', *Sociological Quarterly*, **32**, 251–66.

Hasseldine, J. (2000), 'Using persuasive communications to increase tax compliance: what experimental research has (and has not) told us', *Australian Tax Forum*, **15**, 227–4.

Henrich, J., P. Young, R. Boyd, K. McCabe, W. Albers, A. Ockenfels and G. Gigerenzer (1999), 'What Is the role of culture in bounded rationality?', unpublished manuscript.

Henrich, J., R. Boyd, S. Bowles, C. Camerer, E. Fehr, H. Gintis and R. McElreath (2001), 'In search of Homo economicus: behavioral experiments in 15 small-scale societies', *American Economic Review*, **91**, 73–8.

Hirschi, T. and R. Stark (1969), 'Hellfire and delinquency', *Social Problems*, **17**, 202–13.

Hirschman, A.O. (1970), *Exit, Voice, and Loyalty*, Cambridge MA: Harvard University Press.

Hull, B. B. (2000), 'Religion still matters', *Journal of Economics*, **26**, 35–48.

Hull, B.B. and F. Bold (1989), 'Towards an economic theory of the church', *International Journal of Social Economics*, **16**, 5–15.

Inglehart, R. (1997), *Modernization and Postmodernization: Cultural, Economic and Political Change in 43 Societies*, Princeton: Princeton University Press.

Inglehart, R. (2000), 'Globalization and postmodern values', *Washington Quarterly*, **23**, 215–28.

ISSP (2000), ISSP 1998, Religion II, Codebook, Köln Zentralarchiv für Empirische Sozialforschung.

Jackson, B.R. and V.C. Milliron (1986), 'Tax compliance research: findings, problems, and prospects', *Journal of Accounting Literature*, **5**, 125–66.

Knack, S. and P. Keefer (1997), 'Does social capital have an economic payoff: a cross-country investigation', *Quarterly Journal of Economics*, **112**, 1251–88.

Leijonhufvud, A. (1973), 'Life Among the Econ', *Western Economic Journal*, **11**, 327–37.

Leitzel, J. (2003), *The Political Economy of Rule Evasion and Policy Reform*, London: Routledge.

Lewis, A. (1982), *The Psychology of Taxation*, Oxford: Martin Robertson.

Lipford, J., R.E. McCormick and R.D. Tollison (1993), 'Preaching matters', *Journal of Economic Behavior and Organization*, **21**, 235–50.

Long, S. and J. Swingen (1991), 'The conduct of tax-evasion experiments: validation, analytical methods, and experimental realism', in P. Webley, H. Robben, H. Elffers and D. Hessing, *Tax Evasion: An Experimental Approach*, Cambridge: Cambridge University Press, pp. 128–38.

Martinez-Vazquez, J. (2001), 'Mexico: an evaluation of the main features of the tax administration', Working Paper, 01–12, Georgia State University, Atlanta.

McCloskey, D.N. and S.T. Ziliak (1996), 'The Standard Error of Regressions', *Journal of Economic Literature*, **34**, 97–114.

Mummert, A. and F. Schneider (2002), 'The German shadow economy: parted in a United Germany?', *FinanzArchiv*, **58**, 287–317.

Ockenfels, A. and J. Weimann (1999), 'Types and patterns: an experimental East–West-German comparison of cooperation and solidarity', *Journal of Public Economics*, **71**, 275–87.

Orviska, M. and J. Hudson (2002), 'Tax evasion, civic duty and the law abiding citizen', *European Journal of Political Economy*, **19**, 83–102.

Pommerehne, W.W., A. Hart and B.S. Frey (1994), 'Tax morale, tax evasion and the choice of policy instruments in different political systems', *Public Finance*, **49**, (Supplement), 52–69.
Putnam, R. (1993), *Making Democracy Work*, Princeton: Princeton University Press.
Pyle, D.J. (1991), 'The economics of taxpayer compliance', *Journal of Economic Surveys*, **5**, 163–98.
Pyle, D.J. (1993), 'The economics of taxpayer compliance', in P.M. Jackson (ed.), *Current Issues in Public Sector Economics*, Houndsmills: Macmillan, pp. 58–93.
Robben, H. S. J. (1991), *A Behavioral Simulation and Documented Behavior Approach to Tax Evasion*, Deventer: Kluwer.
Roth, A. E. (1995), 'Introduction to experimental economics', in J.H. Kagel and A.E. Roth (eds), *The Handbook of Experimental Economics*, Princeton: Princeton University Press, pp. 1–98.
Roth, J.A., J.T. Scholz and A.D. Witte (eds) (1989), *Taxpayer Compliance*, Vols. 1 and 2, Philadelphia: University of Pennsylvania Press.
Schelker, M. and R. Eichenberger (2003), 'Starke Rechnungsprüfungskommissionen: Wichtiger als direkte Demokratie und Föderalismus? Ein erster Blick auf die Daten', *Swiss Journal of Economics and Statistics*, **139**, 351–73.
Schmölders, G. (1951/1952), 'Finanzpsychologie', *FinanzArchiv*, **13**, 1–36.
Schmölders, G. (1960), *Das Irrationale in der öffentlichen Finanzwissenschaft*, Hamburg: Rowolt.
Schmölders, G. (1962), *Volkswirtschaftslehre und Psychologie*, Berlin: Reinbek.
Schmölders, G. (1970a), 'Survey research in public finance: a behavioral approach to fiscal theory', *Public Finance*, **25**, 300–6.
Schmölders, G. (1970b), *Finanz- und Steuerpsychologie*, Hamburg: Rowolt.
Schwartz, R. and S. Orleans (1967), 'On legal sanctions', *University of Chicago Law Review*, **34**, 282–300.
Slemrod, J. (1992), *Why People Pay Taxes. Tax Compliance and Enforcement*, Ann Arbor: University of Michigan Press.
Slemrod, J. (2002), 'Trust in public finance'. NBER Working Paper 9187, September, Cambridge, MA.
Starmer, C. (1999), 'Experiments in economics ... Should we trust the dismal scientists in white coats?', *Journal of Economic Methodology*, **6**, 1–30.
Streim, H. (1994), 'Agency problems in the legal political system and supreme auditing institutions', *European Journal of Law and Economics*, **1**, 177–91.
Strümpel, B. (1969), 'The contribution of survey research to public finance', in A.T. Peacock (ed.), *Quantitative Analysis in Public Finance*, New York: Praeger, pp. 14–32.
Stutzer, A. (1999), 'Demokratieindizes für die Kantone der Schweiz', Working Paper No. 23, Institute for Empirical Research in Economics, University of Zurich.
Tittle, C. (1980), *Sanctions and Social Deviance: the Question of Deterrence*, New York: Praeger.
Torgler, B. (2001), 'Is tax evasion never justifiable?', *Journal of Public Finance and Public Choice*, **19**, 143–68.
Torgler, B. (2002), 'Speaking to theorists and searching for facts: tax morale and tax compliance in experiments', *Journal of Economic Surveys*, **16**, 657–84.
Torgler, B. (2003a), 'Why do people go to war?', *Defence and Peace Economics*, **14**, 261–80.

Torgler, B. (2003b), 'Ancestors of the contemporary Homo Economicus', *Homo Oeconomicus*, **19**, 519–41.

Torgler, B. (2003c), 'Tax morale and tax evasion: evidence from the United States', WWZ-Discussion Paper 03/01, Basel: WWZ.

Torgler, B. (2003d), 'Does culture matter? Tax morale in an East–West-German comparison, *FinanzArchiv*', **59**, 504–28.

Torgler, B. (2003e), 'To evade taxes or not: that is the question', *Journal of Socio-Economics*, **32**, 283–302.

Torgler, B. (2003f), 'Tax morale in transition countries', *Post-Communist Economies*, **15**, 357–81.

Torgler, B. (2003g), 'Tax morale, rule governed behaviour and trust', *Constitutional Political Economy*, **14**, 119–40.

Torgler, B. (2003h), 'Beyond punishment: a tax compliance experiment with taxpayers in Costa Rica', *Revista de Análisis Económico*, **18**, 27–56.

Torgler, B. (2004a), 'Tax morale in Asian countries', *Journal of Asian Economics*, **15**, 237–66.

Torgler, B. (2004b), 'Cross culture comparison of tax morale and tax compliance: evidence from Costa Rica and Switzerland', *International Journal of Comparative Sociology*, **45**, 17–43.

Torgler, B. (2004c), 'Moral suasion: an alternative tax policy strategy? Evidence from a controlled field experiment in Switzerland', *Economics of Governance*, **5**, 235–53.

Torgler, B. (2005a), 'Tax morale in Latin America', *Public Choice*, **122**, 133–57.

Torgler, B. (2005b), 'Tax morale and direct democracy', *European Journal of Political Economy*, **21**, 525–31.

Torgler, B. (2006a), 'The importance of faith: tax morale and religiosity', *Journal of Economic Behavior and Organization*, **61**, 81–109.

Torgler, B. (2006b), 'A knight without a sword? The effects of audit courts on tax morale', *Journal of Institutional and Theoretical Economics*, **161**, 735–60.

Torgler, B. and K. Murphy (2004), 'Tax morale in Australia: What factors shape it and has it changed over time?', *Journal of Australian Taxation*, **7**, 298–335.

Torgler, B. and F. Schneider (2007), 'What shapes attitudes toward paying taxes? Evidence from multicultural European countries', forthcoming in *Social Science Quarterly*, **88**.

Verhorn, C.L. and J. Brondolo (1999), 'Organizational options for tax administration', *Bulletin for International Fiscal Documentation*, **53**, 499–512.

Webber, C. and A. Wildavsky (1986), *A History of Taxation and Expenditure in the Western World*, New York: Simon and Schuster.

Webley, P., H. Robben, H. Elffers and D. Hessing (1991), *Tax Evasion: An Experimental Approach*, Cambridge: Cambridge University Press.

Weck, H. (1983), *Schattenwirtschaft: Eine Möglichkeit zur Einschränkung der öffentlichen Verwaltung? Eine ökonomische Analyse*, Finanzwissenschaftliche Schriften 22, Bern: Lang.

Wilde, L. (1980), 'On the use of laboratory experiments in economics', in J. Pitt (ed.), *The Philosophy of Economics*, Dordrecht: Reidel, pp. 137–48.

Witte, A.D. and D.F. Woodbury (1985), 'The effect of tax laws and tax administration on tax compliance', *National Tax Journal*, **38**, 1–14.

2. What do we know about tax morale and tax compliance?

INTRODUCTION

Tax morale is a societal phenomenon that is difficult to explain. Questions about tax compliance are as old as taxes themselves, and will remain an area of discovery as long as taxes exist. To understand the impact of a tax system, it is important to know who complies with the tax law as well as who does not. Tax evasion is a large and growing problem in almost all countries. Unfortunately, we know very little about tax morale. Economists see the problem as one of rational decision made under uncertainty. This means that cheating on taxes is a gamble paying off in lower taxes or, with the probability of detection, ending in sanctions.

This view of taxpayer behaviour was first presented in a formal model by Allingham and Sandmo (1972), influenced by the economics-of-crime approach (see Becker, 1968). Nevertheless, such a portfolio analysis can't explain why many households comply more fully than predicted by this approach. A lot of economic approaches to tax compliance continue on this framework (see Cowell, 1990).

This survey focuses on tax morale and tax compliance and intends to outline alternative theories and empirical findings. Andreoni et al. (1998) write: 'adding moral and social dynamics to models of tax compliance is as yet a largely undeveloped area of research' (p. 852).

Over twenty years ago, Pommerehne (1985) wrote in the *Rivista Internazionale di Scienze Economiche e Commerciali*:

> the attitude can extend to ... supposed factors influencing tax morale, particularly the subjective sense of tax burden ..., the individual perception of fairness of the tax system ..., the relation between taxpayer and administration, but also to what is seen as a fair exchange between the subjective sense of tax burden and the service offered by the state (translated, p. 1164).

This is therefore an opportunity to take a stroll through theoretical and empirical findings in the tax morale literature, focusing on personal income tax morale. The question about tax morale is more why people do not cheat rather than why they do. Most people pay their taxes. Tax compliance is a finally observable action. Complying or not complying is not only a function of opportunity, tax rates and probability of detection, but also the function of an individual's willingness to comply or evade. When tax morale is high, tax compliance will be relatively high too. To analyse the puzzle of tax compliance, it is thus important to go one step back to explain tax morale. The focus is on the process rather than just on outcomes.

In this chapter, I discuss three key factors that seem to be important for understanding tax morale: moral rules and sentiments, fairness, and the relationship between taxpayer and government. First, I examine moral rules and sentiments and present two theories to explain tax morale. In the next section, the issue of fairness is analysed. In the fourth section, the relationship between taxpayer and government is discussed and the last section offers concluding remarks.

MORAL RULES AND SENTIMENTS

Analysing morale poses some problems for economic analysis. The only way to quantify it is to look at its effects. Researchers such as Günter Schmölders (1951/1952, 1960, 1962, 1970a,b) and George Kantona (1975) have emphasized that economic phenomena should not only be analysed from the traditional point of view. It has been noted that compliance cannot be explained entirely by the level of enforcement (Graetz and Wilde, 1985; Elffers, 1991). Countries set the levels of audit and penalty[1] so low that most individuals would evade taxes if they were rational, because it is unlikely that cheaters would be caught and penalized. Nevertheless, a high degree of compliance is observed.

Compliance decisions must be affected by other factors. How can moral rules and sentiments directly guide tax morale? In the literature, we find psychological theories that are discussed in the context of tax morale. It may seem astonishing, but a lot of people do comply with the rules and laws. Kelman's (1965) work, adapted to tax compliance by Vogel (1974), illustrates how people comply for different reasons. Compliance, identification and internalization are Kelman's tripartite typology. 'Compliers' pay their taxes, because people are required to do so and fear the consequences if they do not. 'Identifiers' are influenced by social norms and the beliefs and behaviour of people close to or of importance to them. 'Internalizers' have a consistency between their beliefs and their behaviour (see also Torgler, 2003). In the first section, I will focus on social norms and discuss the four sentiments guilt, shame, duty and fear. In the second section, I will present two interesting economic theories that intend to explain tax morale and tax compliance by showing the limits of traditional economics. The theories imply an extension of the economic model of man.

Social Norms

One factor is social norms. There has been a renewed interest in the social basis of political and economic life (see Knight, 1998). Putnam (1993) claims the importance of social capital for the effective governance of democracy. Other authors have singled out trust as an important feature of productive social relationship (e.g. Gambetta, 1988; Hardin, 1993). Slemrod (1998) argues that the social capital derived from the willingness to pay taxes voluntarily lowers the cost of the operating government and of equitably assigning its cost to citizens. Knack and Keefer (1997) tested the impact of civic duty and trust on growth and investment rates in a cross-sectional analysis. To measure civic norms they used the World Values Surveys of 1981 and 1990–1991. One of the five particular actions to assess the strength of the civic norm was 'cheating on taxes if you have the chance'. In this way, tax compliance emerges as one dimension of civic norm. Knack and Keefer (1997) found a strong and significant positive relationship between social capital variables and economic growth. Schaltegger and Torgler (2006) have observed a strong correlation between trust measured with surveys and accountability with field data. Moreover, they have found that in Swiss cantons with high levels of government accountability, the level of indebtedness is significantly lower, indicating that accountability supports fiscal discipline.

When working with social norms, it is difficult to specify their exact meaning. Social norms consist of a pattern of behaviour that must be shared by other people and sustained by their approval and disapproval (Elster, 1989). Fehr and Gächter (1997) define a social norm as a behavioural regularity that is based on a socially shared belief about how one ought to behave that triggers the enforcement of the prescribed behaviour by informal social sanctions (p. 12) and state:

> Reciprocity provides a key mechanism for the enforcement of social norms. In view of the fact that most social relations in neighborhoods, families and work places are not governed by explicit agreements but by social norms the role of reciprocity as a norm enforcement device is perhaps its most important function (p. 11).

If others behave according to a socially accepted mode of behaviour, the individual will also behave appropriately. Thus, individuals will comply and pay taxes as long as they believe that compliance is a social norm (see Alm et al., 1999).

Polinsky and Shavell (2000), who present a survey of the economic theory of public enforcement of law, emphasize the aspect of social norms for future research. Social norms can be seen as a general alternative to law enforcement[2] in channelling individuals' behaviour. The violation of social norms has consequences such as internal sanctions (guilt, remorse) or external legal and social sanctions, such as gossip and ostracism. As Polinsky and Shavell (2000) state, there is an expanding literature on social norms because of the influence that social norms have on behaviour, their role as a substitute for and supplement to formal laws and the possibility that laws themselves can influence social norms.[3]

There is evidence that many countries with similar fiscal systems have different compliance experiences – see Alm et al. (1995) for the United States, Yankelovich, Skelly and White, Inc. (1984) and Vogel (1974) for Sweden, Lewis (1979) for the United Kingdom and De Juan et al. (1993) for Spain. The main conclusions are that: (i) individuals who comply tend to view tax evasion as immoral; (ii) compliance is higher if moral appeals are made to the taxpayer; (iii) individuals with tax evaders as friends are more likely to be evaders themselves; and (iv) compliance is greater in societies with a stronger sense of social cohesion. Alm et al. (1995) found, in their experimental results, strong evidence that in compliance the role of social norms is the most important determinant.

However, some points remain unexplained. How do social norms arise in the first place? How can these norms be changed by deliberate government policies? There are limits for a government to increase compliance using traditional policies such as audits and fines. If the government can influence a norm, tax evasion can be reduced by policy activities.

Taxpayers may be aware that their evasion could damage the welfare of the community in which they live. As a consequence, evasion can produce psychological costs. People may not be comfortable with dishonesty (Spicer, 1986). However, when a taxpayer is convinced that she pays too much taxes compared with the provided public goods, her psychological costs will be reduced.

In the literature, we find two interesting theories that enable us to integrate moral constraints in a rational taxpayer model. The first theory is an altruistic approach (e.g. Chung, 1976). Here, taxpayers are not only interested in their own welfare but also concerned about the general welfare. The decision to evade is constrained by the knowledge that their evasion will reduce the amount of resources available for social welfare. The second is the 'Kantian' morality approach (see Laffont, 1975; Sugden, 1984). This approach, broadly related to Kant's definition of morality, is based on the assumption that a fair tax is a tax that a taxpayer believes to be fair for all other taxpayers to pay. A false declaration will generate anxiety, guilt or a reduction in the taxpayer's self-image. It is assumed that a taxpayer feels these costs only if he believes that his tax share is not higher than whatever is defined as fair. If he is paying a higher amount, evasion can be seen as a sort of self-defence. Here we have the connection to the third section, which is based on the idea that tax evasion can be reduced if a large majority of taxpayers feel that their tax burden is fair.

Guilt and shame

The sentiments guilt and shame may influence reporting behaviour, reducing the perceived benefits of cheating. According to Lewis (1971), guilt arises when individuals realize that they have acted irresponsibly and in violation of a rule or social norm that they have internalized. Since the obligation of paying taxes to the government is an accepted social norm, it makes sense that individuals who choose not to pay all of their taxes may feel guilty. Aitken and Bonneville (1980) found in a Taxpayer Opinion Survey that over 50 per cent of the respondents claimed that their consciences would be bothered 'a lot' after having engaged in any of the following activities: (i) padding business activities, (ii) overstating medical expenses, (iii) understating income, (iv) not filing a return or (v) claiming an extra dependent. Grasmick and Bursik (1990) interviewed 355 individuals in another survey, regarding their future inclination to perform various legal offences, including tax evasion. Their findings indicated that the anticipated guilt associated with committing tax evasion served as a much greater deterrent than the perceived threat of legal sanctions.

While guilt is associated with an impersonal rule or norm, shame has a 'human face', implicating the self-image. Lewis (1971) writes that shame is an experience in which an internalized other 'seems to scorn, despise, or ridicule the self' (p. 39).

Erard and Feinstein (1994) incorporate shame and guilt directly into the taxpayer's utility. They hypothesize that a taxpayer feels guilty when he under-reports and escapes detection. He also feels ashamed when he under-reports and gets caught. The authors also looked at the issue of misperceptions. Many taxpayer surveys indicate that taxpayers tend to overestimate the probability of an audit (e.g. Harris and Associates Inc., 1988; for evidence from psychology experiments, see Kahneman et al., 1982). Individuals tend to overestimate the probability of unlikely events, such as a tax audit, in a wide variety of contexts (Alm et al., 1992b). Kahneman and Tversky (1979) have developed the theory of 'representativeness', influenced by the principles of cognitive psychology. Individuals form a rough assessment of the likelihood of an event by constructing scenarios of the future. They use these scenarios to estimate the probability of the event occurring. Some scenarios are more available than others; for example, rare and dramatic events. A tax audit can be seen as such a salient event. Memories of audits that a taxpayer has personally experienced or of which he was informed support the imagination of a possible future audit. Erard and Feinstein (1994) argue that their results indicated that moral sentiments and audit misperceptions are necessary to provide a reasonable explanation of actual compliance behaviour. Their results suggest that taxpayers have substantial and varied misperceptions of the probability of an audit. Taxpayers overestimate its level and the rate at which it rises as the reported income falls. They anticipate guilt when filling out their return, under-reporting and escaping from detection, and they anticipate shame if subsequently caught.

Nevertheless, this approach has some weaknesses. How guilt and shame should enter into the utility function cannot be derived from economic or psychological theory. Furthermore, as guilt and shame are not directly observable, identification is based on the form of the assumptions.

Duty and fear

Citizens' sense of duty could play a role in the analysis of tax morale. Scholz and Pinney (1995) argue that the uncertainty about the probability of getting caught imposes sufficient difficulties that citizens rely on heuristics to derive subjective estimates of risk. They focus on the implications of the 'duty heuristic'[4] for the relationship between fear and duty, and hypothesize that the taxpayers' sense of duty to pay taxes significantly influences the perceived probability and risk of being caught when cheating. The empirical findings support the idea that the subjective risk of getting caught is more closely related to the sense of duty than to objective risk factors. Duty influences taxpayers tempted to cheat as much as anyone else. Objective audit probabilities, on the other hand, affect only taxpayers who are more subject to the temptation to cheat. These findings have an interesting implication for tax policies. Increasing audits and penalties will not increase tax compliance significantly. Scholz and Lubell (1998) find that duty and fear increase significantly when taxes decrease, and decrease when taxes increase. So, a citizen's attitude towards compliance with a collective obligation and his or her fear of retribution varies according to changes in costs or benefits associated with the collective.

Theories

I will now present two theories and show their relevance for explaining tax morale and tax compliance. The approach of both theories is characterized by the inclusion of a partially specific psychological effect to catch the relative importance of an effect without losing the spirit of the integrated psychological effect and without giving up economic foundations. Frey (1993) states:

> Inspirations from other social (and literary) sciences are very well compatible with the basis of modern economics, which has proved to be so useful. Indeed, the economic model of human behaviour properly understood perfectly lends itself to the integration of so far neglected aspects of people's actions. What is needed, however, is an effort to overcome the model of 'homunculus economicus' who is at all times in full control of his or her emotions, who does not know any cognitive limitations, who is not embedded in a personal network, who is but extrinsically motivated and whose preferences are not influenced by processes of discussion ... It is time now to embark on a new course and to switch from an exporter to an importer of ideas (p. 97 ff.).

Intrinsic motivation

Other sciences, such as sociology and psychology, have stressed the importance of behaviour based on moral and ethical considerations. In economic analysis, internalized values are taken as exogenously given and not influenced by prices or regulations (see Becker, 1976; Hirshleifer, 1985). However, a few economists, such as Hirschman (1965) and Sen (1977), have taken the relationship between external and internal human motivation into account. Frey (1997) demonstrates that intrinsic versus extrinsic motivation is also relevant for explaining compliance behaviour.[5] He looks at tax morale as a particular kind of intrinsic motivation – an attempt to introduce a psychological effect into economics without giving up the rational choice framework. His approach includes a crowding-out effect of intrinsic motivation in the analysis of tax compliance. When monitoring and penalties for non-compliance are increased, individuals notice that extrinsic motivation has increased, which on the other hand crowds out the intrinsic motivation to comply with taxes. Thus, the net effect of a stricter tax policy is unclear. If the intrinsic motivation is not recognized, taxpayers get the feeling that they can also be opportunistic. This takes into account the relevance of policy instruments in supporting or damaging the intrinsic motivation. Intrinsic motivation depends on the application of policy instruments (see the following sections). But Frey (1997) claims that tax morale is not expected to be crowded out if the honest taxpayers perceive the stricter policy to be directed against the dishonest taxpayers. Regulations that prevent free-riding by others and establish fairness and equity help to preserve tax morale.

Ipsative theory

Under certain circumstances, human actions can be constrained by a set of possibilities that are considered to be relevant only for the individual. Other alternatives are disregarded (see Frey and Foppa, 1986). Frey (1997) calls it the 'ipsative possibility set' (p. 196). The underlying theory strongly relies on psychological evidence and can be seen as an attempt to model an aspect of a human imperfection. The ipsative possibility sets are characterized by Frey (1997) as (i) non-marginal (alternatives are either considered fully or not at all), (ii) asymmetric (alternatives outside the set are left out of consideration) and (iii) personal (relevant to a certain person). Frey claims that an underextension of the ipsative set is a common phenomenon among rational actors. Tax morale can be seen as such an issue, which is not open to a marginal but, rather, an absolute evaluation. There are taxpayers who do not even search for ways to cheat on taxes, while others act contrarily. Relative price changes, as a reason of higher punishment, are only considered by taxpayers with a low tax morale who cheat. Frey even speaks of a perverse effect that arises when the government threatens citizens of high tax morale with increased punishment. Citizens can take this as an indication that the government does not honour compliant behaviour. If the government distrusts them, tax morale can be undermined.

FAIRNESS

Another important factor is the taxpayer's perception of the fairness of his tax burden. For a long time, fairness was considered to be of no relevance in economic analysis. Aspects of justice and fairness have been discussed by Rawls (1971), Buchanan (1976), Baumol (1986) and Sen (1987). Closely related theories were analysed – such as, for example, altruism by Becker (1981), social norms by Opp (1983), Elster (1989) and Coleman (1990), and cognitive dissonance by Schlicht (1984). Empirical research is rarer than theoretical studies. We find first studies in the context of the analysis of behavioural anomalies (see Frey and Eichenberger, 1989; Thaler, 1992). The most common types of analysis are natural experiments (see Kahneman et al., 1986; Frey and Pommerehne, 1993) and laboratory experiments (see, e.g., Rabin, 1993; Fehr and Kirchsteiger, 1994).

How do we know what is fair and what is not? Binmore (1998) states:

> When a dish in short supply is shared at a polite dinner party, there is seldom any verbal dispute ... If things go well, the dish gets divided without any discussion or intervention by the host. When questioned, everybody will agree that each person should take his fair share ... What is judged to be fair according to our current standards of morality depends on a complex combination of contingent circumstances – such as who is fat and who dislikes cheese. Moreover, if we observe what actually happens, rather than what people say should happen, we will find that it also depends on how each person at the table fits into the social

pecking order. Woe betide the poor relative sitting at the table on sufferance in the last century who helped himself to an over-generous portion of his favorite dish (p. 275).

An unfair tax system could enhance the incentives to rationalize cheating. Different studies analyse the relationship between tax evasion and perceived inequities in tax systems. A number of survey research studies have reported positive correlations between perceptions of fiscal inequity and tax evasion (Spicer, 1974; Song and Yarbrough, 1978). Social psychology research suggests that a lack of equity in an exchange relationship creates a sense of distress, especially for the victim (see Walster et al., 1978). Homans (1961) argues that disadvantage is followed by anger, advantage by guilt. Tax evasion may be seen as a reaction to restore equity (for general empirical evidence, see Adams, 1965). Spicer and Becker (1980) found, in an experiment with 57 students at the University of Colorado, that the percentage of taxes evaded was the highest among those students who were told that their tax rates were higher than average, and lowest among those told their tax rates were lower than average. However, other experiments (see Webley et al., 1991) could not find such an effect.

Bordignon (1993) introduces fairness as an additional motivation to the evasion decision. He rationalizes the ethical norms supporting tax compliance by making them dependent on tax structure, public expenditure and perceived evasion by other taxpayers. According to the approach of Spicer and Lundstedt (1976), taxpayers perceive their relationship with the state not only as a relationship of coercion, but also as one of exchange. Bordignon (1993) assumes that the taxpayer can compute the fair terms of trade between his private consumption and government provision of public goods. Taxpayers wish to evade if the terms of trade differ from the computed fair terms, in order to re-establish fairness, constrained by the risk of being caught. This approach is able to show that some people do not evade even if it would be in their self-interest to do so. Alm et al. (1992b) suggest that compliance occurs because some individuals value the public goods that their tax payments finance. If there is an increase in the amount individuals receive from a given tax payment, their compliance rate increases. Individuals pay in taxes, then, to receive government services even when there is no chance of being detected or punished when evading.

Cowell and Gordon (1988) and Falkinger (1988) attempt to explain the links between public expenditure and tax compliance. They introduce a government-financed public good in the standard portfolio choice model of tax evasion. Their results imply a converse relationship compared to the empirical research. This modification can explain the observed relation of evasion to the tax rate, but not the reasons why non-evasion is so prevalent.

To capture that aspect, Gordon (1989) modifies the standard model by including non-pecuniary costs of evasion. He appeals to the literature on social customs (see Akerlof, 1980; Naylor, 1989) to provide a motive for the reason why there can be a utility loss by the act of evading. Non-pecuniary or psychic cost increases as evasion increases. The developed model can explain why some taxpayers refuse a favourable evasion gamble. Furthermore, dishonesty is endogenized as reputation cost. Non-pecuniary costs have a dynamic component, varying inversely with the number of individuals having evaded in the previous period. Interestingly, there is a stable interior equilibrium where evaders and honest individuals coexist. However, non-pecuniary costs are exogenous to the analysis, so that they can rationalize, but not explain, differences in tax behaviour across consumers or social groups. Myles and Naylor (1996) state that Gordon's model was a step forward but that it lay outside the mainstream of the social customs literature, because the psychic costs depend on the extent of evasion. They saw no reason why such a relation should hold. They argued that if the psychic cost is due to the shame upon prosecution, then the extent of evasion is irrelevant; or if it is due to the fear of detection, then it should be dependent on the detection probability rather than the extent of evasion. On the basis of the social customs literature, where it is accepted that once a social custom is broken, all utility from it is lost, Myles and Naylor (1996) suggest a model in which a social custom utility is derived when taxes are paid honestly, but is lost when evasion is undertaken. In their model, taxpayers face a choice between evading or not. If a taxpayer chooses evasion, the standard model of tax evasion becomes operative. The intention of Myles and Naylor was to combine social customs and social conformity with the standard model of tax evasion as a choice with risk.

Cowell (1992) shows that the economic analysis can come to the same results as psychological research if forms of personalized inequity are incorporated in the economic model. Taxpayers will reduce tax evasion when perceiving equity. Falkinger (1995) has pointed out concrete economic situations in which individuals reduce evasion if the socio-economic system is considered to be relatively equal and fair. The fairness of a system a person lives in may result in bad reputation for evaders if people consider evasion to be blameworthy, so that risk aversion will increase with perceived equity. Falkinger used the notion 'equity' for the perceived exchange relationship between taxpayers and government. He argues that risk aversion increases with equity, if the value of consumption characteristics, produced by the supplied good, increases. This brings us to the next section, where we analyse the relationship between government and taxpayer.

TAXPAYER AND GOVERNMENT

A third topic of moral and social influence is the degree of satisfaction taxpayers have with the government. This topic is strongly correlated with aspects of the last section, especially with regard to the concept of procedural fairness. We find this concept in the regulatory literature, in the literature on disputes and civilians' encounters and institutional analysis, where the relationship between taxpayer and government is modelled as an implicit contract. Positive actions by the state are intended to increase taxpayers' positive attitudes and commitment to the tax system and tax payment, and thus compliant behaviour (e.g. Smith and Stalans, 1991; Smith 1992). One of the most important social psychological reasons for expecting co-operation is reciprocation (see Gouldner, 1960; Regan, 1971; Axelrod, 1984; Cialdini, 1984). We distinguish between positive and negative reciprocity. Positive reciprocity is the impulse to be kind to those who have been kind to us. On the other hand, *an eye for an eye, a tooth for a tooth* is a principal example of negative reciprocity (Fehr and Gächter, 1997). Positive behaviour of the state towards taxpayers will increase the likelihood of compliance. As Smith (1992) argues, cycles of antagonism between the tax administration and the taxpayer might first be broken up by a positive concession of the administrator.[6] Taxpayers are more inclined to comply with the law if the exchange between the paid tax and the performed government services are found to be equitable. Frey and Holler (1998) argue that an increase in deterrence disrupts such a balance based on reciprocity for honest taxpayers. This feeling gets stronger when taxpayers, who consider themselves to pay fair dues, are audited and fined. The balance will also be disrupted when they notice that other taxpayers who are violating the tax law do not get punished.

Tyler's research (1990a,b, 1997) provides support for the importance of legitimacy and allegiance to authority in compliance decisions. The way people are treated by the authorities affects their evaluations of authorities and their willingness to co-operate (see, e.g., Tyler and McGraw, 1986; Lind and Tyler, 1988; Tyler et al., 1989). Tyler (1997) argues that understanding what people want in a legal procedure helps to explain public dissatisfaction with the law and points towards directions for building public support for the law in the future. He proposes the creation of a moral climate that associated various forms of property law with public morality. To do so, a better understanding of public morality would be needed to comprehend what the public viewed as fair and unfair. This leads to the argument that taxpayers who are treated fairly and respectfully by the tax authorities tend to co-operate better. But the question remains how these effects occur. Is personal experience more significant than second-hand information?

The survey findings of Yankelovich, Skelly and White, Inc. (1984) suggest that there may be a problem with Internal Revenue Service (IRS) status as a credible authority. Only a small majority of 58 per cent of the public agreed that the IRS and its staff are 'expert/knowledgeable', while a large minority of 37 per cent did not. The same results were found for perceived trustworthiness (59 per cent versus 38 per cent). There seems to be a problem of credibility. This problem appears to stem from the IRS's association with a tax system that the majority of the public considers as complicated and unfair. Complexity leads to public perception of errors and inconsistencies among IRS personnel in dealing with the public. It also may allow for various tax loopholes that contribute to the view of a biased and unfair tax system.

Spicer and Lundstedt (1976) as well as Smith (1992) hypothesize that taxpayers will feel cheated if they believe that their tax burden is not spent well. Smith (1992) analyses the 1987 Taxpayer Opinion Survey in order to study positive incentives that increase citizens' normative commitment to tax compliance. He draws attention to aspects of reciprocity, legitimacy and procedural fairness for tax compliance, and finds that responsive services and procedural fairness are effective positive incentives to increase the commitment to tax compliance. Alm et al. (1992a) used experiments to test this idea. What they found is a greater willingness to comply when participants perceive that they will receive benefits from a public good funded by the taxes collected. Another examination of the role of taxpayers' satisfaction with the government was undertaken by Webley et al. (1991). They found that those participants whose responses to a survey were noted several months after the experiment indicated alienation from the government or a negative attitude towards laws, and were significantly more likely to have engaged in evasion during the experiments.

To deal with this on a theoretical basis, Pommerehne et al. (1994) used a dynamic, recursive analysis of the relationship between government public good provision, government waste, fairness considerations and taxpayer compliance. The message in their simulation is the need to adjust the output of the political sector to people's needs. They conclude:

> The less severe the principal agent problems due to appropriate choice of political framework, the better the outlook for survival of the system and the better the performance of the political system under conditions of sustainability (p. 66).

They further state that tax payments are higher and the performance might be better in a direct than in a representative democracy.

The importance of the institutional aspect for the extent of tax morale has been shown by Pommerehne and Weck-Hannemann (1996). They used

Switzerland as a suitable test because the various cantons have different degrees of political participation possibilities and, due to strong fiscal decentralization, considerable variance in the potential determinants of tax evasion.[7] They hypothesized that the more extended political participation possibilities in the form of citizens' meetings (obligatory and optional referenda and initiatives), the higher tax morale and so *ceteris paribus* tax compliance. Using a cross-sectional/time-series multiple regression, they found that in cantons with a high degree of direct political control, tax morale was higher. In those cantons tax evasion was – *ceteris paribus* – about SFr 1500 lower than the average of those cantons that do not have such a direct influence. Feld and Kirchgässner (2000) pointed out that these results could be seen as an evidence for higher satisfaction[8] among citizens and therefore for greater efficiency for the provision of public services. If the willingness to pay taxes is higher, the citizens are more satisfied with the supply of public services. The strong link between tax prices, public services and higher tax morale in direct democracy indicates that citizens in direct democracies feel more responsible for their communities. Feld and Kirchgässner saw this as indirect evidence for the opinion that self-interested preferences can partially be reversed in the referendum discourse towards the common interest of the community.

Generalizing the empirical evidence, Frey (1997) notes that there are two kinds of tax systems that can be compared. The first is based on the premise that citizens are generally responsible persons. This presupposes that citizens are prepared to pay a fair share, in order to contribute to the provision of public goods and the redistribution of income by the state, if the process is considered efficient and fair. Tax laws, in such a system, allow citizens to declare their own income and to make generalized deductions. If the tax authorities doubt the declaration's correctness, they bear the burden of proof. A lack of taxable income is, first of all, attributed to an error on the taxpayer's side, rather than a result of tax cheating. The second tax system assumes that citizens want to cheat on taxes. As a consequence, tax laws deduct the taxes directly from gross income. Citizens are then charged to claim back from the government. It is up to the citizens to prove that there are incorrect deductions. Important reactions to such distrustful public laws are tax evasion or efforts to minimize the tax burden by illegal activities. In this case, the interaction between individuals and government is characterized by high transaction costs and low productivity. These empirical results suggest that the standard economic approach to tax evasion should be extended by integrating institutions. Pommerehne and Weck-Hannemann (1996) perceive that:

Only when the interaction between citizens and government is fully accounted for and the often-cited aspects of morale are endogenised, can the model provide a proper base for tax compliance policies, possibly by revealing suitable incentive mechanisms (p. 168).

Feld and Frey (2002) have analysed how tax authorities treat taxpayers. Using a data set of tax authorities' behaviour (26 cantonal tax authorities), they found that tax authorities of cantons with more direct participation rights, compared to cantons with less direct democracy, treated taxpayers more respectfully and are less suspicious if taxpayers report too low incomes.[9] On the other hand, not-submitted tax declarations are more heavily fined.[10] This empirical evidence indicates the importance of institutional differences (here political participation rights) for explaining the relationship between taxpayers and tax authorities which influences tax morale.

CONCLUSIONS

Although a significant body of research has already been accumulated concerning tax compliance and tax morale, there are several topics that can merit further development. The main purpose of this chapter is to present the work that has been done in analysing tax compliance and tax morale in a systematic and comprehensive way, focusing on three important topics: moral sentiments, fairness, and the relationship between taxpayer and government. It can also be seen as an attempt to describe the research that tries to incorporate non-economic factors into the economic analysis of tax compliance. Tax compliance is not just a function of opportunity, tax rates, probability of detection and so on, but of each individual's willingness to comply, shaped by tax morale. This means that if tax morale is favourable, tax compliance will be relatively high.

This survey has shown that for future analysis of tax morale it can be fruitful to work with a model that systematically integrates ideas borrowed from other social sciences. An extension of the economic model of man opens a new working instrument, without losing the main advantages of economic theory, its simpleness and robustness. Frey (1997) proposes *Homo Oeconomicus Maturus* (HOM), endowed with a more refined motivation structure.

If we analyse tax morale and tax compliance, we have problems finding data with adequate quality. Experimental techniques could probably provide a good instrument to gain new insights. The second section has also shown us that some points remain relatively unexplained: (i) How do social norms arise in the first place? (ii) How can these norms be changed by deliberate government policies? One possibility is to pay more attention to the institutional framework of tax morale. Experimental studies also help to isolate the impact of fairness motives. As Fehr and Schmidt (2000) state, 'In experiments real subjects make decisions with real monetary consequences in carefully controlled laboratory settings' (p. 4).

Analysing the previous sections, we can implement another agent besides *Homo Oeconomicus Maturus*, *Homo Reciprocans*, which according to Bowles et al. (1997) is 'neither the selfless altruist of utopian theory, nor the selfish hedonist of neoclassical economics. Rather, he is a conditional cooperator whose penchant for reciprocity can be elicited under the proper circumstances' (p. 5).

Studies show that reciprocity plays an important role, as explained first by David Hume (1969 [1739–1740]). Positive reciprocity signifies that positive behaviour by the state towards taxpayers can increase the likelihood of compliance. On the other hand, tax evasion or tax avoidance can be a reaction of negative reciprocity. Accordingly, the influence of the institutional environment on the dominance of positive and negative reciprocity is an important question. As Fehr and Gächter (1997) state, 'The influence of one type on the behaviour of the other is no "one-way street". Ultimately, the institutional environment is decisive, too' (p. 4).

Empirical evidence in tax compliance analysis shows the need to adjust the output of the political sector to the needs of the population to support tax morale. According to Rawls (1971), we have a 'fundamental natural duty ... to comply with just institutions' (p. 115).

It is clear that governments all over the world wish to increase tax morale and tax compliance. Government policy should take the significance of tax morale into account. The considered topics demonstrate that, despite the many improvements and fascinating insights, much future research can be done for a better understanding of tax morale.

NOTES

1. According to Andreoni et al. (1998), in 1995 the audit rate in the United States for individual tax returns was 1.7 per cent, the civil penalty for underpayment of taxes being calculated as 20 per cent of the underpayment that results from wrongful conduct.
2. It is interesting that one of the earliest economically oriented writings on the subject of law enforcement dates from the eighteenth century. The work of Montesquieu (1748/1977), Beccaria (1767/1995) and Bentham (1789/1973) should be mentioned. After Bentham, it took nearly two hundred years before Becker (1968) published his important article on this topic.
3. Posner (1997, pp. 365–366) looks at the incentives for obeying norms. He finds four: (i) norms that are self-enforcing because obedience confers private benefits; (ii) norms that are enforced by emotions; (iii) milder sanctions by expressions of disapproval or ridicule; and (iv) internalized norms, out of a sense of guilt or shame.

4. The duty heuristic is an extension of the low-information rationality approach (see Popkin, 1991) that we find in electoral studies and democratic theory. (For example, Downs (1957) discusses the advantage of following the advice of opinion leaders, while Fiorina (1981) suggests that party identification provided low-cost means to track the behaviour of incumbents). An heuristic can be interpreted as an aid used to minimize cognitive efforts for routine decision situations (see Payne et al., 1993).
5. For a recent survey, see Frey and Jegen (2001). They have shown that crowding effects are an empirically relevant phenomenon.
6. The incentive of enforcement agents to discover violations have not been examined in this chapter. Polinsky and Shavell (2000) have argued that it is an important topic for two reasons. First, the incentive of enforcement agents to discover violations is affected by the structure of their payments. Second, it is possible that enforcement agents are corrupt and might demand payments in exchange for not reporting violations (see, e.g., Becker and Stigler, 1974; Polinsky and Shavell, 1999). The standard models of optimal tax systems assume benevolent bureaucrats, without any thought of using the tax system for their own advantage. Some economic theorists have taken note of the aspect of corruption (see, e.g., Chu, 1990; Virmani, 1987; Chander and Wilde, 1992).
7. Stutzer (1999) compiled an index (varying on a continuum from 1 to 6) to measure voters' possibility of participating in the different cantons.
8. Frey and Stutzer (1999, 2000) present evidence that institutions of direct democracy and federalism systematically affect individual well-being. They note that research in this field underlines the importance of a process rather than an outcome-oriented economic policy.
9. Feld and Frey argue that 'Nobody is perfect, and to cheat a little bit on taxes is a common and minor human weakness and should be considered as such. Such minor violations should not be interpreted as an action intended to breach the psychological contract' (pp. 95–96).
10. This is important to protect honest taxpayers from crowding out tax morale.

REFERENCES

Adams, J.S. (1965), 'Inequity in social exchange', in L. Berkowitz (ed.), *Advances in Experimental Social Psychology*, New York: Academic Press, pp. 167–299.

Aitken, S. and L. Bonneville (1980), 'A general taxpayer opinion survey', Washington, DC: Internal Revenue Service.

Akerlof, G.A. (1980), 'A theory of social custom of which unemployment may be one consequence', *Quarterly Journal of Economics*, 94, 749–95.

Allingham, M.G. and A. Sandmo (1972), 'Income tax evasion: a theoretical analysis', *Journal of Public Economics*, 1, 323–38.

Alm, J., B.R. Jackson and M. McKee (1992a), 'Estimating the determinants of taxpayer compliance with experimental data', *National Tax Journal*, 45, 107–15.

Alm, J., G.H. McClelland and W.D. Schulze (1992b), 'Why do people pay taxes?' *Journal of Public Economics*, 48, 21–48.

Alm, J., G.H. McClelland and W.D. Schulze (1999), 'Changing the social norm of tax compliance by voting', *KYKLOS*, 52, 141–71.

Alm, J., I. Sanchez and A. De Juan (1995), 'Economic and noneconomic factors in tax compliance', *KYKLOS*, 48, 3–18.

Andreoni, J., B. Erard and J. Feinstein (1998), 'Tax compliance', *Journal of Economic Literature*, 36, 818–60.

Axelrod, R. (1984), *The Evolution of Cooperation*, New York: Basic Books.

Baumol, W.J. (1986), *Superfairness, Applications and Theory*, Cambridge, MA: The MIT Press.
Beccaria, C. (1767/1995), *On Crimes and Punishment*, New York: Cambridge University Press.
Becker, G.S. (1968), 'Crime and punishment: an economic approach', *Journal of Political Economy*, **76**, 169–217.
Becker, G.S. (1976), *The Economic Approach to Human Behavior*, Chicago: Chicago University Press.
Becker, G.S. (1981), *A Treatise on the Family*, Cambridge, MA: Harvard University Press.
Becker, G.S. and G.J. Stigler (1974), 'Law enforcement, malfeasance, and compensation of enforcers', *Journal of Legal Studies*, **3**, 1–18.
Bentham, J. (1789/1973), *An Introduction to the Principles of Morals and Legislation*, New York: Anchor Books.
Binmore, K.G. (1998), 'The evolution of fairness norms', *Rationality and Society*, **10**, 275–301.
Bordignon, M. (1993), 'A fairness approach to income tax evasion', *Journal of Public Economics*, **52**, 345–62.
Bowles, S., R. Boyd, E. Fehr and H. Gintis (1997), 'Homo Reciprocans: a research initiative on the origins, dimensions, and policy implications of reciprocal fairness', unpublished paper.
Buchanan, J.M. (1976), 'A Hobbesian interpretation of the Rawlsian difference principle', *KYKLOS*, **19**, 5–25.
Chander, P. and L. Wilde (1992), 'Corruption in tax administration', *Journal of Public Economics*, **49**, 333–49.
Chu, C. (1990), 'Income tax evasion with venal tax officials – the case of developing countries', *Public Finance*, **45**, 392–408.
Chung, P. (1976), 'On complaints about high taxes, an analytical note', *Public Finance*, **31**, 36–47.
Cialdini, R.B. (1984), *Influence: The Psychology of Modern Persuasion*, New York: Quill.
Coleman, J.S. (1990), *Foundations of Social Theory*, Cambridge, MA: Harvard University Press.
Cowell, F.A. (1990), *Cheating the Government. The Economics of Evasion*, Cambridge, MA: The MIT Press.
Cowell, F.A. (1992), 'Tax evasion and inequity', *Journal of Economic Psychology*, **13**, 521–43.
Cowell, F.A. and J.P.F. Gordon (1988), 'Unwillingness to pay: tax evasion and public good provision', *Journal of Public Economics*, **36**, 305–21.
Cummings, R.G., J. Martinez-Vazquez, M. McKee and B. Torgler (2005), 'Effects of tax morale on tax compliance: experimental and survey evidence', Working Paper No. 05-16. Atlanta: Georgia State University.
De Juan, A., M.A. Lasheras and R Mayo (1993), 'Voluntary compliance and behavior of Spanish taxpayers', Instituto de Estudios Fiscales, Madrid, Spain.
Downs, A. (1957), *An Economic Theory of Democracy*, Reading, MA: Addison-Wesley.
Elffers, H. (1991), *Income Tax Evasion: Theory and Measurement*, Amsterdam: Kluwer.
Elster, J. (1989), *The Cement of Society: A Study of Social Order*, Cambridge: Cambridge University Press.

Erard, B. and J.S. Feinstein (1994), 'The role of moral sentiments and audit perceptions in tax compliance', *Public Finance*, **49**, 70–89.

Falkinger, J. (1988), 'Tax evasion and equity: a theoretical analysis', *Public Finance*, **43**, 388–95.

Falkinger, J. (1995), 'Tax evasion, consumption of public goods and fairness', *Journal of Economic Psychology*, **16**, 63–72.

Fehr, E. and S. Gächter (1997), 'Reciprocity and economics. The economic implications of Homo reciprocans', working paper, University of Zurich.

Fehr, E. and G. Kirchsteiger (1994), 'Insider power, wage discrimination, and fairness', *Economic Journal*, **104**, 571–83.

Fehr, E. and K.M. Schmidt (2000), 'Theories of fairness and reciprocity – evidence and economic applications', CESifo Working Paper Series No. 403.

Feld, L.P. and B.S. Frey (2002), 'Trust breeds trust: how taxpayers are treated', *Economics of Governance*, **3**, 87–99.

Feld L.P. and G. Kirchgässner (2000), 'Direct democracy, political culture, and the outcome of economic policy: a report on the Swiss experience', *European Journal of Political Economy*, **16**, 287–306.

Fiorina, M. P. (1981), *Retrospective Voting in American National Elections*, New Haven: Yale University Press.

Frey, B.S. (1993), 'From economic imperialism to social science inspiration', *Public Choice*, **77**, 95–105.

Frey, B.S. (1997), *Not Just for Money. An Economic Theory of Personal Motivation*, Cheltenham, UK and Lyme, USA: Edward Elgar.

Frey, B.S. and R. Eichenberger (1989), 'Anomalies and institutions', *Journal of Institutional and Theoretical Economics*, **145**, 423–37.

Frey, B.S. and K. Foppa (1986), 'Human behaviour: possibilities explain action', *Journal of Economic Psychology*, **7**, 137–60.

Frey, B.S. and M.J. Holler (1998), 'Tax compliance policy reconsidered', *Homo Oeconomicus*, **15**, 27–44.

Frey, B.S. and R. Jegen (2001), 'Motivation crowding theory', *Journal of Economic Surveys*, **15**, 589–611.

Frey, B.S. and W.W. Pommerehne (1993), 'On the fairness of pricing – an empirical survey among the general population', *Journal of Economic Behavior and Organization*, **145**, 423–37.

Frey, B.S. and A. Stutzer (1999), 'Measuring preferences by subjective wellbeing', *Journal of Institutional and Theoretical Economics*, **155**, 755–78.

Frey, B.S. and A. Stutzer (2000), 'Maximising happiness?', *German Economic Review*, **1**, 145–67.

Gambetta, D. (1988), *Trust, Making and Breaking Cooperative Relations*, Oxford and New York: Blackwell.

Gordon, J.P.F. (1989), 'Individual morality and reputation costs as deterrents to tax evasion', *European Economic Review*, **33**, 797–805.

Gouldner, A.W. (1960), 'The norm of reciprocity: a preliminary statement', *American Sociological Review*, **25**, 161–78.

Graetz, M.J. and L.L. Wilde (1985), 'The economics of tax compliance: facts and fantasy', *National Tax Journal*, **38**, 355–63.

Grasmick, H.G. and R.J. Bursik (1990), 'Conscience, significant others, and rational choice: extending the deterrence model', *Law and Society Review*, **24**, 837–61.

Hardin, R. (1993), 'The street-level epistemology of trust', *Politics and Society*, **21**, 505–31.

Harris, L. and Associates, Inc. (1988), '1987 taxpayer opinion survey', conducted for the US Internal Revenue Service, Internal Revenue Service Document 7292, Washington, DC.

Hirschman, A.O. (1965), 'Obstacles to development: a classification and a quasi-vanishing act', *Economic Development and Cultural Change*, **13**, 385–93.

Hirshleifer, J. (1985), 'The expanding domain of economics', *American Economic Review*, **75**, 53–68.

Homans, G.C. (1961), *Social Behavior: its Elementary Form*, New York: Harcourt, Brace and World.

Hume, D. (1969), *A Treatise of Human Nature*, London: Penguin.

Kahneman, D., J. Knetsch and R. Thaler (1986), 'Fairness as a constraint on profit seeking: entitlements in the market', *American Economic Review*, **76**, 728–41.

Kahneman, D. and A. Tversky (1979), 'Prospect theory: an analysis of decision under risk', *Econometrica*, **47**, 263–91.

Kahneman, D., P. Slovic and A. Tversky (eds) (1982), *Judgement Under Uncertainty: Heuristics and Biases*, Cambridge: Cambridge University Press.

Kantona, G. (1975), *Psychological Economics*, Amsterdam: Elsevier.

Kelman, H. (1965), 'Manipulation of human behaviour: an ethical dilemma for the social scientist', *Journal of Social Issues*, **21**, 31–46.

Knack, S. and P. Keefer (1997), 'Does social capital have an economic payoff? A cross-country investigation', *Quarterly Journal of Economics*, **4**, 1251–88.

Knight, J. (1998), 'The bases of cooperation: social norms and the rule of law', *Journal of Institutional and Theoretical Economics*, **154**, 757–63.

Laffont, J.J. (1975), 'Macroeconomic constraints, economic efficiency and ethics: an introduction to Kantian economics', *Economica*, **42**, 430–37.

Lewis, A. (1979), 'An empirical assessment of tax mentality', *Public Finance*, **2**, 245–57.

Lewis, H.B. (1971), *Shame and Guilt in Neurosis*, New York: International University Press.

Lind, E.A. and T.R. Tyler (1988), *The Social Psychology of Procedural Justice*, New York: Plenum Press.

Montesquieu, C. (1748/1977), *The Spirit of the Laws*, Berkeley: University California Press.

Myles, G.D. and R.A. Naylor (1996), 'A model of tax evasion with group conformity and social custom', *European Journal of Political Economy*, **12**, 49–66.

Naylor, R.A. (1989), 'Strikes, free riders and social customs', *Quarterly Journal of Economics*, **104**, 771–805.

Opp, K.-D. (1983), *Die Entstehung sozialer Normen. Ein Integrationsversuch soziologischer, sozialpsychologischer und ökonomischer Erklärungen*, Tübingen: Mohr (Siebeck).

Payne, J.W., J.R. Bettman and E.J. Johnson (1993), *The Adaptive Decision Maker*, New York: Cambridge University Press.

Polinsky, M.A. and S. Shavell (1999), 'Corruption and optimal law enforcement', Working Paper 171, John M. Olin Program in Law and Economics, Stanford Law School.

Polinsky, M.A. and S. Shavell (2000), 'The economic theory of public enforcement of law', *Journal of Economic Literature*, **38**, 45–76.

Pommerehne, W.W. (1985), 'Was wissen wir eigentlich über Steuerhinterziehung?' *Rivista Internazionale di Scienze Economiche e Commerciale*, **32**, 1155–86.

Pommerehne, W.W. and H. Weck-Hannemann (1996), 'Tax rates, tax administration and income tax evasion in Switzerland', *Public Choice*, **88**, 161–70.

Pommerehne, W.W., A. Hart and B.S. Frey (1994), 'Tax morale, tax evasion and the choice of policy instruments in different political systems', *Public Finance*, **49** (Supplement), 52–69.

Popkin, S. (1991), *The Reasoning Voter: Communication and Persuasion in Presidential Campaigns*, Chicago: University of Chicago Press.

Posner, R.A. (1997), 'Social norms and the law: an economic approach', *American Economic Review: Papers and Proceedings*, 87, 365–9.

Putnam, R. (1993), *Making Democracy Work*, Princeton: Princeton University Press.

Rabin, M. (1993), 'Incorporating fairness into game theory and economics', *American Economic Review*, **83**, 1281–1302.

Rawls, J. (1971), *A Theory of Justice*, Oxford: Oxford University Press.

Regan, D.T. (1971), 'Effects of a favor and liking on compliance', *Journal of Experimental Social Psychology*, **7**, 627–39.

Schaltegger, C.A. and B. Torgler (2006), 'Government accountability and fiscal discipline: a panel analysis with Swiss data', *Journal of Public Economics*, **91**, 117–40.

Schlicht, E. (1984), 'Cognitive dissonance in economics', in H. Todt (ed.), *Normengeleitetes Verhalten in den Sozialwissenschaften*, Berlin: Duncker & Humblot.

Schmölders, G. (1951/1952), 'Finanzpsychologie', *FinanzArchiv*, **13**, 1–36.

Schmölders, G. (1960), *Das Irrationale in der öffentlichen Finanzwissenschaft*, Hamburg: Rowolt.

Schmölders, G. (1962), *Volkswirtschaftslehre und Psychologie*, Berlin: Reinbek.

Schmölders, G. (1970a), 'Survey research in public finance: a behavioral approach to fiscal theory', *Public Finance*, **25**, 300–6.

Schmölders, G. (1970b), *Finanz- und Steuerpsychologie*, Hamburg: Rowolt.

Scholz, J.T. and M. Lubell (1998), 'Adaptive political attitudes: duty, trust and fear as monitors of tax policy', *American Journal of Political Science*, **42**, 398–417.

Scholz, J.T. and N. Pinney (1995), 'Duty, fear, and tax compliance: the heuristic basis of citizenship behavior', *American Journal of Political Science*, **39**, 490–512.

Sen, A.K. (1977), 'Rational fools: a critique of the behavioral foundations of economic theory', *Philosophy and Public Affairs*, **6**, 317–44.

Sen, A.K. (1987), *On Ethics and Economics*, Oxford: Blackwell.

Slemrod, J. (1998), 'On voluntary compliance, voluntary taxes, and social capital', *National Tax Journal*, **51**, 485–92.

Smith, K.W. (1992), 'Reciprocity and fairness: positive incentives for tax compliance, in J. Slemrod (ed.), *Why People Pay Taxes. Tax Compliance and Enforcement*, Ann Arbor: University of Michigan Press, pp. 223–58.

Smith, K.W. and L.J. Stalans (1991), 'Encouraging tax compliance with positive incentives: a conceptual framework and research directions', *Law and Policy*, **13**, 35–53.

Song, Y. and Y.E. Yarbrough (1978), 'Tax ethics and taxpayer attitudes: a survey', *Public Administration Review*, **38**, 442–57.

Spicer, M.W. (1974), 'A behavioral model of income tax evasion', dissertation, Ohio State University.

Spicer, M.W. (1986), 'Civilisation at a discount: the problem of tax evasion', *Journal of Public Economics*, **46**, 13–20.

Spicer, M.W. and L.A. Becker (1980), 'Fiscal inequity and tax evasion: an experimental approach', *National Tax Journal*, **33**, 171–5.

Spicer, M.W. and S.B. Lundstedt (1976), 'Understanding tax evasion', *Public Finance*, **31**, 295–304.

Stutzer, A. (1999), 'Demokratieindizes für die Kantone der Schweiz', Working Paper No. 23, Institute for Empirical Research in Economics, University of Zurich.

Sugden, R. (1984), 'Reciprocity: the supply of public goods through voluntary contributions', *Economic Journal*, **94**, 772–87.

Thaler, R.H. (1992), *The Winner's Curse. Paradoxes and Anomalies of Economic Life*, New York: Free Press.

Torgler, B. (2003), 'Tax morale, rule governed behaviour and trust', *Constitutional Political Economy*, **14**, 119–40.

Tyler, T.R. (1990a), 'Justice, self-interest, and the legitimacy of legal and political authority', in J.J. Mansbridge (ed.), *Beyond Self-Interest*, Chicago: University of Chicago Press, pp. 171–9.

Tyler, T.R. (1990b), *Why People Obey the Law*, New Haven: Yale University Press.

Tyler, T.R. (1997), 'Procedural fairness and compliance with the law', *Swiss Journal of Economics and Statistics*, **133**, 219–40.

Tyler, T.R. and K.M. McGraw (1986), 'Ideology and the interpretation of personal experience: procedural justice and political quiescence', *Journal of Social Issues*, **42**, 115–28.

Tyler, T.R., J.D. Casper and B. Fisher (1989), 'Maintaining allegiance toward political authorities: the role of prior attitudes and the use of fair procedures', *American Journal of Political Science*, **33**, 629–52.

Virmani, A. (1987), 'Tax evasion, corruption and administration: monitoring the people's agents under symmetric dishonesty', mimeo, the World Bank, Washington, DC.

Vogel, J. (1974), 'Taxation and public opinion in Sweden: an interpretation of recent survey data', *National Tax Journal*, **27**, 499–513.

Walster, E., G.W. Walster and E. Berscheid (1978), *Equity: Theory and Research*, Boston: Allyn and Bacon.

Webley, P., H. Robben, H. Elffers and D. Hessing (1991), *Tax Evasion: an Experimental Approach*, Cambridge: Cambridge University Press.

Yankelovich, Skelly and White, Inc. (1984), 'Taxpayer attitudes survey: final report', Public Opinion Survey Prepared for the Public Affairs Division, Internal Revenue Service, New York.

3. Speaking to theorists and searching for facts: tax morale and tax compliance in experiments

INTRODUCTION

Tax compliance behaviour can be studied theoretically using field data and laboratory experiments. Laboratory experiments have the advantage that tax reporting institutions (enforcement effort, tax rate and income level) can be controlled.[1] Furthermore, measurements of tax evasion and tax compliance involve some problems. It is difficult to obtain information about tax compliance behaviour. Cowell (1991) states:

> Data from official investigation are hardly ever available and data from other sources may be suspect: if you could directly observe and measure a hidden activity, then presumably it could not really have been properly hidden in the first place (p. 123).

Even if data about tax evaders could be obtained, tax evaders' behaviour could be affected by specific circumstances, which are difficult to control. An experimental approach circumvents the problem of obtaining honest responses on illegal behaviour. Researchers can use their own data obtained from experiments (Andreoni et al., 1998).

But a few problems still remain.[2] It is often argued that a shortcoming lies in the artificiality of the laboratory setting, which makes it difficult to generalize results in real-world terms (Spicer and Thomas, 1982). However, Alm et al. (1992a) argue that:

> there is an extensive – and growing – literature that argues convincingly that experimental results can contribute significantly to policy debates, as long as some conditions are met: the payoffs, and the experimental setting must capture the essential properties of the naturally occurring setting that is the object of investigation. Laboratory methods may offer the only opportunity to investigate the behavioral responses to policy changes (p. 325).

So in experimental work it is essential to operationalize the important variables with real-world values to reduce artificiality. Early works in tax compliance did not pay enough attention to this point. According to Aronson and Carlsmith (1968), 'experimental realism' can be achieved if participants who are involved in it take it seriously and if the experiment evokes processes as in reality.

Roth (1995a) states that:

> Experimental evidence appears regularly in the major economics journals, and it has begun to be reflected in the work of economists who do not themselves do experiments – both in research and in teaching (p. 3).

Tax compliance experiments intend to replicate the structure of voluntary income reporting. Subjects receive income and pay taxes on the reported income. The tax administration is simulated by defining a probability of audit and tax penalty on tax evasion. The experiments in tax compliance and tax morale research that will be presented can be divided into two categories according to Roth's (1995a, p. 22) general definition: (i) 'speaking to theorists' and (ii) 'searching for facts'. 'Speaking to theorists' includes experiments designed to test well-articulated theories, which then feed back into the theoretical literature. As Roth argues, such experiments are part of a dialogue between experimenters and theorists. 'Searching for facts' involves experiments analysing the effects of variables that the existing theory has little to say about. Such experiments are motivated by earlier experiments. Experimenters are thus in a dialogue with one another, so that facts begin to accumulate.

After this introduction, the next section focuses upon the traditional tax compliance topics, such as threat of detection and punishment and the level of tax rates. The third and fourth sections are the core of this chapter. The third section analyses the role of social factors and the fourth one the relevance of institutions. Until now, both topics have only been paid limited attention. Therefore, the purpose of this survey is to examine the impact of these alternative factors on tax morale and tax compliance, focusing on experiments.

TRADITIONAL FOCUS: ECONOMIC AND DETERRENCE VARIABLES

The tax rate, the audit probability and the fine rate seem to be important policy variables. First of all, a deeper look into the pioneering simulation study of Friedland et al. (1978) is presented.

Friedland et al. (1978) conducted an experiment with 15 Israeli undergraduate psychology students. They attempted to find out the effects of fines and audits on tax evasion behaviour using different tax rates. They found that large fines were more effective deterrents than frequent audits. An increase of the tax rate from 25 per cent to 50 per cent, on the other hand, leads to an increase in the probability of under-reporting income and to an extension of under-reporting income. In rounds where the random check was five out of 15 and the fine three times the sum evaded, tax compliance was less high than in rounds with a random check of one out of 15 and a fine magnitude of 15 times the sum evaded. The empirical results suggest that the state should use the instrument of fines instead of controls. However, the work of Friedland et al. has some shortcomings, which are also found in other early studies. Subjects were instructed as follows: 'Your objective is to maximize your net income (gross income less tax less fines)' (p. 110). The aim of such an instruction is to exclude moral considerations. However, involving the participants in a self-contained 'game' might frame participants to follow behavioural rules that are different from those followed in the actual tax declaration process. Thus, it might be useful to tell the subjects not to maximize net income but just to complete their tax returns, giving information about the procedures. The fine magnitudes (three times and 15 times the evaded sum) are not too high, compared to reality. Furthermore, it should be noted that only 15 students participated in the experiment. A small amount of participants reduces the validation of the experiment. In a small sample minor mistakes may have a substantial influence on the results. Rubinstein (2001) points out:

> I suspect that the uncertainty surrounding such mistakes is of higher magnitude than that which is put into routinely calculated 'significance measures' and render many of the 'significance' calculations meaningless (p. 625).

Thus, small experiments should be replicated and experiments should systematically vary the number of participants as one of the treatments.

New works intend to simulate endogenous audit selection rules (see Alm et al., 1993; Alm and McKee, 2000). Tax agencies do not select tax returns randomly for audit but, instead, use information from the returns to determine audit.[3] So the probability of audit is endogenous, depending on the behaviour of taxpayers and tax agencies. There are different ways to simulate endogenous audit selection rules. For example, taxpayers known to have been non-compliant in the past will be audited more frequently in the future, or are faced with the situation that tax agency goes back in time to previous periods' declarations. A third possibility is a cut-off rule, which means that a taxpayer who reports less than some cut-off level of income will be audited with certainty. Experimental results indicate that such endogenous audit rules are able to generate significantly greater compliance than random audit rules. Endogenous audit rules are also able to smooth the level of tax collection over time by reducing the variation in the individual compliance rate (Alm et al., 1993). Alm and McKee (2000) implemented a treatment in which subjects were permitted to discuss their strategies with each other prior to beginning the experiment. This mimics the provision of information within a cohort via tax professionals or publications. According to their findings, they argue that in the face of communication, the addition of a random audit rule is useful to the tax authority. Thus, they propose the combination of endogenous audit rules and random audits to generate substantially more compliance than would an endogenous audit rule alone.

Slemrod et al. (2001) used a controlled field experiment in Minnesota to analyse taxpayer response to an increased probability of audit: 1724 randomly selected taxpayers were informed by letter that the return they were about to file (state and federal) would be closely examined. They used two years' income return data from the same taxpayers, which enabled them to compare changes in reported income, deductions and tax liability between those taxpayers who received the treatments and similar groups of taxpayers who were not subject to any treatment. They found that the treatment effect varies depending on the income. In the treatment group, low- and middle-income taxpayers increased their reported income between 1993 and 1994 relative to the control group. The effect was much stronger for those with a higher opportunity to evade. In 1994, the reported income of high-income taxpayers fell sharply in relation to the control group. According to the authors, the perception that tax evasion will not be detected and punished automatically could be one reason for these results, and thus they propose that a 'heightened audit threat should be carried out simultaneously with a rethinking of how the audits themselves are carried out' (p. 482).

As the authors state, the analysis had a comparably small sample size of high-income taxpayers, which reduces the inference to be drawn. Follow-up experiments should start the field experiment at the beginning of the tax year, to analyse avoidance behaviour as well. Such field experiments are a great enrichment in the tax compliance literature. One of the main advantages is that they are implemented by tax authorities and not experimenters, and thereby they are less artificial.

Generally, early tax compliance experiments tried to test the relevance of the well-articulated expected utility theory, influenced by the model of Allingham and Sandmo (1972) and other authors such as, for example, Yitzhaki (1974). These models helped to analyse the change in tax compliance as a response to different deterrence policies. However, experiments mostly report a higher level of income reporting than the expected utility model would predict (see Alm, 1998). This motivated tax compliance researchers to expand the traditional expected utility theory and to check the relevance of other theories, or to implement new experiments focusing on new variables, searching for facts without a clear theory. Thus, we find an intensive dialogue between experimenters and theorists and Baldry (1987), for example, states, discussing his findings:

> Rather than question the experimental method, these results suggest that it is perhaps the theory which needs revision ... The question asked here is whether simple and reasonable modifications to the basic theory can explain these observations (p. 377).

Influenced by the work of Kahneman and Tversky (1979), researchers started to analyse whether people systematically misjudge or misapply the low audit probability. Alm et al. (1992c) show that subjects appear to overweight the probability of an audit, so that there is more compliance than expected utility theory would predict. They designed an experiment structure in which, according to the expected utility theory, the single-period dominant strategy for a risk-neutral individual is to report zero income. However, they found a substantial compliance rate. Furthermore, the authors found some evidence that compliance is not always caused by overweighting the audit probability or by an extreme risk aversion. They investigated a treatment in which there was no chance of detection. The average compliance rate was 20 per cent, with a variation between 5.3 and 35.8 per cent across the groups.

Generally, the experimental findings show that the direction of the change in tax compliance as a response to different deterrence policies is not always consistent. However, the results tend to suggest that a higher audit rate leads to more compliance, and that tax compliance is an increasing function of income and a decreasing function of the tax rate. Experiments that only analyse deterrence effects enable the examination of the interaction between taxpayers and the tax administration's policy instruments. However, they omit the interaction among taxpayers (see Alm, 1991). Furthermore, early experiments used higher probability and penalty rates than we observe in reality.

Tax compliance experiments were first strongly motivated by theory. The experimental results that indicate a higher compliance rate than traditional models would predict strongly influenced economic theory making as it considers now new factors. At the same time, it increased the incentive for researchers to let deterrence parameters remain constant and to analyse the relevance of social and institutional factors, as we will see in the next two sections.

SOCIAL FACTORS

Tax compliance seems to depend upon numerous factors and is not only affected by deterrence and economic factors. How, for example, can social norms affect compliance? As we will see in this section, experiments in recent years have started to analyse such factors and have provided a new impulse to incorporate these factors in formal theories of compliance. We will see that subjects do not respond only to deterrence factors of a tax evasion game, but also to the context provided to them.

The co-operation observed is not specific to the tax compliance literature. Similar results can be found in the literature on ultimatum and bargaining games. Güth et al. (1982) first introduced the ultimatum bargaining game. Player 1 proposes a division of a fixed sum. Player 2 can either accept or reject, in which case each player receives nothing. In such a situation, the perfect equilibrium would predict that player 1 asks and gets almost 100 per cent. However, the results observed were different. The average demand of player 1 was below 70 per cent and about 20 per cent of the offers were rejected. Ultimatum experiments have shown that in many experiments the modal offer is (50, 50) and the mean offer is somewhere around (40, 60); and that the smaller the offer, the higher is the probability that it is rejected (see Ochs and Roth, 1989; Roth, 1995b).

Even in dictator games, where player 1 proposes a division of some resource between the two and player 2 cannot reject this proposal, we find some co-operation. The difference between the ultimatum and the dictator game is that player 2 cannot reject this proposal. Thus, players receive whatever player 1 proposes. Forsythe et al. (1994) studied dictator games with and without monetary rewards and found that 62 per cent of the dictators still gave two dollars or more out of ten dollars to player 2. Fehr and Schmidt (2000) argue that attempts to explain the results in terms of simple games, such as the Ultimatum Game, that assume selfish preferences, are misplaced: 'It is difficult to believe that they make systematic mistakes and reject money or reward generous offers although their true preferences would require them not to do so' (p. 10).

Thus, more recent efforts in tax compliance research have increasingly analysed non-traditional economic factors such as social norms. Alm et al. (1995) argue that

> a government compliance strategy based only on detection and punishment may well be a reasonable starting point but not a good ending point. Instead, what is needed is a multi-faceted approach ... Put differently, explaining tax compliance requires recognizing the myriad factors that motivate individual behavior, factors that go much beyond the standard economics-of-crime approach to include theories of behavior suggested by psychologists, sociologists, and other social

scientists. Until this effort is made, it seems unlikely that we will come much closer to unraveling the puzzle of tax compliance (p. 15).

Social Norms

There is a lack of empirical evidence regarding the effects of social norms or social capital. Paldam (2000) states:

> Social capital is a new field, suffering from a great lack of good, reliable data. Both time series and cross-country evidence are missing. In the meantime much speculation is going on ... it is hopefully clear that social capital is a promising concept, which can be operationalized by relatively simple measurement. However, it will take some time and a lot of work has to be done before it is known if social capital can deliver what it promises (p. 649).

Alm et al. (1999) argue that there is a social norm of tax compliance affecting individual reporting decisions. They argue furthermore that this social norm can be affected by voting on different aspects of the fiscal system. Their experimental results show that individual compliance behaviour after the vote's announcement is different from the pre-vote behaviour under the identical fiscal regime. Surprisingly, when raising the level of enforcement is rejected, compliance always falls. The authors believe that such a group decision on enforcement destroys any pre-vote social norm of tax compliance. They argue:

> When the group rejects stricter sanctions, this outcome sends a signal to each individual that others do not wish to enforce the tax laws, that it is now socially acceptable to evade one's taxes because others will do the same, and that post-vote individual noncompliance is justified by the actions of others (p. 162).

Furthermore Alm et al. (1999) suggest that the social norm of tax compliance can be influenced by group communication. They find that a subject selects a greater level of enforcement after communicating with others. But communication combined with the vote changes the social norm of tax compliance, so that paying taxes becomes the accepted mode of behaviour. Discussion gives the opportunity to clarify benefits and costs from greater enforcement and increases co-operation among group members. As Bohnet and Frey (1994) argue, communication transforms a group decision into a private one. The information requirements can be fulfilled with institutions such as elections that enforce the incentive to produce information. The pre-election process involves individuals in face-to-face[4] interactions and so induces them to demand information, which clarifies 'the order and ranking of their preferences, to build commensurable scales and to take care of the effect of differences in time and place' (Bohnet and Frey, 1994, p. 345).

And Frey and Eichenberger (1999) argue:

> The market is a discovery mechanism. The same could be said about discourse. By talking to one another, people discover the means of fulfilling their preferences. By relating to other people's positions, they find out where they stand. In economic terms, it could be said that communication changes the production function to fulfil individuals' preferences (p. 22).

Bosco and Mittone (1997) conducted an experiment to test the hypotheses on whether feelings of collective blame influence the decision to evade taxes and whether the awareness of damaging others by reducing social welfare reduces tax evasion. To test the existence and effectiveness of the moral constraints, one group (collective moral constraints) was informed in advance that the audit process would be public. In another group (subjective moral constraint), a system of partial redistribution of the tax money among the participants was introduced. Participants might dislike the idea that they might suffer because of tax evasion, which reduces the total yield and so leaves less money for redistribution. The results of their experiment seem to confirm that moral constraint worked as a powerful disincentive to evade. A serious limitation is the nature of their experiment, which was static (only one round). The decision to evade or not is a dynamic rather than a static problem, because taxes are paid regularly every year. To analyse the dynamic process, Mittone (1997) designed a dynamic, repeated experiment. He found that tax yield redistribution (subjective moral constraint) reduced tax evasion.

Cummings et al. (2005) argue that laboratory experiments have the advantage of holding the tax-reporting institutions constant, in order to investigate compliance behaviour across various cultural settings. Thus, it is possible to isolate cultural effects as a factor in tax compliance. For this, the authors used experiments in two different countries (South Africa and Botswana), with the same tax-reporting setting. The observed difference in tax compliance behaviour can be explained by differences in institutional features and by differences in social norms between those countries. They found that compliance rates vary between the states. It could be argued that differences in the behaviour between the subjects are due to differences in risk attitudes. Therefore, the authors conducted a risk experiment. According to their findings, the observed differences in behaviour are not due to differences in risk attitudes between the pools. The authors state that observed differences in compliance are related to the differences in tax institutions and government behaviour. These experimental results are shown to be robust after replicating them for the same countries using survey response measures of tax compliance. A key strength of the paper is to utilize both field and laboratory data to investigate the effects of cultural norms on compliance behaviour. In their experimental results, Alm et al. (1995) found strong evidence for social norms being a very important determinant of compliance. They compared compliance experiments conducted in Spain and the United States, two countries with different cultures and histories of compliance, and found differences in the level of and the change in compliance (response to policy innovations). The authors concluded that societal attitudes towards tax compliance have exerted a significant impact and argued that:

> Both sets of results suggest that there may well be different factors at work in the compliance decisions in the two countries. As implied by Frey and Weck-Hannemann (1984), perhaps the tax morality – or the social norm of compliance – differs in the two countries, a difference that becomes evident in behavior under controlled laboratory conditions (p. 14).

However, they were unable to test this suggestion directly. Using WVS data on Spain versus the United States from three different waves, Alm and Torgler (2006) were able to estimate the determinants of tax morale in Spain and the United States directly. They find consistent evidence that individuals in the United States have a statistically significant higher tax morale than those in Spain, controlling in a multivariate analysis for additional factors, with quite high marginal effects. Together with the experimental results, these estimation results clearly support the notion that there is a higher social norm of compliance in the United States than in Spain.

In general, there are some problems that arise when conducting a cross-cultural experiment. Roth (1995b, pp. 282–4) points out three main problems:

1. *The experimenter effect*: If different experimenters are involved between the countries, differences arise because of uncontrolled procedural differences or uncontrolled personal differences among the experimenters.
2. *Language effect*: If the instructions for the experiment are presented in different languages, systematic differences between countries might be observed because of the way the instructions are translated.
3. *Currency effect*: If subjects are paid in different currencies, systematic differences between countries might be observed because of different incentives that the potential payments give to the subjects, or because of the different numerical payment scale.

In both studies, it is not really clear why the researchers chose to compare these particular countries. It would be interesting, for example, to carry out cross-country tax compliance experiments in the former East and

West Germany, as Ockenfels (1999) has already done with public good and solidarity experiments (see also Ockenfels and Weimann, 1999). As eastern subjects grew up in a socialist planned economy and western subjects in a market-oriented environment, social differences could be compared. This would help to control for many factors and would reduce methodological problems such as language and currency effects. Future research should expand the number of observed countries to get more reliable cross-country comparisons. Henrich et al. (2001) undertook a large cross-cultural study of behaviour using ultimatum, public good and dictator games. Subjects were recruited from 15 small-scale societies. The authors found a large variation across the different cultural groups and they argue that preferences and/or expectations are affected by group-specific conditions such as institutions or cultural fairness norms.

Positive Inducements

Rewards could be more effective than punishments for eliminating undesired behaviour or for providing motivation (see, e.g., Nuttin and Greenwald, 1968). Falkinger and Walther (1991) have theoretically analysed the impact of rewards on tax compliance. Feld et al. (2007) discuss the importance of rewards and refer to the design possibilities of a controlled field experiment. Alm et al. (1992a) have used experiments to analyse the effects of four alternative forms of positive inducements upon tax compliance behaviour: (i) a lottery treatment, where subjects who were checked and found to be fully compliant for the current and the previous four rounds could enter in a lottery in which the chances of winning were 1 in 25; (ii) a fixed-reward session, where fully compliant participants received a reward of two tokens; (iii) an audit reduction; and (iv) a public good. The results indicate that positive inducements have a significant and positive impact on compliance. However, although (i) and (ii) have the same expected value, the lottery session had the largest effect on compliance. In the public good session, compliance was not as high as in either the lottery or the fixed-reward session, even when the expected value was higher. A reduction in the audit rate also increased compliance, but less than other rewards. The authors finally concluded that rewards must be immediate and salient to have a numerically significant effect. What the paper disregards is a clear comparison between enforcement and positive inducement. The analysis of positive rewards in tax compliance research is an important topic and just in its infancy. Future efforts could, for example, examine whether some sorts of taxpayer subgroups – such as honest taxpayers – crowd out their intrinsic motivation when positive inducements are implemented.

Equity

Spicer and Becker (1980) examined the relationship between perceived fiscal inequity and tax evasion. Survey findings have already reported this relationship (see, e.g., Spicer and Lundstedt, 1976; Song and Yarbrough, 1978). Experiments help better to analyse the causal relationship between inequity and tax evasion. The experiment of Spicer and Becker (1980) is based on the theoretical background of the equity theory. The relationship between taxpayers and the government can be viewed as an exchange relationship. Tyler and Smith (1998) state that the equity theory is important because it hypothesizes that satisfaction and behaviour are linked not only to the objective outcome levels, but also to the relation of one's own outcome to what would be judged fair. Furthermore, a lack of equity between taxpayers' own and others' exchange creates a sense of distress. Disadvantage in such a situation creates anger, and advantage feelings of guilt (see Homans, 1961; Adams, 1965). People will engage in forms of behaviour, such as tax evasion, that are designed to restore equity. The experiment procedure of Spicer and Becker closely followed the experiment by Friedland et al. (1978). Fifty-seven students were told that their own tax tables were based on a tax of 40 per cent. To test the equity theory, 19 participants were told that the average tax rate was 65 per cent, 19 were told that the average tax rate was 15 per cent and the others were told that all participants had the same tax rate. On average, 23.13 per cent of total taxes payable were evaded. The group with the high tax evaded 32 per cent, the group with the low tax 12.26 per cent and the group with the medium taxation 24.50 per cent. Furthermore, perceived relative tax rates were positive, and significant at a 95 per cent confidence level. The results seem to support the hypothesis developed from the equity theory. However, the experiment only took horizontal equity into account, because at start-up all participants received the same amount of money. Furthermore, the instructions may have produced a bias towards a higher non-compliance rate, because participants were asked to maximize their net income.

Webley et al. (1985) used a similar design to investigate equity. They manipulated equity by altering the information about taxation: 'Your tax rate is 30% and the average tax rate is x'. The variable x had the values 15 per cent, 30 per cent and 45 per cent. Contrary to Spicer and Becker (1980), equity did not have a significant effect on tax evasion (see also Webley et al. 1988). Thus, according to the work presented here, the effect of equity on tax compliance does not seem to be clear. However, in some aspects the study of Webley et al. (1985) was different. First, the difference in the tax rates was only 15 per cent, and second, the information about the tax rates was just a part of the initial instructions. However, it should be noted that in the series of experiments by Paul Webley and his co-authors, the subjects were not paid real money; instead, for example, the 'most successful volunteers' were awarded a prize (Webley and Halstead, 1986). Such a payment method may induce the subjects to compete against each other and not against the tax authority. Furthermore, experimental questions showed that many subjects were not particularly aware of the different equity treatments, which might be an indicator that inequity was not implemented well into the design (see Webley et al., 1991).

Tax compliance researchers have started to use cross-country studies. These developments are in line with experiments in other areas. A further step forward in the tax compliance literature has been made by integrating 'cheap talk' and democratic elements such as voting into the experimental design. The findings show that cheap talk raises tax compliance. This is a wide open area for additional experiments. Further, experiments present mixed results on how equity manipulations influence tax compliance. However, these experiments have only analysed the effect of horizontal equity, which implies a different treatment of particular taxpayers relative to others, without analysing the perceived fairness of a taxpayer's exchange with the government. This topic will be treated in the next section.

INSTITUTIONAL VARIABLES

This section focuses on the relevance that transparency of information, individuals' participation in the decision process and output adjustments to the needs of the taxpayers have in supporting tax morale and tax compliance.

Institutional Uncertainty

Influenced by the theoretical analysis, experiments have started to analyse institutional uncertainty and thus the relevance of the available information. The role of fiscal uncertainty has been analysed by comparing the compliance behaviour when key fiscal parameters are known with certainty with situations in which these parameters are made uncertain.

Spicer and Thomas (1982) examined whether more precise information leads to more responses to changes in the audit probability. Eighteen participants out of 54 were given precise information regarding the audit probabilities in each round (first round 1/20, second 5/20 and third 3/20). Eighteen participants received imprecise information (audit probabilities low, high and medium). The remaining participants were given no information about the audit probability. The results indicated that the percentage of taxes evaded was negatively and significantly correlated with the audit probabilities only if respondents received precise information regarding the probabilities. Spicer and Thomas state that in the absence of precise information, taxpayers pay far less attention to the amount evaded: 'The taxpayer can be viewed here as using rules of thumb or heuristics to help his tax evasion decision' (p. 245). As a consequence, Spicer and Hero (1985) examined the rules of thumb or heuristics. They implemented a deception. Although there had not been a previous game, 12 participants out of 36 were told that in the previous game participants paid only 10 per cent of taxes due, 12 were told 50 per cent, and the rest 90 per cent. However, the results indicated that the amount of taxes evaded was not affected significantly by the information provided. So, contrary to survey findings, taxpayers did not use the behaviour of others as a guide to their own evasion. The results seem to suggest that despite the deception, taxpayers use rules of thumb or heuristics. But it should be mentioned that the experiment was not specially designed clearly to identify these rules.

Alm et al. (1992b) analysed the role of fiscal uncertainty by comparing the compliance behaviour of individuals when the fiscal parameters were known with certainty with the compliance when these parameters were under a 'veil of uncertainty'. The results indicate that introducing uncertainty into the fiscal parameters tax rate, fine rate and probability of detection increases tax compliance, when the decision is made independently, which means that individuals receive nothing in return for their tax payments. Compliance is affected in the opposite way, when individuals receive a benefit from the government for their tax payments (see next subsection). The authors finally state that:

> a policy, intentional or not, of increasing the level of fiscal uncertainty is a risky tool for generating increased compliance. Individuals may well respond by reducing their compliance. If that occurs, then not only are individuals made worse off by the uncertainty, but the government may also lose tax revenues (p. 1025).

Public Services

Mackscheidt (1984) stresses the relevance of personal benefit derived from public expenditure. The degree of taxpayers' satisfaction with government seems to play an important role. Taxpayers are more inclined to comply with the law if the exchange between the paid tax and the performed government services are found to be equitable. Alm et al. (1992b) argue that theoretical and experimental work ignores much evidence that tax compliance depends in part upon the use of tax revenue, and stress that:

> Ignoring government expenditures means that individual compliance decision can be treated as independent across individuals, so that each individual need take only his or her own behavior into account when deciding to report income. In practice, however, an individual's choice may not be independent of the choices of others (p. 1019).

Güth and Mackscheidt (1985) designed an experiment that took public transfer expenditures into consideration. Public transfer depended on the actual total revenue of taxes and fines, and was paid according to individual transfer coefficients. With this, Güth and Mackscheidt intended to investigate vertical equity. The results indicate that subjects were consistently honest or dishonest (93 per cent). Becker et al. (1987) analysed the effect of transfer payments. Students received transfers that were independent of the amount of their personal income. They were not informed of the auditing probability. Furthermore, the earned income was based on a test, in which they were confronted with 25 numerical series. Individuals were informed about their individual share of total transfer payments, but not about the amount. The results of the study indicate that individual transfer payment received from the public sector plays an important role. Evasion rises if taxpayers suppose that they receive less than others. Generally, experiments show that compliance is greater with public goods than without.[5] Many earlier experiments did not pay attention to the dynamic process of paying taxes. They used only one or relatively few rounds. Treatments without an adequate number of rounds reduce the possibility that subjects reach an equilibrium decision strategy. There is some evidence in public good games that behaviour changes over the rounds (see, e.g., Andreoni, 1988; Dawes and Thaler, 1988; Isaac and Walker, 1988).

It could also be interesting to consider the effect of an inefficient state. In order to treat this, Güth and Mackscheidt (1985) propose the introduction of an efficiency parameter e. The amount e of the tax revenues that is utilized for the transfer payments can be interpreted as an indicator of the state's efficiency. Thus, the hypothesis that the state's inefficiency leads to a reduction in tax morale can be tested.

Alm et al. (1992b) implemented treatments in which public good is provided. Taxes paid in a round were multiplied by two, and the resulting amount was then redistributed in equal shares to the members of the group. The data indicates that the average compliance is always higher in the presence of the public good. However, the introduction of fiscal uncertainty in the presence of a public good lowers the average compliance rate relatively to the base case.

Alm et al. (1992d) analysed the recognition of government services. They changed consumers' surplus derived from government provision of the public good by changing the group surplus multiplier (0, 2 and 6). In the treatment where the subjects received nothing for their tax payments, the average group compliance rate was 43.5 per cent. The compliance rate of the treatment with the multiplier 2 was 53.7 per cent. Increasing the multiplier to 6 increased compliance to 59.2 per cent. Although compliance increased with the surplus multiplier, the increase was non-linear. The authors conclude that there appear to be limits to how much governments can influence compliance by increasing the individual pay-off to tax payments, and point out that

> government can increase compliance by providing goods that their citizens prefer more, by providing these goods in a more efficient manner, or by more effectively emphasising that taxes are necessary for receipt of government services (p. 34).

However, a problem with such designs is the separation between the effect of public goods and the effect of taxpayers' interaction. One way to deal with this problem is to build an experimental design with a fixed public transfers treatment, regardless of how much taxes subjects pay, and a treatment in which public transfers depend on the amount of paid taxes, where subjects take the compliance of others into account (see Kim, 1994).

If taxpayers can vote on the way taxes will be spent, they may feel more inclined to pay their taxes. Furthermore, the outcome of the vote gives the taxpayers information about the level of group support for the collective decision, and this information can be useful in building expectations about the tax compliance behaviour of other taxpayers (Alm et al., 1993). Kidder and McEwen (1989) argue that the more people are involved in establishing rules, the stronger is their sense of obligation. Tyran and Feld (2006) analysed under which circumstances the enactment of mild law induces law-abiding behaviour. For this, they compared exogenously imposed law (enacted by the experimenter) and endogenously chosen law (participants could vote in a referendum). The results show that mild law imposed by an exogenous authority does not induce widespread law-abiding behaviour. But mild law induces voluntary compliance if it is accepted in a referendum. The authors state that voting for mild law can be interpreted as a signal for co-operation and so induces expectations of co-operation, which increases co-operation. Furthermore, if mild law is accepted endogenously, individuals expect others to be committed not to free-ride.

Alm et al. (1993) analysed the effects of fiscal institutions on compliance by varying the process by which tax collection becomes a public good (voting versus imposition). Donations given to a campus organization were taken as public good. So, the public good was not distributed directly to the subjects, but sent to a specific organization. The experimental results provide evidence that tax compliance is higher when individuals can vote on the use of their taxes than when there is no voting over alternatives. Furthermore, if individuals know that the group is strongly in favour of a particular expenditure, compliance is enhanced. However, compliance falls if the vote count is not revealed. The authors conclude that

> government can generate greater compliance by ensuring that individuals feel that citizens are well-informed of the outcome of the vote, and that taxes are spent in ways consistent with the preferences of the citizens (p. 302).

The studies presented here have enriched tax compliance research, expanding the experiments based on a game between taxpayers and the tax authority to situations in which taxpayers' interactions are considered. The findings show that taxpayers report more income when they receive public goods than when they do not.

FUTURE RESEARCH AND CONCLUSIONS

This section analyses the limits and possibilities of experiments on tax morale and tax compliance, and mentions some topics for future research endeavours that could shed some new light on the tax compliance puzzle. The section concludes with some final remarks.

Sophistication of the Design

Webley et al. (1991) argue that a tax-evasion experiment might be a good instrument to study factors that affect optimizing or cheating. But they doubt that psychological processes can be captured well enough. They argue that 'unless these experiments are carefully designed, the results may reflect a person's understanding of economics rather than the behaviour that would be displayed in the real situation' (p. 46). To obtain experimental results from a more general setting, Webley et al. (1985) constructed a more sophisticated design and conducted two experiments. The authors intended the tax aspect to be less obvious. In a small business simulation, the purpose of income tax was just one of a series of decisions (advertising, service charges, market research) that a subject had to make. Interestingly, compared to previous studies, evading tax was less common. Subjects rarely declared zero income.

In other recent studies, income distribution is not endowed exogenously by the experimenter, but endogenously. In Maciejovsky et al. (2001), participants had to earn their income on an experimental asset market (see also Giese and Hoffmann, 2000; Anderhub et al., 2002). Another way of treating the income endogenously is to use a test in which participants are confronted with, for example, numerical series following certain numerical patterns. Thus, income distribution is based on individuals' test results (see Becker et al., 1987).

Should experiments use a neutral language? Alm (1998) argues that neutral terms allow masking of the context of the experiment, increase control over subject preferences and avoid making subjects invoke different mental scripts. However, some investigations have concluded that there is no difference in behaviour between experiments using neutral terminology and experiments that use tax-specific language (see, e.g., Alm et al., 1992). Wartick et al. (1998) found behavioural differences with adult subjects, but not with students.

Alm (1998) argues that the income declaration is not a single choice decision, but consists of a number of other decisions such as, for example, deductions. He stresses that more analysis of the multidimensional nature of the reporting decision is needed. Webley and Halstead (1986) point out that participants must have the possibility of evading in many ways. However, Cowell (1991) offers the criticism that making experiments more complicated can make them harder to interpret. He argues:

> It is tempting to think that experimental design can be made richer and more lifelike by switching from a game of draughts to a game of chess; but this may not be of much practical advantage if, in real life, people just kick over the chessboard (p. 127).

Limitations?

Many tax compliance games use students as participants. Do students have enough experience of filling in tax forms? Are students a satisfactory sample for studies on tax behaviour? It can be argued that students are not useless, but that the results should be interpreted carefully (see Webley et al., 1991). However, there is evidence that students' responses are no different from those of other subjects (see, e.g., Baldry, 1987). Alm (1998) states that 'There is also no reason to believe that the cognitive processes of students are different from those of "real" people' (p. 43).

Future researchers could check this point by using old designs with mixed subjects. This also helps to check another important concern: the design sensitivity. Experiment replication and small design changes are essential to analyse robustness.

And what about sanctions? It is not possible to implement severe punishments, such as jail, in tax compliance games. The absence of social pressures could inhibit the psychological processes that are important in the real world. Recent experiments have aimed to capture social stigma as a factor (see, e.g., Bosco and Mittone, 1997). Quite a lot of experiments in tax compliance research are computer simulations. It could be argued that the real-life situation of taxation does not involve the use of computers. Furthermore, if the computer is seen as a gaming machine, the results could be biased. However, Webley et al. (1991) point out that: 'We feel that it is not the computer per se that conveys the message that the situation is a game but the content of the program' (p. 52). Moreover, in some countries tax forms can be filled out using the computer.

Experiments should not be too long or complicated, and the instructions should be understandable, so that subjects don't become bored or confused. Furthermore, according to Alm (1998), experiments should be administered in a uniform and consistent manner to allow replicability. This allows testing of the robustness of the design and the avoidance of erroneous conclusions. However, Rubinstein (2001) stresses that the current incentive system does not reward replications. He provides an appropriate example:

> Let us say you are a researcher who is interested in a paper by Prof. X who claims to have found something quite interesting. Let us say that you find the results plausible but you are not sure that the experiment was done properly and that indeed conclusion is valid. Do you have any incentive to repeat the experiment? No, because no one would publish it. Yet, you are interested in the subject matter and you probably think that Prof. X's finding is sensitive to a certain key detail of the experiment. Now you are quite eager to demonstrate your point and to publish a paper. In order to do that you have to first confirm Prof. X's basic claim. If you fail to repeat Prof. X's result, your point is lost. Thus, you approach the experiment with a desire to confirm the published result (p. 626).

Possibilities

In recent years, experimental research aided our understanding of tax morale and tax compliance by, for example, analysing the response of individuals to changes in policy instruments such as the tax rate, the audit rate, the fine rate and so on. Furthermore, experiments have illuminated aspects with regard to which other methods, such as empirical or survey investigations, have difficulties. Experiments can be used to analyse relatively unexplored areas, such as moral and social sentiments, social norms and so on. In the early stages, Schwartz and Orleans (1967) carried out an interesting field experiment. The approach was to determine the effects of moral appeals and threats of punishment on behavioural compliance with tax laws. They found that moral appeals had a much stronger influence than punishment threats. These findings were important in focusing the attention on different potential compliance factors. However, since then, little work has been done to analyse the relevance of moral appeals.

Cowell (1991) argues that it would be useful if the

> set-up of future experiments and the processing of the results could be set up in such a way as to clarify (1) the factors which predispose individuals as to whether they will obey or break the rules about paying taxes, and (2) amongst those who do break the rules the (possibly different) factors which influence by how much they underreport or overclaim (p. 127).

Future research could pay more attention to intertemporal components of tax evasion and tax compliance. Hessing et al. (1992) argue, following their observations, that there are probably three groups of taxpayers: (i) taxpayers who never evade taxes, (ii) taxpayers who will try to evade now and then and (iii) habitual tax evaders. These interesting findings could be examined more closely. However, an individual's willingness to comply could change over time. Can we observe a crowding-out of honest taxpayers by changing policy instruments? And if there is crowding-out, can tax morale be recovered with or without any policy influence? Is the process of recovery symmetric or asymmetric to the crowding-out? The first steps towards taking the intertemporal aspect into account have been taken by, for example, using endogenous audit rules. Alm et al. (1990) analysed the tax amnesty, which has a long-run impact on voluntary tax compliance. Honest taxpayers may perceive the amnesty as a 'special' treatment for tax cheaters and could conclude that the amnesty is unfair to them. In response to this, their compliance may decline. In one treatment, the authors introduced an amnesty in the middle of the experiment, with no prior warning. In other treatments, individuals were told at the beginning that there might be an amnesty at some point in the experiment. Their results indicate that the average level of compliance generally falls after an amnesty is offered. Interestingly, participants who complied either completely or not at all were unaffected by the amnesty. Furthermore, according to the authors, the decline in compliance stems from those participants who engaged in moderate levels of compliance prior to the amnesty.

Besides the two categories 'speaking to theories' and 'searching for facts', Roth (1995a, p. 22) mentioned a third one: 'whispering in the ears of princes'. 'Whispering in the ears of princes' deals with the dialogue between experimenters and policymakers. As already mentioned, most experiments on tax compliance and tax morale fall into the first two categories. However, future research could change this picture. As Roth states, 'whispering in the ears of princes' offers the possibility of utilizing scientific methods to formulate advice on questions of policy. Tax compliance and tax morale research should be qualified for this, because an experimental environment can be designed to mirror the naturally occurring environment by working with policy instruments such as the tax rate, the audit rate, the fine rate and so on. Nevertheless, researchers should be careful to take into consideration the limitations and problems of experiments, especially the design sensitivity. Furthermore, the question remains as to how policymakers classify the ability of experiments to analyse tax compliance and tax morale.

Conclusions

A significant body of research using experiments on tax compliance and tax morale has been accumulated. However, much work has concentrated on traditional topics such as the audit, penalties and the tax rate. There are several other issues that would merit further development. The main purpose of this chapter is to present the work that has been done on issues that have been treated less intensively than the traditional ones and that could merit further development. The focus has been on social and institutional factors.

Tax compliance experiments show that traditional tax compliance models have difficulties predicting the level of tax compliance. In most cases, the level of tax compliance was higher than predicted. Experiments that have analysed the effect of deterrence determinants have given mixed insights into changes in tax compliance as a response to different policies. However, despite the mixed results, the findings tend to suggest that a higher audit rate leads to more compliance, and that tax compliance is an increasing function of income and a decreasing function of the tax rate.

This survey indicates that, holding the probability of a penalty, the fine rate and the taxpayer's risk aversion constant, social and institutional factors systematically matter. Experiments that consider the interaction between subjects indicate that moral constraint works as a disincentive to evade taxes. Furthermore, cheap talk raises compliance. It would be an enrichment to develop a model incorporating the thesis of Bohnet and Frey (1994), that information created in a discussion helps individuals to clarify the order and ranking of their preferences, instead of starting from the assumption that individuals already have well-defined preferences.

Cross-country studies show that differences in tax compliance behaviour can be explained by differences in social and institutional factors. Experiments also show that tax compliance increases when individuals receive public goods. The analysis of horizontal equity has produced mixed results. More experiments should be carried out to gain better insights. It would be interesting to expand the cross-country studies to analyse equity considerations.

The experimental findings have given a new impulse to the theoretical analysis aimed at developing tax compliance models. However, the observed level of compliance still cannot really be predicted by the models. One approach tries to incorporate such findings into a more sophisticated expected utility theory. Another approach moves beyond classical expected utility theory in the direction of social psychology, or sociology theories such as prospect theory. Alm (1998) points out that research should recognize the 'full house' (p. 49) of theories, each explaining the behaviour of different taxpayers. Based on the concept of different kinds of taxpayer, future research should give more structure to the findings. The challenge is to identify the basic themes of other social sciences and include them in a sophisticated manner without abandoning the economic foundations. Tax morale and tax compliance experiments have shown impressively that many taxpayers seem to have a more refined motivation structure than that assumed by traditional economics.

NOTES

1. As Wilde (1980) points out, the objective behind a laboratory experiment is to create a 'microeconomic environment in the laboratory where adequate control can be maintained and accurate measurement of relevant variables guaranteed' (p. 138).
2. See one of the following sections. Smith (1982, pp. 931 ff.) describes sufficient conditions for an experiment. He states that the control over preferences is the most significant element distinguishing this method from other methods. The following conditions must be established: (i) non-satiation – subjects must prefer more to less; (ii) saliency – subjects must recognize that actions affect outcomes, and thus the received rewards have to be related to the decision; (iii) reward dominance – the reward must set off subjective costs or benefits, by an amount comparable to the outside earnings; and (iv) privacy – subjects must only know their own pay-offs.
3. The Internal Revenue Service (IRS), for example, uses the Discrimination Index Function (DIF) formula based on items reported on current tax returns, in its selection of returns (Alm et al., 1993). Other countries follow similar practices (Roth et al., 1989).
4. Experimental studies have shown that face-to-face communication significantly increases co-operation in public good games (see, e.g., Sally, 1995; Bohnet, 1997).
5. For exceptions, see Alm et al. (1995). They did not find evidence that public goods increase compliance.

REFERENCES

Adams, J.S. (1965), 'Inequity in social exchange', in L. Berkowitz (ed.), *Advances in Experimental Social Psychology*, New York: Academic Press, pp. 167–299.
Allingham, M.G. and A. Sandmo (1972), 'Income tax evasion: a theoretical analysis', *Journal of Public Economics*, **1**, 323–38.
Alm, J. (1991), 'A perspective on the experimental analysis of taxpayer reporting', *The Accounting Review*, **66**, 577–93.
Alm, J. (1998), 'Tax compliance and administration', working paper, University of Colorado at Boulder.

Alm, J. and M. McKee (2000), 'Tax compliance as a coordinated game', working paper, University of Colorado at Boulder.
Alm, J. and B. Torgler (2006), 'Culture differences and tax morale in the United States and Europe', *Journal of Economic Psychology*, **27**, 224–46.
Alm, J., M.B. Cronshaw and M. McKee (1993), 'Tax compliance with endogenous audit selection rules', *KYKLOS*, **1**, 27–45.
Alm, J., B. Jackson and M. McKee (1992a), 'Deterrence and beyond: toward a kinder, gentler IRS', in J. Slemrod (ed.), *Why People Pay Taxes*, Ann Arbor: University of Michigan Press, pp. 311–29.
Alm, J., B.R. Jackson and M. McKee (1992b), 'Institutional uncertainty and taxpayer compliance', *American Economic Review*, **82**, 1018–26.
Alm, J., B.R. Jackson and M. McKee (1993), 'Fiscal exchange, collective decision institutions, and tax compliance', *Journal of Economic Behavior and Organization*, **22**, 285–303.
Alm, J., G.H. McClelland and W.D. Schulze (1992c), 'Why do people pay taxes?' *Journal of Public Economics*, **48**, 21–48.
Alm, J., G.H. McClelland and W.D. Schulze (1999), 'Changing the social norm of tax compliance by voting', *KYKLOS*, **52**, 141–71.
Alm, J., G.H. McKee and W. Beck (1990), 'Amazing grace: tax amnesties and tax compliance', *National Tax Journal*, **43**, 23–37.
Alm, J., I. Sanchez and A. De Juan (1995), 'Economic and noneconomic factors in tax compliance', *KYKLOS*, **48**, 3–18.
Anderhub, V., S. Giese, W. Güth, A. Hoffmann and T. Otto (2002), 'Tax evasion with earned income – an experimental study', *FinanzArchiv*, **58**, 188–206.
Andreoni, J. (1988), 'Why free ride? Strategies and learning in public goods experiments', *Journal of Public Economics*, **37**, 291–304.
Andreoni, J., B. Erard and J. Feinstein (1998), 'Tax compliance', *Journal of Economic Literature*, **36**, 818–60.
Aronson, E. and J. Carlsmith (1968), 'Experimentation in social psychology', in G. Lindzey and E. Aronson (eds), *Handbook of Social Psychology*, Reading, MA: Addison-Wesley, pp. 99–142.
Baldry, J.C. (1987), 'Income tax evasion and the tax schedule: some experimental results', *Public Finance*, **42**, 357–83.
Becker, W., H.J. Büchner and S. Sleeking (1987), 'The impact of public transfer expenditures on tax evasion: an experimental approach', *Journal of Public Economics*, **34**, 243–63.
Bohnet, I. (1997), *Kommunikation und Kooperation*, Tübingen: Mohr.
Bohnet, I. and B.S. Frey (1994), 'Direct-democratic rules: the role of discussion', *KYKLOS*, **47**, 341–54.
Bosco, L. and L. Mittone (1997), 'Tax evasion and moral constraints: some experimental evidence', *KYKLOS*, **50**, 297–324.
Cowell, F.A. (1991), 'Tax-evasion experiments: an economist's view', in P. Webley, H. Robben, H. Elffers and D. Hessing (eds), *Tax Evasion: An Experimental Approach*, Cambridge: Cambridge University Press, pp. 123–7.
Cummings, R.G., J. Martinez-Vazquez, M. McKee and B. Torgler (2005), 'Effects of tax morale on tax compliance: experimental and survey evidence', Working Paper No. 05–16. Atlanta: Georgia State University.
Dawes, R.M. and R.H. Thaler (1988), 'Anomalies: cooperation', *Journal of Economic Perspectives*, **2**, 187–97.

Falkinger, J. and H. Walther (1991), 'Rewards versus penalties: on a new policy against tax evasion', *Public Finance Quarterly* **19**, 67–79.

Feld, L.P., B.S. Frey and B. Torgler (2007), 'Rewarding honest taxpayers', forthcoming in H. Elffers, P. Verboon and W. Huisman (eds), *Managing and Maintaining Compliance*, The Hague: Boom Legal publisher, pp. 45–61.

Fehr, E. and K.M. Schmidt (2000), 'Theories of fairness and reciprocity – evidence and economic applications', CESifo Working Paper Series No. 403.

Forsythe, R., J. Horowitz, N.E. Savin and M. Sefton (1994), 'Replicability, fairness and pay in experiments with simple bargaining games', *Games and Economic Behavior*, **6**, 347–67.

Frey, B.S. and R. Eichenberger (1999), *The New Democratic Federalism for Europe*, Cheltenham, UK and Northampton, MA, USA: Edward Elgar.

Friedland, N., S. Maital and A. Rutenberg (1978), 'A simulation study of income tax evasion', *Journal of Public Economics*, **10**, 107–16.

Giese, S. and A. Hoffmann (2000), 'Tax evasion and risky investments in an intertemporal context: an experimental study', Discussion Paper No. 30, Humbold-Universität zu Berlin.

Güth, W. and K. Mackscheidt (1985), 'Die Erforschung der Steuermoral', mimeo, Universität zu Köln.

Güth, W., R. Schmittberger and B. Schwarz (1982), 'An experimental analysis of ultimatum bargaining', *Journal of Economic Behavior and Organization*, **3**, 367–88.

Henrich, J., R. Boyd, S. Bowles, C. Camerer, E. Fehr, H. Gintis and R. McElreath (2001), 'In search of Homo Economicus: behavioral experiments in 15 small-scale societies', *American Economic Review*, **91**, 73–8.

Hessing, D. J., H. Elffers, H.S.J. Robben and P. Webley (1992), 'Does deterrence deter? Measuring the effects of deterrence on tax compliance in field studies and experimental studies', in J. Slemrod (ed.), *Why People Pay Taxes. Tax Compliance and Enforcement*, Ann Arbor: The University of Michigan Press, pp. 291–305.

Homans, G.C. (1961), *Social Behavior: its Elementary Form*, New York: Harcourt.

Isaac, R.M. and J.M. Walker (1988), 'Group size effects in public goods provision: the voluntary contributions mechanism', *Quarterly Journal of Economics*, **53**, 179–200.

Kahneman, D. and A. Tversky (1979), 'Prospect theory: an analysis of decision under risk', *Econometrica*, **47**, 263–91.

Kidder, R. and C. McEwen (1989), 'Taxpaying behavior in social context: a tentative typology of tax compliance and noncompliance', in J.A. Roth and J.T. Schulz (eds), *Taxpayer Compliance, Vol. 2*, Philadelphia: University of Pennsylvania, pp. 46–75.

Kim, C.K. (1994), 'The effects of public transfers and tax rate changes on reported income: experimental evidence', Ph.D. dissertation, University of Pittsburgh.

Maciejovsky, B., E. Kirchler and H. Schwarzenberger (2001), 'Mental accounting and the impact of tax penalty and audit frequency on the declaration of income: an experimental analysis', Discussion Paper No. 16, Humboldt-Universität zu Berlin.

Mackscheidt, K. (1984), 'Konsolidierung durch Erhöhung von Steuern und Abgaben?', in H.H. v. Arnim and Konrad Littmann (eds), *Finanzpolitik im Umbruch: Zur Konsolidierung öffentlicher Haushalte*, Berlin: Duncker & Humblot, pp. 145–61.

Mittone, L. (1997), 'Subjective versus objective probability: results from seven experiments on fiscal evasion', CEEL Working Papers, No. 4.
Nuttin, J. and A.G. Greenwald (1968), *Reward and Punishment in Human Learning*, New York: Academic Press.
Ochs, J. and A.E. Roth (1989), 'An experimental study of sequential bargaining', *American Economic Review*, **79**, 355–84.
Ockenfels, A. (1999), *Fairness, Reziprozität und Eigennutz*, Tübingen, Mohr Siebeck.
Ockenfels, A. and J. Weimann (1999), 'Types and patterns: an experimental East–West-German comparison of cooperation and solidarity', *Journal of Public Economics*, **71**, 275–87.
Paldam, M. (2000), 'Social capital: One or many? Definition and measurement', *Journal of Economic Surveys*, **14**, 629–53.
Roth, A.E. (1995a), 'Introduction to experimental economics', in J.H. Kagel and A.E. Roth (eds), *The Handbook of Experimental Economics*, Princeton: Princeton University Press, pp. 1–98.
Roth, A.E. (1995b), 'Bargaining experiments', in J.H. Kagel and A.E. Roth (eds), *The Handbook of Experimental Economics*, Princeton: Princeton University Press, pp. 253–342.
Roth, J.A., J.T. Scholz and A.D. Witte (eds) (1989), *Taxpayer Compliance*, Vols 1 and 2, Philadelphia: University of Pennsylvania Press.
Rubinstein, A. (2001), 'A theorist's view of experiments, Joseph Schumpeter Lecture', *European Economic Review*, **45**, 615–28.
Sally, D. (1995), 'Conversation and cooperation in social dilemmas', *Rationality and Society*, **7**, 58–92.
Schwartz, R. and S. Orleans (1967), 'On legal sanctions', *University of Chicago Law Review*, **34**, 282–300.
Slemrod, J., M. Blumenthal and C. Christian (2001), 'Taxpayer response to an increased probability of audit: evidence from a controlled experiment in Minnesota', *Journal of Public Economics*, **79**: 455–83.
Smith, V. L. (1982), 'Microeconomic systems as an experimental science', *American Economic Review*, **72**, 923–55.
Song, Y. and Y.E. Yarbrough (1978), 'Tax ethics and taxpayer attitudes: a survey', *Public Administration Review*, **38**, 442–57.
Spicer, M.W. and L.A. Becker (1980), 'Fiscal inequity and tax evasion: an experimental approach', *National Tax Journal*, **33**, 171–5.
Spicer, M.W. and S.B. Lundstedt (1976), 'Understanding tax evasion', *Public Finance*, **31**, 295–304.
Spicer, M.W. and R.E. Hero (1985), 'Tax evasion and heuristics. A research note', *Journal of Public Economics*, **26**, 263–7.
Spicer, M.W. and J.E. Thomas (1982), 'Audit probabilities and the tax evasion decision: an experimental approach', *Journal of Economic Psychology*, **2**, 241–5.
Tyler, T.R. and H.J. Smith (1998), 'Social justice and social movements', in D.T. Gilbert, S.T. Fiske and G. Lindzey (eds), *The Handbook of Social Psychology*, Vol. 3, Boston: McGraw-Hill, pp. 595–629.
Tyran, J.-R. and L.P. Feld (2006), 'Achieving compliance when legal sanctions are non-deterrent', *Scandinavian Journal of Economics*, **101**, 135–56.
Wartick, M.L., B. Madio and C. Vines (1998), 'Reward dominance in tax reporting experiments: the role of context', working paper, University of Kentucky.

Webley, P. and S. Halstead (1986), 'Tax evasion on the micro: significant simulations or expedient experiments?', *Journal of Interdisciplinary Economics*, **1**, 87–100.

Webley, P., I. Morris and F. Amstutz (1985), 'Tax evasion during a small business simulation', in H. Brandstätter and E. Kirchler (eds), *Economic Psychology*, Linz: Trauner, pp. 233–42.

Webley, P., H. Robben and I. Morris (1988), 'Social comparison, attitudes and tax evasion in a shop simulation', *Social Behaviour*, **3**, 219–28.

Webley, P., H. Robben, H. Elffers and D. Hessing (1991), *Tax Evasion: an Experimental Approach*, Cambridge: Cambridge University Press.

Wilde, L. (1980), 'On the use of laboratory experiments in economics', in J. Pitt (ed.), *The Philosophy of Economics*, Dordrecht: Reidel, pp. 137–48.

Yitzhaki, S. (1974), 'A note on income tax evasion: a theoretical analysis', *Journal of Public Economics*, **3**, 201–2.

PART II

What shapes tax morale?

Most studies treat 'tax morale' as a black box without discussing or even considering how it might arise or how it might be maintained. It is usually perceived as being part of the meta-preferences of taxpayers and used as the residuum in the analysis capturing unknown influences to tax evasion. The more interesting question then is which factors shape the emergence and maintenance of tax morale (pp. 88–9).

Lars P. Feld and Bruno S. Frey (2002), 'Trust breeds trust: how taxpayers are treated', *Economics of Governance*, **3**, 87–99.

That taxation is a boring topic is demonstrably rubbish. In reality, it appears boring only to those who are uninterested in human nature and the institutions that have been designed to channel human nature to build productive civilizations. Taxation is about the relationship between individuals and the state, about how a society overcomes the free-rider impulse that threatens to undermine beneficial collective action, and about honesty and trust (p. 145).

Joel Slemrod (2003), 'Tax from any angle: reflections on multi-disciplinary tax research', *National Tax Journal*, **56**, 145–51.

4. The importance of faith: tax morale and religiosity

INTRODUCTION

I analyse in this chapter religiosity as a potential factor that affects tax morale, which we define as the intrinsic motivation to pay taxes. Religiosity has been analysed using different measurements such as church attendance, religious education, being an active member of a church or a religious organization, perceived religiosity, religious guidance, and trust in the church, controlling for the specific religion of a person to check also whether some religions are more tax compliant than others. To the author's knowledge, there are only two papers that examine the effect of religiosity on tax cheating (Tittle, 1980; Grasmick et al., 1991). Grasmick et al. used data collected from the annual Oklahoma City Survey in spring 1989 with a random sample of 330 adults. In our analysis, we use the World Values Surveys (1995–1997). Compared to Grasmick et al., for example, our analysis has a higher sample size covering more than 30 countries, more measurements of religiosity, and more control variables. Since in some countries in our analysis corruption is quite high, it cannot be assumed that the obligation of paying taxes to the government is an accepted social norm. Thus, it is relevant to include a measurement of corruption in the analysis to check the robustness of results. Furthermore, we investigate whether trustworthiness, such as lying ('claiming government benefits to which someone is not entitled'), cheating ('avoiding a fare on public transport') and buying a stolen product ('buying something you knew was stolen') also explain tax morale.

As most empirical research on tax compliance has generally been done with US data, there is a lack of research within countries outside the United States. Thus, this chapter contributes to expanding the focus, as it includes a great number of countries to get a general idea of the effect of religiosity on tax morale. The empirical findings indicate that religiosity has a significant positive effect on tax morale, even if other determinants such as corruption, trustworthiness, and demographic and economic factors are controlled for. Before approaching empirical discussion, the next section will provide an introduction to the economics of religiosity and will argue that religiosity works as a constraint on individual behaviour.

RELIGIOSITY AS A CONSTRAINT ON INDIVIDUAL BEHAVIOUR

Theoretical Considerations

There are many behavioural norms, such as, for example, moral constraints, that are not formally laid down, but are crucially influenced by religious motivations. North (1981) uses the term 'ideology' to refer to a system of internalized constraints that influences individuals' behaviour. He points out that 'Their myopic vision has prevented neoclassical economists from seeing that even with a constant set of rules, detection procedures, and penalties there is immense variation in the degree to which individual behavior is constrained' (p. 47).

Adam Smith (1976), in his *Theory of Moral Sentiments*, analysed religiosity from a rational point of view and noted that it acts as a kind of internal moral enforcement mechanism (for a broad discussion, see Anderson, 1988). Such an opinion is contrary to the one that emerged in the nineteenth century and has been strongly present in the twentieth century – for example, in the works of Freud (1927)[1] and Davis (1949), who see religion as non-rational or even irrational (see Stark et al., 1996). Religious behaviour results from religious beliefs, which are shaped by benefit and cost considerations (see Hardin, 1997).

New research movements follow Adam Smith and use the notion of rationality to address ethical capabilities of rational human behaviour (see, e.g., Iannaccone, 1998; van Staveren, 2001). Religion can be seen as a moral commitment to acting in a determinate way. As Sen (1977) states, commitment 'drives a wedge between personal choice and personal welfare' (p. 329). Van Staveren argues that commitment to values shared within a community can provide an explanation for unselfish behaviour, since the motive resides in the value itself. Sen (1992) gives an example in which a man stops a fight, even if he gets hurt in doing so. Such behaviour can be judged as rational. Stopping the fight can be interpreted as an action motivated by his values, based on a commitment, for example, to peaceful conflict resolution (see van Staveren, 2001).

Previous works that have used economic instruments in non-market areas have been based on given preferences (see Becker, 1981). However, today many economists argue that individuals' preferences are not to be taken as given. Mueller (2001), for example, points out that

The importance of faith

> If preferences are truly exogenous, and all individual choices are attempts by rational actors to maximize their utilities, it is difficult to understand why individuals in northern Germany overwhelmingly choose to be Protestants, while southern Germans opt to be Roman Catholics; why Italy is overwhelmingly Roman Catholic, while neighboring Greece is overwhelmingly Greek Orthodox (p. 161).

According to Mueller, religious instructions are able to shape individual preferences so that a particular religion is favoured. Networks of people, such as family or colleagues, can influence a person's decision. Someone invests in a set of positively valued social relations by conforming to the norms and the behaviour of such a network. To act conformably and thus imitate the behaviour can enforce acceptance within such a group (see Smith et al., 1998).

Hardin develops an economic theory of knowledge that focuses on the way in which people come to hold their beliefs. He demonstrates how belief might change. One way is to reduce cognitive dissonance:

> Suppose I am in a community of people who believe x and who generally support those who seem to believe x and to shun those who do not. I might see it as in my interest now to profess belief x even though I do not actually believe it. I thereby enjoy the camaraderie of my group.
>
> Now, as a result of my participation in the life of the group, I hear many things that actually support the belief that I merely pretend to have. After some – perhaps long – time, I may begin to have difficulty separating various things I seemingly know from the belief x, which begins to be reinforced by this growing body of related knowledge (p. 266).

Thus, Hardin notes that preferences might change without leaving the area of rational choice. New knowledge is acquired because it is more comfortable when someone is accepted rather then excluded from the group's various activities. People internalize the values of their communities and act in line with their ideology. Higgs (1987) has reformulated the traditional utility function, including the identity with groups of like-minded people as an essential argument. From this point of view, there is no reason for human beings to be irreligious. He states that 'By acting in concert with others who embrace the same ideology, they enjoy a solidarity essential to the maintenance of their identities' (p. 53).

Religious organizations provide moral constitutions for a society. Religion provides a certain level of enforcement to adhere to accepted rules and it acts as a 'supernatural police' (Anderson and Tollison, 1992).

Similar to habits, religiosity has the function of economizing and simplifying our actions.[2] It makes our social lives more predictable and provides a sense of security to counteract the anxiety associated with uncertainty (Heiner, 1983). Religiosity settles habits of thoughts common to all individuals. As a consequence, transaction and enforcement costs decrease. Twenty-five centuries ago, Confucius emphasized the importance of ritual in creating harmonious, predictable human behaviour.

Religious behaviour can be socially enforced with quasi-moral judgements and sanctions. Hull and Bold (1994) analyse the role of religious organizations in encouraging the production of social goods as moral behaviour, which we can, for example, find in the Ten Commandments. The relative costs for religious inputs to produce social goods are quite low. The demand side is influenced by the culture's complexity. In complex communities, individuals are less able to recognize social costs of misbehaviour, and the individual gain from proper behaviour is lower than in a small societal group. The authors state that religion has a comparative advantage in producing or encouraging social goods in large cultures of intermediate complexity, where the central government is too weak to enforce property rights. Such a strategy attracts members, and this helps a church to prosper and survive. One church 'institution' that promotes compliance and punishes misbehaviour is the afterlife doctrine: 'Heaven rewards desirable behavior and hell increases the expected cost of misbehavior, causing an increase in enforcement effectiveness' (Hull and Bold, 1994, p. 449).

Margolis (1997) analysed the question of why morality and religiosity are tied together. Religiosity includes beliefs about the right behaviour. He argues that the right behaviour has two components:

> Right behavior in the sense of proper performance or rituals honoring what is sacred in the society and hence serving also to bind the society together; and right behavior in the secular sense of what is fair and just (p. 247).

According to Hirschi and Stark (1969), religion might inhibit illegal behaviour because it is a sanctioning system that legitimizes and reinforces social values. Empirical studies have shown that states and counties with higher rates of religious memberships have significantly less violent and non-violent crime (see, e.g., Hull and Bold, 1989; Lipford et al., 1993; Hull, 2000).

Grasmick et al. (1991) argue that there are agents other than the state that threaten violators. They argue that agents in the near surroundings restrict the possibility of setting or reducing crime's expected utility by informal and 'interpersonal' sanctions (e.g., loss of respect). They state that

> While embarrassment's most immediate consequence probably is physiological discomfort, more long-term consequences include loss of valued relationships and perhaps restricted opportunities to achieve other valued goals (p. 253).

As a second factor, Grasmick et al. (1991) mention feelings of shame or guilt. These sentiments may influence reporting behaviour, reducing the perceived benefits of cheating. According to Lewis (1971), guilt arises when individuals realize that they have acted irresponsibly and in violation of a rule or social norm that they have internalized. Since the obligation of paying taxes to the government is an accepted social norm, it makes sense that individuals who choose not to pay all of their taxes may feel guilty. Aitken and Bonneville (1980) found in a Taxpayer Opinion Survey that more than 50 per cent of the respondents claimed that their consciences would be bothered 'a lot' as a result of engaging in any of the following activities: (i) padding business activities, (ii) overstating medical expenses, (iii) understating income, (iv) not filing a return or (v) claiming an extra dependent. Grasmick and Bursick (1990) interviewed 355 individuals in another survey regarding their future inclination to perform various legal offences, including tax evasion. Their findings indicated that the anticipated guilt associated with committing tax evasion served as a much greater deterrent than the perceived threat of legal sanctions. Grasmick et al. point out that depression, anxiety and affected self-image might have long-term consequences that could impede normal social functioning.

Measurement of Religiosity

There are different measurements of religiosity. On the one hand, we have variables that can be observed, such as frequency of church attendance, being an active member of a church or a religious organization, or having been brought up religiously at home. On the other hand, there are beliefs that are not observable, such as being religious, trust in the church, the importance of religion in a person's life or having absolutely clear guidance on what is good and what is evil. Analysing all these different factors helps create a picture of how religiosity affects tax morale (for the derivation of the variables, see Table A4.1 in the Appendix).

The frequency of CHURCH ATTENDANCE and the involvement in a church or a religious organization (ACTIVE IN CHURCH GROUP) indicate that people devote time to religion. Both involve ties to others, and religious activities might support the norms of a larger community (see Tittle and Welch, 1983). Iannaccone (2002) points out that traditional research has neglected the aspect of the time that people devote to religion: 'Attendance takes time, time that has an opportunity cost because it preempts other activities' (p. 209).

Similarly, being an active member in a church also takes time. However, with this variable we cannot measure the amounts of time spent. On the other hand, an *active* role in the community might produce a stronger interaction with others than simply attending church *routinely*. Higgs (1987) points out that people join groups that are closely connected to the way they see themselves: 'People crave the comfort of association with those they recognize as their "own kind"' (p. 42). In general, someone's reputation will be affected and a greater likelihood of embarrassment will be created by non-compliance if religiosity implies a strong interaction with 'conventional significant others' (see Grasmick et al., 1991).

Associated with these variables are the degree of religiosity (RELIGIOUS) and the measure of how important people believe religion is in their life (IMPORTANCE OF RELIGION). Neither of these variables measures the exact time spent on religious activities, but they try to capture the extent of individuals' internalized religious convictions (religious identity salience).

The variable RELIGIOUS EDUCATION measures whether someone acquired religious human capital as a child. Smith et al. (1998, p. 29) point out that there is a positive link between religious education and the extent of adult religious practice and involvement. Education helps to internalize religious norms and rules and thus reinforces religious socialization.

RELIGIOUS GUIDANCE measures the obligation to follow particular rules that define what is good and what is evil. It coordinates behaviour by enforcing rules, allowing the formation of more stable expectations about individuals' behaviour.

The church as an institution is a producer and a distributor of ideologies. If individuals believe the church as an institution to be fair and worthy, the costs of participating in the church and internalizing religious norms decrease. As a consequence, individuals might be more willing to follow certain norms. TRUST IN CHURCH might be strongly correlated with an individual's belief in the church's authority to enforce norms. Trust often goes hand in hand with loyalty, which raises the cost of not participating.

EMPIRICAL FINDINGS

Model and Variables

The data used are from the World Values Survey (WVS 1995–1997). The WVS permits cross-country comparisons of people's tax morale in more than 40 societies around the world, representing about 70 per cent of the world population, by representative national samples. The WVS has been broadly used by political scientists (see, e.g., Inglehart, 1997, 2000a) as well as economists such as Knack and Keefer (1997), Slemrod (2003) and Torgler (2003). Weighted ordered probit models are estimated, as some groups might be over-sampled. A weighted variable helps us to correct the samples and thus to reflect national distributions. The weighted ordered probit models help us to analyse the ranking information of the scaled dependent variable tax morale. As in the ordered probit estimation, the equation has a non-linear form; only the sign of the coefficient can be directly interpreted, not its size. Calculating the marginal effects is therefore a way of finding the quantitative effect that a variable has on tax morale. The marginal effect indicates the change in the share of taxpayers (or the probability of) belonging to a specific tax morale level when the independent variable increases by one unit. In the weighted ordered probit estimation, only the marginal effects for the highest value 'tax evasion is never justified' are shown. Thirty-two countries have been included in the estimations.[3] Furthermore, in order to deal with the high number of observations (the too-large sample size problem; see Kennedy, 1998), we adjusted the significance level downwards.

The general question to assess the level of tax morale in a society is as follows:

> Please tell me for the following statement whether you think it can always be justified, never be justified, or something in between: ... 'Cheating on tax if you have the chance' (% 'never justified' – code 1 from a ten-point scale where 1 = never and 10 = always).

The dependent variable TAX MORALE is developed by recoding the ten-point scale into a four-point scale, with the value 3 as never justifiable, and 0 as an aggregation of the last seven scores. As the last seven scores were not chosen often, the aggregation allows the use of ordered probit models. The estimation equations regress the indices of tax morale on the following further variables:[4]

1. *Age*. Instead of using age as a continuous variable, four classes have been formed: 16–29, 30–49, 50–64 and 65+, with 16–29 as the reference group. Tittle argues that older people are more sensitive to the threats of sanctions, and that over the years they have acquired greater social stakes, such as material goods, status and a stronger dependency on the reactions from others, so that the potential costs of sanctions increase. However, another reason might be that many older people (65+) might have a different attitude towards tax compliance (a higher tax morale) because they are often no longer subject to income tax.

The findings of the tax compliance studies show that the impact of age on compliance is still uncertain. Many studies have found that age increases the level of tax compliance (for survey studies, see, e.g., Vogel, 1974; Aitken and Bonneville, 1980; Tittle, 1980; Westat, Inc., 1980a; Groenland and van Veldhoven, 1983; Grasmick et al., 1991: for experimental results, see Friedland et al., 1978; Kaplan and Reckers, 1985; Baldry, 1987). While there are few studies that report a negative correlation between age and tax compliance, the results of quite a few studies imply no influence (for surveys, see Spicer, 1974; Minor, 1978; Song and Yarbrough, 1978; Yankelovich, Skelly and White, Inc., 1984; Mason and Calvin, 1984: for experiments, see Spicer and Becker, 1980; Jackson and Jones, 1985). To the author's knowledge, only Clotfelter's (1983) findings show that under-reporting is significantly higher for younger taxpayers than for those aged 65 and older, which would imply a curvilinear relationship between age and tax compliance. To clarify the importance of the age variable, more empirical evidence is needed.

2. *Gender.* Social psychological research suggests that women are more compliant and less self-reliant than men (e.g. Tittle, 1980). Evidence from the tax compliance literature shows the tendency that men are less compliant than women (for survey studies, see, e.g., Vogel, 1974; Minor, 1978; Aitken and Bonneville, 1980: Tittle, 1980; for experiments, see Spicer and Becker, 1980; Spicer and Hero, 1985; Baldry, 1987). However, if social psychology argues that the difference is based on the traditional female role, it follows that today's female generation, which is more independent, would have a lower tax morale or tax compliance. Grasmick et al. (1991) find evidence that supports this argument. However, as the study was done many years ago, further evidence would help to clarify this result.

In the past decade, experimental research findings have shown that gender may influence aspects such as charitable giving, bargaining and household decision making (see Andreoni and Vesterlund, 2001; Eckel and Grossman, 2001). In public good games, the results are not clear. Some have found men to be more co-operative (see Brown-Kruse and Hummels, 1993), while others have found that women are more co-operative (Nowell and Tinkler, 1994). Using dictator games, Andreoni and Vesterlund (2001) observed individuals taking decisions with different budgets and, interestingly, found that in expensive giving situations, women are more generous than men, and when the price of giving decreases, men start to give more than women.

3. *Marital status* (dummy variables, SINGLE, LIVING TOGETHER, MARRIED, DIVORCED, SEPARATED, WIDOWED; reference group, SINGLE). Marital status might influence legal or illegal behaviour. Tittle (1980) states that

> A long tradition in sociology, extending back to Durkheim, postulates that proneness toward rule breaking varies inversely with the extent to which individuals are involved in social networks with constraining content (p. 111).

This would imply that married people are more compliant than others, especially compared to singles, because they are more constrained by their social network. Tittle found significant differences among the different marital statuses, with the greatest evidence for the singles, followed by the separated or divorced. However, controlling for age, the results show that the association between deviance and marital status was a reflection of age differences, as older persons are more likely to be married or widowed and age was a strong predictor concerning deviance.

In the tax compliance literature, we do not find many studies that systematically analyse marital status. Some studies have found that non-compliance is more common and of greater magnitude among married taxpayers (see Clotfelter, 1983; Feinstein, 1991). One reason could be that in the United States, dual incomes are treated as one, and one thus taxed in a higher bracket than two separate incomes (Hays, 2000). However, much remains to be done before we clearly understand the correlation between tax compliance or tax morale and marital status.

4. *Education* (continuous variable; 1 = poorly educated, 9 = highly educated). Education is related to taxpayers' knowledge of tax law. Better-educated taxpayers are supposed to know more about tax law and fiscal connections, and thus would be in a better position to assess the degree of compliance (see Lewis, 1982). They might be more aware of government waste and benefits. However, it should be noted that there might possibly be people with a lower education who have acquired a high degree of knowledge of taxation (see Eriksen and Fallan, 1996). They could invest in such specific knowledge because of the lower opportunity costs of their time. On the other hand, Vogel's (1974, p. 500) survey findings indicate that less-educated taxpayers had less access to tax compliance information, were less informed about relevant tax regulations and needed assistance more often.

More educated people may be less compliant because they better understand the opportunities for evasion. Furthermore, fiscal knowledge may also positively influence the practice of avoidance (see Geeroms and Wilmots, 1985). Witte and Woodbury (1985) found that compliance is higher in established but growing areas that are populated largely by middle-class, native-born whites. Areas with a better-educated population and with a large share of students have low levels of compliance. Furthermore, areas with large proportions of poverty and unemployment have a low level of compliance for all groups.

Fiscal ignorance might be an important contributor to the development of negative feelings towards taxation. After reviewing the literature of the 1970s, Lewis (1982) reports that more educated taxpayers have in general higher 'sympathetic' fiscal preferences than those with a lower education. They are better aware of the benefits and services that the state provides for the citizens from the revenues.

Generally, three aspects of education can be distinguished: (i) the degree of fiscal knowledge, (ii) the degree of knowledge involving evasion or avoidance opportunities and (iii) knowledge involving government waste as well as the benefits and services that the state provides by means of the taxes. Thus, the effect of education is not clear at all. More empirical studies will help to give an idea of which effects are stronger and define the influence on tax morale and tax compliance.

5. *Economic class* (UPPER CLASS, UPPER MIDDLE CLASS, LOWER MIDDLE CLASS; in the reference group, WORKING CLASS and LOWER CLASS). We have not used the income variable because of difficulties in comparing this variable across different countries. Thus, we have added a variable that measures the economic situation of an individual without producing biases for different nations. In general, the effects of income on tax morale are difficult to assess theoretically. Depending on risk preferences and the progression of the income tax schedules, income may increase or reduce tax morale. In countries with a progressive income tax rate, taxpayers with a higher income realize a higher dollar return by evading, but with possibly less economic utility. On the other hand, lower-income taxpayers might have lower social 'stakes' or restrictions, but are less in a position to take these risks, because of a high marginal utility loss (wealth reduction) if they are caught and penalized (Jackson and Milliron, 1986). The empirical findings are mixed. Clotfelter (1983) found that the coefficient on the after-tax income variable significantly reduces tax compliance (others, e.g., Witte and Woodbury, 1985; in survey studies Westat, Inc., 1980a; Groenland and van Veldhoven, 1983; and in experiments Friedland et al., 1978). On the other hand, Feinstein did not find a significant relationship between income and evasion, paying more attention to the positive dependent relationship between the tax rate and income (for further studies that came to the same result, see, e.g., Spicer, 1974; Grasmick and Scott, 1982; Yankelovich, Skelly and White, Inc., 1984: and in experiments, Spicer and Becker, 1980; Jackson and Jones, 1985). A positive relationship has been found by Mason and Calvin (1984) and Song and Yarbrough (1978). Researchers such as Witte and Woodbury (1985) state that low- and high-income taxpayers are relatively less compliant than the income groups in the middle. Jackson and Milliron (1986, p. 133) argue that there are two main explanations for the differences in the empirical findings: (i) many early studies have used linear models, which might produce biased correlation coefficients if the relationship between income level and compliance is not linear but, for example, curvilinear; and (ii) it might be that the observed level of compliance varies with the level of earned income.

6. *Occupational status* (FULL TIME EMPLOYED (reference group), PART TIME EMPLOYED, SELF-EMPLOYED, UNEMPLOYED, AT HOME, STUDENT, RETIRED, OTHER). Does occupational status influence tax morale? Here, we should differentiate between tax morale and tax evasion. The standard argument is that self-employed taxpayers evade more taxes. Vogel's (1974) survey in Sweden reports that self-employed taxpayers are more likely to think that large parts of taxes are used for meaningless purposes, that the government has made a great number of unnecessary social reforms, that they have gained less benefit from government programmes than the average taxpayer, and that the burden of taxes is too high and the exchange rate unfavourable. Lewis (1982) argues that the self-employed have higher compliance costs and taxes become more visible. Furthermore, tax evasion might depend on the opportunity to evade or avoid taxes. Westat, Inc. (1980b) show that 'white-collar' taxpayers have a higher non-compliant level in terms of overstating deductions, but that 'blue-collar' workers more often understate their income. However, all these arguments affect tax evasion and not necessarily tax morale. Thus, it is difficult to make a clear prediction about the influence of occupational status on tax morale.

7. *Financial satisfaction* (scale 1 = dissatisfied to 10 = satisfied). Financial dissatisfaction might negatively influence TAX MORALE. Such dissatisfaction might create a sense of distress, especially when taxes have to be paid and there is a discrepancy between the actual and the aspired financial situation.[5] Thus, taxes might be perceived as a strong restriction, increasing the incentives to reduce tax honesty. As the income variable is integrated into the equation, we can analyse the 'stress' component of this financial dissatisfaction. This argumentation is in line with prospect theory, which argues that people evaluate utility gains and losses not according to an absolute change but relative to a reference point (see, e.g., Kahneman and Tversky, 1979; Tversky and Kahneman, 1992). Taxpayers might compare their wealth and earnings with those of other taxpayers ('references') in their social environment (see Festinger, 1957).

8. *Risk aversion*: dummy variable (1 = RISK AVERSE). The individual tax compliance decision could also be a function of risk attitudes. Prior survey studies have rarely controlled for risk attitudes. Risk aversion reduces the incentive to act illegally. Furthermore, controlling for risk attitudes allows for better insights regarding the variables of age, gender or economic situation. It could be argued that the obtained difference between women and men, or between different age groups, is influenced by different risk attitude functions. Hartog et al. (2002), for example, found in an empirical survey analysis that an increase in income reduces risk aversion.

Results

In the first estimations presented in Table 4.1 we analyse the different faiths in separate estimations, controlling for the specific religion of an individual. We include the main religions around the world, such as CATHOLIC, PROTESTANT, JEWISH, HINDU, MOSLEM, BUDDHIST and ORTHODOX, in our analysis. The results indicate that there is a strong correlation between religiosity and tax morale. All coefficients are highly significant, with marginal effects between 1.8 and 9.3 percentage points. Strong effects can be observed for those people who had a religious education and for those people who are actively involved in a church or a religious organization. For example, being an active member of a church group increases the probability of stating that tax evasion is never justifiable by 8.5 percentage points. Looking at the religions, we observe a tendency for Catholics, Hindus, Buddhists and people with another religion to have a higher tax morale than people without a religious denomination. On the other hand, Orthodox and Protestants tend to have to a lower tax morale than the reference group, although the coefficient PROTESTANT is not always significant. This result is in line with the study by Furnham (1983), who found that a higher degree of protestant work ethic leads to more opposition to taxation. High protestant work ethic scorers believe more than low scorers that 'we should say "good luck" to people who avoid taxes; that taxes are an imposition, and that the taxes they pay are unreasonably high' (p. 119). According to Furnham, one reason might be that people with stronger protestant ethics 'are naturally against certain aspects of taxation' (p. 125), believing that success is based 'purely upon effort, and that the poor and unemployed are to blame for their plight' (p. 125). The negative coefficient of the variable ORTHODOX is surprising. In history, the Orthodox Church had a close relationship with the state (see, e.g., Stan and Turcescu, 2000). Thus, offences against the state were also religious offences. However, individuals in post-communist countries might have been influenced by anti-religious policies during the communist era.

In general, the results obtained from the variables JEWISH, BUDDHIST, HINDU and OTHER RELIGION should be treated with caution, as the number of observations is relatively low. Thus, they react more sensitively to a variation in the number of observations in the estimations.[6] Furthermore, it should be noted that in different countries individuals' exposure to the tax system is quite different. For example, the positive effect of the variable HINDU might be influenced by the fact that in India, for example, the great majority of citizens are not subject to income tax. The coefficient MUSLIM is mostly not significant. McGee (1998) reports that Muslims are not always obligated to pay all taxes. If the government engages in activities that are not legitimated, tax evasion might not be immoral (for a list of possible immoral state activities, see Yusuf, 1971). It would not be immoral for a Muslim not to pay indirect taxes, to avoid paying tariffs, to evade income taxes or not to comply with a law that causes prices to rise. However, evasion of property taxes might be immoral (McGee, 1998). The result of the variable BUDDHIST is not surprising, taking into consideration the strong guiding principles based on moral and ethical values (see, e.g., Alexandrin, 1993; Mendis, 1998), that might have an impact on the obligation to pay taxes.

In general, the coefficients of the confession variables are not significant for all religious denominations. This may indicate that it is not confession *per se* that increases tax morale and possibly inhibits illegal behaviour, but religiosity.

Looking at the control variables, we observe that a greater age is significantly correlated with a higher tax morale. Furthermore, women report a significantly higher tax morale than men. Married people have a higher tax morale and people living together a lower tax morale than singles. People who are employed part-time, at home or retired have a higher tax morale than people employed full-time. An increase in the financial satisfaction level by one unit increases the share of individuals arguing that tax evasion is never justifiable by around 1.3 percentage points. All economic classes higher than the reference group (WORKING CLASS and LOWER CLASS) have a lower tax morale, with the highest marginal effects for the upper class. Finally, risk-averse people have a higher tax morale than the reference group.

Sensitivity Analysis

To check the reliability of the effect of religiosity on tax morale, the perceived level of corruption has been included in additional equations.[7] In countries where corruption is systemic and the government budget lacks transparency, it *cannot* be assumed that the obligation to pay taxes is an accepted social norm. Friedman et al. (2000) show empirically that countries with more corruption have a higher share of unofficial economy. Corruption generally undermines the tax morale of the citizens, who become frustrated. Furthermore, there might be a crowding-out effect of morality among the tax administrators when there are a great number of corrupt colleagues. Taxpayers will feel cheated if they believe that corruption is widespread and their tax burden is not spent well. A corrupt bureaucracy will not award the services to the most efficient producers, but to the producer who offers

Table 4.1 Tax morale and religiosity

Weighted ordered probit	Coeff.	Marg.	Coeff.	Marg.	Coeff.	Marg.	Coeff.	Marg.	Coeff.	Marg.	Coeff.	Marg.
(a) Demographic factors												
AGE 30–49	0.127***	0.050	0.130***	0.051	0.126***	0.050	0.142***	0.056	0.117***	0.046	0.123***	0.048
AGE 50–64	0.280***	0.110	0.282***	0.111	0.282***	0.111	0.304***	0.120	0.269***	0.105	0.285***	0.112
AGE 65+	0.410***	0.161	0.396***	0.156	0.406***	0.159	0.437***	0.172	0.389***	0.152	0.402***	0.158
WOMAN	0.103***	0.041	0.115***	0.045	0.112***	0.044	0.111***	0.044	0.100***	0.039	0.111***	0.043
EDUCATION	−0.025***	−0.010	−0.017***	−0.007	−0.025***	−0.010	−0.017***	−0.007	−0.029***	−0.011	−0.023***	−0.009
(b) Marital status												
MARRIED	0.044*	0.017	0.061***	0.024	0.048**	0.019	0.050*	0.020	0.069***	0.027	0.043*	0.017
LIVING TOGETHER	−0.087**	−0.034	−0.059	−0.023	−0.087***	−0.034	−0.077***	−0.030	−0.103***	−0.040	−0.094***	−0.037
DIVORCED	−0.062	−0.024	−0.038	−0.015	−0.058	−0.023	−0.049	−0.019	−0.054	−0.021	−0.064	−0.025
SEPARATED	0.025	0.010	0.043	0.017	0.021	0.008	0.042	0.016	0.012	0.005	0.009	0.003
WIDOWED	0.009	0.004	0.034	0.013	0.022	0.009	0.029	0.011	0.025	0.010	0.014	0.006
(c) Employment status												
PART TIME EMPLOYED	0.068***	0.027	0.067**	0.026	0.075***	0.029	0.071***	0.028	0.075***	0.029	0.080***	0.032
SELF-EMPLOYED	0.023	0.009	−0.007	−0.003	0.031	0.012	0.015	0.006	0.026	0.010	0.018	0.007
UNEMPLOYED	0.032	0.012	0.036	0.014	0.033	0.013	0.039	0.015	0.001	0.000	0.038	0.015
AT HOME	0.134***	0.053	0.127***	0.050	0.135***	0.053	0.141***	0.055	0.095***	0.037	0.141***	0.055
STUDENT	0.058*	0.023	0.053	0.021	0.056	0.022	0.064*	0.025	0.058	0.023	0.069**	0.027
RETIRED	0.149***	0.059	0.150***	0.059	0.153***	0.060	0.159***	0.063	0.123***	0.048	0.155***	0.061
OTHER	−0.002	−0.001	0.013	0.005	−0.004	−0.002	0.010	0.004	−0.017	−0.007	−0.003	−0.001
(d) Economic situation												
FINANCIAL SATISFACTION	0.033***	0.013	0.032***	0.013	0.033***	0.013	0.034***	0.013	0.034***	0.013	0.035***	0.014
UPPER CLASS	−0.180***	−0.071	−0.199***	−0.078	−0.189***	−0.074	−0.192***	−0.076	−0.196***	−0.077	−0.176***	−0.069
UPPER MIDDLE CLASS	−0.050**	−0.019	−0.072***	−0.028	−0.052***	−0.020	−0.073***	−0.029	−0.031	−0.012	−0.050***	−0.020
LOWER MIDDLE CLASS	−0.105***	−0.041	−0.113***	−0.045	−0.107***	−0.042	−0.125***	−0.049	−0.100***	−0.039	−0.106***	−0.041

	(1)		(2)		(3)		(4)		(5)		(6)		(7)	
(e) Risk														
RISK AVERSE	0.129***	0.051	0.111***	0.044	0.129***	0.051	0.117***	0.046	0.125***	0.049	0.108***	0.043	0.132***	0.052
(f) Religiosity														
CHURCH ATTENDANCE	0.046***	0.018												
RELIGIOUS EDUCATION[a]			0.237***	0.093										
ACTIVE IN CHURCH GROUP					0.216***	0.085								
RELIGIOUS[a]							0.085***	0.033						
IMPORTANCE OF RELIGION									0.128***	0.050				
RELIGIOUS GUIDANCE											0.113***	0.045		
TRUST CHURCH													0.059***	0.023
(g) Religion														
CATHOLIC	0.044**	0.017	0.049***	0.019	0.109***	0.043	0.116***	0.045	−0.066***	−0.026	0.090***	0.035	0.094***	0.037
PROTESTANT	−0.050*	−0.020	−0.028	−0.011	−0.020	−0.008	−0.023	−0.009	−0.154***	−0.060	−0.061***	−0.024	−0.029	−0.011
ORTHODOX	−0.241***	−0.094	−0.186***	−0.073	−0.178***	−0.070	−0.204***	−0.080	−0.351***	−0.137	−0.220***	−0.086	−0.220***	−0.086
JEWISH	0.198	0.078	0.265	0.104	0.235	0.092	0.229	0.090	0.100	0.039	0.263	0.103	0.228	0.090
MUSLIM	0.011	0.004	0.039	0.015	0.103*	0.040	0.030	0.012	−0.138***	−0.054	0.038	0.015	0.072	0.028
HINDU	0.563***	0.221	0.609***	0.240	0.669***	0.263	0.680***	0.267	0.444***	0.173	0.777***	0.305	0.619***	0.243
BUDDHIST	0.231***	0.091	0.282	0.111	0.299***	0.117	0.239	0.094	0.132	0.051	0.227	0.089	0.315***	0.124
OTHER RELIGION	0.239***	0.094	0.287***	0.113	0.271***	0.107	0.334	0.131	0.120***	0.047	0.295***	0.116	0.331***	0.130
Number of observations	34265		31251		34497		31660		35062		33000		33317	
Prob(LM-statistic)	0.000		0.000		0.000		0.000		0.000		0.000		0.000	

Notes: Dependent variable: tax morale on a four-point scale (0 to 3). In the reference group are AGE 16–29, MAN, SINGLE, FULL TIME EMPLOYED, WORKING CLASS AND LOWER CLASS, NOT RISK AVERSE, NOT ACTIVELY IN A CHURCH GROUP, NO ABSOLUTELY GUIDANCE OF WHAT IS GOOD OR EVIL and NO RELIGIOUS DENOMINATION. Significance levels: * $0.005 < p < 0.010$; ** $0.001 < p < 0.005$; *** $p < 0.001$. Marginal effect = highest tax morale score (3). [a] South Korea is not included in these estimations.

Table 4.2 Tax morale and corruption

Weighted ordered probit	Coeff.	Coeff.	Coeff.	Coeff.	Coeff.	Coeff.
(a) Demographic factors	Included	Included	Included	Included	Included	Included
(b) Marital status	"	"	"	"	"	"
(c) Employment status	"	"	"	"	"	"
(d) Economic situation	"	"	"	"	"	"
(e) Risk attitude	"	"	"	"	"	"
(f) Religiosity						
Behaviour						
CHURCH ATTENDANCE	0.048*** (0.019)					
RELIGIOUS EDUCATION [a]		0.240*** (0.095)				
ACTIVE IN CHURCH GROUP			0.223*** (0.088)			
Attitude						
RELIGIOUS [a]				0.087*** (0.034)		
IMPORTANCE OF RELIGION					0.142*** (0.056)	
RELIGIOUS GUIDANCE						0.113*** (0.045)
TRUST CHURCH						0.062*** (0.024)

(g) Religion						
CATHOLIC	0.043*	0.054***	0.111***	0.121***	-0.005	0.172***	0.094***
	(0.017)	(0.021)	(0.044)	(0.048)	(-0.002)	(0.068)	(0.037)
PROTESTANT	-0.078***	-0.051*	-0.045	-0.049	-0.115***	-0.006	-0.057**
	(-0.031)	(-0.020)	(-0.018)	(-0.019)	(-0.045)	(-0.002)	(-0.022)
ORTHODOX	-0.249***	-0.190***	-0.183***	-0.208***	-0.300***	-0.148***	-0.230***
	(-0.098)	(-0.075)	(-0.072)	(-0.082)	(-0.118)	(-0.058)	(-0.090)
JEWISH	0.098	0.172	0.137	0.131	0.063	0.246	0.163
	(0.038)	(0.068)	(0.054)	(0.052)	(0.025)	(0.097)	(0.064)
MUSLIM	0.046	0.084	0.141	0.063	-0.050	0.145***	0.113**
	(0.018)	(0.033)	(0.055)	(0.025)	(-0.020)	(0.057)	(0.044)
HINDU	0.593***	0.647***	0.705***	0.718***	0.550***	0.891***	0.647***
	(0.233)	(0.255)	(0.277)	(0.283)	(0.216)	(0.351)	(0.254)
BUDDHIST	0.236***	0.297	0.307***	0.249	0.218**	0.312	0.321***
	(0.093)	(0.117)	(0.121)	(0.098)	(0.086)	(0.123)	(0.126)
OTHER RELIGION	0.247***	0.299	0.281***	0.348***	0.186***	0.382***	0.334***
	(0.097)	(0.118)	(0.111)	(0.137)	(0.073)	(0.151)	(0.131)
(h) Corruption	-0.048***	-0.046	-0.045***	-0.049	-0.055***	-0.045***	-0.046
	(-0.019)	(-0.018)	(-0.018)	(-0.019)	(-0.022)	(-0.018)	(-0.018)
Number of observations	31 545	30 133	31 731	29 107	31 113	29 293	30 780
Prob (LM–statistic)	0.000	0.000	0.000	0.000	0.000	0.000	0.000

Notes: Dependent variable: tax morale on a four point scale (0 to 3). In the reference group are AGE 16–29, MAN, SINGLE, FULL TIME EMPLOYED, WORKING CLASS AND LOWER CLASS, NOT RISK AVERSE, NOT ACTIVELY IN A CHURCH GROUP, NO ABSOLUTE GUIDANCE OF WHAT IS GOOD OR EVIL, and NO RELIGIOUS DENOMINATION. Significance levels: * $0.005 < p < 0.010$; ** $0.001 < p < 0.005$; *** $p < 0.001$. Marginal effects in parenthesis (highest tax morale score, 3). [a] South Korea is not included in these estimations.

Table 4.3 Religion and religiosity

Weighted ordered probit	Coeff.	Marg.	Coeff.	Marg.	Coeff.	Marg.	Coeff.	Marg.	Coeff.	Marg.	Coeff.	Marg.
CHURCH ATTEND.	−0.007	0.003			0.050***	0.020	0.040***	0.016				
ACTIVE IN CHURCH GROUP			−0.3E−03***	0.1E−03					0.213***	0.084	0.188***	0.074
RELIGIOUS[a]					0.033**	0.013			0.070***	0.027		
TRUST CHURCH							0.036***	0.014			0.047***	0.018
Religion												
CATHOLIC	0.014	0.006	0.137***	0.054	0.046*	0.018	0.027	0.011	0.095***	0.037	0.073***	0.029
PROTESTANT	−0.389***	−0.153	−0.091***	−0.036	−0.089***	−0.035	−0.098***	−0.038	−0.073***	−0.029	−0.078***	−0.031
ORTHODOX	−0.313***	−0.123	−0.174***	−0.068	−0.260***	−0.102	−0.276***	−0.108	−0.212***	−0.084	−0.230***	−0.091
JEWISH	−0.024	−0.0095	0.232	0.091	0.057	0.022	0.080	0.031	0.069	0.027	0.111	0.043
MUSLIM	0.025	0.0095	0.155***	0.061	−0.012	−0.004	0.041	0.016	0.060	0.024	0.110**	0.043
HINDU	0.722***	0.2835	0.879***	0.345	0.607***	0.239	0.553***	0.217	0.702***	0.2763	0.635***	0.249
BUDDHIST	0.556***	0.2186	0.073	0.029	0.189	0.074	0.246***	0.097	0.229	0.090	0.305***	0.119
OTHER RELIGION	0.174	0.069	0.222	0.087	0.243***	0.096	0.241***	0.095	0.262***	0.103	0.261***	0.102
Interaction terms												
CATH * CHURCH A.	0.030**	0.012										
PROT * CHURCH A.	0.114***	0.045										
ORTH * CHURCH A.	0.038***	0.015										
JEWS * CHURCH A.	0.053	0.021										
MUSL * CHURCH A.	0.027	0.011										
HIND * CHURCH A.	−0.0013	−0.001										
BUDD * CHUR. A.	−0.065	−0.026										
O. REL * CHUR. A.	0.041	0.016										

CATH * CHUR. G.	0.149***	0.059
PROT * CHUR. G.	0.475***	0.187
ORTH * CHUR. G.	0.223***	0.088
JEWS * CHUR. G.	−0.0053	−0.002
MUSL * CHUR. G.	0.260	0.102
HINDU * CHUR. G.	−0.595***	−0.234
BUDD * CHUR. G.	0.171	0.067
O. REL * CHUR. G.	0.371***	0.146
Prob(LM–statistic)	0.000	0.000	0.000	0.000	0.000

Notes: Dependent variable: tax morale on a four point scale (0 to 3). All other variables included, in the reference group are AGE 16–29, MAN, SINGLE, FULL TIME EMPLOYED, WORKING CLASS AND LOWER CLASS, NOT RISK AVERSE, NOT ACTIVELY IN A CHURCH GROUP, NO ABSOLUTE GUIDANCE OF WHAT IS GOOD OR EVIL and NO RELIGIOUS DENOMINATION. Significance levels: * $0.005 < p < 0.010$; ** $0.001 < p < 0.005$; *** $p < 0.001$. Marginal effects in parenthesis (highest tax morale score, 3). [a] South Korea is not included in the estimation.

Table 4.4 Tax morale and lying

Weighted ordered probit	Coeff.	Coeff.	Coeff.	Coeff.	Coeff.	Coeff.
(a) **Demographic factors**	Included	Included	Included	Included	Included	Included
(b) **Marital status**	"	"	"	"	"	"
(c) **Employment status**	"	"	"	"	"	"
(d) **Economic situation**	"	"	"	"	"	"
(e) **Risk attitude**	"	"	"	"	"	"
(f) **Religiosity**						
Behaviour						
CHURCH ATTENDANCE	0.059*** (0.023)					
RELIGIOUS EDUCATION [a]		0.246*** (0.097)				
ACTIVE IN CHURCH GROUP			0.231*** (0.091)			
Belief						
RELIGIOUS				0.109** (0.043)		
IMPORTANCE OF RELIGION					0.148*** (0.058)	
RELIGIOUS [a] GUIDANCE					0.095*** (0.037)	
TRUST CHURCH						0.074*** (0.029)

132

(g) Religion					
CATHOLIC	0.105***	0.098**	0.193***	0.156***	0.072**	0.220***	0.168***
	(0.042)	(0.039)	(0.076)	(0.061)	(0.028)	(0.087)	(0.066)
PROTESTANT	−0.146***	−0.128***	−0.104***	−0.136***	−0.173***	−0.078**	−0.119***
	(−0.058)	(−0.050)	(−0.041)	(−0.053)	(−0.068)	(−0.031)	(−0.047)
ORTHODOX	−0.146***	−0.099**	−0.065**	−0.130***	−0.183***	−0.059**	−0.119***
	(−0.057)	(−0.039)	(−0.025)	(−0.051)	(−0.072)	(−0.023)	(−0.047)
JEWISH	0.213	0.279	0.259	0.253	0.188	0.358	0.294
	(0.084)	(0.110)	(0.102)	(0.099)	(0.074)	(0.141)	(0.116)
MUSLIM	0.093*	0.109	0.205**	0.083	0.018	0.174**	0.165**
	(0.037)	(0.043)	(0.081)	(0.033)	(0.007)	(0.068)	(0.065)
HINDU	0.535***	0.558***	0.670***	0.634***	0.513**	0.776***	0.609***
	(0.210)	(0.219)	(0.263)	(0.249)	(0.202)	(0.305)	(0.239)
BUDDHIST	0.421	0.488	0.498	0.418	0.366	0.504	0.493
	(0.165)	(0.192)	(0.196)	(0.164)	(0.144)	(0.198)	(0.193)
OTHER RELIGION	0.219**	0.268**	0.275**	0.297***	0.178**	0.360**	0.323***
	(0.086)	(0.105)	(0.108)	(0.117)	(0.070)	(0.142)	(0.127)
(h) Corruption	−0.041***	−0.036**	−0.037**	−0.041***	−0.048***	−0.037**	−0.038***
	(−0.016)	(−0.014)	(−0.015)	(−0.016)	(−0.019)	(−0.015)	(−0.015)
(i) Trustworthiness							
LYING	0.410**	0.408**	0.408**	0.411**	0.409**	0.405**	0.407**
	(0.161)	(0.160)	(0.160)	(0.161)	(0.161)	(0.159)	(0.160)
Number of observations	29 629	29 400	29 784	28 464	29 230	28 644	28 895
Prob(LM-statistic)	0.000	0.000	0.000	0.000	0.000	0.000	0.000

Notes: Dependent variable: tax morale on a four-point scale (0 to 3). All other variables included, in the reference group are AGE 16–29, MAN, SINGLE, FULL TIME EMPLOYED, WORKING CLASS AND LOWER CLASS, NOT RISK AVERSE, NOT ACTIVELY IN A CHURCH GROUP, NO ABSOLUTE GUIDANCE OF WHAT IS GOOD OR EVIL, NO RELIGIOUS DENOMINATION. Significance levels: * 0.005 < *p* < 0.010; ** 0.001 < *p* < 0.005; *** *p* < 0.001. Marginal effects in parenthesis (highest tax morale score, 3). [a] South Korea is not included in these estimations.

Table 4.5 Tax morale and buying a stolen product

Weighted ordered probit	Coeff.	Coeff.	Coeff.	Coeff.	Coeff.	Coeff.	Coeff.	Coeff.
(a) **Demographic factors**	Included	Included	Included	Included	Included	Included	Included	Included
(b) **Marital status**	"	"	"	"	"	"	"	"
(c) **Employment status**	"	"	"	"	"	"	"	"
(d) **Economic situation**	"	"	"	"	"	"	"	"
(e) **Risk attitude**	"	"	"	"	"	"	"	"
(f) Religiosity								
Behaviour								
CHURCH ATTENDANCE	0.040*** (0.016)							
RELIGIOUS EDUCATION [a]		0.224*** (0.088)						
ACTIVE IN CHURCH GROUP			0.224*** (0.088)					
Belief								
RELIGIOUS				0.050*** (0.020)				
IMPORTANCE OF RELIGION					0.109*** (0.043)			
RELIGIOUS GUIDANCE [a]						0.075*** (0.030)		
TRUST CHURCH								0.040*** (0.016)

	(1)	(2)	(3)	(4)	(5)	(6)	(7)
(g) Religion							
CATHOLIC	0.020	0.021	0.069***	0.105***	−0.009	0.134***	0.070***
	(0.008)	(0.008)	(0.027)	(0.041)	(−0.004)	(0.053)	(0.028)
PROTESTANT	−0.132***	−0.116***	−0.112***	−0.102***	−0.157***	−0.072***	−0.108***
	(−0.052)	(−0.046)	(−0.044)	(−0.040)	(−0.062)	(−0.029)	(−0.042)
ORTHODOX	−0.222***	−0.168***	−0.170***	−0.169***	−0.255***	−0.128***	−0.200***
	(−0.087)	(−0.066)	(−0.067)	(−0.067)	(−0.100)	(−0.051)	(−0.079)
JEWISH	0.012	0.073	0.032	0.056	−0.004	0.161	0.067
	(0.005)	(0.029)	(0.013)	(0.022)	(−0.002)	(0.063)	(0.026)
MUSLIM	0.025	0.060	0.106**	0.067	−0.037***	0.129***	0.091
	(0.010)	(0.024)	(0.042)	(0.026)	(−0.015)	(0.051)	(0.036)
HINDU	0.603***	0.645***	0.688***	0.727***	0.579***	0.851***	0.651***
	(0.237)	(0.254)	(0.270)	(0.286)	(0.227)	(0.336)	(0.256)
BUDDHIST	0.286***	0.196	0.342***	0.176	0.280	0.216	0.348*
	(0.112)	(0.077)	(0.135)	(0.069)	(0.110)	(0.085)	(0.137)
OTHER RELIGION	0.173***	0.206	0.186***	0.275***	0.140***	0.288***	0.250***
	(0.068)	(0.081)	(0.073)	(0.108)	(0.055)	(0.114)	(0.098)
(h) Corruption	−0.051***	−0.051***	−0.050***	−0.053***	−0.057***	−0.051***	−0.049***
	(−0.020)	(−0.020)	(−0.020)	(−0.021)	(−0.022)	(−0.020)	(−0.019)
(i) Trustworthiness							
BUYING A STOLEN PRODUCT	0.505***	0.509***	0.505***	0.508***	0.500***	0.505***	0.503***
	(0.198)	(0.200)	(0.198)	(0.200)	(0.196)	(0.199)	(0.197)
Number of observations	31 312	29 905	31 496	28 898	30 894	29 082	30 562
Prob(LM-statistic)	0.000	0.000	0.000	0.000	0.000	0.000	0.000

Notes: Dependent variable: tax morale on a four point scale (0 to 3). All other variables included, in the reference group are AGE 16–29, MAN, SINGLE, FULL TIME EMPLOYED, WORKING CLASS AND LOWER CLASS, NOT RISK AVERSE, NOT ACTIVELY IN A CHURCH GROUP, NO ABSOLUTE GUIDANCE OF WHAT IS GOOD OR EVIL and NO RELIGIOUS DENOMINATION. Significance levels: * $0.005 < p < 0.010$; ** $0.001 < p < 0.005$; *** $p < 0.001$. Marginal effects in parenthesis (highest tax morale score, 3). [a] South Korea is not included in these estimations.

Table 4.6 Tax morale and cheating

Weighted ordered probit	Coeff.	Coeff.	Coeff.	Coeff.	Coeff.	Coeff.
(a) Demographic factors	Included	Included	Included	Included	Included	Included
(b) Marital status	"	"	"	"	"	"
(c) Employment status	"	"	"	"	"	"
(d) Economic situation	"	"	"	"	"	"
(e) Risk attitude	"	"	"	"	"	"
(f) Religiosity						
Behaviour						
CHURCH ATTENDANCE	0.038*** (0.015)					
RELIGIOUS EDUCATION [a]		0.159*** (0.063)				
ACTIVE IN CHURCH GROUP			0.190*** (0.074)			
Belief						
RELIGIOUS [a]				0.068*** (0.027)		
IMPORTANCE OF RELIGION					0.114*** (0.044)	
RELIGIOUS GUIDANCE						0.077*** (0.030)
TRUST CHURCH						0.065*** (0.025)

	(1)	(2)	(3)	(4)	(5)	(6)	(7)
(g) Religion							
CATHOLIC	−0.009	0.025	0.040*	0.063***	−0.005**	0.101***	0.017
	(−0.004)	(0.010)	(0.016)	(0.025)	(−0.020)	(0.040)	(0.007)
PROTESTANT	−0.177***	−0.157***	−0.153***	−0.164***	−0.206***	−0.126***	−0.170***
	(−0.069)	(−0.062)	(−0.060)	(−0.064)	(−0.080)	(−0.050)	(−0.067)
ORTHODOX	−0.133***	−0.069***	−0.083***	−0.090***	−0.177***	−0.043	−0.133***
	(−0.052)	(−0.027)	(−0.033)	(−0.036)	(−0.069)	(−0.017)	(−0.052)
JEWISH	0.104	0.190	0.137	0.153	−0.074	0.250	0.146
	(0.041)	(0.075)	(0.054)	(0.060)	(−0.029)	(0.098)	(0.057)
MUSLIM	−0.080	−0.018	−0.002	−0.042	−0.144***	0.074	−0.040
	(−0.031)	(−0.007)	(−0.001)	(−0.017)	(−0.057)	(0.007)	(−0.016)
HINDU	0.269***	0.348***	0.353***	0.395***	0.235**	0.530***	0.283***
	(0.105)	(0.137)	(0.138)	(0.155)	(0.92)	(0.208)	(0.111)
BUDDHIST	0.443***	0.332	0.503***	0.281	0.427***	0.344	0.512***
	(0.173)	(0.131)	(0.197)	(0.110)	(0.167)	(0.135)	(0.200)
OTHER RELIGION	0.170***	0.231***	0.190***	0.262	0.125**	0.285***	0.221***
	(0.067)	(0.091)	(0.074)	(0.103)	(0.049)	(0.112)	(0.086)
(h) Corruption	−0.029***	−0.029***	−0.028***	−0.032***	−0.036***	−0.029	−0.029
	(−0.012)	(−0.012)	(−0.011)	(−0.013)	(−0.014)	(−0.012)	(−0.011)
(i) Trustworthiness							
CHEATING	0.511***	0.514***	0.511***	0.516***	0.506***	0.513***	0.511***
	(0.200)	(0.202)	(0.200)	(0.203)	(0.198)	(0.202)	(0.200)
Number of observations	31 299	29 892	31 482	28 886	30 876	29 071	30 556
Prob(LM-statistic)	0.000	0.000	0.000	0.000	0.000	0.000	0.000

Notes: Dependent variable: tax morale on a four-point scale (0 to 3). All other variables included, in the reference group are AGE 16–29, MAN, SINGLE, FULL TIME EMPLOYED, WORKING CLASS AND LOWER CLASS, NOT RISK AVERSE, NOT ACTIVELY IN A CHURCH GROUP, NO ABSOLUTE GUIDANCE OF WHAT IS GOOD OR EVIL and NO RELIGIOUS DENOMINATION. Significance levels: * $0.005 < p < 0.010$; ** $0.001 < p < 0.005$; *** $p < 0.001$. Marginal effects in parenthesis (highest tax morale score, 3). [a] South Korea is not included in these estimations.

the larger bribes. Thus, corruption reduces the efficiency of allocation and produces delays in transactions to acquire additional payments (see, e.g., Rose-Ackerman, 1997; Jain, 2001). Thus, paid taxes are not spent in line with taxpayers' preferences. Table 4.2 indicates that there is a significant negative correlation between tax morale and the perceived size of corruption. An increase in the corruption scale by one unit increases the share of subjects indicating the highest tax morale by around 1.8 percentage points. Thus, the results indicate that a higher degree of perceived corruption crowds out tax morale. If taxpayers notice that many public officials are corrupt and that many others evade taxes, they might feel that their intrinsic motivation is not recognized or honoured. Thus, taxpayers may decide that they can also be opportunistic. The moral costs of evading taxes decrease. The positive effects of religiosity on tax morale remain robust, with a small increase in the marginal effects for some variables.

In a next step, we will analyse whether the impact of religiosity depends on which religion the person adheres to. Thus, we will analyse whether active followers of some religions are more tax compliant than others. We choose the two main observable variables (church attendance and being an active member of a church group) and interact them with the different confessions. It can be supposed that the effect of a specific confession depends on the degree of religiosity. The results in Table 4.3 indicate that in *both* estimations the product terms of the variables CATHOLIC, PROTESTANT and ORTHODOX, contrary to the others, are statistically significant with a positive sign, so we may conclude that there is an interaction between these religions and the two measurements that we used for religiosity. The marginal effects are very large, especially for the variable PROTESTANT. This result is interesting since, previously, the variables PROTESTANT and ORTHODOX were not statistically significant as single terms. Thus, the positive effect on tax morale in these two religions strongly depends on the extent to which someone is an active follower.

In a next step, we analyse to what extent religious beliefs (being religious and trusting the church as an institution) that are not observable and religious behaviour (observable, measured with the same two previous variables) affect tax morale. Thus, we integrate both types of variables together in further estimations. The results in Table 4.3 indicate that both factors matter. Thus, religiosity affects tax morale as a social norm and as a way of establishing a reputation for trustworthiness. However, it should be noted that compared to Table 4.2, the marginal effects for the 'behavioural' variables remain more stable than for the 'belief' variables.

Finally, we check whether questions about trustworthiness explain tax morale as well as religiosity. This also helps us to check the robustness of the correlation between religiosity and tax morale. Thus, the following variables have been integrated separately into different equations (see Tables 4.4–4.6): (1) Claiming government benefits to which you are not entitled, (2) Avoiding a fare on public transport, and 3) Buying something you knew was stolen. It can be expected that a high intrinsic motivation to pay taxes is correlated with a moral obligation not to lie or to cheat. Thus, it is not surprising that the results indicate that trustworthiness has a strong impact on tax morale. The marginal effects vary between 15.9 (lying) and 20.3 (cheating) percentage points. However, the significant positive correlation between tax morale and religiosity and the quantitative effects measured by the marginal effects remain quite robust. On the basis of these results, it might be interesting to analyse whether the impact of religiosity works through its impact on trustworthiness or whether there is an independent effect. Therefore, we have built interaction terms between religiosity and trustworthiness. The results are presented in Tables A4.2 to A4.4 in the Appendix. In most of the estimations, the coefficient of the product is significant. However, in many estimations the marginal effects are relatively small, which indicates that religiosity does not only work through its impact on trustworthiness, but also has an independent effect.

CONCLUSIONS

The basic contribution of this chapter is to analyse religiosity as a factor that potentially affects tax morale. With data from the World Values Survey 1995–97, strong evidence has been adduced that religiosity factors exert a systematic influence on tax morale. This effect tends to persist even after controlling for factors such as corruption, trustworthiness, age, economic situation, education, gender, marital status and employment status.

The empirical findings support the relevance of incorporating non-economic factors into the analysis of tax compliance. Tax morale and tax compliance are not just functions of the opportunity to evade taxes, tax rates and the probability of detection. It might therefore be fruitful to work with models that systematically integrate ideas borrowed from other social sciences. An extension of the economic model of man integrating factors such as religiosity opens up a new working instrument without losing simplicity and robustness. As Iannaccone (1998) points out,

> The economics of religion will eventually bury two myths – that of homo economicus as a cold creature with neither need nor capacity for piety, and that of homo religiosus as a benighted throwback to pre-rational times (p. 1492).

APPENDIX

Table A4.1 The derivation of some variables

Variable	Derivation
TAX MORALE (dependent variable)	Please tell me for each of the following statements whether you think it can always be justified, never be justified, or something in between: [...] Cheating on tax if you have the chance (3=never and 0=always)
CHURCH ATTENDANCE	Apart from weddings, funerals and christenings, about how often do you attend religious services these days? More than once a week, once a week, once a month, only on special holy days, once a year, less often, never practically never. (7 = more than once a week to 1 = never, practically never)
CHURCH PARTICIPATION	Now I am going to read off a list of voluntary organizations; for each one, could you tell me whether you are an active member or not: Church or religious organization (dummy variable)
RELIGIOUS EDUCATION	Were you brought up religiously at home (dummy variable)? 1. Yes 0. No
RELIGIOUS	Independently of whether you go to church or not, would you say you are: 1. A convinced atheist 2. Not a religious person 3. A religious person
IMPORTANCE OF RELIGION	Please say, for each of the following, how important it is in your life. Would you say ... Religion (1 = not at all important, 4 = very important)
RELIGIOUS GUIDANCE	Here is a statement that people sometimes make when discussing good and evil: There are absolutely clear guidelines about what is good and evil. These always apply to everyone, whatever the circumstances. (dummy variable)
TRUST CHURCH	I am going to name a number of organizations. For each one, could you tell me how much confidence you have in them: is it a great deal of confidence, quite a lot of confidence, not very much confidence or none at all? The churches (4 = a great deal, 1 = not very much)
EDUCATION	What is the highest educational level that you have attained? 1. No formal education 2. Incomplete primary school 3. Completed primary school 4. Incomplete secondary school: technical/vocational type 5. Complete secondary school: technical/vocational type 6. Incomplete secondary: university–preparatory type 7. Complete secondary: university–preparatory type 8. Some university–level education, without degree 9. University–level education, with degree

FINANCIAL SATISFACTION	How satisfied are you with the financial situation of your household? (scale 1 = dissatisfied to 10 = satisfied)
RISK AVERSE	Now I would like to ask you something about the things that would seem to you, personally, most important if you were looking for a job. Here are some of the things many people take into account in relation to their work. Regardless of whether you're actually looking for a job, which one would you, personally, place first if you were looking for a job? 1. A good income so that you do not have any worries about money 2. A safe job with no risk of closing down or unemployment 3. Working with people you like 4. Doing an important job which gives you a feeling of accomplishment And what would be your second choice? A dummy variable was built with the value 1, if someone has chosen 2 as first or as second choice.
ECONOMIC CLASS	People sometimes describe themselves as belonging to the working class, the middle class, or the upper or lower class. Would you describe yourself as belonging to the: 1. Upper class 2. Upper middle class 3. Lower middle class 4. Working class 5. Lower class
LYING	Please tell me for each of the following statements whether you think it can always be justified, never be justified, or something in between: [...] Claiming government benefits to which you are not entitled (3 = never and 0 = always)
CHEATING	Please tell me for each of the following statements whether you think it can always be justified, never be justified, or something in between: [...] Avoiding a fare on public transport (3 = never and 0 = always)
BUYING A STOLEN PRODUCT	Please tell me for each of the following statements whether you think it can always be justified, never be justified, or something in between: [...] Buying something you knew was stolen (3 = never and 0 = always)

Source: Inglehart (2000b).

Table A4.2 Tax morale and trustworthiness (lying)

Weighted ordered probit	Coeff.	Coeff.	Coeff.	Coeff.	Coeff.	Coeff.	Coeff.
Behaviour							
CHURCH ATTENDANCE [a]	0.055*** (0.022)						
RELIGIOUS EDUCATION		0.215*** (0.085)					
ACTIVE IN CHURCH GROUP			0.158*** (0.062)				
Belief							
RELIGIOUS [a]				0.115*** (0.045)			
IMPORTANCE OF RELIGION					0.100*** (0.039)		
RELIGIOUS GUIDANCE						0.015 (0.006)	
TRUST CHURCH							0.037*** (0.015)

Trustworthiness

LYING	0.403***	0.399***	0.403***	0.419***	0.345***	0.391***	0.358***
	(0.158)	(0.157)	(0.159)	(0.164)	(0.135)	(0.154)	(0.141)
RELDENOM * LYING	0.002	0.015	0.036*	−0.003	0.024***	0.039***	0.018***
	(0.001)	(0.006)	(0.014)	(−0.001)	(0.009)	(0.016)	(0.007)
Number of observations	29 629	29 400	29 784	28 464	29 230	28 644	28 895
Prob(LM-statistic)	0.000	0.000	0.000	0.000	0.000	0.000	0.000

Notes: Dependent variable: tax morale on a four point scale (0 to 3). All other variables included, in the reference group are AGE 16–29, MAN, SINGLE, FULL TIME EMPLOYED, WORKING CLASS AND LOWER CLASS, NOT RISK AVERSE, NOT ACTIVELY IN A CHURCH GROUP, NO ABSOLUTE GUIDANCE OF WHAT IS GOOD OR EVIL and NO RELIGIOUS DENOMINATION. Significance levels: * $0.005 < p < 0.010$; ** $0.001 < p < 0.005$; *** $p < 0.001$. Marginal effects in parenthesis (highest tax morale score, 3). [a] South Korea is not included in these estimations.

Table A4.3 *Tax morale and trustworthiness (buying a stolen product)*

Weighted ordered probit	Coeff.	Coeff.	Coeff.	Coeff.	Coeff.	Coeff.	Coeff.
Behaviour							
CHURCH ATTENDANCE	−0.010 (−0.004)						
RELIGIOUS EDUCATION [a]		0.012 (0.005)					
ACTIVE IN CHURCH GROUP			−0.090 (−0.035)				
Belief							
RELIGIOUS [a]				−0.036 (−0.014)			
IMPORTANCE OF RELIGION					0.006 (0.002)		
RELIGIOUS GUIDANCE						−0.078 (−0.031)	
TRUST CHURCH							−0.046* (−0.018)

144

Trustworthiness

BUYING A STOLEN PRODUCT	0.442*** (0.174)	0.461 (0.181)	0.491*** (0.193)	0.416*** (0.164)	0.393*** (0.154)	0.484*** (0.191)	0.414*** (0.163)
RELIGIOSITY * BUYING A STOLEN PRODUCT	0.020*** (0.008)	0.087 (0.034)	0.127*** (0.050)	0.036*** (0.014)	0.042*** (0.017)	0.062*** (0.024)	0.035*** (0.014)
Number of observations	31312	29905	31496	28898	30894	29082	30562
Prob(LM–statistic)	0.000	0.000	0.000	0.000	0.000	0.000	0.000

Notes: Dependent variable: tax morale on a four-point scale (0 to 3). All other variables included, in the reference group are AGE 16–29, MAN, SINGLE, FULL TIME EMPLOYED, WORKING CLASS AND LOWER CLASS, NOT RISK AVERSE, NOT ACTIVELY IN A CHURCH GROUP, NO ABSOLUTE GUIDANCE OF WHAT IS GOOD OR EVIL and NO RELIGIOUS DENOMINATION. Significance levels: * $0.005 < p < 0.010$; ** $0.001 < p < 0.005$; *** $p < 0.001$. Marginal effects in parenthesis (highest tax morale score, 3). [a] South Korea is not included in these estimations.

Table A4.4 Tax morale and trustworthiness (cheating)

Weighted ordered probit	Coeff.	Coeff.	Coeff.	Coeff.	Coeff.	Coeff.	Coeff.
Behaviour							
CHURCH ATTENDANCE	0.015*** (0.006)						
RELIGIOUS EDUCATION [a]		0.099*** (0.039)					
ACTIVE IN CHURCH GROUP			0.080** (0.031)				
Belief							
RELIGIOUS[a]				0.045 (0.018)			
IMPORTANCE OF RELIGION					0.083*** (0.032)		
RELIGIOUS GUIDANCE						−0.027 (−0.009)	
TRUST CHURCH							−0.025*** (−0.001)

Trustworthiness

CHEATING	0.469***	0.495***	0.504***	0.481***	0.460***	0.493***	0.452***
	(0.184)	(0.194)	(0.197)	(0.189)	(0.180)	(0.194)	(0.177)
RELIGIOSITY * CHEATING	0.013***	0.035***	0.060***	0.014	0.018***	0.054***	0.022***
	(0.005)	(0.014)	(0.023)	(0.005)	(0.007)	(0.022)	(0.009)
Number of observations	31 299	29 892	31 482	28 886	30 876	29 071	30 556
Prob(LM–statistic)	0.000	0.000	0.000	0.000	0.000	0.000	0.000

Notes: Dependent variable: tax morale on a four point scale (0 to 3). All other variables included, in the reference group are AGE 16–29, MAN, SINGLE, FULL TIME EMPLOYED, WORKING CLASS AND LOWER CLASS, NOT RISK AVERSE, NOT ACTIVELY IN A CHURCH GROUP, NO ABSOLUTE GUIDENCE OF WHAT IS GOOD OR EVIL and NO RELIGIOUS DENOMINATION. Significance levels: * $0.005 < p < 0.010$; ** $0.001 < p < 0.005$; *** $p < 0.001$. Marginal effects in parenthesis (highest tax morale score, 3). [a] South Korea is not included in these estimations.

NOTES

1. Freud (1927) uses words such as 'neurosis', 'illusion', 'poison' to describe religion (p. 8).
2. For a treatment of habits, see Twomey (1999).
3. Germany (differentiating between West and East Germany), Spain, the United States, Australia, Norway, Argentina, Finland, South Korea, Poland, Switzerland, Brazil, Chile, Belarus, India, Slovenia, Bulgaria, Lithuania, Latvia, Estonia, Ukraine, Russia, Peru, Venezuela, Uruguay, Moldova, Azerbaijan, Dominican Republic, Serbia, Montenegro, Macedonia and Bosnia. These are reasons why other countries don't appear in the investigation (dependent and independent variables not included in the survey, other religion codings, low number of observations; e.g., Ghana).
4. For a description of the variables, see Table A4.1 in the Appendix.
5. For the theory of aspirations, see Frank (1941), Simon (1955) and Siegel (1957).
6. The data used had the following distribution: Catholic (28.2 per cent), Protestant (12.3 per cent), Orthodox (17.4 per cent), Jews (0.2 per cent), Muslim (7 per cent), Hindu (4 per cent), Buddhist (1.7 per cent) and other religious denomination (2.5 per cent).
7. Aggregated (country) values of the perceived corruption are strongly correlated (−0.745, significant at the 0.01 level) with the Transparency International Index of Corruption (CPI ranking 1996, the higher the value, the lower is the corruption).

REFERENCES

Aitken, S. and L. Bonneville (1980), 'A general taxpayer opinion survey', Washington, DC: Internal Revenue Service.
Alexandrin, G. (1993), 'Elements of Buddhist economics', *International Journal of Social Economics*, **20**, 3–11.
Anderson, G. M. (1988), 'Mr. Smith and the preachers: the economics of religion in *The Wealth of Nations*', *Journal of Political Economy*, **96**, 1066–88.
Anderson, G.M. and R.D. Tollison (1992), 'Morality and monopoly: the constitutional political economy of religious rules', *CATO Journal*, **13**, 373–391.
Andreoni, J. and L. Vesterlund (2001), 'Which is the fair sex? Gender differences in altruism', *Quarterly Journal of Economics*, **116**, 293–312.
Baldry, J.C. (1987), 'Income tax evasion and the tax schedule: some experimental results', *Public Finance*, **42**, 357–83.
Becker, G.S. (1981), 'Altruism in the family and selfishness in the market place', *Economica*, **48**, 1–15.
Brown-Kruse, J. and D. Hummels (1993), 'Gender effects in laboratory public goods contribution: do individuals put their money where their mouth is?', *Journal of Economic Behavior and Organization*, **22**, 255–67.
Clotfelter, C.T. (1983), 'Tax evasion and tax rate: an analysis of individual return', *The Review of Economics and Statistics*, **65**, 363–73.
Davis, K. (1949), *Human Society*, New York: Macmillan.
Eckel, C.C. and P.J. Grossman (2001), 'Chivalry and solidarity in ultimatum games', *Economic Inquiry*, **39**, 171–88.
Eriksen, K. and L. Fallan (1996), 'Tax knowledge and attitudes towards taxation: a report on a quasi-experiment', *Journal of Economic Psychology*, **17**, 387–402.
Feinstein, J.S. (1991), 'An econometric analysis of income tax evasion and its detection', *RAND Journal of Economics*, **22**, 14–35.
Festinger, L. (1957), *A Theory of Cognitive Dissonance*, Evanston: Row and Peterson.

Frank, J.D. (1941), 'Recent studies of the level of aspiration', *Psychological Bulletin*, **28**, 218–26.
Freud, S. (1927), *The Future of an Illusion*, Garden City: Doubleday.
Friedland, N., S. Maital and A. Rutenberg (1978), 'A simulation study of income tax evasion', *Journal of Public Economics*, **10**, 107–16.
Friedman, E., S. Johnson, D. Kaufmann and P. Zoido-Lobaton (2000), 'Dodging the grabbing hand: the determinants of unofficial activity in 69 countries', *Journal of Public Economics*, **76**, 459–93.
Furnham, A. (1983), 'The protestant work ethic, human values and attitudes towards taxation', *Journal of Economic Psychology*, **3**, 113–28.
Geeroms, H. and H. Wilmots (1985), 'An empirical model of tax evasion and tax avoidance', *Public Finance*, **40**, 190–209.
Grasmick, H.G. and R.J. Bursick (1990), 'Conscience, significant others, and rational choice: extending the deterrence model', *Law and Society Review*, **24**, 837–61.
Grasmick, H.G. and W. Scott (1982), 'Tax evasion and mechanisms of social control: a comparison with grand and petty theft', *Journal of Economic Psychology*, **2**, 213–20.
Grasmick, H.G., R.J. Bursik and J.K. Cochran (1991), '"Render unto Caesar what is Caesar's": religiosity and taxpayers' inclinations to cheat', *Sociological Quarterly*, **32**, 251–66.
Groenland, E.A.G. and G.M. van Veldhoven (1983), 'Tax evasion behavior: a psychological framework', *Journal of Economic Psychology*, **3**, 129–44.
Hardin, R. (1997), 'The economics of religious belief', *Journal of Institutional and Theoretical Economics*, **153**, 259–78.
Hartog, J., A. Ferrer-i-Carbonell and N. Jonker (2002), 'Linking measured risk aversion to individual characteristics', *KYKLOS*, **55**, 3–26.
Hays, S. (2000), 'An empirical analysis of taxpayers' attitudes and behavioral intentions regarding compliance with federal income tax laws', Dissertation, College of Adminstration and Business, Louisiana Tech University.
Heiner, R. A. (1983), 'The origins of predictable behavior', *American Economic Review*, **73**, 560–95.
Higgs, R. (1987), *Crisis and Leviathan. Critical Episodes in the Growth of American Government*, Oxford: Oxford University Press.
Hirschi, T. and R. Stark (1969), 'Hellfire and delinquency', *Social Problems*, **17**, 202–13.
Hull, B.B. (2000), 'Religion still matters', *Journal of Economics*, **26**, 35–48.
Hull, B.B. and F. Bold (1989), 'Towards an economic theory of the church', *International Journal of Social Economics*, **16**, 5–15.
Hull, B.B. and F. Bold (1994), 'Hell, religion, and cultural change', *Journal of Institutional and Theoretical Economics*, **150**, 447–64.
Iannaccone, L.R. (1998), 'Introduction to the economics of religion', *Journal of Economic Literature*, **46**, 1465–96.
Iannaccone, L. R. (2002), 'A marriage made in heaven? Economic theory and religious studies', in S. Grossbard-Shechtman and C. Clague (eds), *The Expansion of Economics*, New York: M.E. Sharpe, pp. 163–193.
Inglehart, R. (1997), *Modernization and Postmodernization: Cultural, Economic and Political Change in 43 Societies*, Princeton: Princeton University Press.
Inglehart, R. (2000), 'Globalization and postmodern values', *Washington Quarterly*, **23**, 215–28.

Inglehart, R. et al. (2000), *Codebook for World Values Survey*, Ann Arbor: Institute for Social Research.
Jackson, B.R. and S. Jones (1985), 'Salience of tax evasion penalties versus detection risk', *Journal of the American Taxation Association*, **6**, 7–17.
Jackson, B.R. and V.C. Milliron (1986), 'Tax compliance research: findings, problems, and prospects', *Journal of Accounting Literature*, **5**, 125–66.
Jain, A.K. (2001), 'Corruption: a review', *Journal of Economic Surveys*, **15**, 71–121.
Kahneman, D. and A. Tversky (1979), 'Prospect theory: an analysis of decision under risk', *Econometrica*, **47**, 263–91.
Kaplan, S.E. and P.M.J. Reckers (1985), 'A study of tax evasion judgments', *National Tax Journal*, **38**, 97–102.
Kennedy, P. (1998), *A Guide to Econometrics*, Cambridge, MA: The MIT Press.
Knack, S. and P. Keefer (1997), 'Does social capital have an economic payoff: a cross-country investigation', *Quarterly Journal of Economics*, **112**, 1251–88.
Lewis, A. (1982), *The Psychology of Taxation*, Oxford: Martin Robertson.
Lewis, H.B. (1971), *Shame and Guilt in Neurosis*, New York: International University Press.
Lipford, J., R.E. McCormick and R.D. Tollison (1993), 'Preaching matters', *Journal of Economic Behavior and Organization*, **21**, 235–50.
Margolis, H. (1997), 'Religion as paradigm', *Journal of Institutional and Theoretical Economics*, **153**, 242–52.
Mason, R. and L.D. Calvin (1984), 'Public confidence and admitted tax evasion', *National Tax Journal*, **37**, 490–96.
McGee, R.W. (1998), 'The ethics of tax evasion in Islam', in R.W. McGee (ed.), *The Ethics of Tax Evasion*, South Orange: The Dumont Institute for Public Policy Research, pp. 214–19.
Mendis, P. (1998), 'Ethics into economics: Are we Homo economicus or Homo religious?' *Journal of Interdisciplinary Economics*, **9**, 169–84.
Minor, W. (1978), 'Deterrence research: problems of theory and method', In J.A. Cramer (ed.), *Preventing Crime*, Beverly Hills: Sage, pp. 21–45.
Mueller, D.S. (2001), 'Centralism, federalism, and the nature of individual preferences', *Constitutional Political Economy*, **12**, 161–72.
North, D.C. (1981), *Structure and Change in Economic History*, New York, London: Norton.
Nowell, C. and S. Tinkler (1994), 'The influence of gender on the provision of a public good', *Journal of Economic Behavior and Organization*, **25**, 25–36.
Rose-Ackerman, S. (1997), 'The political economy of corruption', in K.A. Elliott (ed.), *Corruption and the Global Economy*, Washington, DC: Institute for International Economics, pp. 31–60.
Sen, A. (1977), 'Rational Fools: a critique of the behavioural foundation of economic theory', *Philosophy and Public Affairs*, **6**, 317–44.
Sen, A. (1992), *Inequality Reexamined*, Oxford: Blackwell.
Siegel, S. (1957), 'Level of aspiration and decision making', *Psychological Review*, **64**, 253–62.
Simon, H.A. (1955), 'A behavioral model of rational choice', *Quarterly Journal of Economics*, **69**, 174–83.
Slemrod, J. (2003), 'Trust in public finance', NBER Working Paper 9187, September, Cambridge, MA.

Smith, A. (1976 [1759]), *Theory of Moral Sentiments*, Oxford: Oxford University Press.
Smith, I., J.W. Sawkins and P.T. Seaman (1998), 'The economics of religious participation: a cross-country study', *KYKLOS*, **51**, 25–43.
Song, Y. and Y.E. Yarbrough (1978), 'Tax ethics and taxpayer attitudes: a survey', *Public Administration Review*, **38**, 442–57.
Spicer, M.W. (1974), 'A behavioral model of income tax evasion', dissertation, Ohio State University.
Spicer, M.W. and L.A. Becker (1980), 'Fiscal inequity and tax evasion: an experimental approach', *National Tax Journal*, **33**, 171–5.
Spicer, M.W. and R.E. Hero (1985), 'Tax evasion and heuristics. A research note', *Journal of Public Economics*, **26**, 263–7.
Stan, L. and L. Turcescu (2000), 'The Romanian Orthodox Church and post-communist democratization', *Europe-Asia Studies*, **52**, 1467–88.
Stark, R., L.R. Iannaccone and R. Finke (1996), 'Linkages between economics and religion', *American Economic Review*, **86**, 433–7.
Tittle, C. (1980), *Sanctions and Social Deviance: the Question of Deterence*, New York: Praeger.
Tittle, C. and M. Welch (1983), 'Religiosity and deviance: toward a contingency theory of constraining effects', *Social Forces*, **61**, 653–82.
Torgler, B. (2003), 'Why do people go to war?' *Defence and Peace Economics*, **14**, 261–80.
Tversky, A. and D. Kahneman (1992), 'Advances in prospect theory: cumulative representation of uncertainty', *Journal of Risk and Uncertainty*, **5**, 297–323.
Twomey, P.J. (1999), 'Habit', in P.E. Earl and S. Kemp (eds), *The Elgar Companion to Consumer Research and Economic Psychology*, Cheltenham, UK and Northampton, MA, USA: Edward Elgar, pp. 270–5.
van Staveren, I. (2001), *The Values of Economics. An Aristotelian Perspective*, London: Routledge.
Vogel, J. (1974), 'Taxation and public opinion in Sweden: an interpretation of recent survey data', *National Tax Journal*, **27**, 499–513.
Westat, Inc. (1980a), 'Self-reported tax compliance: a pilot survey report', prepared for the Internal Revenue Service, 21 March.
Westat, Inc. (1980b), 'Individuals income tax compliance factors study qualitative research', prepared for the Internal Revenue Service, 4 February.
Witte, A.D. and D.F. Woodbury (1985), 'The effect of tax laws and tax administration on tax compliance', *National Tax Journal*, **38**, 1–14.
Yankelovich, Skelly and White, Inc. (1984), 'Taxpayer attitudes survey: final report', public opinion survey prepared for the Public Affairs Division, Internal Revenue Service, New York.
Yusuf, S.M. (1971), *Economic Justice in Islam*, Lahore: Sh. Muhammad Ashraf.

5. Tax morale and institutions

INTRODUCTION

The purpose of this chapter is to identify which factors have an impact on tax morale at the national level. It can be supposed that the extent of tax morale depends on the type of constitution. In general, there are fewer studies that systematically analyse the influence of institutions on tax morale or tax compliance. Thus, we will analyse whether institutions such as direct democracy and federalism have an influence on tax morale, controlling for additional variables. It is essential to analyse under which institutional conditions citizens are more willing to pay their taxes. For this, the study analyses a cross-section of individuals throughout Switzerland, using the World Values Survey (WVS) data for 1995–1997 and the International Social Survey Programme (ISSP) data set 'Religion II'. Switzerland has been chosen because it allows us to observe the influence of institutional factors such as direct democracy (via initiatives and referenda) and federalism (local autonomy). In Switzerland, cantons have different degrees of possible political participation and fiscal decentralization (see Table A5.1 in the Appendix).

The Swiss WVS survey was conducted in 1996 and the ISSP survey in 1999. Both data sets allow us to control for many factors that are unrelated to institutional variables. Working with two data sets allows us to check the robustness of our main variables. The findings suggest that institutional factors in the form of direct democratic participation rights and federalism raise tax morale. Furthermore, trust in government and trust in the courts and the legal system have a positive effect on tax morale. In the next section, theoretical considerations on tax morale are presented, focusing on direct democracy, local autonomy and trust in institutions. The third section presents the empirical findings and the chapter ends with some concluding remarks.

THEORETICAL CONSIDERATIONS AND HYPOTHESES

Tax Morale and Political Participation

Tax morale might depend on the type of institutional setting. Institutions that respect the preferences of the citizens will have more support from the people than a state that acts as a Leviathan (see Prinz, 2002). Such supportive behaviour has a positive effect on tax morale. Levi (1988) points out that a possibility to create or maintain compliance is to provide reassurance by the government. A government that precommits itself to direct democratic rule imposes restraints on its own power and thus sends a signal that taxpayers are seen as responsible persons. Furthermore, direct democratic rule indicates that citizens are not ignorant or uncomprehending voters, which might create or maintain a certain social capital stock. The government thus indicates that taxpayers' preferences are taken into account in the political process. The more taxpayers can participate in political decision making by popular rights, the more this contract is based on trust and the higher is tax morale. As Frey (2003) points out, taxpayers are treated as '*citizens* rather than subjects, and have extensive rights *and* obligations to their state' (p. 9).

Taxpayers are in the position better to monitor and control politicians via referenda, and in the position of being rule setters via initiative and thus able to renegotiate the tax contract with the government influencing, for example, tax laws and tax rates that enhance civic virtue. Thus, the possibility for taxpayers to vote on fiscal issues positively influences tax morale. Being involved in the political decision-making process enhances taxpayers' sense of civic duty (Feld and Frey, 2002a) and thus tax morale. The instrument of direct democracy helps taxes to be spent according to their preferences, and their motivation to contribute by paying their taxes increases. Thus, the following hypothesis can be developed:

Hypothesis 1: The more extensive the citizens' possibilities for direct political participation, the higher is the intrinsic motivation to comply in the form of tax morale.

Torgler (2001) has surveyed the empirical evidence about the effects of political participation on tax compliance. Looking at the experimental evidence, Alm et al. (1999), Feld and Tyran (2002) and Torgler and Schaltegger (2005) found that voting on tax issues has a positive effect on tax compliance.

Tax Morale and Trust in the Government, the Courts and the Legal System

Trust can reinforce co-operation, hence maintaining the psychological contract between the state and the taxpayers (see Torgler, 2001, 2003). It is an important institution that influences citizens' incentive to commit themselves to obedience. And this trust can only be created if the government's commitment is in line with citizens' needs and desires (see Hardin, 1998). Not only trust in the government but also trust in the courts and the legal system, and thus in the way in which the relationship between the state and its citizens is established, might have an effect on tax morale.

Slemrod (2002) points out that the cost of raising taxes and running the government is lower if taxpayers are more willing to pay their taxes voluntarily:

> It is as if there is a stock of goodwill, or social capital, the return to which is the more efficient operation of government. This social capital stock may be reduced by a policy change that decreases the incentive to be a law-abiding citizen (p. 13).

In the light of this, the following hypothesis will be tested:

Hypothesis 2: The more extensive the citizens' trust in the government and the legal system, the higher is the intrinsic motivation to comply in the form of tax morale.

Kucher and Götte (1998) used data from Switzerland (Zurich), where taxpayers have to file a declaration of liable revenue and property, to analyse trust in government. As a dependent variable, they used the ratio of submitted tax declarations between 1964 and 1996. Trust has been measured as the ratio of concurrence between the city government's recommendation for an issue put to a vote and the actual outcome at the ballot. The results indicate that trust does significantly raise the ratio of submitted tax declarations. Furthermore, Feld and Frey (2002a) show, in their empirical analysis from Switzerland, that respectful treatment by the tax administrations reduces tax evasion.

Tax Morale and Decentralization

A second institution is federalism. Small structures have the advantage that citizens' preferences can be met better. There is an intensive everyday interaction between taxpayers and local politicians and bureaucrats. This closeness between taxpayers, the tax administration and the local government may induce trust and thus enhance tax morale. Politicians and members of the administration are better informed about the preferences of the local population. Furthermore, if politicians are elected at the local level, they have an incentive to take citizens' preferences into account (see Frey and Eichenberger, 1999) and thus to spend the tax revenues according to their preferences. Decentralization moves the government closer to the people. Many economists point out the relevance of giving sub-national governments the taxing power (see, e.g., Bahl, 1999). The strength of decentralized systems is that this input–output relationship is more transparent. The tax system must be visible to the local taxpayers. Income tax is a good instrument for a local structure. It is easy to administer and it is always under the scrutiny of individuals who have the opportunity to use the instruments of exit and voice (see Hirschman, 1970). The mechanism of entry and exit in federal states provides a strong incentive to produce public services in accordance with taxpayers' preferences. Thus, the third hypothesis states:

Hypothesis 3: The more extensive the local autonomy, the higher is the intrinsic motivation to comply in the form of tax morale.

EMPIRICAL RESULTS

Model

In order to examine our hypotheses derived in this second section, the following estimation equation is postulated:

$$TM_i = \beta_0 + \beta_1 \cdot p_c + \beta_2 \cdot f_c + \beta_3 \cdot t_i + \beta_4 \cdot y_i + \beta_5 \cdot CTL_i + \beta_6 \cdot TR_i + \beta_7 \cdot INST_c + \varepsilon_i$$

where TM_i denotes the individual degree of tax morale measured with the WVS for the years 1996 and 1999 with the ISSP data set in Switzerland. In both data sets, we have the same tax morale scale. The independent variables are specified as follows:

1. p_c: As an approximation for the probability of detection, the number of tax auditors as a percentage of the total number of taxpayers in each canton c is used.
2. f_c: The penalty tax rate is approximated by the standard legal fine as a multiple of the evaded tax amount (in per cent) in a canton c.[1]
3. t_i: The individual tax rate.
4. y_i: The individual income class of a taxpayer (see the Appendix).
5. CTL_i: A panel of control variables at the individual level, covering age, gender, education, marital status and employment status.
6. TR_i: Trust in government in the WVS data set[2] and confidence in the courts and the legal system in ISSP.[3]
7. $INST_c$: Institutional factors at the cantonal level c. For the degree of direct democracy, the six-point scale index developed by Stutzer (1999) and applied, for example, by Frey and Stutzer (2000, 2002) and Frey and

Feld (2002), Feld and Frey (2002a,b) has been used. The index reflects the extent of direct democratic participation (1 = lowest and 6 = highest degree of participation) at the cantonal level.[4] As indexes do not tell us as much as a single instrument, we will measure the degree of direct democratic participation with a dummy on legislative referendum and the signature requirements for legislative initiatives. Local autonomy is measured with an index developed by Ladner (1994), based on survey results where chief local administrators in 1865 Swiss municipalities were asked to report how they perceived their local autonomy on a ten-point scale. (1 = no autonomy, 10 = very high communal autonomy; see Table A5.2 in the Appendix.)

The economics-of-crime approach would predict that the extent of tax *evasion* would depend negatively on the probability of being caught, and on the magnitude of the punishment in the case of being caught. However, empirical and experimental findings indicate that the expected utility-maximization approach does not work well. The pooled cross-sectional time-series estimation for Swiss cantons over the years 1970, 1978, 1985, 1990 and 1995 done by Frey and Feld (2002), using tax evasion as the dependent variable, indicates that the probability of detection has a theoretically unexpected positive sign, which is not statistically significant, while the size of the fine is statistically significant at the 5 per cent level. Beron et al. (1992) found, using tax return data from 1969, a weak deterrent effect from audits on tax compliance. Similarly, experiments show a mixed picture of the effects of deterrence factors, with the tendency for a higher audit rate to lead to greater compliance (see Torgler, 2002). Slemrod et al. (2001) used a controlled field experiment in Minnesota to analyse taxpayers' response to an increased probability of audit. While low- and middle-income taxpayers increased their reported tax between 1993 and 1994 relative to the control group, the reported income of high-income taxpayers fell sharply in relation to the control group.

It is difficult to predict the effects of deterrence factors on tax morale. Deterrence imposed by the tax authority might crowd out taxpayers' intrinsic motivation to pay their taxes and thus crowd out tax morale. On the other hand, deterrence factors might prevent taxpayers with a low tax morale from exploiting the more honest taxpayers. Tax morale is therefore not expected to be crowded out if the honest taxpayers perceive the stricter policy to be directed against dishonest taxpayers. Regulations that prevent free-riding by others, reducing the possibility of their escaping from their tax payments, may help to preserve tax morale (see Frey, 1997).

The effects of the tax rate and income on tax evasion are difficult to assess theoretically. They depend on the individual's risk preference and the progression of the income tax schedule (see Andreoni et al., 1998). A higher marginal tax rate makes tax evasion marginally more profitable, but a contrary effect works depending on the risk aversion of taxpayers. The results are influenced by the tax schedule (proportional, progressive, regressive; see Frey and Feld, 2002).

Regarding the control variables, it might be worthwhile to point out that it can be expected that older people have a higher tax morale than younger people. Over the years, they have acquired greater social stakes, in the form of material goods, status and a stronger dependency on the reactions from others (Tittle, 1980), as they mostly have lived for a certain time in the same place and thus are more attached to the community (see Pommerehne and Weck-Hannemann, 1996). In the tax compliance literature, evidence concerning the variable gender indicates the tendency for males to be less compliant than females (see, e.g., Vogel, 1974; Spicer and Becker, 1980; Tittle, 1980). Looking at marital status, it can be argued that married people might be more constrained by their social network and thus more compliant but, on the other hand, in Switzerland they are taxed in a higher bracket than two separate incomes, which might have a negative impact on tax morale. Better-educated taxpayers are supposed to know more about tax law and fiscal connections, and thus would be in a better position to assess the degree of compliance, being more aware of the benefits and services that the state provides for the citizens from the revenues (see Lewis, 1982). On the other hand, they may be less compliant because they better understand the opportunities for evasion and avoidance, and they might be more critical about and more aware of how the state uses tax revenues. Self-employed persons do not have a lower tax morale than other taxpayers *per se*, but they have better possibilities for evading taxes. Most empirical results that indicate that they have a lower tax compliance are not found in Switzerland, but in other countries, where labour income earners pay taxes at source.

Results

Deterrence factors

Our estimations start with an analysis of the effects that the traditional variables of an economics-of-crime approach have on tax morale. Thus, our first estimations will consider three basic variables of this approach: the fine rate of tax evasion, the probability of detection and the individual tax rate. Therefore, weighted least-squares models and weighted ordered probit models are estimated in Table 5.1.

In the weighted ordered probit estimation, only the marginal effects for the highest value 'tax evasion is never justified' (WVS 1996) and 'seriously wrong not to report all the income' (ISSP 1999) are shown.

Table 5.1 presents the results. As we can see, most results are robust regarding the estimation methods. The weighted least-squares estimations using tax morale as a cardinal variable offer qualitatively quite similar results to the weighted ordered probit model. Looking at the variables FINE RATE, AUDIT PROBABILITY and INDIVIDUAL INCOME TAX RATE, we observe similar values for both data sets. The results indicate that the basic tax evasion model does not perform in a satisfactory way. The coefficients are mostly not significant. Only in one estimation is the coefficient of the variable AUDIT PROBABILITY significant at the 10 per cent level, showing a positive sign. On the other hand, the coefficient of the variable FINE RATE is statistically not significant, with a negative tendency. In further estimations, we will see that these coefficients are often not significant. In the estimations where the coefficient is significant, we find a tendency for a higher audit probability to be correlated with a higher tax morale, and a higher fine rate with a lower tax morale. One reason might be that stronger controls help to catch tax evaders and thus honest taxpayers perceive the audit probability to be directed against dishonest taxpayers. On the other hand, however, a higher fine rate might crowd out more the intrinsic motivation to comply with taxes, as it is settled in the laws and more evident for the taxpayers, thus signalling stronger external interventions.

The individual tax rate has a notable negative effect on tax morale, which is significant at the 10 per cent level in the weighted ordered probit estimation with the WVS data set.

It is difficult to get a clear picture of the effects of the control variables on tax morale. There is a tendency for females to have a higher tax morale than males. The marginal effects indicate, for example, in the WVS survey estimation that being female rather than male increases the probability of a person stating that tax evasion is never justified by 27.5 percentage points. Furthermore, married people seem to have a higher tax morale than the reference group (singles). In the ISSP data set, which does not differentiate between married people and people living together, the coefficient is positive, but not significant. A higher education correlates with a higher tax morale, at a statistically significant rate in the ISSP data set.

Different results can be observed regarding the effects of income and the employment status on tax morale. Only the coefficients of the ISSP estimations are statistically significant, indicating a positive correlation between tax morale and income. Part-time employees have a higher tax morale than full-time employees in the WVS, but a lower one in the ISSP data set.

In general, the main finding in these estimations is that the standard model of tax evasion does not work well. The findings do not indicate that coercion does not play any role, but it reduces the emphasis of the significance of such an instrument for resolving the social dilemma of tax payments. Monitoring and penalties for non-compliance might have the effect that individuals crowd out the intrinsic motivation to comply with taxes (see Frey, 1997). Empirical findings in Switzerland also indicate that the expected utility-maximization approach does not work well. The pooled cross-sectional time-series estimations for Swiss cantons over the years 1970, 1978, 1985, 1990 and 1995 done by Frey and Feld (2002) using tax evasion as the dependent variable indicate that probability of detection has a positive sign, being statistically significant in some equations, while the size of the fine is statistically significant with a negative sign. Torgler and Schaltegger (2005) even found, in a tax compliance experiment carried out in Switzerland and Costa Rica, a negative effect of penalties on tax compliance (see Chapter 9).

These findings indicate that the basic evasion model has to be extended using additional factors. Thus, the chapter analyses the extent to which important insights can be obtained by including formal and informal institutions to evaluate what shapes tax morale. Switzerland is characterized by a constitution that combines direct democracy elements such as initiatives and referenda with a high degree of federalism, which means that the cantons and local authorities have large competences. The degree of institutionalized rights of political participation strongly varies between the 26 Swiss cantons.

Direct democratic participation rights and trust in the government and the legal system

First, we will analyse the effect of direct democracy and trust in the government, the courts and the legal system on tax morale.[5] The degree of direct democratic participation rights of taxpayers is measured using an index developed by Stutzer (1999). The results for both data sets are presented in Tables 5.2 and 5.3. The index of direct democratic rights has a highly significant positive effect on tax morale, with high marginal effects. Thus, the first hypothesis cannot be rejected. Equation 2a (Equation 2b) in Table 5.2 indicates that an increase in the index of direct democracy by one point raises the share of persons indicating the highest tax morale by 6.4 (2.9) percentage points. Thus, the results show that the institution of direct democracy raises the individual's tax morale.[6]

In a next step, we will analyse whether trust in the government and the legal system have a positive effect on tax morale. With the WVS question, we focus more closely on the current politico-economic level. On the other hand, with the ISSP data set we focus on how the relationship between the state and its citizens is established. Since democracy works as an institution that enhances the psychological tax contract between citizens and the

Table 5.1 The determinants of tax morale in Switzerland in 1996 and 1999 (dependent variable: tax morale)

Independent variables	World Values Survey, 1996						ISSP, 1999					
	Weighted least squares		Weighted ordered probit				Weighted least squares		Weighted ordered probit			
	Coeff.	t-Stat.	Coeff.	z-Stat.	Marg.		Coeff.	t-Stat.	Coeff.	z-Stat.	Marg.	
(a) Deterrence factors												
FINE RATE	−0.001	−1.187	−0.001	−1.615	−0.001		−0.001	−0.682	−0.001	−0.834	0.000	
AUDIT PROBABILITY	0.001	1.121	0.002*	1.856	0.001		0.001	1.073	0.001	1.074	0.000	
(b) Tax rate												
INDIVIDUAL INC. TAX RATE	−0.008	−1.327	−0.009*	−1.916	−0.004		−0.019	−1.568	−0.022	−1.772	−0.006	
(c) Demographic factors												
AGE 30–49	0.028	0.211	0.025	0.249	0.010		−0.041	−0.447	−0.032	−0.332	−0.009	
AGE 50–64	0.403**	2.553	0.396***	3.163	0.157		−0.020	−0.191	−0.020	−0.167	−0.006	
AGE 65+	0.348	1.380	0.347	1.554	0.138		0.013	0.082	−0.002	−0.011	−0.001	
FEMALE	0.284***	2.882	0.275***	3.397	0.109		0.064	0.930	0.082	1.066	0.024	
EDUCATION	0.013	0.510	0.013	0.617	0.005		0.033*	1.870	0.040**	2.042	0.012	
(d) Marital status												
MARRIED	0.319**	2.296	0.317**	2.963	0.126		0.001	0.015	0.005	0.063	0.002	
LIVING TOGETHER	0.071	0.400	0.070	0.528	0.028							
DIVORCED	0.183	0.941	0.174	1.135	0.069		−0.292**	−2.189	−0.334**	−2.120	−0.098	
SEPARATED	0.292	0.819	0.190	0.693	0.075		0.158	0.844	0.232	1.290	0.068	
WIDOWED	0.013	0.059	−0.133	−0.736	−0.053		−0.021	−0.149	−0.026	−0.147	−0.008	

(e) Economic variable

INCOME	−0.007	−0.398	−0.007	−0.490	−0.003	0.000*	1.706	0.000*	1.853	−0.066	0.000

(f) Employment status

PART TIME EMPLOYED	0.286**	2.103	0.283***	2.581	0.112	−0.176*	−1.786	−0.225**	−2.046	−0.066	0.011
LESS THAN PART TIME						0.047	0.351	0.038	0.253		
SELF-EMPLOYED	0.150	0.865	0.139	0.934	0.055						
UNEMPLOYED	−0.051	−0.173	−0.047	−0.223	−0.019	−0.041	−0.167	−0.076	−0.270	−0.022	
AT HOME	0.237	1.488	0.240*	1.862	0.095	0.132	1.003	0.142	0.931	0.041	
STUDENT	0.030	0.125	0.012	0.066	0.005	0.177	1.285	0.228	1.627	0.066	
RETIRED	0.514**	2.288	0.590***	2.728	0.234	0.207	1.377	0.252	1.475	0.074	
OTHER	0.432	1.235	0.468	1.628	0.186						
SICK						0.244	1.003	0.245	0.483	0.071	
Observations	922					1130					
R-squared	0.114					0.034					
Prob(F-statistic)	0.000					0.000					
Prob(LM-statistic)			0.000					0.000			

Notes: Dependent variable: tax morale on a four-point scale. In the reference group are AGE 16–29, MALE, SINGLE and FULL TIME EMPLOYED. In the ISSP data, married and people living together are added into one group. Furthermore, they include people working less than part time and sick persons, omitting instead self-employed persons. Significance levels: * $0.05 < p < 0.10$; ** $0.01 < p < 0.05$; *** $p < 0.01$. Marginal effect = highest tax morale score (4).

state and thus induces trust, we first analyse the trust variables in separate estimations (see Equations 3a and 3b). The results indicate that hypothesis 2 cannot be rejected either. Both trust coefficients are highly significant, showing a statistically significant positive effect on tax morale. An increase in the trust in government scale (trust in the courts and the legal system) by one unit increases the share of subjects indicating the highest tax morale by 8.9 (3.4) percentage points. To investigate whether the positive correlation between direct democracy and tax morale is largely driven by a higher trust, we include them together in the same equations (see Equations 4a and 5b). Furthermore, in order to test for alternative explanations we include additional variables (religiosity and individuals' financial satisfaction in the WVS and religiosity in the ISSP data set). Religiosity might influence people's habits and might provide a restriction on engaging in tax evasion (for empirical evidence, see Torgler, 2006 or Chapter 4). As a religious variable we take the variable frequency of church attendance (CHURCH ATTENDANCE). This shows approximately how much time individuals devote to religion. It says more about behaviour than, for example, religious attitudes. To the author's knowledge, there are only three papers that examine the effect of religiosity on tax cheating (Tittle, 1980; Grasmick et al., 1991; Torgler, 2006). All three studies indicate that religiosity affects the degree of rule breaking, tax compliance and tax morale. Our findings in Tables 5.2 and 5.3 are in line with these results, showing a positive correlation between tax morale and the degree of church attendance.

Financial dissatisfaction might negatively influence tax morale. Such a dissatisfaction might create a sense of distress, especially when taxes have to be paid and there is a discrepancy between the actual and the aspired financial situation.[7] Thus, taxes might be perceived as a strong restriction, which increases the incentives to reduce tax honesty. As the income variable is integrated into the equation, we can analyse the 'stress' component of the financial dissatisfaction. The results in Table 5.2 show that an increase in the financial satisfaction level by one unit increases the share of individuals arguing that tax morale is never justifiable by two percentage points. The coefficients of direct democracy and trust in government and trust in the courts and the legal system remain statistically highly significant. Thus, it can be concluded that both variables have a robust influence on tax morale.

However, it can be argued that the index of direct democratic participation possibilities disregards substitutive and complementary relationships between the single components, as it is a non-weighted composite index (Frey and Stutzer, 2002). Furthermore, factors that are more closely related to taxation might have a stronger impact on tax morale than other factors. Thus, Equations 8 to 11 evaluate each single component of the direct democratic participation index (see Tables 5.4 and 5.5). For both data sets, all the coefficients for the single components are highly significant, and it is interesting to note that the index with the strongest direct connection to taxes (financial referendum) has the highest coefficient value and the strongest marginal effects. An increase in the index of legislative financial referendum by one point raises the proportion of taxpayers with the highest tax morale by 6.2 (2.6) percentage points in the WVS (ISSP) data set.

Including the single items separately in the equations disregards the fact that the instruments of initiative and referendum have different rationales. Referenda impose severe restrictions on the autonomy of the politicians and the legislature to act in their personal interest (see Feld and Kirchgässner, 2000). As a consequence, tax revenues might be spent more in accordance with the preferences of the taxpayers, restricting a possible politicians' cartel. Furthermore, the referendum possibility leads the politicians to adopt a relatively consensual position in order to avoid policy rejections. Contrary to a referendum, with an initiative taxpayers are in the position of 'agenda setters' (see Feld and Kirchgässner, 2000). This means that issues that the government would prefer not to have to discuss get submitted to a vote because of the leverage of the voters or taxpayers as 'agenda setters'. An initiative helps to express the taxpayers' preferences on what should be done with the taxes and thus opens the door for new and innovative ideas. As indexes do not tell us as much as a single instrument, in Equations 12a and 12b we include a dummy on legislative referenda (mandatory) and the signature requirements for legislative initiatives, to assess the (marginal) impact of both instruments (see Table A5.3 in the Appendix).[8] Furthermore, such a procedure reduces the problems of multicorrelation, as the correlation between the subindexes for legislative referendum and legislative initiative is very high (0.772). For both data sets, the coefficient of the dummy LEGISLATIVE REFERENDUM is highly significant, with high marginal effects (9.7 percentage points in the WVS, 6.8 in the ISSP data set). Similarly, higher signature requirements lead to a lower tax morale, but are not statistically significant. The mandatory referendum seems to be a stronger instrument to enhance tax morale than the initiative. A possible reason for the differences between the two instruments might be that the mandatory referendum is the strongest form of direct democratic control, as a referendum has to be held on all new fiscal decisions (see Feld and Kirchgässner, 2001). An initiative, on the other hand, imposes costs by forcing a vote on a given issue. In Switzerland, there is evidence that the interests of the political elite do not always correspond to taxpayers' preferences. Frey and Eichenberger (1999, p. 20) report an interesting example from Switzerland in 1992, where taxpayers were not prepared to pay additional expenses, rejecting – in an optional referendum – a proposal to increase the salaries and the staff of Swiss Members of Parliament. In

Table 5.2 *The effects of direct democracy and trust on tax morale (WVS 1996) (weighted ordered probit, dependent variable: tax morale)*

Independent variables	Equation 2a			Equation 3a			Equation 4a		
	Coeff.	z-Stat.	Marg.	Coeff.	z-Stat.	Marg.	Coeff.	z-Stat.	Marg.
(a) Deterrence factors									
FINE RATE	-0.002***	-2.591	-0.001	-0.001	-1.037	-0.098	-0.002**	-2.096	-0.001
AUDIT PROBABILITY	0.001	0.809	0.000	0.002*	1.822	0.000	0.001	1.176	0.001
(b) Tax rate									
INDIVIDUAL INC. TAX RATE	-0.008	-1.544	-0.003	-0.008*	-1.691	0.001	-0.007	-1.404	-0.003
(c) Institutional variable									
DIRECT DEMOCRATIC RIGHTS	0.162***	4.517	0.064				0.184***	5.033	0.073
(d) Trust									
TRUST IN GOVERNMENT				0.225***	5.214	0.089	0.170***	3.810	0.067
(e) Demographic factors									
AGE 30–49	0.055	0.562	0.022	0.038	0.372	0.015	0.014	0.137	0.006
AGE 50–64	0.427***	3.440	0.170	0.407***	3.143	0.162	0.310**	2.355	0.123
AGE 65+	0.385*	1.739	0.153	0.277	1.297	0.110	0.215	0.951	0.086
FEMALE	0.286***	3.485	0.114	0.259***	3.117	0.103	0.261***	3.108	0.104
EDUCATION	0.010	0.468	0.004	-0.009	-0.433	-0.004	-0.013	-0.595	-0.005

(f) Marital status											
MARRIED	0.320***	3.012	0.127	0.314***	2.784	0.125	0.346***	3.047	0.137		
LIVING TOGETHER	0.051	0.378	0.020	0.098	0.701	0.039	0.089	0.600	0.035		
DIVORCED	0.139	0.893	0.055	0.164	1.055	0.065	0.210	1.288	0.083		
SEPARATED	0.197	0.697	0.078	0.206	0.725	0.082	0.242	0.834	0.096		
WIDOWED	−0.140	−0.755	−0.056	−0.144	−0.807	−0.057	−0.139	−0.759	−0.055		
(g) Economic variable											
INCOME	−0.014	−1.006	−0.006	−0.013	−0.861	−0.005	−0.026*	−1.666	−0.010		
FINANCIAL SATISFACTION							0.050***	2.894	0.020		
(h) Employment status											
PART TIME EMPLOYED	0.276**	2.502	0.110	0.270**	2.377	0.107	0.238	2.090	0.094		
SELF-EMPLOYED	0.160	1.060	0.064	0.102	0.701	0.041	0.139	0.921	0.055		
UNEMPLOYED	−0.061	−0.292	−0.024	−0.024	−0.108	−0.010	0.072	0.331	0.029		
AT HOME	0.244*	1.896	0.097	0.208	1.594	0.083	0.214*	1.658	0.085		
STUDENT	0.039	0.216	0.015	−0.084	−0.463	−0.033	−0.065	−0.336	−0.026		
RETIRED	0.582***	2.729	0.231	0.599***	2.933	0.238	0.503**	2.372	0.200		
OTHER	0.496*	1.755	0.197	0.549*	1.762	0.218	0.607	1.910	0.241		
(i) Religiosity											
CHURCH ATTENDANCE							0.078***	3.623	0.031		
Observations	922			891			879				
Prob(LM-statistic)	0.000			0.000			0.000				

Notes: Dependent variable: tax morale on a four-point scale. In the reference group are AGE 16–29, MALE, SINGLE and FULL TIME EMPLOYED. Significance levels: * $0.05 < p < 0.10$; ** $0.01 < p < 0.05$; *** $p < 0.01$. Marginal effect = highest tax morale score (4).

Table 5.3 The effects of direct democracy and trust on tax morale (ISSP 1999) (weighted ordered probit, dependent variable: tax morale)

Independent variables	Equation 2b			Equation 3b			Equation 4b		
	Coeff.	z-Stat.	Marg.	Coeff.	z-Stat.	Marg.	Coeff.	z-Stat.	Marg.
(a) Deterrence factors									
FINE RATE	−0.001	−1.207	0.000	−0.001	−0.677	0.000	−0.001	−0.663	0.000
AUDIT PROBABILITY	0.38E−03	0.418	0.000	0.001	0.677	0.000	−0.47E−04	−0.051	0.000
(b) Tax rate									
INDIVIDUAL INC. TAX RATE	−0.010	−0.779	−0.003	−0.021*	−1.681	−0.006	−0.010	−0.770	−0.003
(c) Institutional variable									
DIRECT DEMOCRATIC RIGHTS	0.100***	3.346	0.029				0.104***	3.410	0.030
(d) Trust									
TRUST IN COURTS AND LEGAL SYSTEM				0.116***	3.782	0.034	0.093***	2.936	0.027
(e) Demographic factors									
AGE 30–49	−0.027	−0.287	−0.008	0.047	0.482	0.014	0.064	0.640	0.018
AGE 50–64	−0.017	−0.145	−0.005	0.049	0.411	0.014	0.050	0.401	0.014
AGE 65+	−0.008	−0.043	−0.002	0.053	0.270	0.016	0.005	0.027	0.002
FEMALE	0.090	1.162	0.026	0.075	0.948	0.022	0.076	0.950	0.022
EDUCATION	0.044**	2.273	0.013	0.034*	1.676	0.010	0.038*	1.861	0.011

	Coef.	z-stat	Marg.	Coef.	z-stat	Marg.	Coef.	z-stat	Marg.
(f) Marital status									
MARRIED/LIVING TOGETHER	0.011	0.131	0.003	−0.019	−0.237	−0.006	−0.061	−0.723	−0.018
DIVORCED	−0.314*	−1.941	−0.091	−0.344*	−2.157	−0.100	−0.300*	−1.816	−0.087
SEPARATED	0.236	1.307	0.069	0.193	1.063	0.057	0.178	0.961	0.051
WIDOWED	−0.038	−0.221	−0.011	−0.029	−0.161	−0.008	−0.103	−0.565	−0.030
(g) Economic variables									
INCOME	0.23E−04	0.997	0.000	0.37E−04*	1.708	0.000	0.21E−04	0.957	0.000
(h) Employment status									
PART TIME EMPLOYED	−0.203*	−1.828	−0.059	−0.214	−1.902	−0.062	−0.172	−1.489	−0.050
LESS THAN PART TIME	0.049	0.331	0.014	0.020	0.131	0.006	−0.002	−0.014	−0.001
UNEMPLOYED	0.006	0.020	0.002	0.011	0.037	0.003	−0.039	−0.116	−0.011
STUDENT	0.283**	2.020	0.082	0.255*	1.741	0.075	0.366**	2.457	0.106
RETIRED	0.302*	1.751	0.088	0.257	1.453	0.075	0.319*	1.751	0.092
AT HOME	0.172	1.130	0.050	0.142	0.917	0.042	0.151	0.952	0.044
SICK	0.290	0.549	0.084	0.215	0.390	0.063	0.250	0.379	0.072
(i) Religiosity									
CHURCH ATTENDANCE							0.085***	4.750	0.025
Observations	1130			1083			1068		
Prob(LM-statistic)	0.000			0.000			0.000		

Notes: Dependent variable: tax morale on a four-point scale. In the reference group are AGE 16–29, MALE, SINGLE and FULL TIME EMPLOYED. Significance levels: * $0.05 < p < 0.10$; ** $0.01 < p < 0.05$; *** $p < 0.01$. Marginal effect = highest tax morale score (4).

Table 5.4 A sensitivity analysis for the effects of direct democracy on tax morale (WVS 1996) (weighted ordered probit, dependent variable: tax morale)

Independent variables	8a	9a	10a	11a	12a	13a
(a) Deterrence factors						
FINE RATE	−0.003***	−0.003***	−0.001	0.001	−0.001	−0.002*
	(−0.001)	(−0.001)	(−0.001)	(0.000)	(0.000)	(0.001)
AUDIT PROBABILITY	0.002*	0.002**	0.002*	−0.5E−03	0.002**	0.001
	(0.001)	(0.001)	(0.001)	(0.000)	(0.001)	(0.000)
(b) Tax rate						
INDIVIDUAL INCOME TAX RATE	−0.008	−0.008	−0.007	−0.007	−0.007	−0.007
	(−0.003)	(−0.003)	(−0.003)	(−0.003)	(−0.003)	(−0.003)
(c) Direct democracy						
INDEX DIRECT DEMOCRACY						0.161***
						(0.064)
Subindices						
CONSTITUTIONAL INITIATIVE	0.148***					
	(0.059)					
LEGISLATIVE INITIATIVE		0.154***				
		(0.061)				

LEGISLATIVE REFERENDUM			0.099***			
			(0.040)			
LEGISLATIVE FINANCIAL REFERENDUM				0.157***		
				(0.062)		
Single instruments						
DUMMY LEGISLATIVE REFERENDUM					0.244***	
					(0.097)	
SIGNATURE REQUIREMENT					−0.067	
LEGISLATIVE INITIATIVE					*(−0.026)*	
(d) Trust						
TRUST IN GOVERNMENT	0.179***	0.180***	0.158***	0.168***	0.152***	0.169***
	(0.071)	(0.072)	(0.063)	(0.067)	(0.060)	(0.067)
(e) Language						
GERMAN SPEAKING						0.081
						(0.032)
(f) Further variables	Yes	Yes	Yes	Yes	Yes	Yes

Notes: Marginal effects for the highest tax morale score are given in parentheses. Dependent variable: tax morale on a four-point scale. In the reference group are AGE 16–29, MALE, SINGLE and FULL TIME EMPLOYED. Significance levels: * $0.05 < p < 0.10$; ** $0.01 < p < 0.05$; *** $p < 0.01$.

Table 5.5 A sensitivity analysis for the effects of direct democracy on tax morale (ISSP 1999) (weighted ordered probit, dependent variable: tax morale)

Independent variables	8b	9b	10b	11b	12b	13b
(a) Deterrence factors						
FINE RATE	−0.001	−0.001	−0.001	0.001	−0.50E−03	0.42E−03
	(0.000)	(0.000)	(0.000)	(0.000)	(0.000)	(0.000)
AUDIT PROBABILITY	0.4E−03	0.4E−03	0.31E−03	−0.001	0.001	0.17E−03
	(0.000)	(0.000)	(0.000)	(0.000)	(0.000)	(0.000)
(b) Tax rate						
INDIVIDUAL INCOME TAX RATE	−0.018	−0.017	−0.004	−0.013	−0.20E−03	−0.001
	(−0.005)	(−0.005)	(−0.005)	(−0.004)	(0.000)	(0.000)
(c) Direct democracy						
Subindices						
CONSTITUTIONAL INITIATIVE	0.051*					
	(0.015)					
LEGISLATIVE INITIATIVE		0.064**				
		(0.018)				
LEGISLATIVE REFERENDUM			0.088***			
			(0.026)			
LEGISLATIVE FINANCIAL REFERENDUM				0.090***		
				(0.026)		

170

Single instruments

DUMMY LEGISLATIVE REFERENDUM					0.237***	0.226***
					(0.068)	(0.065)
SIGNATURE REQUIREMENT					−0.043	−0.002
LEGISLATIVE INITIATIVE					(−0.012)	(−0.001)
(d) Trust						
TRUST IN COURTS AND LEGAL SYSTEM	0.095***	0.096***	0.097***	0.084***	0.094***	0.090***
	(0.028)	(0.028)	(0.028)	(0.024)	(0.027)	
(e) Language						
GERMAN SPEAKING						0.168
						(0.049)
(f) Further variables	Yes	Yes	Yes	Yes	Yes	Yes

Notes: Marginal effects for the highest tax morale score are given in parentheses. Dependent variable: tax morale on a four point scale. In the reference group are AGE 16–29, MALE, SINGLE, FULL TIME EMPLOYED and FRENCH AND ITALIAN SPEAKING. Significance levels: * $0.05 < p < 0.10$; ** $0.01 < p < 0.05$; *** $p < 0.01$.

general, between 1848 and 1997, in 36 per cent of the 316 referenda, the opinions of the voters differed from the opinion of Parliament (see also Frey and Eichenberger, 1999).

In order to account for different cultural backgrounds and thus better to isolate the institutional effect from the cultural one, a language dummy variable (German-speaking individuals) has been integrated.[9] Culture can be seen as a kind of language, based on rule systems such as ideas and values, and internal institutions such as customs and conventions (see Henrich et al., 1999). An essential question in the tax compliance context is whether culture influences co-operation, solidarity or, in our analysis, tax morale. We can see in the last equation that the coefficients for direct democratic participation rights remain highly significant. On the other hand, the language factor does not show a statistically significant effect on tax morale. Thus, it can be concluded that, when controlling for cross-regional differences, the extent of direct democracy remains robust.

Local autonomy

Federalism is a second important political institution in Switzerland. Tables 5.6 and 5.7 present the estimations. First, we integrate the variable LOCAL AUTONOMY into the equation without the variables TRUST IN GOVERNMENT (COURTS AND THE LEGAL SYSTEM) and INDEX OF DIRECT DEMOCRACY. In both data sets, the coefficients show a statistically significant positive effect on tax morale. The share of individuals indicating the highest tax morale increases in the WVS data set (ISSP) by 6.2 (5.4) percentage points, with an increase in autonomy of one index point. The introduction of the trust variables does not affect the size or the significance of the variable. The last equation jointly includes local autonomy and direct democracy. The results indicate that the two constitutional factors interact with each others and thus work as complements.[10] Both determinants help citizens to express their demands and to control the government. As we can see, the coefficient for local autonomy loses its significance and its size in the WVS, while the direct democracy index remains robust. On the other hand, the ISSP data indicates that the variable LOCAL AUTONOMY remains highly significant, with a slightly lower coefficient and a smaller marginal effect. On the other hand, the index of direct democracy is still significant, but at a lower significance level and with lower coefficient and marginal effect values.

Frey and Stutzer (2000) argue that direct democracy and local autonomy are interdependent. Direct democracy and federal structures foster each other because individuals are interested in strong federalism. They are bearing the costs and benefits of the government's activities, which helps

Table 5.6 Tax morale and local autonomy (WVS 1996) (weighted ordered probit, dependent variable: tax morale)

Independent variables	Equation 5a		Equation 6a		Equation 7a	
	Coeff.	Marg.	Coeff.	Marg.	Coeff.	Marg.
(a) Deterrence factors						
FINE RATE	−0.001	0.000	−0.39E−03	0.000	−0.002	−0.001
AUDIT PROBABILITY	0.002**	0.001	0.002**	0.001	0.001**	0.001
(b) Tax rate						
INDIVIDUAL INCOME TAX RATE	−0.009*	−0.003	−0.008	−0.003	−0.007	−0.003
(c) Local autonomy						
INDEX LOCAL AUTONOMY	0.156**	0.062	0.165***	0.066	0.015	0.006
(d) Trust						
TRUST IN GOVERNMENT			0.165***	0.066	0.169***	0.067
(e) Direct democracy						
INDEX DIRECT DEMOCRACY					0.180***	0.072
(f) Further variables	Yes		Yes		Yes	
Number of observations	910		879		879	
Prob(LM–statistic)	0.000		0.000		0.000	

Notes: Dependent variable: tax morale on a four-point scale. In the reference group are AGE 16–29, MALE, SINGLE and FULL TIME EMPLOYED. Significance levels: * $0.05 < p < 0.10$; ** $0.01 < p < 0.05$; *** $p < 0.01$.

Table 5.7 *Tax morale and local autonomy (ISSP 1999) (weighted ordered probit, dependent variable: tax morale)*

Independent variables	Equation 5b		Equation 6b		Equation 7b	
	Coeff.	Marg.	Coeff.	Marg.	Coeff.	Marg.
(a) Deterrence factors						
FINE RATE	0.85E–04	0.000	0.28E–03	0.000	–0.10E–03	0.000
AUDIT PROBABILITY	0.001	0.000	0.24E–03	0.000	–0.34E–04	0.000
(b) Tax rate						
INDIVIDUAL INCOME TAX RATE	–0.006	–0.002	–0.005	–0.001	–0.002	–0.001
(c) Local autonomy						
INDEX LOCAL AUTONOMY	0.187***	0.054	0.197***	0.057	0.142**	0.041
(d) Trust						
TRUST IN COURTS AND THE LEGAL SYSTEM			0.094***	0.027	0.093***	0.027
(e) Direct democracy						
INDEX DIRECT DEMOCRACY					0.061*	0.018
(f) Further variables	Yes		Yes		Yes	
Number of observations	1114		1068		1068	
Prob(LM–statistic)	0.000		0.000		0.000	

Notes: Dependent variable: tax morale on a four-point scale. In the reference group are AGE 16–29, MALE, SINGLE and FULL TIME EMPLOYED. Significance levels: * $0.05 < p < 0.10$; ** $0.01 < p < 0.05$; *** $p < 0.01$.

taxpayers to get a better identification with the aims and objectives of the government. In general, Feld and Kirchgässner (2001) point out that:

> The more important regional and local jurisdictions are in the internal organization of a nation-state, the more important is the question of the proper decision-making procedures at the different government levels. The assignment of competencies to different government levels is linked to decision-making procedures (p. 333).

The two variables are significantly correlated at the 0.01 level (WVS, $r = 0.392$; ISSP, $r = 0.574$). Thus, it is difficult to separate the effects of the two variables in one model.

In general, the criticism could be offered that including aggregated variables such as direct democracy or local autonomy might produce downward-biased standard errors (see, e.g., Frey and Stutzer, 2000). To check whether a correction regarding the standard errors has an effect on the significance level of the aggregated variables, in the Appendix we present, in Tables A5.3 and A5.4, a summary of the main estimations, with standard errors adjusted to clustering in 20 cantons (WVS) and 26 cantons (ISSP). Tables A5.3 and A5.5 indicate that no changes are observable regarding our main aggregated variables: direct democracy and federalism each have a significant positive effect on tax morale.

CONCLUSIONS

The basic intention of this chapter was to analyse how formal and informal institutions affect tax morale. Empirical and experimental findings in the tax compliance literature have shown that the standard model of tax evasion, based on an expected utility-maximization approach, predicts a higher degree of tax evasion than observed. Thus, the tax compliance puzzle is why people pay taxes. It has been argued that tax morale might explain such a high compliance. However, hardly any empirical studies have analysed what shapes tax morale. This chapter has tried to fill this gap by analysing tax morale as a dependent variable and by working with two different data sets from Switzerland, the WVS and the ISSP. Special attention has been given to two constitutional determinants that are rarely analysed in the empirical tax compliance literature: direct democracy and local autonomy. Institutions that respect the preferences of the citizens will gain more support from the people than a state that acts as a Leviathan, and thus will enhance tax morale. Both instruments help taxes to be spent according to the citizens' preferences, which increases their motivation to pay the taxes. Furthermore, we have checked whether trust in the government and trust in the courts and the legal system correlate with a higher tax morale.

Using these two data sets, strong evidence has been found that formal and informal institutions significantly influence tax morale. This effect tends to persist even after controlling for the basic variables from the traditional tax evasion models (probability of detection, the fine for tax evasion, and individuals' tax rates) and socio-demographic and socio-economic factors (age, income, education, gender, marital status and employment status) and carrying out sensitivity tests. In line with a recent empirical study undertaken by Feld and Frey (2002a,b) in Switzerland, in pooled cross-sectional time-series estimations for Swiss cantons the traditional deterrence factors do not perform in a satisfactory way. In many estimations carried out using our two data sets, the coefficients were not significant.

APPENDIX

Table A5.1 Direct democratic rights in Swiss cantons

Canton	Index for constitutional initiative	Index for legislative initiative	Index for legislative referendum	Index for financial referendum	Composite index for direct democratic rights	Dummy legislative referendum (mandatory)	Signature requirement legislative initiative[a]	Local autonomy
Aargau	5.67	5.67	6	4.5	5.46	1	0.88	4.9
Appenzell I. Rh.	6	6	6	3	5.25	1	0.00	5
Appenzell A. Rh.	6	6	6	4	5.5	1	0.00	5.8
Bern	2.67	2.67	3.67	5	3.5	0	2.22	4.6
Basel–Landschaft	6	6	6	4.75	5.69	1	0.87	4.3
Basel–Stadt	4.67	4.67	4	4.25	4.4	0	3.20	5.5
Fribourg	2.67	2.67	2.33	2	2.42	0	3.98	4.2
Genève	2	2	2	1	1.75	0	4.84	3.2
Glarus	6	6	6	4	5.5	1	0.00	5.6
Graubünden	4	5	6	4	4.75	1	2.42	5.8
Jura	4.67	4.67	3	2.5	3.71	0	3.92	4
Luzern	4.67	5.33	3.67	4.25	4.48	0	1.77	4.1
Neuchâtel	2.67	2.67	1.67	1.5	2.13	0	5.86	3.7
Nidwalden	2.67	6	6	5	4.92	1	0.00	5.5
Obwalden	5.33	6	6	5	5.58	1	0.00	6
Sankt Gallen	3.33	4	3	3.25	3.4	0	1.44	4.9

Table A5.1 continued

Canton	Index for constitutional initiative	Index for legislative initiative	Index for legislative referendum	Index for financial referendum	Composite index for direct democratic rights	Dummy legislative referendum (mandatory)	Signature requirement legislative initiative[a]	Local autonomy
Schaffhausen	5.33	5.33	5.17	4.5	5.08	1	2.09	6.1
Solothurn	5.33	5.33	6	5	5.42	1	1.84	4.9
Schwyz	5.33	5.33	4.67	4.38	4.93	1	2.50	4.6
Thurgau	3.67	3.67	4.33	4.5	4.04	0	2.93	5.9
Ticino	1.33	2.67	1.67	2.75	2.1	0	3.66	4.3
Uri	5.67	5.67	5.33	5	5.42	1	1.19	5.4
Vaud	2.33	2.33	2	3	2.42	0	3.37	4.7
Valais	3	3.67	6	1	3.42	0	2.28	5.5
Zug	5	5	3.67	4	4.42	0	3.30	6
Zürich	3.33	3.33	6	4	4.17	1	1.31	5.4

Notes: [a] Relative value (signature requirements/total number of voters). The cantons which have or had until recently the 'Landsgemeinde' (town meeting) (Appenzell I. Rh., Obwalden, Glarus, Appenzell A. Rh. and Nidwalden) have been coded with the value 1 for the dummy of legislative referendum and the value 0 for the signature requirements (absolute value = 1).

Sources: Index Direct Democracy, Frey and Stutzer (2000, p. 937); Dummy Legislative Referendum and Signature Requirement Legislative Initiative, Stutzer (1999, pp. 18–19). Local Autonomy, Ladner (1994), Frey and Stutzer (1999, p. 27). See also Trechsel and Serdült (1999).

Table A5.2   The derivation of variables (WVS)

Variable	Derivation
Tax morale (dependent variable)	Please tell me for the following statement whether you think it can always be justified, never be justified, or something in between: Cheating on tax if you have the chance. (% 'never justified' – code 1 from a ten-point scale where 1 = never and 10 = always) The ten-point scale has been recoded into a four-point scale, with the value 4 standing for 'never justifiable'. Values 4–10 have been integrated into group 1 because of a lack of variance.
FINE RATE	Standard legal fine (in per cent) as a multiple of the evaded tax amount, based on questionnaire data of Frey and Feld (2002) and Feld and Frey (2002a,b).
PROBABILITY OF DETECTION	Number of tax auditors as a percentage of the total number of taxpayers, based on questionnaire data of Frey and Feld (2002) and Feld and Frey (2002a,b).
INDIVIDUAL TAX RATE	Own calculations based on the average weighted value (in per cent) using the WVS income groups. From the tax table (Steuerbelastung in der Schweiz, 1996, p. 48) the value closest to the average found in the WVS groups is used, groups 6 and 7 being pooled. For the highest value an average income of SFr300 000 has been assumed (midpoint). For simplicity, no differentiation between singles and married people has been made, working with the individual tax rate table for singles.
TRUST IN GOVERNMENT	Could you tell me how much confidence you have in the government in your capital: is it a great deal of confidence, quite a lot of confidence, not very much confidence or none at all? (4 = a great deal to 1 = none at all)
CHURCH ATTENDANCE	Apart from weddings, funerals and christenings, about how often do you attend religious services these days? More than once a week, once a week, once a month, only on special holidays, once a year, less often, never practically never? (7 = more than once a week to 1 = never, practically never)

Table A5.2   continued

Variable	Derivation
INCOME	Here is a scale of incomes (1–10). We would like to know in what group your household is, counting all wages, salaries, pensions and other incomes that come in. Just give the letter of the group your household falls into, before taxes and other deductions. 1. Less than SFr20 000 2. SFr20 000–26 999 3. SFr27 000–31 999 4. SFr32 000–37 999 5. SFr38 000–44 999 6. SFr45 000–51 999 7. SFr52 000–59 999 8. SFr60 000–69 999 9. SFr70 000–89 999 10. More than SFr90 000
EDUCATION	What is the highest educational level that you have attained? 1. Never went to school 2. Incomplete primary school 3. Primary school (up to 12 years of age) 4. Apprenticeship 5. Lower secondary school (up to 16 years of age) 6. Secondary school without diploma (16–19 years) 7. Technical school 8. Secondary school with diploma 9. University or Federal Polytechnical School without degree 10. University or Federal Polytechnical with degree
INDIVIDUAL FINANCIAL SATISFACTION	How satisfied are you with the financial situation of your household? (scale 1 = dissatisfied to 10 = satisfied)

Source: Inglehart et al. (2000).

Table A5.3   The derivation of variables (ISSP)

Variable	Derivation
TAX MORALE (dependent variable)	Do you feel it is wrong or not wrong if a taxpayer does not report all of his or her income in order to pay less income taxes? (1 = not wrong, 2 = a bit wrong, 3 = wrong, 4 = seriously wrong)
TRUST IN COURTS AND THE LEGAL SYSTEM	How much confidence do you have in the courts and the legal system? (5 = complete confidence to 1 = no confidence at all)
FINE RATE	Standard legal fine (in per cent) as a multiple of the evaded tax amount, based on questionnaire data of Frey and Feld (2002) and Feld and Frey (2002a,b).
PROBABILITY OF DETECTION	Number of tax auditors as a percentage of the total number of taxpayers based on questionnaire data of Frey and Feld (2002) and Feld and Frey (2002a,b).
INDIVIDUAL TAX RATE	Own calculations based on the average weighted value (in per cent) working with the income information given by the ISSP. From the tax table (Steuerbelastung in der Schweiz, 1999, p. 48) the value closest to the ISSP income values (midpoint) is used. For simplicity, no differentiation between singles and married people has been made, working with the individual tax rate table for singles.
CHURCH ATTENDANCE	How often do you take part in the activities or organisations of a church or a place of worship, other than attending services? Never (1), less than once a year, about once or twice a year, several times a year, about once a month, 2–3 times a month, nearly every week, every week, several times a week (9)
INCOME	Monthly earnings from employment in Swiss francs (midpoints)
EDUCATION	What is the highest educational level that you have attained? 1. Incomplete primary school 2. Primary school (up to 12 years of age) 3. Incomplete secondary 4. Secondary completed 5. Incomplete + complete semi–higher qualification, incomplete university, others 6. University completed

Source: ISSP (1998).

Table A5.4 *Determinants of tax morale (WVS 1996; standard error adjusted to clustering in 20 cantons) (weighted ordered probit, dependent variable: tax morale)*

Independent variables	14a	15a	16a	17a	18a
(a) Deterrence factors					
FINE RATE	−0.002**	−0.002*	−0.001*	−0.39E−03	−0.002*
	(−2.206)	(−1.680)	(−1.943)	(0.810)	(−1.794)
AUDIT PROBABILITY	0.001	0.001	0.002	0.002	0.001
	(0.749)	(0.631)	(1.294)	(1.146)	(0.773)
(b) Tax rate					
INDIVIDUAL INCOME TAX RATE	−0.007*	−0.007	−0.007	−0.008*	−0.007*
	(−1.714)	(−1.646)	(−1.512)	(−1.909)	(−1.710)
(c) Institutions					
INDEX DIRECT DEMOCRACY	0.184***	0.161***			0.180***
	(3.929)	(3.036)			(3.371)

Single instruments				
DUMMY LEGISLATIVE REFERENDUM	0.170***			
	(3.125)			
SIGNATURE REQUIREMENT			0.244***	
LEGISLATIVE INITIATIVE			(2.638)	
INDEX LOCAL AUTONOMY			−0.067	
			(−1.315)	
(d) Trust				
TRUST IN GOVERNMENT		0.169***		0.165
		(3.153)		(1.611)
(e) Language				
GERMAN SPEAKING		0.081	0.152***	0.165***	0.015
		(0.453)	(2.976)	(3.262)	(0.092)
					0.169***
					(3.159)
(f) Further variables	Yes	Yes	Yes	Yes	Yes

Notes: z-values are given in parentheses. Dependent variable: tax morale on a four-point scale. In the reference group are AGE 16–29, MALE, SINGLE, FULL TIME EMPLOYED and FRENCH AND ITALIAN SPEAKING. Significance levels: * $0.05 < p < 0.10$; ** $0.01 < p < 0.05$; *** $p < 0.01$.

Table A5.5 *Determinants of tax morale (ISSP 1999; standard error adjusted to clustering in 26 cantons) (weighted ordered probit, dependent variable: tax morale)*

Independent variables	14b	15b	16b	17b	18b
(a) Deterrence factors					
FINE RATE	−0.001	−0.50E−03	−0.42E−03	0.28E−03	−0.15E−03
	(−0.686)	(−0.570)	(−0.487)	(0.255)	(−0.201)
AUDIT PROBABILITY	−0.47E−04	0.001	0.17E−03	0.24E−03	0.49E−03
	(−0.047)	(0.671)	(0.162)	(0.253)	(0.559)
(b) Tax rate					
INDIVIDUAL INCOME TAX RATE	−0.010	−0.20E−03	−0.001	−0.005	0.004
	(−0.461)	(−0.010)	(−0.034)	(−0.212)	(0.184)
(c) Institutions					
INDEX DIRECT DEMOCRACY	0.104***				
	(2.736)				

Single instruments				
DUMMY LEGISLATIVE REFERENDUM		0.237***	0.226**	0.219**
		(2.674)	(2.398)	(2.533)
SIGNATURE REQUIREMENT		−0.043	−0.002	−0.015
		(−0.945)	(−0.028)	(−0.339)
LEGISLATIVE INITIATIVE				0.111*
				(1.833)
INDEX LOCAL AUTONOMY			0.197***	
			(2.742)	
(d) Trust				
TRUST IN COURTS AND LEGAL SYSTEM	0.093***	0.094***	0.090***	0.094***	0.096***
	(3.159)	(3.261)	(2.996)	(3.190)	(3.311)
(e) Language				
GERMAN SPEAKING			0.168	
			(1.165)	
(f) Further variables	Yes	Yes	Yes	Yes	Yes

Notes: z-values are given in parentheses. Dependent variable: tax morale on a four-point scale. In the reference group are AGE 16–29, MALE, SINGLE, FULL TIME EMPLOYED and FRENCH AND ITALIAN SPEAKING. Significance levels: * $0.05 < p < 0.10$; ** $0.01 < p < 0.05$; *** $p < 0.01$.

NOTES

1. The information about the probability of detection and the fine for tax evasion has been collected by Lars P. Feld and Bruno S. Frey, and is based on a questionnaire. The following contributions are based upon this data set: Feld and Frey (2002a,b) and Frey and Feld (2002).
2. Could you tell me how much confidence you have in the government in your capital: is it a great deal of confidence, quite a lot of confidence, not very much confidence or none at all? (4 = a great deal to 1 = none at all)
3. How much confidence do you have in courts and the legal system? (5 = complete confidence to 1 = no confidence at all)
4. The index includes the four legal instruments: the popular initiative to change the canton's constitution, the popular initiative to change the canton's law, the compulsory and optional referenda to prevent new laws or the changing of a law, and the compulsory and optional referenda to prevent new state expenditure. The index is based on the degree of restrictions in form of the necessary signatures to use an instrument, the time span to collect the signatures and the level of new expenditure (for a detailed discussion, see Stutzer, 1999).
5. It should be noted that the Swiss World Values Survey was not random-random but quota-random, based on a random sample of communes and then on quotas in terms of sex, age and so on in the selected communes. Thus, the smallest cantons are not necessarily represented (not represented are: Appenzell a. Rh., Glarus, Jura, Nidwalden, Uri and Zug).
6. What about the causality between direct democracy and tax morale? Do taxpayers with a higher tax morale choose direct democratic institutions? In line with Frey (2001) and Frey and Stutzer (2000), it could be argued that direct democratic institutions have a long tradition in Switzerland and are quite stable over time, which suggests that the causality runs from direct democratic rights to tax morale and not the other way round. However, on the basis of this kind of data set, it is not possible fully to rule out the causality problem.
7. For the theory of aspirations, see e.g., Frank (1941), Simon (1955) and Siegel (1957).
8. The dummy of the legislative referenda indicates whether a canton has the power to inaugurate a referendum (mandatory). The signature requirement for legislative initiatives is the major parameter in this form of direct democracy and an indicator of the costs of using the initiative instrument. The higher the number of signatures, the more difficult and costly it is to realize the initiative. This was measured as a relative value (signature requirements/total number of voters).
9. In order to save degrees of freedom, only the index of direct democracy has been integrated in the WVS estimation and not both single direct democratic participation instruments, as in the estimation used with the ISSP data set, which covers more observations at the cantonal level.
10. For similar results that analyse happiness, see Frey and Stutzer (2002).

REFERENCES

Alm, J., G.H. McClelland and W.D. Schulze (1999), 'Changing the social norm of tax compliance by voting', *KYKLOS*, **52**, 141–71.

Andreoni, J., B. Erard and J. Feinstein (1998), 'Tax compliance', *Journal of Economic Literature*, **36**, 818–60.

Bahl, R. (1999), 'Implementation rules for fiscal decentralization', working paper, International Studies Program, School of Policy Studies, Georgia State University, Atlanta.

Beron, K.J., H.V. Tauchen, and A.D. Witte (1992), 'The effect of audits and socioeconomic variables on compliance', in J. Slemrod (ed.), *Why People Pay Taxes. Tax Compliance and Enforcement*, Ann Arbor: The University of Michigan Press, pp. 67–89.

Feld, L.P. and B.S. Frey (2002a), 'Trust breeds trust: how taxpayers are treated', *Economics of Governance*, **3**, 87–99.

Feld, L.P. and B.S. Frey (2002b), 'The tax authority and the taxpayer. An exploratory analysis', paper presented at the 2002 Annual Meeting of the European Public Choice Society, Belgirate.

Feld, L.P. and G. Kirchgässner (2000), Direct democracy, political culture, and the outcome of economic policy: a report on the Swiss experience', *European Journal of Political Economy*, **16**, 287–306.

Feld, L.P. and G. Kirchgässner (2001), 'The political economy of direct legislation: direct democracy and local decision-making', *Economic Policy*, **16**, 331–67.

Feld L.P. and J.-R. Tyran (2002), 'Tax evasion and voting: an experimental analysis', *KYKLOS*, **55**, 197–222.

Frank, J.D. (1941), 'Recent studies of the level of aspiration', *Psychological Bulletin*, **28**, 218–26.

Frey, B.S. (1997), *Not Just for the Money. An Economic Theory of Personal Motivation*, Cheltenham, UK and Lyme, USA: Edward Elgar.

Frey, B.S. (2001), *Inspiring Economics. Human Motivation in Political Economy*, Cheltenham, UK and Northampton, MA, USA: Edward Elgar.

Frey, B. S. (2003), 'The role of deterrence and tax morale in taxation in the European Union', Jelle Zijlstra Lecture, Netherlands Institute for Advanced Study in the Humanities and Social Sciences (NIAS).

Frey, B.S. and R. Eichenberger (1999), *The New Democratic Federalism for Europe*, Cheltenham, UK and Northampton, MA, USA: Edward Elgar.

Frey, B.S. and L.P. Feld (2002), 'Deterrence and morale in taxation: an empirical analysis', CESifo Working Paper No. 760, August 2002.

Frey, B.S. and A. Stutzer (2000), 'Happiness, economy and institutions', *Economic Journal*, **110**, 918–38.

Frey, B. S. and A. Stutzer (2002), *Happiness and Economics*, Princeton: Princeton University Press.

Grasmick, H.G., R.J. Bursik and J.K. Cochran (1991), '"Render unto Caesar what is Caesar's": religiosity and taxpayers' inclinations to cheat', *Sociological Quarterly*, **32**, 251–66.

Hardin, R. (1998), 'Trust in government', in V. Braithwaite and M. Levi (eds), *Trust and Governance*, New York: Russell Sage Foundation, pp. 9–27.

Henrich, J., P. Young, R. Boyd, K. McCabe, W. Albers, A. Ockenfels and G. Gigerenzer (1999), 'What is the role of culture in bounded rationality?', Unpublished manuscript.

Hirschman, A.O. (1970), *Exit, Voice, and Loyalty*, Cambridge, MA: Harvard University Press.

Inglehart, R. et al. (2000), *Codebook for World Values Survey*, Ann Arbor: Institute for Social Research.

ISSP (1998), Codebook, Religion II, ZA Study 3190, Zentralarchiv für Empirische Sozialforschung, Köln.

Kucher, M. and L. Götte (1998), 'Trust me: an empirical analysis of taxpayer honesty', *FinanzArchiv*, **55**, 429–44.

Ladner, A. (1994), 'Finanzkompetenzen der Gemeinden – ein Überblick über die Praxis', in F. Eng, A. Glatthard and B.H. Koenig (eds), *Finanzföderalismus*, Bern: Emissionszentrale der Schweizer Gemeinden, pp. 64–85.

Levi, M. (1988), *Rules and Revenue*, Berkeley: University of California Press.

Lewis, A. (1982), *The Psychology of Taxation*, Oxford: Martin Robertson.

Pommerehne, W.W. and H. Weck-Hannemann (1996), 'Tax rates, tax administration and income tax evasion in Switzerland', *Public Choice*, 88, 161–70.

Prinz, A. (2002), 'A moral theory of tax evasion', unpublished manuscript, Westfälische Wilhelms-Universität Münster.

Siegel, S. (1957), 'Level of aspiration and decision making', *Psychological Review*, **64**, 253–62.

Simon, H. A. (1955), 'A behavioral model of rational choice', *Quarterly Journal of Economics*, **69**, 174–83.

Slemrod, J. (2002), 'Trust in Public Finance', NBER Working Paper 9187, September, Cambridge, MA.

Slemrod, J., M. Blumenthal and C. Christian (2001), 'Taxpayer response to an increased probability of audit: evidence from a controlled experiment in Minnesota', *Journal of Public Economics*, **79**, 455–83.

Spicer, M.W. and L.A. Becker (1980), 'Fiscal inequity and tax evasion: an experimental approach', *National Tax Journal*, **33**, 171–5.

Stutzer, A. (1999), 'Demokratieindizes für die Kantone der Schweiz', Working Paper No. 23, Institute for Empirical Research in Economics, University of Zurich.

Tittle, C. (1980), *Sanctions and Social Deviance: the Question of Deterrence*, New York: Praeger.

Torgler, B. (2001), 'What do we know about tax morale and tax compliance?', *International Review of Economics and Business (RISEC)*, **48**, 395–419.

Torgler, B. (2002), 'Speaking to theorists and searching for facts: tax morale and tax compliance in experiments', *Journal of Economic Surveys*, **16**, 657–84.

Torgler, B. (2003), 'Tax morale, rule governed behaviour and trust', *Constitutional Political Economy*, **14**, 119–40.

Torgler, B. (2006), 'The importance of faith: tax morale and religiosity', *Journal of Economic Behavior and Organization*, **61**, 81–109.

Torgler, B. and C.A. Schaltegger (2005), 'Tax amnesties and political participation', *Public Finance Review*, **33**, 403–31.

Trechsel, A. and U. Serdült (1999), *Kaleidoskop Volksrechte: Die Institutionen der direkten Demokratie in den schweizerischen Kantonen 1970–1996*, Basel: Helbing & Lichtenhahn.

Vogel, J. (1974), 'Taxation and public opinion in Sweden: an interpretation of recent survey data', *National Tax Journal*, **27**, 499–513.

6. Tax morale in Latin America

INTRODUCTION

Tax morale and tax compliance are important factors for guaranteeing an adequate provision of public goods. Especially in times when the costs of running public offices have strongly increased, governments search for strategies to generate revenues. A high degree of tax evasion creates misallocations in resource use (see Alm and Martinez-Vazquez, 2003). In developing countries, tax evasion is often widespread (see, e.g., de Soto, 2000). Such a high level of tax evasion reduces the government's ability to work and thus to provide adequate services. Over recent decades, developing countries in, for example, Latin America have made considerable efforts to implement major reforms in tax policies and to improve the effectiveness of their tax administrations:

> These efforts frequently took place under unfavourable macroeconomic circumstances. Tax administrators often had to cope with a barrage of tax reforms, interspersed with numerous ad hoc changes in tax rates, exemptions, and payment periods introduced largely for revenue reasons (Casanegra de Jantscher and Bird, 1992, pp. 1–2).

Empirical evidence is rare in the tax compliance literature. Pyle (1993) points out in a survey that 'The solution should lie in the results of empirical studies. Alas, the current harvest of such studies is remarkably thin' (p. 73).

However, it is interesting to notice that there is hardly any empirical evidence about the degree of tax morale in developing countries. Thus, the focus on Latin America in this chapter is novel. We analyse tax morale as a dependent variable and search for factors that systematically affect tax morale. It is important to analyse the determinants that influence tax morale in developing countries, as the environment is different from that of developed countries. On the other hand, if we observe similar tendencies, some effects might be independent of cultural environments. To get a robust picture, we will analyse two different data sets: the World Values Survey (WVS) and the Latinobarómetro. The WVS covers the years from 1981 to 1997 and the Latinobarómetro the year 1998. In the next section, I will give an overview of the tax system and tax administration in Latin America. The third section in this chapter starts with a descriptive analysis evaluating the degree of tax morale in different Latin American countries, and checking whether there is a correlation between tax morale, tax avoidance and the size of the shadow economy. In a second step, a cross-sectional analysis will be made with multiple regressions pooling developing countries and differentiating between Central and South America. The chapter finishes with some concluding remarks.

TAX MORALE, TAX EVASION AND THE STATE

Taxation in developing countries is a challenging topic and has attracted increasing attention in the past two decades. Many problems have been observed, such as, for example, poor administration performance resulting in a lack of tax revenues, tax structures where considerations of horizontal and vertical tax equity are not integrated, and governmental and economic instability. The levels of tax revenues as percentages of the GDP are much lower than in OECD countries (around 18 per cent, compared to around 40 per cent in OECD countries; see, e.g., Tanzi and Zee (2000, p. 303).

Most countries traditionally have no self-filling procedure, but apply deductions. Bahl and Martinez-Vazquez (1992) offer the criticism that developing countries imitate the complex tax structures of developed countries despite their disadvantage of having lower tax administration capabilities. Tax reforms in the 1980s had the intention of increasing the stability in the revenue system. The 1990s fiscal crises might have been motivating factors for reforms (see Das-Gupta and Mookherjee, 1995). Jenkins (1995) points out that income tax has performed very badly in Latin America, tending to yield modest amounts of revenue. According to Tanzi and Zee (2000), characteristics such as, for example, a large agricultural sector, a strong shadow economy, small firms, and a small proportion of wage income make it difficult for developing countries to rely on modern taxes such as personal income tax (see also Burgess and Stern, 1993). The uneven income distribution and the concentration of political and financial power at the top prevent modern tax reforms that would introduce personal income or property taxes. Thus, it is not surprising that radical reforms can hardly be seen in such countries (for an overview of reforms, see, e.g., Cabezas, 1992; McLure and Pardo, 1992; Silvani and Radano, 1992; Burgess and Stern, 1993; Bejaković, 2000; Martinez-Vazquez, 2001).

An important aim of a tax reform is, in general, to find a good way of raising revenues, and promoting equity and efficiency, without crowding out tax morale.

Tax Morale and Tax Evasion

There is a lively discussion on how tax attitudes are related to the actions of individuals. Is there a correlation between tax morale and tax evasion? In a general context, the social psychology literature has focused intensively on this topic (see, e.g., Ajzen and Fishbein, 1980). Lewis (1982) points out that

> it could be that tax evasion is the only channel through which taxpayers can express their antipathy [...] we can be confident in our general prediction that if tax attitudes become worse, tax evasion will increase (pp. 165 and 177).

The connection between attitude and behaviour is an interesting question that can be analysed empirically. Weck (1983) found, in an empirical analysis, that there is a negative correlation between tax morale and the size of the shadow economy. Compared to other variables, tax morale had the most significant impact on the size of the shadow economy. Torgler (2003) shows, in a multivariate analysis for the United States, using the *Taxpayer Opinion Survey*, that tax morale and tax evasion are negatively correlated. Furthermore, integrating European and transition countries, Torgler (2001a) observed a significant negative correlation between tax morale and the shadow economy.

The informal sector plays an important role in developing countries. Employment in the informal sector seems to be a relevant source of income for many people. Tanzi (2000) points out that it is realistic to assume that informal activities are more important in developing than in developed countries because it is easier to be underground, as the exemption levels for income and value added taxes are lower, social security taxes are higher and the obstacles to starting activities in the formal economy are also higher than in developed countries.

We will analyse whether there is a correlation between the size of the shadow economy, measured as the degree of informal employment as a percentage of the total population (2000/2001 average; estimated in Schneider 2002, p. 6), and tax morale, which we define as the intrinsic motivation to pay taxes. The general question for assessing the level of tax morale in a society is as follows:

> On a scale of 1 to 10, where 1 means not at all justifiable and 10 means totally justifiable, how justifiable do you believe it is to: 'Manage to avoid paying all tax'.

The question is developed from the Latinobarómetro, an annual public opinion survey carried out in 17 Latin American countries (data from

1998). It reports the opinions, attitudes and behaviour of the roughly 400 million inhabitants of the region, covering most of Latin America with the exception of Cuba, the Dominican Republic and Puerto Rico. Figure 6.1 gives the mean value for all countries based on a scale from 0 to 3, where 3 is the highest tax morale and 0 the lowest (value 0 integrates the values 4–10). The results indicate a strong negative correlation between both variables (–0.511), which is significant at the 0.05 level (significance, two-tailed test = 0.043). Countries with a low tax morale show a clear tendency to have a large shadow economy.

However, it should be noted that in some developing countries, law-breaking helps people to survive, as the transaction costs of behaving honestly are too high. The key problem is that the government is not able to secure property rights sufficiently. On the other hand, a combination of interventionism and bureaucracy is observed. Thus, a situation of 'over-

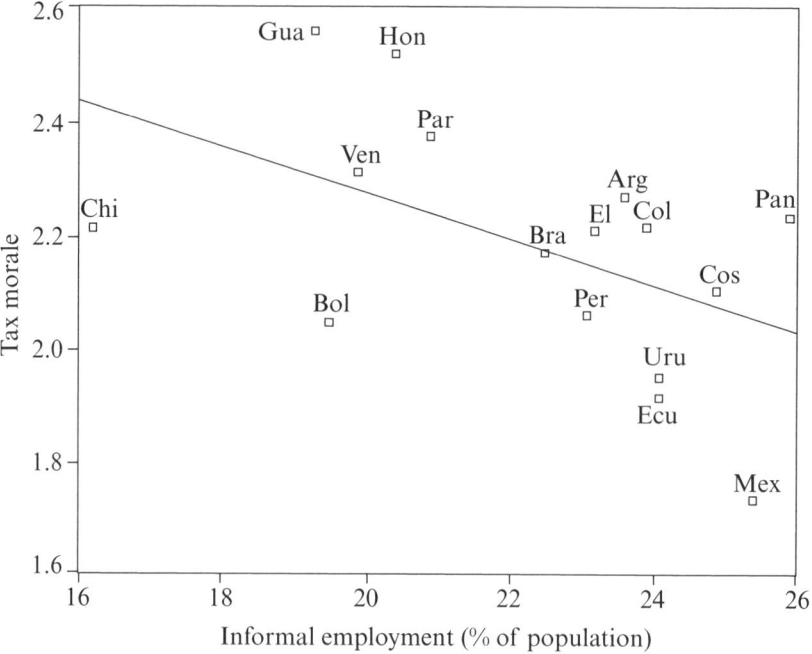

Notes: Arg, Argentina; Bol, Bolivia; Bra, Brazil; Col, Columbia; Cos, Costa Rica; Chi, Chile; Ecu, Ecuador; El, El Salvador; Gua, Guatemala; Hon, Honduras; Mex, Mexico; Nic, Nicaragua; Pan, Panama; Par, Paraguay; Per, Peru; Uru, Uruguay; Ven, Venezuela.

Figure 6.1 The correlation between tax morale and the size of the shadow economy

government' and 'under-government' arises, as Frey and Eichenberger (1999, p. 89) point out. The government and the administration have a strong discretionary power over the allocation of resources, which enhances corruption. Thus, individuals' tax evasion can be seen as an 'exit' option, a signal through which taxpayers can express their disagreement. De Soto (1989) and his research team conducted an experiment, setting up a small garment factory in Lima, with the aim of complying with the bureaucratic procedures and thus behaving in accordance with the law. He reports that they were asked ten times for a bribe to speed up the process, and on two occasions it was the only possible way to continue the experiment. It took ten months in total to start the business (see also de Soto, 2000).

Government and the Administration

The way in which people are treated by the authorities affects their evaluation of these authorities and thus their willingness to co-operate (see, e.g., Tyler and McGraw, 1986; Lind and Tyler, 1988; Tyler et al., 1989). Whether or not they feel fairly treated influences their willingness to pay taxes. An unfair tax system could enhance the incentives to rationalize cheating. On the basis of equity theory, it can be argued that taxpayers perceive their relationship with the state not only as a relationship of coercion, but also as one of exchange (for an overview, see Torgler, 2001b; see also Chapter 2). Taxpayers are more inclined to comply with the law if the exchange between the tax paid and the performed government services is found to be equitable. Thus, positive actions by the state are intended to increase taxpayers' positive attitudes and commitment to the tax system and tax payment, and thus to enhance compliant behaviour. If the taxpayers are concerned about the burden of taxation and the way in which the government uses the taxes, this might indicate that the relationship between input (paid taxes) and output (what comes back from the government) is not in equilibrium. An individual's tax compliance might thus be influenced by the relation between the benefits received from the government in the form of public goods and the price paid for them. Individuals might feel cheated if taxes are not spent adequately. The moral costs of evading taxes decrease and tax morale is crowded-out. Table 6.1 indicates that over 46 per cent of the respondents in Latin America believe a high tax burden to be the reason why people do not pay taxes: 'because taxes are too high' has the highest percentage of all reasons mentioned. Thus, anti-tax feelings arise if the tax burden is perceived to be too heavy. In particular, self-employed people might sense the tax burden more distinctly, as taxes become more perceptible to them. Furthermore, on average, 32.4 per cent mention that people evade taxes 'because taxes are ill spent'. The highest value is measured in Mexico (50.3 per cent), followed by El Salvador (46.4 per cent) and Ecuador (45.8 per cent), and the lowest values are observed in Guatemala (20.1 per cent), Chile (22.6 per cent) and Peru (23.2 per cent).

In the empirical section of this chapter, we will analyse whether greater trust in the authorities tends to increase tax morale and thus taxpayers' intrinsic motivation to pay taxes. If the state acts trustworthily, taxpayers might be more willing to comply with the taxes. On the other hand, perceived unfairness increases the incentive to act against the tax law, as the psychological costs are reduced. The relationship between the taxpayers and the state can be seen as a relational or psychological contract, which involves strong emotional ties and loyalties (see Feld and Frey, 2002a). Such a psychological tax contract can be maintained by positive actions, based on trust. More trust might enhance citizens' incentive to commit themselves to obedience. Governments with an authoritarian political structure are quite typical in developing countries. The presidents often have a strong political role, and active democratic political participation is often non-existent. Thus, the government plays an important role in developing countries, where greater difficulties must be confronted than in developed countries. Taxes can be seen as a price paid for the government's positive actions. If the president acts trustworthily, people might be more inclined to pay their taxes. However, we will not only analyse the trust in the president, but also whether a higher satisfaction with officials has a positive effect on tax morale. This allows us to check the robustness of the trust variable, expanding it to other agents of the state. Furthermore, the administration (in our case, the tax administration) plays an essential role in tax policy, especially in those countries where formal institutions are less stable and credible. In many developing countries, we observe a low capacity of the tax administration to monitor taxpayers' compliance. Tanzi (2000) reports a case in Peru where corruption in the tax administration was so common that the government had to close down the existing administration and replace it completely.[1] In many countries, there was a very high demand for poorly paid jobs in the tax administration, which indicates that applicants were aware of the possibility of gaining extra income. Furthermore, in some countries these jobs can be bought (see also Tanzi, 2000). There are many opportunities for a tax official to demand bribes. The effective tax burden might therefore be much higher than the official tax burden, for example, due to the 'special payments' to the tax officials. Tanzi (2000) offers a set of arguments why corruption is likely to be a major problem in tax administrations (p. 113):

> 1. the laws are difficult to understand and can be interpreted differently so that taxpayers need assistance in complying with them;

2. the payment of taxes requires frequent contacts between taxpayers and tax administrators;
3. the wages of the tax administrators are low;
4. acts of corruption on the part of the tax administrators are ignored, not easily discovered or, when discovered, are penalized only mildly;
5. the administrative procedures (for example, the criteria for the selection of taxpayers for audits) lack transparency and are not closely monitored within the tax or customs administrations;
6. tax administrators have discretion over important decisions, such as those related to the provision of tax incentives, determination of tax liabilities, selection of audits, litigations, and so on; and
7. more broadly, when the controls of the state (the principal) over the agents charged with carrying out its functions are weak.

Corruption generally undermines the tax morale of the citizens, who become frustrated. Furthermore, there might be a crowding-out effect of morality among the tax administrators when there is a large number of corrupt colleagues. Corruption can be reduced by following fair procedures. In the tax compliance literature, most studies include the assumption that tax collectors are intrinsically motivated (see, e.g., Hindriks et al., 1999). Discretionary power over resource allocation can induce corruption. Especially in developing countries, agents such as the political elite, administration staff and legislators have a discretionary power, because institutions are neither credible nor working well. Over-regulation on the one hand and a lack of democratic procedures on the other offer good grounds for illegal activities. Corruption reduces the efficiency of allocation and produces delays in transactions to acquire additional payments (see, e.g., Rose-Ackerman, 1997; Jain, 2001). In some countries, tax collectors' wages have been raised to reduce the incentive for them to engage in corruption. Interestingly, such a strategy can also be reported from Ancient Egypt, where the pharaohs increased the salary of tax agents (scribes) or trained special agents to check corruption in the revenue bureaus (see Adams, 1993).

Hindriks et al. (1999) searched for anecdotal evidence in the literature and reported that in Taiwan 94 per cent of interviewed tax administrators admitted having let themselves be bribed, and that in India 76 per cent of all government tax inspectors took bribes. Similar to these findings, our descriptive analyses indicate that people believe corruption to be a real problem in Latin America. As we can see in Table 6.1, on average 44.2 per cent of the respondents in Latin America state that individuals evade taxes because there is corruption. Ecuador, Mexico and El Salvador have the highest values, and Argentina, Chile and Peru the lowest.

A further important factor mentioned in Table 6.1 is the lack of civic conscience and honesty. Honesty restricts the possibility set for an individual to act illegally. Taxpayers may be aware that their evasion could damage the welfare of the community in which they live. As a consequence, evasion can produce psychological costs. People may not be comfortable with dishonesty (see Spicer, 1986). The findings of Orviska and Hudson (2002), evaluating the 1996 British Social Attitudes Survey, indicate that civic conscience has an impact on individuals' perceptions of whether tax evasion is right or wrong. Furthermore, Torgler (2003) shows, using the Taxpayer Opinion Survey, that a higher level of obedience and respect for the authority leads to a significantly higher tax morale.

On the other hand, people in Latin America do not believe that the deterrence instruments are not good enough, which is measured using 'because those that evade taxes go unpunished'. This reason has been mentioned less often than the other factors, having, at 23.1 per cent, the lowest average value of all the reasons (Table 6.1). Thus, this result indicates that an increase in detection and punishment should not be the only strategy to increase tax morale and tax compliance. As Frey (1997, p. 44) points out, 'the spirit of law, including specific rules, should acknowledge the citizens' basic good will'.

EMPIRICAL EVALUATION

In our analysis, we will use two data sets: the World Values Survey and the Latinobarómetro. The World Values Survey data covers ten countries (WVS 1995–1997), including Puerto Rico and the Dominican Republic, which are not available in the Latinobarómetro data set. In the WVS, the general question for assessing the level of tax morale in a society is as follows:

> Please tell me for the following statement whether you think it can always be justified, never be justified, or something in between: ... 'Cheating on tax if you have the chance' (% 'never justified' – code 1 from a ten-point scale where 1 = never and 10 = always).

Both data sets help to give a relatively robust picture of the degree of tax morale and the determinants that shape tax morale in Latin America. Certainly, subjective surveys are always prone to significant reporting errors. Thus, the way in which tax morale is measured in this study is not free of bias. It can be argued that a taxpayer who has taken part in some illegal behaviour in the past will tend to excuse this kind of behaviour, declaring a high tax morale. Furthermore, people might overstate their willingness to pay taxes, as there are no sanctions involved. However, our results have indicated previously that there is a negative correlation between the degree of tax morale and the size of the shadow economy. A further point might be the delicate nature of tax compliance. However, the way in which we define

Table 6.1 Reasons why individuals evade taxes

Why do people not pay their taxes?	Arg	Bol	Braz	Col	Cos	Chi	Ecu	El	Gua	Hon	Mex	Nic	Pan	Par	Per	Uru	Ven	Average
Lack of honesty	17.7	47.0	45.5	31.3	54.0	54.7	53.8	58.5	49.6	53.5	39.2	36.0	49.8	47.3	41.6	20.3	57.5	44.5
Because nationals are quick-witted and sly	14.8	17.6	31.8	17.8	29.2	44.4	47.2	25.8	12.8	28.3	25.4	16.2	32.7	8.9	25.6	30.5	39.9	26.4
They don't see the point of paying taxes	19.7	28.5	25.9	24.4	21.2	30.3	37.8	44.8	15.3	41.3	49.9	30.4	26.9	29.9	21.4	23.4	29.2	29.4
Lack of civic conscience	15.3	35.3	32.0	28.9	24.9	39.5	49.3	40.4	20.2	49.3	38.3	33.4	41.1	37.4	34.2	24.2	40.7	34.4
Because those that evade taxes go unpunished	26.0	23.0	24.3	16.6	19.2	18.1	31.3	36.4	13.4	24.6	36.5	21.0	18.6	19.9	14.6	26.5	22.3	23.1
Because the taxes are ill-spent	26.7	40.4	29.7	40.4	27.8	22.6	45.8	46.4	20.1	35.1	50.3	33.7	27.5	29.9	23.2	25.1	26.6	32.4
Because the taxes are too high	65.6	37.1	50.0	62.8	37.6	32.0	50.8	54.3	24.1	47.2	55.8	57.6	38.5	42.9	50.2	63.7	25.3	46.8
Because there is corruption	32.0	42.4	48.9	48.7	43.7	32.5	59.0	52.5	43.2	44.4	54.6	41.9	40.5	47.0	32.8	41.0	45.7	44.2

Note: The percentage of individuals that mentioned reasons why people do not pay their taxes.

tax morale is less delicate than if we were to ask whether or not a person has evaded taxes. A further advantage is the fact that both data sets cover a broad variety of questions on different topics, which reduces framing effects compared to a survey based only on tax compliance questions. The use of different data sources combined with a huge range of countries reduces biases that could arise from a momentary mood at the time of the survey. Certainly, the criticism can be offered that a tax morale variable deduced from more than one question would be more reliable and valid. On the other hand, it might be important to focus on a specific tax compliance question, to constitute a reliable measure of tax morale. The use of a single question has also the advantage that problems associated with the construction of an index – such as complexity, especially regarding the measurement procedure or a feeble correlation between the items – can be reduced.

The descriptive analysis shows that the average tax morale values in both data sets are similar: 63.2 per cent of the respondents stated that managing to avoid paying all of their tax is never justified, with a mean value of 2.19 using the scale from 0 to 3 (3 = highest tax morale) in the Latinobarómetro. On the other hand, the WVS reports that 66.8 per cent argue that cheating on tax if you have the chance is never justified, with a mean value of 2.22.

In this subsection, we will carry out a multivariate regression analysis in order to gain deeper insights. First, we will present some theoretical considerations about key determinants that may influence tax morale and thus allow us to develop hypotheses. After that, weighted ordered probit estimations will be presented using both data sets (Latinobarómetro and World Values Survey), pooling the countries but differentiating between regions.

The descriptive analysis shows that Mexico is a special case, indicating a very low tax morale in both data sets. Furthermore, Mexico can be classified as a region on its own, building the bridge between the United States and Central America. Thus, we use a separate dummy variable for Mexico.[2] In general, a cross-country analysis with attitude survey questions might cause difficulties. Because of the biases connected with cross-country comparisons, we restrict our analysis to the relatively homogeneous region of Latin America, building dummy variables to detect regional differences. We start with the Latinobarómetro, as this data set with 17 countries offers a broader picture of Latin America than the World Values Survey. As a dependent variable, we use tax morale (scale from 0 to 3, where 3 measures the highest tax morale).

Multivariate Analysis with the Latinobarómetro

Research commonly treats tax evasion as an important reaction in expressing preferences. However, there are other possibilities such as, for example, tax avoidance. Tax avoidance and tax evasion are often not distinguished in economic studies. We have the possibility of analysing both components. Whereas the World Values Survey focuses on evasion, the Latinobarómetro takes into account tax avoidance. Tax evasion might produce higher moral costs than tax avoidance, as the latter is more broadly accepted being closer to a legal strategy to escape from tax payments.

Main variables

1. Avoid paying taxes
Compared to the World Values Survey, the Latinobarómetro has the advantage of covering additional tax compliance questions. We have focused on the following variable, which we define as TAX AVOIDANCE:

> Could you tell me if recently you have known someone or have heard someone you know comment about somebody who has: Managed to avoid paying all his tax (1 = yes, 0 = no).

If individuals notice that many others evade taxes, their willingness to contribute may decrease, crowding out their intrinsic motivation to comply with taxes. Taxpayers get the feeling that they can also be opportunistic. The moral costs to evade taxes decrease. Thus, we would hypothesize that taxpayers who know or have heard about citizens who have managed to avoid taxes have a lower tax morale than others. The behaviour of other taxpayers is of great importance in understanding taxpayers' compliance. As a consequence, theories on pro-social behaviour, that take the behaviour of others into account, may be a promising concept (see Frey and Torgler, 2007). Lewis (1982, p. 144) points out that there might be a

> tax subculture, with its own set of unwritten rules and regulations. Thus I am more likely to evade not only because I have friends who, I know, have got away with it (so why shouldn't I?) but also because evasion is ethically acceptable among my friends [...] Furthermore, 'no friends of mine can be criminals' may come the reply: 'What's good enough for fine, upstanding citizens like Fred Bloggs, John Doe, Donald Campbell, Herman Schmitt and Hans Anderson is good enough for me.'

Frey and Torgler (2007) find, in their empirical analysis using data from Western and Eastern Europe, that tax morale decreases if people perceive that tax evasion is common. On the other hand, if people believe that others are honest, their own willingness to pay taxes increases. The size of the effect is substantial. The results remain robust after exploiting endogeneity and conducting several robustness tests.

2. Trust that people obey the law
This variable measures the contrary effect of the previous one. If we believe that most people obey the law and pay their taxes, the moral costs of not being obedient increase.[3] The hypothesis would be that an increase in the level of 'trust that other people obey the law' increases tax morale.

3. Perceived probability of being caught
Traditionally, the tax compliance literature stresses the relevance of deterrence factors such as the probability of being caught and fine rates. However, complying or not complying is not only a function of opportunity, tax rates and probability of detection, but also depends on social and moral attitudes, institutions and procedures. Especially when we analyse tax morale as a dependent variable, it can be doubted that the perceived probability of being caught has a positive effect on tax morale.[4] Frey (1997) points out that a severe punishment can be an indicator that the government distrusts individuals and that compliance is not honoured, which may undermine tax morale.

4. Trust in the president
We will analyse whether trust in the president has a positive effect on tax morale.[5] If taxpayers trust the president, they are more inclined to be honest. Our hypothesis is therefore that a higher degree of trust in the president leads to a higher tax morale.

Results

Table 6.2 presents the results. We have used a *weighted* ordered probit estimation to correct the samples and thus to get a reflection of the national distribution. The ordered probit models are relevant in such an analysis insofar as they help to analyse the ranking information of the scaled dependent variable tax morale. However, as in the ordered probit estimation, the equation has a non-linear form, so that only the sign of the coefficient can be directly interpreted and not its size. Calculating the marginal effects is therefore a method of finding the quantitative effect that a variable has on tax morale (see, e.g., Frey and Stutzer, 2002). The marginal effects are only presented for the highest value, 'tax avoidance is never justified'. We can observe that South America and Mexico have a significantly lower tax morale than Central America. Being from South America (Mexico[6]) rather than from Central America reduces the probability of stating that tax avoidance is never justified by more than ten percentage points (20 percentage points). Knowing about individuals who avoid taxes has a significantly negative effect on tax morale. Thus, the first hypothesis cannot be rejected. It reduces the share of individuals arguing that tax morale is never justifiable by more than six percentage points. On the other hand, if people trust that others obey the law, tax morale increases significantly, by more than eight percentage points. These results show the relevance of maintaining a high level of social capital.

In line with our expectations, the hypothesis regarding the variable TRUST PRESIDENT cannot be rejected either, whereas – not surprisingly – PERCEPTION BEING CAUGHT is not significant, showing a coefficient with a negative sign.

Looking at the control variables, we observe that all age groups from 30 to 65+ have a significantly higher tax morale than the age 16–29 reference group. For example, the proportion of persons of age 65+ who report the highest tax morale is 12.5 percentage points higher than for the reference age group. Marginal effects increase with an increase in age. Furthermore, there is a tendency for married people or people who live together to have a significantly higher tax morale than singles. The share of people reporting the highest tax morale is higher for self-employed persons, salaried individuals working in a private company and people in charge of a household than for salaried people working in a public company. The tax administration's collecting problems affect the monitoring of self-employed individuals, as it is very difficult and costly to gather information about them. Thus many enterprises, especially small ones, remain invisible (Burgess and Stern, 1993). Regarding tax morale, such a situation does not mean that those individuals' morale is lower. On the contrary, they do not feel the tax burden, as the government and the administration find it difficult to capture their existence. This might also explain the difference between salaried people working in private and public companies.

It might be interesting to integrate a proxy for income into the estimations. The Latinobarómetro has no specific information about the income of the subjects. Thus, the following proxies are integrated into further equations: OWN HOUSE, SOCIO-ECONOMIC STATUS[7] and FORTUNE (see Table 6.3).[8] Interestingly, none of the coefficients are significant, showing low marginal effects, but the coefficients for the regional variables remain significant.

Multivariate Analysis with the World Values Survey

In a second step, we will evaluate the World Values Survey (WVS) data. The data set covers a wider range of questions on attitudes, issues and socio-economic characteristics. We evaluate the 1995–1997 wave, which covers the greatest number of Latin American countries. As before, we build regional dummy variables. The WVS has the disadvantage that Central America has not been covered sufficiently. Thus, instead of differentiating between South

Table 6.2 Determinants of tax morale 1998 (Latinobarómetro) (weighted ordered probit)

Variable	Equation 1 Coeff.	Marg.	Equation 2 Coeff.	Marg.	Equation 3 Coeff.	Marg.	Equation 4 Coeff.	Marg.
(a) Demographic factors								
AGE 30–49	0.086***	0.033	0.061**	0.023	0.068***	0.026	0.070***	0.026
AGE 50–64	0.167***	0.063	0.129***	0.048	0.148***	0.056	0.159***	0.060
AGE 65+	0.332***	0.125	0.264***	0.099	0.334***	0.126	0.321***	0.121
FEMALE	0.007	0.003	0.036	0.013	0.022	0.008	0.021	0.008
EDUCATION	0.005**	0.002	0.003	0.001	0.004*	0.002	0.004	0.001
(b) Marital status								
MARRIED/LIVING TOGETHER	0.047*	0.018	0.045*	0.017	0.043*	0.016	0.039	0.015
DIVORCED/WIDOWED	−0.033	−0.012	−0.052	−0.020	−0.040	−0.015	−0.044	−0.017
(c) Employment status								
SELF-EMPLOYED	0.032	0.012	0.063*	0.024*	0.050	0.019	0.056	0.021
SALARIED IN A PRIVATE COMPANY	0.065*	0.025	0.072*	0.027*	0.070*	0.026	0.073**	0.028
UNEMPLOYED	−0.048	−0.018	−0.027	−0.010	−0.039	−0.015	−0.030	−0.011
RETIRED	0.010	0.004	0.058	0.022	0.006	0.002	0.000	0.000
IN CHARGE OF HOUSEHOLD	0.117**	0.044	0.109***	0.041***	0.121***	0.046	0.133***	0.050
STUDENT	0.037	0.014	0.041	0.016	0.036	0.014	0.049	0.018

(f) Regional variable						
SOUTH AMERICA		−0.300***	−0.113	−0.310***	−0.117	−0.289***	−0.109	−0.292***	−0.110
MEXICO		−0.626***	−0.236	−0.631***	−0.237	−0.639***	−0.241	−0.637***	−0.200
(g) Further variables						
AVOID PAYING TAXES	−0.172***	−0.065				
TRUST PEOPLE OBEY THE LAW			0.227***	0.086		
PERCEPTION BEING CAUGHT					−0.002	−0.001		
TRUST PRESIDENT							0.021***	0.008
Observations	14823		14409		15274		15282	
Prob(LM-statistic)	0.000		0.000		0.000		0.000	

Notes: Dependent variable: tax morale on a four-point scale. In the reference group are AGE 16–29, MALE, SINGLE, SALARIED IN A PUBLIC COMPANY and CENTRAL AMERICA. Significance levels: * $0.05 < p < 0.10$; ** $0.01 < p < 0.05$; *** $p < 0.01$. Marginal effect = highest tax morale score (3).

Table 6.3 Tax morale and status in 1998 (Latinobarómetro) (weighted ordered probit)

	Equation 5		Equation 6		Equation 7	
	Coeff.	Marg.	Coeff.	Marg.	Coeff.	Marg.
(a) Demographic variables	Included		Included		Included	
(b) Marital status	Included		Included		Included	
(c) Employment status	Included		Included		Included	
(d) Regional variable						
SOUTH AMERICA	−0.297***	−0.112	−0.283***	−0.107	−0.321***	−0.121
MEXICO	−0.626***	−0.236	−0.624***	−0.236	−0.650***	−0.245
(e) Fortune and status						
OWN HOUSE	0.024	0.009				
SOCIO–ECONOMIC STATUS			−0.007	−0.003		
FORTUNE					0.005	0.002
Number of observations	15 371		14 987		14 567	
Prob(LM-statistic)	0.000		0.000		0.000	

Notes: Dependent variable: tax morale on a four-point scale. In the reference group are AGE 16–29, MALE, SINGLE, SALARIED IN A PUBLIC COMPANY and CENTRAL AMERICA. Significance levels: * $0.05 < p < 0.10$; ** $0.01 < p < 0.05$; *** $p < 0.01$. Marginal effect = highest tax morale score (3).

and Central America, we build additional dummies for Mexico and the Dominican Republic (Caribbean area). In line with the Latinobarómetro findings, Table 6.4 indicates that Mexico has a significantly lower tax morale than the reference group (other Latin American countries).

Instead of trust in the president, we use satisfaction with officials. This allows us to check the robustness of the trust variable, expanding it to other agents of the state. The coefficient is highly significant and the marginal effects show that an increase in the level of satisfaction by one unit raises the share of individuals stating that tax morale is never justifiable by one percentage point.

We have obtained comparable results regarding the control variables. A higher age has a positive effect on tax morale. Furthermore, married people (females) have a higher tax morale than singles (males). The coefficient of the variable EDUCATION now has a negative sign. However, the significant effect on tax morale is not robust throughout all of the equations. We have also controlled for the economic situation of individuals. The results show a tendency for the lowest group (reference group) to have a higher tax morale than those groups with a better economic situation. However, only the coefficient for the variable LOWER MIDDLE CLASS indicates a significant difference to the variable LOWER CLASS. We also checked whether people with a stronger religiosity had a higher tax morale.[9] According to Hirschi and Stark (1969), religion might inhibit illegal behaviour, because religion is a sanctioning system that legitimizes and reinforces social values. Empirical studies have shown that states and counties with higher rates of religious memberships have significantly less violent and non-violent crime (see, e.g., Lipford et al., 1993; Hull and Bold, 1994). Table 6.4 shows a positive correlation between tax morale and religiosity.

Political participation is a social innovation for Latin America and produces beneficial effects. In recent decades we have observed a strengthening of democracy in some Latin American countries, such as Chile, Mexico and Argentina. Democracy offers citizens the possibility of expressing their preferences. A more active role helps citizens better to monitor and control politicians, and thus to reduce the asymmetry of information between them and their agents (the government), which reduces the discretionary power. This might influence citizens' tax morale.[10] Thus we would hypothesize that a stronger pro-democratic attitude has a positive effect on tax morale. We have built variables that measure individuals' support for democratic government (PRO DEMOCRACY 1[11] and PRO DEMOCRACY 2[12]). Table 6.4 indicates that pro-democratic attitudes have a highly significant positive effect on tax morale. An increase in the pro-democracy scale by one unit in both cases raises the proportion of persons indicating the highest tax morale by 7.3 (4.5) percentage points. We also analyse the effect of pride on

Table 6.4 Determinants of tax morale (WVS, 1995–1997) (weighted ordered probit)

Variable	Equation 1 Coeff.	Equation 1 Marg.	Equation 2 Coeff.	Equation 2 Marg.	Equation 3 Coeff.	Equation 3 Marg.	Equation 4 Coeff.	Equation 4 Marg.
(a) Demographic factors								
AGE 30–49	0.090***	0.033	0.086***	0.032	0.101***	0.037	0.086***	0.032
AGE 50–64	0.304***	0.112	0.298***	0.109	0.284***	0.105	0.281***	0.104
AGE 65+	0.509***	0.187	0.500***	0.183	0.501***	0.184	0.441***	0.162
FEMALE	0.109***	0.040	0.101***	0.037	0.091***	0.034	0.109***	0.040
EDUCATION	−0.011	−0.004	−0.018***	−0.007	−0.014**	−0.005	−0.006	−0.002
(b) Marital status								
MARRIED	0.095***	0.035	0.081**	0.030	0.090***	0.033	0.076**	0.028
LIVING TOGETHER	−0.006	−0.002	−0.008	−0.003	−0.004	−0.001	−0.009	−0.003
DIVORCED	−0.067	−0.025	−0.042	−0.015	−0.042	−0.016	−0.045	−0.017
SEPARATED	0.017	0.006	0.019	0.007	−0.008	−0.003	0.034	0.013
WIDOWED	0.158**	0.058	0.116	0.043	0.139*	0.051	0.169**	0.062
(c) Employment status								
PART TIME EMPLOYED	0.013	0.005	0.038	0.014	0.030	0.011	0.018	0.007
SELF-EMPLOYED	0.061	0.023	0.060	0.022	0.056	0.021	0.056	0.021
UNEMPLOYED	0.015	0.005	0.009	0.003	0.027	0.010	0.021	0.008
AT HOME	−0.034	−0.012	−0.008	−0.003	−0.019	−0.007	−0.022	−0.008
STUDENT	0.120***	0.044	0.116***	0.043	0.134***	0.049	0.106***	0.039
RETIRED	0.008	0.003	0.041	0.015	0.056	0.021	0.049	0.018
OTHER	0.021	0.008	−0.008	−0.003	0.015	0.006	−0.009	−0.003

	(1) Coef.	(1) Marg.	(2) Coef.	(2) Marg.	(3) Coef.	(3) Marg.	(4) Coef.	(4) Marg.
(d) Economic situation								
UPPER CLASS	-0.027	-0.010	-0.072	-0.027	-0.015	-0.006	-0.037	-0.014
UPPER MIDDLE CLASS	-0.014	-0.005	-0.050	-0.019	-0.024	-0.009	-0.012	-0.004
LOWER MIDDLE CLASS	-0.098**	-0.036	-0.135***	-0.050	-0.115**	-0.042	-0.079*	-0.029
WORKING CLASS	-0.019	-0.007	-0.061	-0.022	-0.043	-0.016	-0.022	-0.008
(e) Religiosity								
RELIGIOUS	0.092***	0.034	0.094***	0.034	0.091***	0.033	0.060***	0.022
(f) Regional variable								
MEXICO	-0.274***	-0.101	-0.239***	-0.088	-0.264***	-0.097	-0.285***	-0.105
DOMINICAN REPUBLIC	0.313***	0.115	0.239***	0.088	0.269***	0.099	0.280***	0.103
(g) Further variables								
SATISFACTION WITH NATIONAL OFFICERS	0.028***	0.010						
PRO DEMOCRACY 1			0.200***	0.073				
PRO DEMOCRACY 2					0.123***	0.045		
PRIDE							0.249***	0.092
Observations	7422		7233		7146		7483	
Prob(LM-statistic)	0.000		0.000		0.000		0.000	

Notes: Dependent variable: tax morale on a four–point scale. In the reference group are AGE 16–29, MALE, SINGLE, FULL TIME EMPLOYED, LOWER CLASS and SOUTH AMERICA. Significance levels: * $0.05 < p < 0.10$; ** $0.01 < p < 0.05$; *** $p < 0.01$. Marginal effect = highest tax morale score (3).

tax morale. Being proud of one's country enhances identification with the state. This might be a reason for behaving co-operatively and thus finding it important to pay taxes. The expected sign for the variable PRIDE[13] is therefore positive. Table 6.4 indicates that this hypothesis cannot be rejected. We find a positive correlation between pride and tax morale. An increase in pride by one unit raises the share of persons arguing that tax morale is never justifiable by 9.2 percentage points.

We also explore the effects of satisfaction variables on tax morale. We start with the variable FINANCIAL SATISFACTION,[14] which is more strongly related to tax payments. If the financial situation in a household is poor, tax payments might be seen as a severe restriction of their possibility set, which might reduce tax honesty. To get a broader view, we include the variables SATISFACTION[15] and HAPPINESS.[16] Table 6.5 presents the results. All three variables significantly affect tax morale in a positive way. Interestingly, the variable HAPPINESS has the highest marginal effects.

CONCLUSIONS

There are a couple of publications about the informal sector in Latin America, but hardly any study that has analysed tax morale. Most of the empirical evidence is centred on the United States, evaluating, for example, the TCMP program or amnesty data. Thus, it is difficult to know to what extent findings from the United States can be transferred to other countries. Furthermore, audit and amnesty data have a selection bias, as only specific individuals participate in an amnesty, and not all individuals (especially tax evaders) are measured using audit data. Our data sets have also the advantage that they include a broad variety of socio-economic data. Working with two data sets (Latinobarómetro and World Values Survey) allows us to gain a robust picture of tax morale in Latin America. These two data sets offer the possibility of carrying out a more refined study covering more than one year.

Our findings indicate that there is a significant correlation between tax morale and the size of the shadow economy. Looking at individuals' perceptions of reasons for tax evasion, we find that the tax burden, the lack of honesty and corruption are seen as the main factors. A tax system must be fair from the taxpayers' viewpoint. If a taxpayer feels that he or she is in some sort of unfair contract, he or she will probably be less likely to comply. As Smith (1992) argues, cycles of antagonism between the tax administration and the taxpayer might begin to break down following a positive concession by the administrator. Taxpayers are more inclined to

Table 6.5 Tax morale and satisfaction (WVS, 1995–1997) (weighted ordered probit)

	Equation 5		Equation 6		Equation 7		Equation 8	
	Coeff.	Marg.	Coeff.	Marg.	Coeff.	Marg.	Coeff.	Marg.
(a) Demographic variables	Included		Included		Included		Included	
(b) Marital status	Included		Included		Included		Included	
(c) Employment status	Included		Included		Included		Included	
(d) Economic situation								
INCOME	Included		Included		Included		0.052^{***}	0.019
(e) Religiosity	Included		Included		Included		Included	
(f) Regional variable								
MEXICO	-0.302^{***}	-0.111	-0.306^{***}	-0.112	-0.256^{***}	-0.094	-0.292^{***}	-0.108
DOMINICAN REPUBLIC	0.289^{***}	0.106	0.277^{***}	0.102	0.299^{***}	0.110	0.289^{***}	0.107
(g) Satisfaction								
FINANCIAL SATISFACTION	0.018^{***}	0.006						
SATISFACTION			0.038^{***}	0.014				
HAPPINESS					0.199^{***}	0.073		
Number of observations	7572		7580		7572		7052	
Prob(LM-statistic)	0.000		0.000		0.000		0.000	

Notes: Dependent variable: tax morale on a four–point scale. In the reference group are AGE 16–29, MALE, SINGLE, FULL TIME EMPLOYED, LOWER CLASS and SOUTH AMERICA. Significance levels: * $0.05 < p < 0.10$; ** $0.01 < p < 0.05$; *** $p < 0.01$. Marginal effect = highest tax morale score (3).

comply with the law if the exchange between the tax paid and the performed government services is found to be equitable.

In our multivariate analysis, we used entire pooled samples to check the robustness of the findings. We could observe a significantly lower tax morale in South America and Mexico than in the Central America/Caribbean area. Mexico in particular has a very low tax morale. Furthermore, people who said they knew, or had heard about, practised tax avoidance had a significantly lower tax morale than others. On the other hand, if people believed that others were obeying the law, their intrinsic motivation to pay taxes increased. In general, the findings show that a tax policy should maintain a high level of social capital. If people believe that others are honest, their willingness to pay taxes increases. Otherwise, the government and the tax administration get into hot water, as the tax morale of individuals who notice that many others evade taxes is reduced. Evasion is a signal that intrinsic motivation is not approved. Thus, taxpayers get the feeling that they can also be opportunistic and the moral costs of evading taxes decrease.

In general, the results indicate that there are alternative tax policy strategies to those that assume that people are knaves, who must be controlled to reduce their self-interested behaviour and thus tax evasion. It is not necessary to develop a constitution designed for knaves. Tax law should consider the 'spirit of trust'; in other words, it should include specific rules such as self-declaration, which gives taxpayers more scope of their own and supports trustfulness as a motivation to pay taxes. Trust in the president and the officials, the belief that other individuals obey the law and a pro-democratic attitude have a significant positive effect on tax morale. The government and the tax administration have to create confidence in their credibility and their capacity to deliver promised returns for taxes. The relationship between taxpayers and tax authorities, seen as a relational or psychological contract, involves strong emotional ties and loyalties. Such a psychological tax contract can be maintained by positive actions, based on trust (see Feld and Frey, 2002b). If such rules yield good results and taxpayers make their decisions to comply with taxation according to past experiences, the social capital associated with paying taxes can be created or maintained.

NOTES

1. In 1991, important reforms were enacted in Peru, creating an increase in revenues measured as a percentage of the GDP. The tax administration (the Superintendencia Nacional de Administracion Tributaria) reduced its workforce while implementing higher standards, and increased salaries to be competitive with the private sector (Bejaković, 2000).

2. The low tax morale in Mexico corresponds to the low revenue performance (also compared to other developing countries), despite the fact the tax structure is comparable to those of many OECD countries. Martinez-Vazquez (2001) tries to explain this so-called paradox. As he mentions, the modern tax system structure is undermined by factors such as (i) *ad hoc* policy measures, (ii) the lack of ability of tax administrations to deal with a modern tax system, and (iii) the policy of the Mexican authorities to keep tax efforts (measured as the ratio of revenues to GDP) relatively constant, which derives from an agreement between the government and the private sector.
3. The following question has been asked: 'In general, would you say that people always obey the law, or are there exceptions or particular occasions when people can follow their consciences even if it means breaking the law?' (1 = always obey the law, 0 = follow their consciences)
4. The Latinobarómetro has asked respondents the following question: 'Would you say that it is very possible, fairly, a little, or not at all possible that a person in our country who has committed an illegal act gets caught?'
5. Trust in government has been measured as follows: 'Please tell me how much confidence you have in the president' (1 = not at all, 4 = a lot).
6. It is interesting to note that Mexico has had many tax reforms. However, it seems that too many reforms can produce instability in the tax system. In Mexico, reforms took place in 1978–80, 1983, 1985, 1986, 1988, 1989, 1990–91, 1993, 1994, 1995–97 and 1998 (Martinez-Vazquez, 2001, p. 29). Martinez-Vazquez (2001) points out that the instability of the tax system makes tax enforcement more difficult and might lead to lower tax revenues. Changes demand too much of the tax administration, create uncertainty and confusion among taxpayers, and increase tax compliance costs. Contrary to other Latin American countries, Mexico has a very modern tax revenue structure based on income tax as the most important source of revenue (31 per cent of total federal revenues in 1998).
7. Socio-economic status (4 = very good, 1 = very bad).
8. As a proxy for FORTUNE, we take the aggregated sum of the following factors: colour TV, freezer, computer, washing machine, phone, car, second house, drinking water and sewage system (value 0 to 9).
9. We have developed a religiosity variable from the following question in the WVS: 'Independently of whether you go to church or not, would you say you are a religious person (value 3), not a religious person (2), a confirmed atheist (1)?'
10. Empirical evidence from Switzerland presented by Pommerehne and Weck-Hannemann (1996) shows that in cantons with a high degree of direct political control, tax evasion is – *ceteris paribus* – about SFr1500 lower as compared to the average of the cantons without such direct influence. Furthermore, using two different data sets at the individual level (the World Values Survey and the International Social Survey Programme), Torgler (2005) found that direct democratic rights had a significantly positive effect on tax morale (see also Chapter 5).
11. The question is: 'Would you say that having a democratic political system is a very good (4), fairly good (3), fairly bad (2) or very bad (1) way of governing this country?' (scale 1 to 4)
12. 'Democracy may have problems but it's better than any other form of government.' (4 = strongly agree, 1 = strongly disagree).
13. How proud are you to be …? (substitute your own nationality for …, 1 = not at all proud, 4 = very proud).
14. How satisfied are you with the financial situation of your household? (scale 1 = dissatisfied to 10=satisfied).
15. All things considered, how satisfied are you with your life as a whole these days? (scale 1 = dissatisfied to 10 = satisfied)
16. Taking all things together, would you say you are: very happy (4), quite happy (3), not very happy (2), not at all happy (1)?

REFERENCES

Adams, C. (1993), *For Good and Evil. The Impact of Taxes on the Course of Civilization*, London: Madison Books.

Ajzen, I. and Fishbein, M. (1980), *Understanding Attitudes and Predicting Social Behaviour*, Englewood Cliffs: Prentice-Hall.

Alm, J. and J. Martinez-Vazquez (2003), 'Institutions, paradigms, and tax evasion in developing and transition countries', in J. Martinez-Vazquez and J. Alm (eds), *Public Finance in Developing and Transition Countries. Essays in Honor of Richard Bird*, Cheltenham, UK and Northampton, MA, USA: Edward Elgar.

Bahl, R. and J. Martinez-Vazquez (1992), 'The nexus of tax administration and tax policy in Jamaica and Guatemala', in M. Casanegra de Jantscher and R.M. Bird (eds), *Improving Tax Administration in Developing Countries*, Washington, DC: International Monetary Fund, pp. 66–110.

Bejaković, P. (2000), 'Improving the tax administration in transition countries', paper presented at the Conference Global Entrepreneurship in the New Millenium, School of Management Syracuse University, Syracuse, New York, August 2000.

Burgess, R. and N. Stern (1993), 'Taxation and Development', *Journal of Economic Literature*, **31**, 762–830.

Cabezas, R.M. (1992), 'Comments to: Tax administration reform in Bolivia and Uruguay'. In M. Casanegra de Jantscher and R.M. Bird (eds), *Improving Tax Administration in Developing Countries*, Washington, DC: International Monetary Fund, pp. 60–65.

Casanegra de Jantscher, M. and R.M. Bird (1992), 'The reform of tax administration', in M. Casanegra de Jantscher and R.M. Bird (eds), *Improving Tax Administration in Developing Countries*, Washington, DC: International Monetary Fund, pp. 1–18.

Das-Gupta, A. and D. Mookherjee (1995), 'Reforming Indian income tax enforcement', IED Discussion Paper Series, No. 52, Institute for Economic Development, Boston University.

de Soto, H. (1989), *The Other Path. The Invisible Revolution in the Third World*, New York: Harper & Row.

de Soto, H. (2000), *The Mystery of Capital: Why Capitalism Triumphs in the West and Fails Everywhere Else*, New York: Basic Books.

Feld, L.P. and Frey, B.S. (2002a), 'The tax authority and the taxpayer. An exploratory analysis', paper presented the 2002 Annual Meeting of the European Public Choice Society Belgirate.

Feld, L.P. and Frey, B.S. (2002b), 'Trust breeds trust: how taxpayers are treated', *Economics of Governance*, **3**, 87–99.

Frey, B.S. (1997), *Not Just for the Money. An Economic Theory of Personal Motivation*, Cheltenham, UK and Lyme, USA: Edward Elgar.

Frey, B.S. and R. Eichenberger (1999), *The New Democratic Federalism for Europe*, Cheltenham, UK and Northampton, MA, USA: Edward Elgar.

Frey, B.S. and A. Stutzer (2002), *Happiness and Economics. How the Economy and Institutions Affect Well-Being*, Princeton: Princeton University Press.

Frey, B.S. and B. Torgler (2007), 'Tax morale and conditional cooperation', *Journal of Comparative Economics*, **35**, 136–59.

Hindriks, J., M. Keen and A. Muthoo (1999), 'Corruption, extortion and evasion', *Journal of Public Economics*, **74**, 395–430.

Hirschi, T. and R. Stark (1969), 'Hellfire and delinquency', *Social Problems*, **17**, 202–13.
Hull, B.B. and F. Bold (1994), 'Hell, religion, and cultural change', *Journal of Institutional and Theoretical Economics*, **150**, 447–64.
Jain, A.K. (2001), 'Corruption: a review', *Journal of Economic Surveys*, **15**, 71–121.
Jenkins, G.P. (1995), 'Perspectives for tax policy reform in Latin America in the 1990's', working paper, Harvard Institute for International Development (HIID).
Lewis, A. (1982), *The Psychology of Taxation*, Oxford: Martin Robertson.
Lind, E.A. and Tyler, T.R. (1988), *The Social Psychology of Procedural Justice*, New York: Plenum Press.
Lipford, J., R.E. McCormick and R.D. Tollison (1993), 'Preaching matters', *Journal of Economic Behavior and Organization*, **21**, 235–50.
Martinez-Vazquez, J. (2001), 'Mexico: an evaluation of the main features of the tax administration', Working Paper 01–12, Georgia State University, Atlanta.
McLure, C. Jr. and S.R. Pardo (1992), 'Improving the administration of the Colombian Income Tax', in M. Casanegra de Jantscher and R.M. Bird (eds), *Improving Tax Administration In Developing Countries*, Washington, DC: International Monetary Fund, pp. 66–110.
Orviska, M. and J. Hudson (2002), 'Tax evasion, civic duty and the law abiding citizen', *European Journal of Political Economy*, **19**, 83–102.
Pommerehne, W.W. and H. Weck-Hannemann (1996), 'Tax rates, tax administration and income tax evasion in Switzerland', *Public Choice*, **88**, 161–70.
Pyle, D.J. (1993), 'The economics of taxpayer compliance', in P.M. Jackson (ed.), *Current Issues in Public Sector Economics*, Houndsmills: Macmillan, pp. 58–93.
Rose-Ackerman, S. (1997), 'The political economy of corruption', in K.A. Elliott (ed.), *Corruption and the Global Economy*, Washington, DC: Institute for International Economics, pp. 31–60.
Schneider, F. (2002), 'The size and development of the shadow economies and shadow economy labor force of 16 Central and South American and 21 OECD countries: first results for the 90s', working paper, Johannes Kepler University of Linz.
Silvani, C.A. and A.H.J. Radano (1992), 'Tax administration reform in Bolivia and Uruguay', in M. Casanegra de Jantscher and R.M. Bird (eds), *Improving Tax Administration in Developing Countries*, Washington: International Monetary Fund, pp. 19–59.
Smith, K.W. (1992), 'Reciprocity and fairness: positive incentives for tax compliance', in J. Slemrod (ed.), *Why People Pay Taxes. Tax Compliance and Enforcement*, Ann Arbor: University of Michigan Press, pp. 223–58.
Spicer, M.W. (1986), 'Civilisation at a discount: the problem of tax evasion', *Journal of Public Economics*, **46**, 13–20.
Tanzi, V. (2000), *Policies, Institutions and the Dark Side of Economics*, Cheltenham, UK and Northampton, MA, USA: Edward Elgar.
Tanzi, V. and Zee, H. H. (2000), 'Tax policy for emerging markets: developing countries', *National Tax Journal*, **53**, 299–322.
Torgler, B. (2001a), 'Is tax evasion never justifiable?', *Journal of Public Finance and Public Choice*, **XIX**: 143–68.
Torgler, B. (2001b), 'What do we know about tax morale and tax compliance?', *RISEC: International Review of Economics and Business*, **48**, 395–419.

Torgler, B. (2003), 'Tax morale and tax evasion: evidence from the United States', WWZ-Discussion Paper 03/01, Basel: WWZ.

Torgler, B. (2005), 'Tax morale and direct democracy', *European Journal of Political Economy*, **21**, 525–31.

Tyler, T.R. and K.M. McGraw (1986), 'Ideology and the interpretation of personal experience: procedural justice and political quiescence', *Journal of Social Issues*, **42**, 115–28.

Tyler, T.R., J.D. Casper and B. Fisher (1989), 'Maintaining allegiance toward political authorities: the role of prior attitudes and the use of fair procedures', *American Journal of Political Science*, **33**, 629–52.

Weck, H. (1983), *Schattenwirtschaft: Eine Möglichkeit zur Einschränkung der öffentlichen Verwaltung? Eine ökonomische Analyse*, Finanzwissenschaftliche Schriften 22, Bern: Lang.

7. Does culture matter? A comparison of tax morale in the former East and West Germany

INTRODUCTION

The purpose of this chapter is to analyse tax morale in the former East and West Germany. Before starting with the empirical discussion, the next section analyses whether there is a cultural difference between the two parts of the country. The empirical discussion in the third section starts with a descriptive analysis to see whether there is a difference between the former East and West Germany. As observed differences might be explained in terms of specific differences, in the second part of the section multiple regressions are conducted. First, cross-sections of individuals in each part of the country are analysed separately for the year 1997. This helps us to analyse factors that influence tax morale. In a second step, we check whether there is a significant difference between the former East and West Germany. In a third step, we will do the same comparison with data from 1990, just after reunification. After focusing on the differences between east and west, we will analyse the development of tax morale over time. Such a comparison is interesting, due to the historical event of German reunification following the fall of the Berlin Wall on 9 November 1989. Eastern and western taxpayers grew up in different social environments. German reunification allows us better to isolate so-called cultural factors from other factors and is close to a natural experiment. Many factors can be controlled because they are similar, such as as, for example, a common language, similar education systems and a shared cultural and political history prior to the separation after the Second World War. As a consequence, a comparison between the former East and West Germany has a methodological advantage compared to cross-country studies.

IS THERE A CULTURAL DIFFERENCE BETWEEN THE FORMER EAST AND WEST GERMANY?

Culture is a difficult term to define. Henrich et al. (1999) define culture as

> information stored in people's heads, which can be transmitted among individuals. This information can be thought of as the ideas, values, beliefs, behavioural strategies, perceptual models and organizational structures that reside in individual brains, and can be learned by other individuals through imitation, observation (plus inference), interaction, discussion and/or teaching (p. 2).

According to Kasper and Streit (1999, p. 162), culture bridges the tension between individuals and the social group, and hinges on learned institutions and their underpinned values. Similar to Henrich et al. (1999), they see culture as a kind of language that is based on rule systems, such as ideas, values, internal institutions such as customs and conventions and external institutions. It covers the tools, techniques, works of art, rituals and symbols. They point out that 'We may thus see culture as a largely implicit rule system that is underpinned by symbols and other reminders of its institutional content' (p. 162).

Henrich et al. (1999) argue that cultural transmission mechanisms provide a means of solving the problem of co-operation, building a mechanism similar to conformism, which creates a force that maintains common behaviour and thus maintains co-operation. Thus, an essential question in the tax compliance context is whether culture influences co-operation, solidarity or, as we will analyse using World Values Survey data, tax morale. Tax morale reflects whether complying with the law is a social norm. The German reunification allows us to analyse the effects of different cultures on tax morale using two World Values Survey waves. A comparison between the former East and West Germany might provide important insights into the effects of social norms. Ockenfels and Weimann (1999) report that there is the common belief that former East Germans are still more co-operative and less selfish than former West Germans. Many people in the eastern part miss the solidarity and co-operative spirit that was present in the years before reunification. Ockenfels and Weimann (1999) conducted public good and solidarity experiments in the former East and West Germany. They found differences in co-operation and solidarity. Former East Germans were less co-operative than former West Germans. They argue that socialistic systems create a social dilemma:

> Individual effort to expand production was not rewarded and therefore not rational. Each person had to develop strategies to overcome the scarcity resulting from the unsolved dilemma (p. 285).

Thus, people were *forced* to defect. Furthermore, the authors point out that possibly, after the reunification, selfish behaviour was seen as linked to the free market-oriented system, thus justifying selfish behaviour.

Mummert and Schneider (2002, p. 292) report a significantly lower share of black labour in the former East Germany than in the former West Germany. In the east, only 12.9 per cent stated that they had been working in the shadow economy, compared to 24.5 per cent in the west. Furthermore, in 1997 the German institute Forschungsstelle für empirische Sozialökonomik conducted a survey in the former West and East Germany. The authors defined tax morale in a similar way as we do: 'tax evasion is morally not justifiable at all'. The results show that in 1997 eastern taxpayers had a higher tax morale than western taxpayers. Sixty-six per cent of eastern individuals agreed with this statement, compared to 53 per cent in former West Germany. Compared to this study, we will use higher sample units for both regions and analyse tax morale as a dependent variable with multivariate regressions, controlling for many factors in order to avoid biased estimates.

Social norms are learned through daily experience. An important aim of the GDR regime was adherence to norms. The regime served as norm entrepreneurs. The East German regime tried to integrate the population into its structure (e.g. mass organizations). Interpreting their findings, Mummert and Schneider (2002) point out that living in a totalitarian state for many years had led to a deep trust in authority as people gradually internalized norms that are forced to be respected for years. Once the norms of honesty are internalized, a person feels guilty when not acting according to them. Thus, people develop a preference for not violating social norms (Posner, 2000). Polinsky and Shavell (2000) argue that social norms can be seen as a general alternative to law enforcement in channelling individuals' behaviour. The violation of social norms has consequences such as internal sanctions (guilt, remorse) or external legal and social sanctions and as gossip and ostracism. The results of Mummert and Schneider (2002) show the effects of social norm enforcements. Former East Germans had a higher inclination to want actors in the shadow economy to be punished. Such a norm enforcement 'might as well be the outcome of a "public reflex"cultivated over decades in a socialist system where differing private opinions had no right to exist' (p. 300).

If norms are learned, we would expect tax morale to decrease in the East over time and to increase with age, as individuals were exposed for a longer time to an environment in which social norm adherence was important. Our empirical data analysis will help to analyse this point.

DATA ANALYSIS

Descriptive Statistics

First, we will analyse whether there are different levels of tax morale in the former East and West Germany, presenting descriptive statistics. To assess the level of tax morale, we use the following question: 'Please tell me for the following statement whether you think it can always be justified, never be justified, or something in between: ... "Cheating on tax if you have the chance".' The question leads to a ten-point scale index of tax morale with the two extreme points 'never justified' and 'always justified'. The ten-point scale has been recoded into a four-point scale (0,1,2,3), with the value 3 standing for 'never justifiable'. Values 4–10 have been integrated in the value 0 due to a lack of variance. In order to analyse the development over time, we display in Figure 7.1 a histogram that refers to the distribution of tax morale scores in the former East and West Germany for the year 1990, and in Figure 7.2 the distribution for the year 1997. We can observe that there is a difference between east and west. In both years, former East Germans reported a higher tax morale than former West Germans. In East Germany in 1990, 67.2 per cent of the respondents considered that tax evasion was never justifiable, compared to 40 per cent in West Germany. However, we can observe a decay over time in the former East Germans' highest tax morale score, from 67.2 per cent in 1990 to 53.7 per cent in 1997. On the other hand, tax morale development in the former West Germany seems to be quite stable.

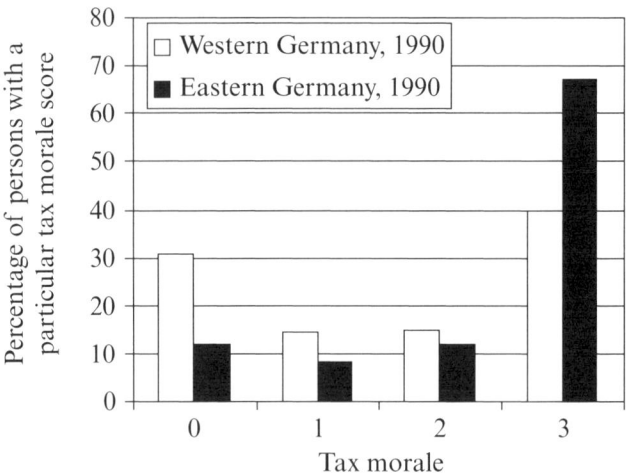

Figure 7.1   Tax morale in eastern and western Germany in 1990

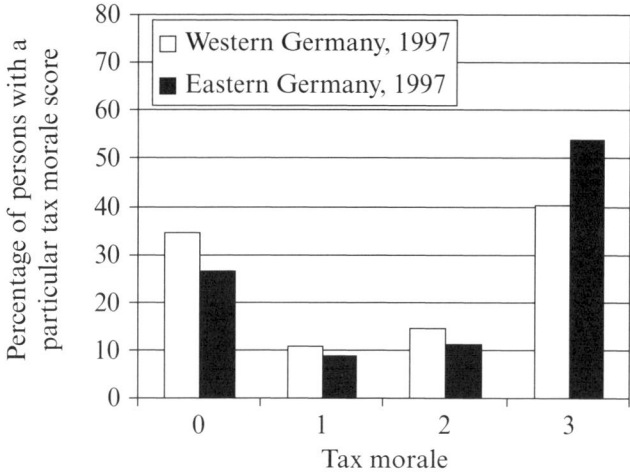

Figure 7.2   Tax morale in eastern and western Germany in 1997

We test the hypothesis of whether our different samples have the same distribution using the Wilcoxon rank-sum test (Mann–Whitney). The results presented in Table 7.1 indicate that there is a significant difference between the former East and West Germany for both years, with higher z-values for the year 1990. Furthermore, tax morale has significantly decreased over time in the east, contrary to the west, where no significant difference is observed. However, it should be noted that a descriptive analysis provides information about the raw effects and not the partial effects. The observed differences between east and west might be explained in terms of differences in socio-demographic and socio-economic factors. Multiple regressions will be conducted, which help to disentangle the effects of socio-demographic and socio-economic factors from a possible cultural difference.

Table 7.1   The two-sample Wilcoxon rank-sum (Mann–Whitney) test

Hypothesis	z-value	Prob > $|z|$
H_0: TM Western Germany 1990 = TM Eastern Germany 1990	–16.159	0.000
H_0: TM Western Germany 1997 = TM Eastern Germany 1997	–5.602	0.000
H_0: TM Eastern Germany 1990 = TM Eastern Germany 1997	–7.914	0.000
H_0: TM Western Germany 1990 = TM Western Germany 1997	0.812	0.417

Note: TM = tax morale.

Can we also observe a high tax morale in other societies that experienced communist rule? The World Values Survey allows us to analyse the degree of tax morale in other transition countries. We will differentiate between the Former Soviet Union (FSU) and Central/Eastern European (CEE) countries. In Table 7.2 we present the descriptive analysis, showing in column 2, for

Table 7.2 Tax morale in transition countries

Countries	Tax evasion is never justifiable (%)		Mean	
	1990–1993	1995–1997	1990–1993	1995–1997
Eastern Germany	67.2	53.7	2.344	1.919
Former Soviet Union				
Armenia		41.1		1.508
Azerbaijan		47.8		1.634
Belarus	44.4	40.7	1.617	1.518
Estonia	64.6	42.4	2.250	1.560
Georgia		49.7		1.760
Latvia	64.4	31.3	2.155	1.379
Lithuania	57.0	46.1	2.089	1.687
Moldova		39.0		1.426
Russia	54.2	46.4	1.857	1.662
Ukraine		41.4		1.558
Average	56.9	42.8	1.994	1.576
Central and Eastern Europe				
Bulgaria	57.4	65.3	2.038	2.240
Bosnia		56.4		2.172
Croatia		36.6		1.309
Hungary	56.3		1.913	
Macedonia		61.4		2.109
Montenegro		48.4		1.749
Poland	49.3	55.2	1.829	2.001
Romania	67.7		2.308	
Slovenia	68.5	53.9	2.296	1.913
Serbia		56.0		1.969
Average	60	52.7	2.077	1.718

Notes: Own calculations from the World Values Surveys. Second column: percentage of individuals saying that tax evasion is 'never justified'. Third column: the mean of the degree of tax morale, scaled from 0 to 3, where 3 means the highest tax morale.

each country, the percentage of individuals who say that tax evasion is never justifiable, and in column 3 the mean value for all countries based on the same scale used for the former East and West Germany (0 to 3, where 3 is the highest tax morale). The tax morale in the former East Germany compared to other former communist countries is quite high, exceeding the average tax morale in FSU and CEE in both years. In general, CEE countries show a higher tax morale than FSU countries. Furthermore, we can see a decay of tax morale over time, similar to the findings in the former East Germany. This effect is much stronger for FSU than for CEE countries.

Model and Variables

The World Values Survey (WVS) allows us to analyse many factors and thus better isolate a possible cultural factor. Thus, personality and demographic factors should be integrated into a multiple regression analysis. As the dependent variable we use tax morale. The reported tax morale can be modelled in a micro-econometric tax morale function, $TM_{it} = \alpha + \beta X_{it} + \varepsilon_{it}$, which is estimated by ordered probit or logit. In this subsection, we will focus on the independent variables $X = x_1 + x_2 + \ldots + x_n$. These variables are socio-demographic and socio-economic characteristics, as well as formal and information constraints (e.g. institutions, social norms) on individual i at time t. The specifications used are in line with those used in the previous chapter (see also Table A7.1 in the Appendix).

Results

First, we will use WVS data from 1997. The determinants of tax morale are analysed using least-squares and ordered probit models. The ordered probit models help us to analyse the ranking information of the scaled dependent variable tax morale. Table 7.3 presents the estimated coefficients and marginal effects for the former West and East Germany, taking into account demographic and economic determinants. As in the ordered probit estimation, the equation has a non-linear form, so that only the sign of the coefficient can be directly interpreted and not its size. Calculating the marginal effects is therefore a method of finding the quantitative effect that a variable has on tax morale. The marginal effect indicates the change in the share of taxpayers (or the probability of) belonging to a specific tax morale level, when the independent variable increases by one unit. In the weighted ordered probit estimation, only the marginal effects for the highest value, 'tax evasion is never justified', are shown.

As we can see in Table 7.3, most results are robust regarding the estimation methods. The least-squares estimations with tax morale as a cardinal

Table 7.3 *Determinants of tax morale in western and eastern Germany, 1997*

	Equation 1 Western Germany						Equation 1 Eastern Germany					
	Least squares			Ordered probit			Least squares			Ordered probit		
Variable	Coeff.	t-Stat.	Coeff.	z-Stat.	Marg.		Coeff.	t-Stat.	Coeff.	z-Stat.	Marg.	
(a) Demographic factors												
AGE 30–49	−0.076	−0.596	−0.071	−0.608	−0.027		0.473***	2.974	0.436***	2.914	0.173	
AGE 50–64	0.114	0.650	0.119	0.743	0.046		0.711***	3.861	0.656***	3.694	0.260	
AGE 65+	0.116	0.434	0.148	0.592	0.057		0.950***	3.733	0.860***	3.329	0.341	
FEMALE	0.179*	1.677	0.152	1.539	0.059		0.113	1.220	0.112	1.235	0.444	
EDUCATION	−0.066***	−3.075	−0.060***	−3.051	−0.023		−0.055***	−2.502	−0.062***	−2.796	−0.024	
(b) Economic variable												
INCOME	−0.038*	−1.652	−0.041*	−1.906	−0.016		−0.004	−0.151	−0.002	−0.069	−0.001	
(c) Marital status												
MARRIED	0.459***	3.320	0.432***	3.391	0.166		0.243	1.526	0.221	1.433	0.087	
LIVING TOGETHER	0.364**	2.051	0.329**	1.991	0.127		0.375**	2.014	0.345*	1.875	0.137	
DIVORCED	0.426**	1.986	0.405**	2.117	0.156		0.245	1.114	0.193	0.876	0.077	
SEPARATED	−0.207	−0.528	−0.201	−0.547	−0.077		−0.080	−0.203	−0.067	−0.194	−0.027	
WIDOWED	0.316	1.398	0.305	1.430	0.117		−0.180	−0.765	−0.194	−0.849	−0.077	

(d) Employment status

PART TIME EMPLOYED	−0.001	−0.004	−0.004	−0.034	−0.008	−0.117	−0.536	−0.119	−0.605 −0.047
SELF-EMPLOYED	−0.297	−0.854	−0.283	−0.865	−0.109	−0.654**	−2.363	−0.550**	−2.192 −0.218
UNEMPLOYED	−0.032	−0.128	−0.074	−0.319	−0.029	0.226	1.623	0.210	1.552 0.083
AT HOME	−0.029	−0.170	−0.043	−0.279	−0.017	0.305	0.838	0.154	0.397 0.061
STUDENT	−0.309	−1.605	−0.300	−1.607	−0.115	−0.131	−0.520	−0.045	−0.183 −0.018
RETIRED	0.315	1.472	0.275	1.371	0.106	0.222	1.282	0.268	1.510 0.106
OTHER	0.140	0.268	0.217	0.418	0.008	0.497	1.512	0.533	1.523 0.211
Number of observations	768					784			
Prob(F-statistic)	0.000					0.000			
Prob(LM-statistic)			0.000					0.000	

Notes: Dependent variable: tax morale on a four-point scale. In the reference group are AGE 16–29, MALE, SINGLE and FULL TIME EMPLOYED. Significance levels: * $0.05 < p < 0.10$; ** $0.01 < p < 0.05$; *** $p < 0.01$.

variable yield results quite similar to those of the ordered probit model. It is interesting to observe that we find a sizeably different impact of the age profile on tax morale. While not significant in the West, it exerts a hugely significant influence on tax morale in the East. The marginal effects increase with an increase in age. Thus, the group aged 65 and above reports the highest tax morale of all groups. The proportion of persons aged 65+ and more who report the highest tax morale is 34.1 percentage points higher than for the reference age group (age 16–29). In the least-squares estimation for the former East Germany, the tax morale score reported by individuals between 50 and 64 is on average around 0.7 points higher than the one for the reference group.

In the former West and East Germany, education has a significant negative effect on tax morale. An increase in education by one unit reduces the share of persons indicating that tax evasion is never justifiable by more than two percentage points. In both countries, females mostly do not report a significantly higher tax morale than males. Looking at the marital status, married people, couples who live together and divorced individuals have a higher tax morale compared to singles in the former West Germany. On the other hand, in the former East Germany there is a significant difference only between couples who live together and singles. In the former West Germany, the employment status has no significant effect on tax morale. Interestingly, only self-employed persons in the former East Germany have a significantly lower tax morale than full-time employees. Being self-employed rather than a full-time employee lowers the probability of a person stating that tax evasion is never justifiable by 21.8 percentage points.

East–West Differences in Tax Morale?

In a next step, we will check first whether there is a significant difference in tax morale between the former East and West Germany. The descriptive analysis has shown a significant difference between east and west. However, as already mentioned, we will test whether these results remain robust controlling for other confounding influences such as age, education or income. It might be interesting to analyse first whether there is a difference just after reunification. Thus, we will put the data together and check the differences using a dummy variable for people living in the eastern part of Germany. As the income variable has been scaled differently in the east and the west, we have excluded it from the equations.[1] However, to get a proxy for the economic situation, in Equation 4 we have integrated a variable where people had to classify themselves (lower class, working class, lower middle class, upper middle class or upper class).

Our first estimation (Equation 2) findings in Table 7.4 indicate that tax morale is significantly higher among eastern taxpayers. Only the marginal effects for the highest value (tax morale is never justifiable) are shown. The probability of inhabitants of the former East Germany stating the highest tax morale is 27.0 per cent higher than for those living in the west. For inhabitants of the former East Germany, the probability of a person stating the highest tax morale is increased by 27.9 percentage points. Thus, the findings show that tax morale is unambiguously higher in the east. Furthermore, the age coefficients suggest that an increase in the age level has a positive effect on tax morale, as the marginal effects increase from a lower age group to a higher one. However, as we have pooled the observations from the east and the west, the great differences between the age profiles in the east and the west can produce biases regarding the dummy variable EAST in Table 7.4. To control this problem, we have built interaction terms to Equation 3 and 4. The EAST dummy then captures the differential for the reference group (individuals below age 30). It can be supposed that the effect of cultural differences depends on the age profile in the east. As young people in 1990 had hardly been influenced by western society, it could be hypothesized that younger former East German citizens have a higher tax morale than younger former West Germans. The results show a significant difference between East and West in the age category below 30, with high marginal effects.

We will now analyse whether the significant difference observed between East and West can also be found for the year 1997. If social norms are learned through daily experience as discussed in the second section, we should observe a decay of norms internalized in the GDR regime era. Furthermore, we might expect that older citizens in the East have been more influenced by the norm indoctrination of the GDR regime. The results in Table 7.5 show that the east–west difference has strongly diminished. While the marginal effect of the EAST dummy was 0.297 in 1990, it is only 0.076 in 1997. Thus, in seven years around three-quarters of the east–west differential disappeared. Furthermore, the interaction terms in Equations 3 and 4 indicate that most of the reduction comes from the youngest eastern age group. There is no statistically significant difference between the youngest easterners (16–29) and their western counterparts. The results are in line with the expectations that younger individuals in the east, who were less exposed to the GDR regime, behave more like their counterparts in the west than the older citizens. On the other hand, older eastern citizens still display a higher tax morale than their western counterparts.

Table 7.4 A comparison of eastern and western Germany in 1990 (weighted ordered probit)

	Coeff.	z-Stat.	Marg.	Coeff.	z-Stat.	Marg.	Coeff.	z-Stat.	Marg.
	2			3			4		
(a) Demographic variables									
AGE 30–49	0.145**	2.396	0.058	0.086	1.299	0.034	0.069	1.036	0.028
AGE 50–64	0.389***	5.537	0.155	0.318***	4.170	0.127	0.297***	3.868	0.119
AGE 65+	0.510***	5.047	0.203	0.417***	3.995	0.167	0.404***	3.863	0.161
OTHER FACTORS	Yes			Yes			Yes		
(b) Economic variable							Yes		
(c) Marital status	Yes			Yes			Yes		
(d) Employment status	Yes			Yes			Yes		
(e) Culture effect									
EASTERN	0.699***	12.186	0.279	0.543***	5.149	0.217	0.547***	5.168	0.218
AGE 30–49*EASTERN				0.159	1.170	0.064	0.172	1.257	0.068
AGE 50–64*EASTERN				0.210	1.311	0.084	0.221	1.377	0.088
AGE 65+*EASTERN				0.364*	1.940	0.145	0.348*	1.836	0.139
Number of observations	3340			3340			3340		
Prob(LM-statistic)	0.000			0.000			0.000		

Notes: Dependent variable: tax morale on a four-point scale. In the reference group are AGE 16–29, MALE, SINGLE, FULL TIME EMPLOYED, WORKING CLASS and WESTERN. Significance levels: * $0.05 < p < 0.10$; ** $0.01 < p < 0.05$; *** $p < 0.01$.

Table 7.5 A comparison of eastern and western Germany in 1997 (weighted ordered probit)

	Coeff.	z-Stat.	Marg.	Coeff.	z-Stat.	Marg.	Coeff.	z-Stat.	Marg.
	2			3			4		
(a) Demographic variables									
AGE 30–49	0.088	1.056	0.035	−0.074	−0.733	−0.029	−0.082	−0.762	−0.033
AGE 50–64	0.286***	2.698	0.114	0.105	0.790	0.042	0.022	0.156	0.009
AGE 65+	0.306**	1.967	0.122	0.133	0.753	0.053	0.010	0.053	0.004
OTHER FACTORS	Yes			Yes			Yes		
(b) Economic variable							Yes		
(c) Marital status	Yes			Yes			Yes		
(d) Employment status	Yes			Yes			Yes		
(e) Culture effect									
EASTERN	0.190***	3.308	0.076	−0.148	−1.304	−0.059	−0.117	−0.954	−0.047
AGE 30–49*EASTERN				0.426***	3.037	0.169	0.405***	2.711	0.161
AGE 50–64*EASTERN				0.456***	2.743	0.181	0.486***	2.780	0.194
AGE 65+*EASTERN				0.478**	2.492	0.190	0.500**	2.431	0.199
Number of observations	1947			1947			1782		
Prob(LM–statistic)	0.000			0.000			0.000		

Notes: Dependent variable: tax morale on a four-point scale. In the reference group are AGE 16–29, MALE, SINGLE, FULL TIME EMPLOYED, LOWER CLASS and WESTERN. Significance levels: * $0.05 < p < 0.10$; ** $0.01 < p < 0.05$; *** $p < 0.01$.

Tax Morale Development over Time

Up to this point, we have focused on the differences between the former East and West Germany. However, Figures 7.1 and 7.2 and the size of the marginal effects obtained in the regression estimations might indicate a decay of tax morale in the former East Germany over time. This would imply that the tax morale difference between east and west has eroded over time. Thus, we will analyse the east and the west separately, building a dummy variable for the year 1997. As education has been coded differently in 1997 and in 1990, this variable has been excluded from the estimation. But since the east and the west are being analysed separately, the income variable can be added. It comes as no surprise that the results in Table 7.6 do not indicate any significant difference between 1990 and 1997 for the former West Germany, but we can observe a decay of tax morale over time in the former East Germany. Inhabitants had a significantly lower probability of reporting the highest tax morale in 1997 than in 1990, with high marginal effects of more than 17 percentage points.

These results might indicate that reunification entailed costs in terms of tax morale for eastern inhabitants. This could be due to the great expectations that East Germans had for the unification process, the introduction of the single currency and the massive federal transfers from west to east. But in the Germany of 1997, GDP per capita in the east was still relatively low, standing at 57 per cent of the Western level, the unemployment rate in the east was twice as high, and wages in the east averaged 75 per cent of the Western level (Hunt, 2000). These results, however, contrast with life satisfaction. Frijters et al. (2004), using the German Socio-Economic Panel (GSOEP) between 1991 and 2001, report that former East Germans experienced a continued improvement in life satisfaction leading to a convergence between East and West Germans.

In general, the results obtained in this chapter should be interpreted with caution. It would be wrong to conclude that the communist system always had a positive effect on tax morale. As we have already seen, tax morale is quite high in the former East Germany compared to other former communist countries (see Table 7.2). Cultural differences cannot be compared by testing tax morale only: other factors such as liberty, freedom and happiness are essential. A lower tax morale can express taxpayers' disagreement. Such behaviour restricts the government's possibility to act as a Leviathan, maximizing its own preferences. Furthermore, if we look at the output variable 'tax evasion', it could be argued that, *per se*, such an exit option is never justifiable. Therefore, it is important to see how the tax rules have been implemented. There is a difference between the tax

Table 7.6 A comparison of western and eastern Germany between the years 1990 and 1997 (weighted ordered probit)

	Western Germany			Eastern Germany		
	Coeff.	z-Stat.	Marg.	Coeff.	z-Stat.	Marg.
		5			6	
(a) Demographic variables	Yes			Yes		
(b) Economic variable	Yes			Yes		
(c) Marital status	Yes			Yes		
(d) Employment status	Yes			Yes		
(e) Culture effect						
Western Germany, 1997	0.097	1.448	0.037			
Eastern Germany, 1997				−0.472***	−7.992	−0.177
Number of observations	2704			2165		
Prob(LM-statistic)	0.000			0.000		

Notes: Dependent variable: tax morale on a four-point scale. In the reference group for West Germany: West Germany 1990; for East Germany: East Germany 1990. As education has been coded differently in 1990 and 1997, the variable has been excluded in the equations. As economic variable, we take income.

rules implemented by a democratically legitimated political process and rules forcefully introduced by a dictator, or by a non-legitimated process or government. Paldam and Svendsen (2001, p. 21) cite Bulat Okudzhava, who stated in 1989: during the past 70 years, a new man has been created who is obedient and easily frightened. 'What has been created over the decades cannot be undone in a day'.

In a dictatorship, there is an intention to control and thus achieve an atomization of human relationships (see Wintrobe, 1998). In the former East Germany, the STASI archives were an example of this kind of control. In the former communist countries, the price for exit or voice was high. If a country is able to produce a high price for exit and voice, it acquires a powerful defence against these two potent weapons by means of which individuals can express their preferences (see Hirschman, 1970). Paldam and Svendsen (2001) argue that a dictatorship such as the communist state created conditions that favoured the building of negative social capital, which may have acted as a brake on economic development as soon as the dictatorship was abolished. Plan fulfilment pressure was high, increasing thus the opportunity costs of non-co-operation. Control mechanisms such as the STASI archive reduce trust, networks and voluntary co-operation among individuals. On the other hand, many individuals had to develop strategies to overcome scarcity, which might have increased solidarity and co-operation in small groups such as families or close friends.

McGee (1996) argues that there is nothing immoral about tax evasion, if tax revenues are collected to finance a dictator's war machine. There could even be a moral duty not to pay taxes (McGee, 1996, pp. 17–18). In authoritarian political systems, elections play a lesser role than in democracies. Thus, people's preferences are less integrated in the political system. Should individuals pay taxes without doubting such a system, which does not take their preferences into account? It can hardly be assumed that all citizens have the same preferences and that these preferences match the goals of the authoritarian state. On the contrary, one would predict that such systems would transfer more benefits to specific groups. Thus, the authoritarian government appropriates more resources for its own use. A high level of resources will be used to seek group support by bribing or by suppressing specific groups (see Frey and Eichenberger, 2001). This tendency can also be seen in the development of the constitution of the German Democratic Republic. In 1949, the first constitution was oriented on the constitution of the Weimar Republic. Twenty years later, it was replaced with a more socialist constitution, with the intention of strengthening the communist regime (see Karsten, 1993).

Furthermore, there might be a bias in the analysis, due to the transition process. In the period from 1991 to 1995, around US$ 440 billion was transferred from west to east (around $26 000 for every inhabitant in the East; see Kasper and Streit, 1999). Former West Germans had to shoulder a high transfer burden, which might negatively influence their tax morale. Positive expectations regarding the transfer process in the former East Germany might influence the survey answers in 1990. The survey was conducted in the autumn of 1990. The first free elections for East Germany were held in March 1990, and showed a strong support for parties that intended to speed up unification with the West. In July 1990, monetary, economic and social union was established. Finally, in October, political union followed (see Hunt, 2000). It could, however, be argued that the considerable transfer of funds to the east would have a positive effect on tax morale, but compared to 1990, no higher tax morale was observed. Cialdini and Trost (1998) argue that people might have felt uncomfortable about receiving a gift, favour, services or aid without reciprocating in some way. Reciprocity as a norm obligates individuals to return the form of behaviour that they have received from others. Former East Germans might feel a sense of discomfort caused by the transfer payments from west to east. Kasper and Streit (1999) argue that former East Germans have to unlearn the old institutions and learn new ones (e.g. a different tax system) which takes time and practice. In such a process, expectations were destabilized. The authors offered the criticism that the transformation process failed to demonstrate in the East how effectively a deregulated market system works:

> Unification was based on a 'social justice strategy' whose effect was to destroy existing capital and jobs and delay the restructuring and modernisation of eastern Germany. [...] Despite opportunities at the start that were far better than in most former command economies, a quick transfer of the basic institutions and massive material aid, east German living standards are lagging far behind those of western Germany. As of 1996, average per capita standards in the east are barely half those in the west, and the speed with which the gap is closing has decelerated sharply during the mid-1990s (pp. 447–8).

CONCLUSIONS

This chapter has provided a comparison of tax morale between inhabitants of the former East and West Germany after the post-reunification period, using World Values Survey data for the years 1990 and 1997. The setting of German reunification is particularly interesting with regard to the analysis of tax morale, as it is close to a natural experiment and it reduces problems of multinational cross-studies. The results indicate that the inhabitants of the former East Germany have a higher tax morale than those of the former West Germany, both in 1990 and 1997. The cultural background seems to have an effect on tax morale. Adherence to social norms as practised in the GDR provides a key explanation of why tax morale is higher in the east. In 1997 data, we can observe a higher tax morale for older citizens in the east. On the other hand, we did not find a significant east–west difference between the younger individuals. Not surprisingly, a different result has been found just after reunification in 1990, where in the east citizens below the age of 30 had a higher tax morale than their western counterparts. From 1990 to 1997, we observed a significant decrease in tax morale in the east, but not in the west. A key finding in this chapter is the fact that around three-quarters of the 1990 east–west differential disappeared in a short time period of seven years. Thus, a strong convergence in the level of tax morale between the two populations can be observed over the decade.

However, the results should be interpreted with caution. It can be argued that the findings indicate a higher solidarity to pay taxes in the former East Germany, which might provide a basis for tax compliance. Although, compared to cross-country studies, reunification offers a good possibility of analysing different cultural contexts, survey questions after reunification can have certain biases, which might reduce the possible controlling factor of culture as an important variable in explaining the differences in tax morale.

Nevertheless, the findings indicate that it might be fruitful to go beyond the standard economic model of tax compliance, moving in the direction of social psychology or sociology theories, and thus analysing the effects of social norms on tax morale. Taxpayers' behaviour and values are not just influenced by deterrence factors such as penalties and audits, but also by cultural norms that act as constraints and that vary between different environments.

APPENDIX

Table A7.1   The derivation of some variables

Variable	Derivation
Tax morale (dependent variable)	Please tell me for each of the following statements whether you think it can always be justified, never be justified, or something in between […]: Cheating on tax if you have the chance. (4 = never and 1 = always)

Variable	Derivation
INCOME	Here is a scale of incomes (1–10). We would like to know in what group your household is, counting all wages, salaries, pensions and other incomes that come in. Just give the letter of the group your household falls into, before taxes and other deduction. West Germany: 1. Below 2000 DM per month 2. 2000–2999 DM 3. 3000–3999 DM 4. 4000–4499 DM 5. 4500–4999 DM 6. 5000–5499 DM 7. 5500–5999 DM 8. 6000–6999 DM 9. 7000–7999 DM 10. 8000 DM and over East Germany: 1. Under 1000 Marks per month 2. 1000–1299 Marks 3. 1300–1599 4. 1600–1799 5. 1800–1999 6. 2000–2199 7. 2200–2499 8. 2500–2799 9. 2800–3199 10. 3200 Marks or more per month
CLASS	People sometimes describe themselves as belonging to the working class, the middle class, or the upper or lower class. Would you describe yourself as belonging to the: 1. Upper class 2. Upper middle class 3 Lower middle class 4. Working class 5. Lower class

Table A7.1   continued

Variable	Derivation
EDUCATION	For West and East Germany in 1997: What is the highest educational level that you have attained? 1. No formal education 2. Incomplete primary school 3. Completed primary school 4. Incomplete secondary school: technical/vocational type 5. Complete secondary school: technical/vocational type 6. Incomplete secondary: university–preparatory type 7. Complete secondary: university–preparatory type 8. Some university–level education, without degree 9. University–level education, with degree For western and eastern Germany in 1990: At what age did you or will you complete your full time education, either at school or at an institution of higher education? Please exclude apprenticeships: 14. Completed education at the age of 14 or younger 15. Completed education at the age of 15 16. Completed education at the age of 16 17. Completed education at the age of 17 18. Completed education at the age of 18 19. Completed education at the age of 19 20. Completed education at the age of 20 21. Completed education at 21 years of age or older

Source: Inglehart et al. (2000).

NOTE

1. The income scale structure did not allow us to build useful groups so as to make the income variable comparable (see Table A7.1 in the Appendix).

REFERENCES

Cialdini, R.B. and M. Trost (1998), 'Social influence: social norms, conformity, and compliance', in D.T. Gilbert, S.T. Fiske and G. Lindzey (eds), *The Handbook of Social Psychology*, Boston: McGraw-Hill, pp. 151–92.

Frey, B.S. and R. Eichenberger (2001), 'The political economy of stabilization programmes in developing countries', in B.S. Frey (ed.), *Inspiring Economics. Human Motivation in Political Economy*, Cheltenham, UK and Northampton, MA, USA: Edward Elgar, pp. 163–83.

Frijters, P., J.P. Haisken-DeNew and M.A. Shields (2002), 'The value of reunification in Germany: an analysis of changes in life satisfaction', IZA Discussion Paper No. 419, January.

Fritjers, P., J.P. Haisken-DeNew and M. Shields (2004), 'Money does matter! Evidence from increasing real income and life satisfaction in East Germany following reunification', *American Economic Review*, **94**, 730–40.

Henrich, J., P. Young, R. Boyd, K. McCabe, W. Albers, A. Ockenfels and G. Gigerenzer (1999), 'What is the role of culture in bounded rationality?', unpublished manuscript.

Hirschman, A.O. (1970), *Exit, Voice, and Loyalty*, Cambridge, MA: Harvard University Press.

Hunt, J. (2000), 'Why do people still live in East Germany?', NBER Working Paper No. w7564, February.

Inglehart, R. et al. (2000), *Codebook for World Values Survey*, Ann Arbor: Institute for Social Research.

Karsten, S.G. (1993), 'Justice, solidarity, subsidiarity: the demise of East German communism', *International Journal of Social Economics*, **20**, 44–56.

Kasper, W. and M.E. Streit (1999), *Institutional Economics. Social Order and Public Policy*, Cheltenham, UK and Northampton, MA, USA: Edward Elgar.

McGee, R.W. (1996), 'When is tax evasion unethical?', working paper, Policy Analysis No. 11. International Business & Technical Consultants, Inc.

Mummert, A. and F. Schneider (2002), 'The German shadow economy: parted in a United Germany?' *FinanzArchiv*, **58**, 287–317.

Ockenfels, A. and J. Weimann (1999), 'Types and patterns: an experimental East–West-German comparison of cooperation and solidarity', *Journal of Public Economics*, **71**, 275–87.

Paldam, M. and G.T. Svendsen (2001), 'Missing social capital and the transition in Eastern Europe', *Journal for Institutional Innovation, Development and Transition*, **5**, 21–34.

Polinsky, M.A. and S. Shavell (2000), 'The economic theory of public enforcement of law', *Journal of Economic Literature*, **38**, 45–76.

Posner, E.A. (2000), *Law and Social Norms*, Cambridge, MA: Harvard University Press.

Wintrobe, R. (1998), *The Political Economy of Dictatorship*, Cambridge: Cambridge University Press.

PART III
Tax policy strategies

Certainly, there is tax evasion, draft evasion, and various other forms of disobedience and even outright resistance; yet it is remarkable the extent to which citizens acquiesce and even actively consent to the demand of governments, well beyond the point explicable by coercion. This is a puzzle for social scientists, particularly those who believe that individuals are self-interested, rational actors who calculate only the private, egoistic costs and benefits of possible choices (p. 2).

Levi, Margaret (1997), *Consent, Dissent, and Patriotism*, Cambridge: Cambridge University Press.

8. Moral suasion: an alternative tax policy strategy? Evidence from a controlled field experiment in Switzerland

INTRODUCTION

Tax compliance seems to depend upon numerous factors and is not only affected by deterrence and economic factors (for a survey, see Torgler 2001, 2002a). Many studies have focused on the effect of deterrence factors such as, for example, fines and the audit rate. Recently, researchers have started to put more weight on letting these deterrence factors remain constant and analysing the extent to which other determinants matter (e.g. Bosco and Mittone, 1997). Such studies have worked with experiments. Recently, tax compliance researchers have started to use field experiments to implement 'real' actors such as the tax authority or taxpayers in their natural situation of filling out the tax form (see Blumenthal et al., 2001; Slemrod et al., 2001). In line with these studies, we will analyse the effects of moral suasion on tax morale in a controlled field experiment, in co-operation with the local tax administration in Trimbach (Canton Solothurn, Switzerland). The next section presents theoretical considerations about the effects of moral suasion on tax morale and tax compliance and gives an overview on the related literature. The third section introduces the design of the field experiment, before the results are presented in the fourth section. The chapter ends with some concluding remarks.

MORAL SUASION

Economists are generally sceptical about the effects of moral suasion. We find some studies in the field of monetary or environmental economics. Many years ago, Breton and Wintrobe (1978) analysed the relationship between central and commercial banks. They point out that the techniques of moral suasion 'allow the central and commercial banks to exchange views on the current economic situation and develop a common view of the economy' (p. 214). And Baumol and Oates (1979) stress that 'voluntary compliance does have several significant and useful roles to play and [...] some of our colleagues have been a bit too ready to reject it out of hand' (p. 283).

Experiments can be used to analyse rather undeveloped areas, such as moral and social sentiments, social norms and so on. In the early stages, Schwartz and Orleans (1967) carried out an interesting field experiment. Their approach was to determine the effects of moral appeals and threats of punishment on behavioural compliance with the tax laws. They found that moral appeals had a much stronger influence than punishment threats. These findings were important in focusing attention on different potential compliance factors. However, since then, little work has been done to analyse the relevance of moral appeals. In line with Schwartz and Orleans, McGraw and Scholz (1991) analysed the effects of moral suasion on tax compliance. In the experiment, the participants were shown a video appealing to social responsibility. Researchers could not find a larger increase in income reporting compared to the control group.

In recent years, we have found tendencies in the tax compliance literature for researchers to stress moral considerations (see Chapter 2). Roth et al. (1989) identify moral commitment as an important determinant that affects tax compliance. Erard and Feinstein (1994) point out that

> One important reason why the conventional expected utility model of tax compliance overpredicts the prevalence and extent of tax evasion is that compliance behavior is assumed to be motivated solely by financial considerations, whereas in reality many taxpayers are influenced by a variety of other feelings, which we will call moral sentiments (p. 74).

If moral sentiments or moral commitments play an important role in the degree of tax compliance, it might be interesting to analyse the extent to which moral suasion can influence moral sentiments and thus the degree of co-operation. Surprisingly, the tax compliance literature has rarely analysed the effects of moral suasion on tax compliance. What we find is an analysis of the effects of information and complexity on tax compliance (for a survey, see Torgler, 2002b). However, there is a lack of economic models that do not start from the assumption that individuals have well-defined preferences. Even Gary Becker (1996) argues that values can no longer be treated as exogenous preferences and stresses the power of endogenous preferences as an extension of the utility-maximizing approach, serving to unify often neglected aspects such as habitual, social or political behaviour, addiction, emotions such as love and sympathy and so on. Bowles (1998) states that

If preferences are affected by the policies or institutional arrangements we study, we can neither accurately predict nor coherently evaluate the likely consequences of new policies or institutions without taking account of preference endogeneity (p. 75).

One policy might be to influence individuals' preferences using moral suasion. This instrument is often used in the political process. Frey and Kirchgässner (1994) point out that politicians often try to create an anti-inflation mentality to reduce the expectations about inflation and thus to reduce the costs of disinflation. In general, economists are rather cautious regarding the effects of moral suasion. Frey and Kirchgässner (1994) give two examples (p. 404). In the 1970s, petrol enterprises such as Shell (e.g. in Switzerland and in the United States; see also Baumol and Oates 1979, p. 289) ran large marketing campaigns to promote the use of unleaded petrol, despite its slightly higher price. However, after a short time, a drop in sales of unleaded petrol was observed. Shell's unleaded petrol, 'Shell of the Future', reached only 5 per cent of sales (Baumol and Oates, 1979). The governor of Oregon used large propaganda expenses as well as his personal charisma to reduce electricity consumption. After a reduction of 2 per cent in the first month, no reaction was observed in the following months. The authors point out that moral suasion does not work in situations in which individuals or institutions such as firms are under strong competitive pressure. Frey and Kirchgässner (1994) are more optimistic about the effects of moral suasion in a state of emergency, as were Baumol and Oates (1979). In many countries, moral appeals for voluntary blood donors in emergency situations have been very successful: 'Happily, experience suggests that, in these instances, circumstances for effective voluntary cooperation are likely to be the most favorable' (Baumol and Oates, 1979, p. 283).

De Alessi (1975, p. 127) points out that individuals are more generous towards each other after a disaster. Such a situation shifts the individual utility function towards more 'community feeling'. Baumol and Oates (1979) mention two examples from New York City. In September 1970, the hospitals had a blood shortage. The response to an urgent appeal for voluntary donations was so high that donors were willing to stand in line for up to 90 minutes to donate blood. The appeals during a period of water shortage in the 1960s achieved a reduction in water consumption of between 4 and 6 per cent. Frey (1997) points out that such behaviour is a manifestation of intrinsic motivation. He states that

> Economists should acknowledge that the motivation structure of individuals is more complex than in their traditional model. Once they accept that behaviour is not solely motivated by extrinsic motivation, they must become aware that their cynicism has considerable cost by damaging environmental moral [...] What is

proposed is a partial rehabilitation of moral appeals in environmental policy – without giving up incentive instruments (p. 65).

Baumol and Oates (1979) stress that moral suasion should be used under specific circumstances; otherwise, it can undermine voluntarism. It is interesting to note that India's 1997 tax amnesty was quite successful (additional revenues of 100 billion rupees) as the state had engaged two private marketing enterprises to conduct a marketing campaign (based on moral suasion) to increase tax compliance.

However, some researchers have seen the importance of clarifying this topic. Hasseldine (2000) stresses that moral appeals could help frame tax compliance as a positive act. Blumenthal et al. (2001) worked together with the Minnesota Department of Revenue in a field experiment and analysed the impact of moral persuasion on voluntary income tax compliance. The authors focused on whether taxpayers who were subject to moral appeals changed their reports more than taxpayers who were not, as the authors did not have access to audits of taxpayers' returns. They used the difference-in-difference approach (treatment minus control after tax year 1994 and before tax year 1993). Compliance behaviour was measured by the income reported or the tax paid, and was compared with the reference group (no communication). They found that the average compliance rate of those in the treatment group was $220 higher compared to the control group (0.08 per cent of average income). However, the coefficient was not statistically significant. Similarly, the percentage of income reporting was not statistically significant, with letter two (when using another letter with a different normative appeal). Thus, this study did not find that moral appeals had a significant effect. In a second step, Blumenthal et al. (2001) conducted a multiple regression in which they used the treatments as dummy variables to check other variables. The results indicate that people with greater opportunities to evade or avoid taxes (e.g. the self-employed) are less susceptible to normative appeals.

THE DESIGN OF THE FIELD EXPERIMENT

General Aspects

The tax laws in Switzerland allow citizens to declare their own income and to make generalized deductions. The Trimbach commune has 3497 taxpayers (as of January 2003). Out of these individuals, around 580 people were selected at random before the 2001 tax form was sent out. We divided these people into two groups. The experimental treatment group received a letter just after the tax form (for this letter and a translation, see the Appendix). To simulate real effects, taxpayers were not informed that they were part of the experiment.

Compared to the study of Blumenthal et al. (2001), our analysis looks at two other compliance factors: *timely filling out* and *timely paying*. To the author's knowledge, no other study has analysed this aspect in a controlled field experiment with real taxpayers.

It could be argued that moral suasion might be more efficient at a local level. Due to Switzerland's federal structure, the competence of collecting the tax forms is mostly held by the communities. There is a clear division of competences between the communities and the cantonal government. In Trimbach, where the experiment was conducted, the tax administration has the autonomy to collect tax forms and to remind taxpayers about filling them out. We were careful to choose a small town, as there is intensive contact between the tax administration and the taxpayers. Closeness might play an important role in how well moral suasion works. It means physical proximity, as all households are no more than about one kilometre away from the tax administration. However, there might even be a certain mental closeness and connectedness, based on strong mutual interactions. In small communities, everyone can actually come to know everyone else. In local areas, certain social norms are likely to emerge and give rise to social identification (see Taylor, 1996). Small structures have the advantage that citizens' preferences can be met better. Politicians are informed about the preferences of the local population. They are elected at the local level, and they have an incentive to take citizens' preferences into account. There is strong everyday interaction between taxpayers and local politicians and bureaucrats, which moves the government closer to the citizens. Thus, if there is a moral suasion effect, it might be more common at the local level than at a much more centralized level, as in the experiment conducted by Blumenthal et al. (2001).

We have information regarding timely filling out and timely paying for the tax years 1999, 2000 and 2001. This helped us to analyse the impact of moral suasion on compliance comparing the treatment group with the control group for different years.

The Design of the Letter

In February 2002, the treatment group received a letter signed by the commune fiscal commissioner. The letter was sent just after the 2001 tax form in a separate envelope, to increase the probability that taxpayers who use professional assistance would read it. We chose a pink sheet of paper so that individuals would be more aware of it. Furthermore, the chief tax administrator signed the letter in person. The style (easy to read and to understand) and an adequate letter length (not too long) were chosen to make it easier to capture the taxpayers' attention.

To reduce biases, individuals were not informed that they had been selected at random for a tax compliance study. The letter had the following moral suasion passage in the first paragraph:

> If the taxpayers did not contribute their share, our commune with its 6226 inhabitants would suffer greatly. With your taxes you help keep Trimbach attractive for its inhabitants.

Similar to the design of the letter in Blumenthal et al. (2001), the message points out the importance of paying the taxes voluntarily to guarantee the provision of public goods in an attractive manner. Contrary to Blumenthal et al. (2001), we carried out our experiment at the communal level; we integrated the number of inhabitants (6226) into the message to stress how 'close' people are to each other. In the second paragraph, we indicate that citizens are trusted. The relationship between taxpayers and government can be seen as a relational or psychological contract, which involves strong emotional ties and loyalties (see, e.g., Feld and Frey, 2002a). If the local tax administration acts trustworthily, taxpayers might be more willing to comply with the taxes. Such a psychological tax contract can be maintained by positive actions, based on trust:

> In Switzerland, contrary to other countries, the citizens have the opportunity to actively participate in the legislative procedure. This advantage is also reflected in the tax legislation, which stipulates self-declaration by the taxpayers. This Swiss system presupposes that citizens have a sense of responsibility and are ready to maintain the functioning of municipalities, cantons and the state. With your conscientious tax declaration you contribute to preserving this democratic and liberal structure.

A letter that runs to more than one sentence helps to cover moral suasion factors better, by focusing on different aspects. It enhances the probability that the normative appeals used in our letter will have an effect on taxpayers' attitudes and thus might change their compliance behaviour. It leaves open the question of the extent to which the behaviour will be adjusted because of attitudinal shifts. On the other hand, the more sentences are used, the higher are the 'noise' or 'interpretation difficulties' and the lower is the chance of knowing which sentence finally resulted, or did not result, in shifting attitudes. Furthermore, it increases the possibility that individuals do not read the letter right through to the end. Letters should not be too long or complicated but, rather, understandable, so that subjects become neither bored nor confused, and therefore have an incentive to read the whole letter.

RESULTS

Descriptive Analysis

Tax compliance researchers have paid substantial attention to tax evasion and thus to the decision as to how much income to report in a tax return. Very little is known about individuals' compliance behaviour regarding the timely filling out of the tax form (*TF*) and the extent to which individuals pay their taxes on time (*TP*). This field data analysis tries to overcome these shortfalls. It takes into consideration the fact that compliance has different characteristics. The civic duty of a taxpayer does not just consist of the rightful declaration of income. The timely filling out of the tax form and the timely paying of the taxes are also important compliance determinants for a tax administration. A higher level of compliance leads to lower tax administration costs, and may also contribute to maintaining a good atmosphere between the tax administration and the taxpayers, especially in a system that gives citizens increased responsibility. It will be interesting to observe the extent to which moral suasion has an impact on compliance determinants that go beyond the study of Blumenthal et al. (2001), which focused on reported income. There is a relatively high probability that tax evasion will not be detected by the tax administration. On the other hand, the degree of timeliness is carefully recorded for each taxpayer. Moral suasion may work differently in situations in which taxpayers' reactions can be better observed by the tax administration.

TF and *TP* are coded as follows:
TF: 3 = no submission delay, extension of time
2 = first reminder
1 = second reminder
0 = no submission

TP: 3 = payments on time, remission of taxes
2 = first request for payment
1 = debt collection
0 = not paid the taxes

Thus, a higher value goes hand in hand with higher tax compliance. The value 0 for the *TF* variable covers a group that, according to Erard and Ho

(2001, pp. 25–26), have been neglected by tax compliance research: the non-filers, also known as the 'ghosts'. With a sample from the 1988 US federal individual income tax return file based on a 25 per cent random sub-sample survey, they show that non-filling in of the tax return is more current among self-employed individuals, especially in those professions where income is easier to hide. Furthermore, they point out that a reduction of the burden of filling and programmes educating individuals about the filling in procedure help to reduce non-filling, as for taxpayers near the threshold of filling, the burden serves as a filling restriction: 'Once a ghost is brought into the system, he is likely to remain in the system' (p. 48).

Table 8.1 shows the percentage of non-filers in our field experiment: 4.8 per cent in the control group and 3.1 per cent in the treatment group. Looking back on the years 2001 and 2000, the values vary between 2.1 and 4.8 per cent. These results are in line with the estimated cantonal level (Solothurn, 2.4 per cent of the taxpayers; Swiss average, 2.85 per cent; year 1999).[1]

In general, Table 8.1 indicates that a great amount of taxpayers send their tax forms back on time (control group: 91.3 per cent, treatment group: 92.1 per cent). Thus, we cannot observe a strong variance among the degree of compliance for both variables. For both compliance variables, we can observe that the moral suasion treatment group has a higher compliance rate than the reference group. The mean values for the variable $TF(TP)$ are 2.813 (2.878) for the control group and 2.859 (2.923) for the treatment group. The strongest effects can be observed for the variable TP. Similarly, Table 8.2 also indicates that a great number of taxpayers have a high payment morality.

However, to get a real picture of the extent to which such behaviour is the consequence of a moral suasion effect, the TF and TP values for the years 1999 and 2000 are included. As assignments to treatment and control groups have been made at random, one can simply compare the change in compliance across the treatment and control groups to estimate the treatment effect. For time 1 (before) and 2 (after the experiment), groups A (treatment) and B (control), compliance (TC), $[TC(2,A) - TC(2,B)] - [TC(1,A) - TC(1,B)]$, or equivalently $[TC(2,A) TC(1,A)] - [TC(2,B) - TC(1,B)]$, is the difference-in-difference. Tables 8.3 and 8.4 present the results. To calculate the difference-in-differences, we also take the averages of two time periods before the experiment. The change in compliance regarding timely paying suggests a successful moral suasion effect with mean increases of 0.048 and 0.046 respectively. We can observe the strongest increase in the highest compliance scale (2.1, respectively 2.3 per cent). On the other hand, a positive treatment effect regarding timely compliance is only observable taking the average of the years 1999 and 2000 into consideration. Looking

Table 8.1   Timely filling out, 2001

Timely filling out (*TF*)	Degree		Control group	Treatment group	Total
	0	Count	14	9	23
		% within groups	4.8	3.1	4.0
	1	Count	1		1
		% within groups	0.3		0.2
	2	Count	10	14	24
		% within groups	3.5	4.8	4.1
	3	Count	264	268	532
		% within groups	91.3	92.1	91.7
Total		Count	289	291	580
		% within groups	100.0	100.0	100.0
Mean			2.813	2.859	

Table 8.2   Timely paying, 2001

Timely paying (*TP*)	Degree		Control group	Treatment group	Total
	0	Count	1		1
		% within groups	0.3		0.2
	2	Count	32	22	54
		% within groups	11.1	7.6	9.3
	3	Count	256	267	532
		% within groups	88.6	92.4	90.5
Total		Count (N)	289	289	578
		% within groups	100.0	100.0	100.0
Mean			2.878	2.923	

only at 2000 and 2001, we even observe a small negative treatment effect. In general, we observe an increase in the compliance scale 2 (2.1 and 1.8 per cent respectively). A mixed picture is observed in the highest scale, a decrease (1.4 per cent) looking at the tax year 2001 minus tax year 2000 and a small increase taking into consideration tax year 2001 minus the average of tax years 1999 and 2000 (0.3 per cent).

Table 8.3 Change in compliance: 'timely paying'

		Control	Treatment	Treatment – Control
Means	Before (year 1999)	2.823	2.823	0.000
	Before (year 2000)	2.808	2.804	–0.004
	After (year 2001)	2.879	2.923	0.044
	2001 – 2000	0.071	0.119	0.048
	2001 – average (1999 & 2000)	0.063	0.110	0.046

Compliance degrees (in %)

0	Before (year 1999)	2.9	3.6	0.7
	Before (year 2000)	2.3	3.0	0.7
	After (year 2001)	0.3	1.0	0.7
	2001 – 2000	–2.0	–2.0	0.0
	2001 – average (1999 & 2000)	–2.3	–2.3	0.0
1	Before (year 1999)	1.7	1.2	–0.5
	Before (year 2000)	1.9	2.6	0.7
	After (year 2001)	0.0	0.0	0.0
	2001 – 2000	–1.9	–2.6	–0.7
	2001 – average (1999 & 2000)	–1.8	–1.9	–0.1
2	Before (year 1999)	6.2	4.4	–1.8
	Before (year 2000)	8.7	5.5	–3.2
	After (year 2001)	11.1	7.6	–3.5
	2001 – 2000	2.4	2.1	–0.3
	2001 – average(1999 & 2000)	3.7	2.7	–1.0
3	Before (year 1999)	89.3	90.7	1.4
	Before (year 2000)	87.2	88.9	1.7
	After (year 2001)	88.6	92.4	3.8
	2001 – 2000	1.4	3.5	2.1
	2001 – average(1999 & 2000)	0.3	2.6	2.3

We will use an independent-samples t-test to compare the mean values for the reference group and the treatment group in the year 2001. This test can be applied as subjects have been randomly assigned to the two groups, so that any difference in response is due to the treatment effect. The results indicate that there is a significant difference between the groups for the

Table 8.4 *Change in compliance: 'timely filling out'*

		Control	Treatment	Treatment − Control
Means	Before (year 1999)	2.866	2.830	−0.036
	Before (year 2000)	2.826	2.881	0.055
	After (year 2001)	2.813	2.859	0.046
	2001 − 2000	−0.013	−0.022	−0.009
	2001 − average (1999 & 2000)	−0.033	0.003	0.036
Compliance degrees (in %)				
0	Before (year 1999)	2.8	3.8	1.0
	Before (year 2000)	3.9	2.1	−1.8
	After (year 2001)	4.8	3.1	−1.7
	2001 − 2000	0.9	1.0	0.1
	2001 − average (1999 & 2000)	1.5	0.2	−1.3
1	Before (year 1999)	0.4	0.8	0.4
	Before (year 2000)	1.1	1.4	0.3
	After (year 2001)	0.3	0.0	−0.3
	2001 − 2000	−0.8	−1.4	−0.6
	2001 − average (1999 & 2000)	−0.5	−1.1	−0.7
2	Before (year 1999)	4.4	4.2	−0.2
	Before (year 2000)	3.6	2.8	−0.8
	After (year 2001)	3.5	4.8	1.3
	2001 − 2000	−0.1	2.0	2.1
	2001 − average (1999 & 2000)	−0.5	1.3	1.8
3	Before (year 1999)	92.4	91.3	−1.1
	Before (year 2000)	91.5	93.7	2.2
	After (year 2001)	91.3	92.1	0.8
	2001 − 2000	−0.2	−1.6	−1.4
	2001 − average (1999 & 2000)	−0.7	−0.4	0.3

coefficient of the variable *TP* (significance, two-tailed test = 0.086), but not for the variable *TF*. In a next step, the paired-sample t-test (Wilcoxon) is carried out. This allows us to compare the mean values of a group in different time periods. It computes the differences between values and tests whether the average differs from zero. In our study, taxpayers' *TF* and *TP* values are measured in 2000 and 2001. Thus, each subject has two measures, before and after the field experiment. Table 8.5 presents the results. For the variable *TF*, there is no significant difference between the years 2000 and 2001 for both groups. On the other hand, for the *TP* variable there is a significantly higher compliance in the year 2001 compared to 2000. Table 8.5 shows that the mean coefficient and the t-value are higher for the treatment group than for the control group.

Table 8.5   Paired samples statistics

Pairs	Mean	Standard error of the mean	*t*-value
Treatment group			
TP 2000 – *TP* 2001	−0.12***	0.03	−3.57
TF 2000 – *TF* 2001	0.02	0.03	0.53
Control group			
TP 2000 – *TP* 2001	−0.07**	0.03	−2.46
TF 2000 – *TF* 2001	−0.4E–02	0.03	−0.12

Notes: number of observations in the treatment group, 281 in the control group, 286. Significance levels: * $0.05 < p < 0.10$; ** $0.01 < p < 0.05$; *** $p < 0.01$.

However, the findings of the paired sample *t*-statistics alone cannot determine whether there is a significant *treatment effect*. Thus, in line with Tables 8.3 and 8.4, we analyse whether those in the treatment group changed their payment timeliness more than did those in the control group. A regression framework using time and treatment dummy variables can calculate such a treatment effect. Consider the following model: $TC_{it} = \beta_0 + \beta_1 treatment_{it} + \beta_2 after_{it} + \beta_3 treatment_{it} * after_{it} + \varepsilon_{it}$. The estimated

Table 8.6   The difference-in-difference test

Compliance	Coefficient	*t*-value
Timely paying		
Treatment group	−0.31E–02	−0.08
Year 2001	0.07*	1.77
Treatment group * year 2001	0.05	0.85
Timely filling out		
Treatment group	0.06	1.11
Year 2001	−0.01	−0.25
Treatment group * year 2001	−0.01	−0.14

Note: Significance level: * $0.05 < p < 0.10$.

β_3 will show the treatment effect as in Tables 8.3 and 8.4, but will also indicate the extent to which those differences are statistically significant. Table 8.6 presents the results. While the previous result in Table 8.3 suggested a successful moral suasion effect for the variable *TP*, the coefficient for both interaction terms is not statistically significant. A similar result can be found for the *TF* treatment effect.

Multivariate Analysis

In a next step, we will use the variable *TP* as a dependent variable, controlling in a multivariate analysis for additional factors and working with the 2001 data.[2] A dummy variable MORAL SUASION has been built to compare the control group with the treatment group (1 = treatment group).

Model estimation

Ordered probit models are used to analyse the determinants of *TP*. An ordered probit estimation helps to analyse the ranking information of the scaled dependent variables TP.[3] As the equation has a non-linear form, only the sign of the coefficient can be directly interpreted and not its size. Calculation of the marginal effects is therefore a method for finding the quantitative effects of the variable *TP*. In all estimations, we present the marginal effect for the *TP* values 1 and 2. The basic estimation equation has the following structure:

$$TP_i = \beta_0 + \beta_1 \cdot AGE_i + \beta_2 \cdot CULTURE_i + \beta_3 \cdot GROUP_i + \beta_4 \cdot MARITAL_i + \beta_5 \cdot TF_i + \beta_6 \cdot ECONOMIC_i + \beta_7 \cdot TAXRATE_i + \varepsilon_i$$

The independent variables are specified as follows:

AGE_i: Dummy variables in the first estimations for the following groups: 20–29, 30–49, 50–64 and 65+, with 20–29 as the reference group and a continuous variable in further estimations. Predicted sign: (+). Elderly people are more experienced in tax matters and know the consequences of not paying the taxes and not sending the tax form in on time. Furthermore, they are more strongly attached to their communities, which might be important in our case.

$CULTURE_i$: We are going to differentiate between Swiss and foreigners (dummy variable: 1 = Swiss citizens and 0 = foreigners). It should be noted that a married couple that includes one foreign person have been coded as foreigners. It is difficult to develop a clear prediction of the effects on compliance. Due to their status, foreigners might have an incentive to be honest and to avoid conflicts with the state. On the other hand, they might be less affected by the second paragraph in the letter, as they gain less from direct democracy, being excluded from participation rights.

$GROUP_i$: This is a dummy variable with the value 1 for the treatment group and 0 for the control group. We will see, in a multiple regression analysis, whether the small differences between the control group and the treatment group are significant, controlling for additional variables.

$MARITAL\ STATUS_i$: In the first estimations, dummy variables: (SINGLE, LIVING TOGETHER, MARRIED, DIVORCED, SEPARATED and WIDOWED; reference group, SINGLE). In further estimations, we use only one dummy variable (MARRIED). It should be noted that married couples fill out a joint tax return. Marital status might influence legal or illegal behaviour. Tittle (1980) states that

> A long tradition in sociology, extending back to Durkheim, postulates that proneness toward rule breaking varies inversely with the extent to which individuals are involved in social networks with constraining content (p. 111).

This would imply that married people are more compliant than others, especially compared to singles, because they are more constrained by their social networks. In the tax compliance literature, we do not find many studies that systematically analyse marital status. Some studies have found that non-compliance is more common and of greater magnitude among married taxpayers (see Clotfelter, 1983; Feinstein, 1991). Similar to the previous argumentation, couples might have a lower compliance, being taxed in a higher bracket than two separate incomes. Thus, we would predict that married people would have a lower compliance than singles.

TF_i: We will analyse whether people who are more compliant regarding the timely filling out of the tax form also have better payment behaviour.[4]

$TAX\ RATE_i$ (amount to be paid to the tax administration divided by the taxable income): The individual tax rate has been included, as it is the central variable in the standard tax compliance/evasion models. However, as we are now considering another dependent variable, the effect of the tax rate is difficult to assess theoretically. In previous tax compliance studies, the effect has depended on the risk preference, the progression of the income tax schedule and the penalty structure (see Yitzhaki, 1974; Andreoni et al., 1998).

$ECONOMIC_i$: Some of the variables analysed are proxies for a taxpayer's economic situation:

- INCOME (individuals' self-declared total taxable income)
- HOUSE OWNER (dummy variable)

To check the sensitivity of these variables, we mostly integrate them separately into the estimations. Being a house owner might increase the incentive to act in line with the law, to maintain societal 'stakes'. Homeowners face higher costs in leaving the community compared to people who rent apartments. They may have chosen to buy a house because they like the region and the people. Thus, we would predict that house owners would be more compliant than other individuals. As there is a strong correlation between income and having an own house in our data, we integrate them separately into the estimations.

Results

In the first two estimations, we try to optimize the number of observations. Contrary to estimations 3 and 4, non-filers are included in estimations 1 and 2, as the tax administration collects socio-demographic variables of non-filers. Tables 8.7 and 8.8 present the results. We first look at the variable MORAL SUASION. Although the marginal effects are relatively high, indicating that being in the moral suasion group increases the probability of being in the most compliant group by around three percentage points, the coefficients are not significant. Equations 2 to 4 indicate that a higher compliance regarding the timely filling out of the tax form is correlated with a higher payment compliance.[5] Being at age 65+ rather than 20–29 increases the probability of being totally compliant by between 9 and 14 percentage points. Using age as a continuous variable also indicates a statistically significant positive correlation between age and compliance. There is a tendency for Swiss citizens to be less compliant than foreigners. However, the coefficient is only on the border of statistical significance in Equation 3 (see Table 8.8). Being married rather than single reduces the probability of being on the highest TP scale by between 5.9 and 7.9 percentage points. Equation 4 indicates that having one's own house has a significantly positive effect on compliance. This significant positive impact is compatible with the theoretical considerations. Finally, income and the tax rate have no statistically significant impact on TP. In general, Table 8.8 shows that the reduced number of observations has no effect on the equal distribution between the control group and the reference group. However, on the basis of the lower number of observations, the results should be treated with caution.

CONCLUSIONS

Governments and tax administrations have an incentive to search for tax policy strategies that generate additional revenues, especially in times of

Table 8.7 Determinants of the variable TP (weighted ordered probit, dependent variable: TP (timely paying))

	Equation 1				Equation 2			
	Coeff.	z-Stat.	Marg. $TP=1$	Effects $TP=2$	Coeff.	z-Stat.	Marg. $TP=1$	Effects $TP=2$
(a) Groups								
MORAL SUASION	0.244	1.422	−0.034	0.034	0.209	1.139	−0.026	0.026
(b) Demographic factors								
AGE 30–49	0.099	0.395	−0.014	0.014	−0.109	−0.407	0.014	−0.014
AGE 50–64	0.485	1.541	−0.067	0.068	0.263	0.807	−0.033	0.033
AGE 65+	0.993***	2.678	−0.138	0.140	0.718*	1.871	−0.089	0.090
(c) Culture								
SWISS	−0.056	−0.254	0.008	−0.008	−0.127	−0.524	0.016	−0.016
(d) Marital status								
MARRIED	−0.509**	−2.199	0.071	−0.072	−0.468**	−1.990	0.058	−0.059
DIVORCED	−0.302	−0.922	0.042	−0.043	−0.166	−0.472	0.021	−0.021
SEPARATED	−0.289	−0.609	0.040	−0.041	−0.051	−0.084	0.006	−0.006
WIDOWED	0.207	0.399	−0.029	0.029	0.446	0.495	−0.055	0.056

(e) Timely filling out

		0.496***	4.659	−0.062	0.062

Observations	572
Treatment group	288
Control group	284

Prob(LM-statistic)	0.000

Notes: Dependent variable: *TP* on a three-point scale (0–2). In the reference group are CONTROL GROUP (without moral suasion), AGE 20–29, FOREIGNER and SINGLE. Significance levels: * $0.05 < p < 0.10$; ** $0.01 < p < 0.05$; *** $p < 0.01$.

Table 8.8 The results of further estimations (weighted ordered probit, dependent variable: TP (timely paying))

	Equation 3				Equation 4			
	Coeff.	z-Stat.	Marg. $TP=1$	Effects $TP=2$	Coeff.	z-Stat.	Marg. $TP=1$	Effects $TP=2$
(a) Groups								
MORAL SUASION	0.297	1.522	−0.031	0.032	0.309	1.607	−0.034	0.035
(b) Demographic factors								
AGE	0.014*	1.834	−0.002	0.002	0.017**	2.367	−0.002	0.002
(c) Culture								
SWISS	−0.445*	−1.761	0.046	−0.047	−0.273	−1.057	0.030	−0.031
(d) Marital status								
MARRIED	−0.738***	−3.579	0.077	−0.079	−0.519**	−2.433	0.057	−0.059
(e) Timely filling out	0.220	1.307	−0.023	0.023	0.248	1.601	−0.027	0.028
(f) Economic situation								
OWN HOUSE	0.584**	2.425	−0.061	0.062				
LOG (INCOME)					−0.022	−0.424	0.002	−0.003

(g) Individual tax rate

		0.342	0.123	−0.038	0.039
Observations	502	505
Treatment group	252	253
Control group	250	252
Prob(LM-statistic)	0.000	0.006

Notes: Dependent variable: *TP* on a three-point scale (0–2). In the reference group are CONTROL GROUP (without moral suasion), AGE 20–29, FOREIGNER and WITHOUT OWN HOUSE. Significance levels: * $0.05 < p < 0.10$; ** $0.01 < p < 0.05$; *** $p < 0.01$. Marginal effect = highest TP score (2).

large and persistent deficits. Raising taxes and increasing enforcement strategies are only two of the possible instruments. In the tax compliance literature, we find evidence of the difficulty of increasing tax compliance by means of traditional factors. Turning away from deterrence strategies offers the possibility of checking the effects of alternative factors such as moral suasion. With this field experiment, we have analysed the effects of moral suasion on tax compliance. Tax compliance researchers have paid substantial attention to tax evasion and thus to the decision as to how much income to report in a tax return. But very little is known about individuals' compliance behaviour regarding moral suasion, focusing on the variables *timely filling out of the tax form* and *paying individual taxes on time*. This field data analysis has tried to overcome these shortfalls. Contrary to a previous controlled experiment done by Blumenthal et al. (2001), which found little or no evidence of a positive effect of normative appeals on tax compliance, we chose to co-operate with a *local* tax administration, because moral suasion efforts might be more effective at this lower level. Our results are in line with those of previous findings, indicating that moral suasion has hardly any effect on taxpayers' compliance behaviour. Those in the treatment group did not significantly change their payment timeliness more than did those in the control group.

The use of controlled field experiments has many advantages. Compared to laboratory experiments, one of the main advantages is the implementation by tax authorities and not experimenters, which evokes real processes in the normal environment outside the laboratory setting. It helps better to test the effects of different instruments on taxpayers in the real situation of 'filling out the tax form' and 'paying the taxes'. This helps in the formulation of practical advice on tax policy, based on scientific testing. Certainly, compared to laboratory experiments, these kinds of experiments allow social and economic interactions and are thus less controlled, but causality can be better determined than in non-experimental studies (for the advantages and problems of randomized field trials see Burtless, 1995).

Our field experiment has been carried out in a specific commune in Switzerland. Future research could expand the analysis, integrating different communes in different cantons. This is especially interesting in Switzerland (or in the United States), as among the cantons (states) it covers a certain variation of institutional components such as direct democracy and federalism. Feld and Frey (2002a) found, for example, that tax authorities of cantons with more direct participation rights, compared to cantons with less direct democracy, treat taxpayers more respectfully and are less suspicious. Furthermore, Feld and Frey (2002b) show in their empirical analysis that a respectful treatment of taxpayers by the tax administration reduces tax evasion. Thus, if further communes are included, it will be possible to analyse whether taxpayers are more sensitive to moral appeals when the tax administration treats taxpayers with more respect.

Furthermore, in this controlled field experiment we have only analysed possible short-term effects of moral suasion on compliance, as individuals in the treatment group have received a moral suasion letter only once. It might be interesting to observe what happens in a panel if moral suasion is used regularly. In addition, as our study has been working with the newest data, we have been unable to analyse the long-term effects (several time periods) after the treatment letter.

Finally, referring to advertising research, Blumenthal et al. (2001) point out that 'Communications of a different sort, delivered in a different way, or with greater frequency might still produce a compliance effect' (p. 135). Thus, more field experiments could analyse whether more communication channels, including, for example, local newspapers, radio and publicity events affect compliance behaviour. Positive effects of moral suasion have been observed by looking, for example, at tax amnesties. In India, a successful amnesty was accompanied by intensive media activities organized by a marketing company and integrating sport and film celebrities. In Switzerland, Geneva collected the highest per capita amount among the cantons in an amnesty following intensive efforts, such as using educational advertising and press conferences (see Torgler et al., 2003).

APPENDIX

Gemeinde Trimbach

Finanzverwaltung
062 289 23 10 Tf
062 289 23 30 Fax
trimbach@bluewin.ch

An unsere
geschätzten
EinwohnerInnen

Trimbach, im Februar 2002

Sehr geehrte Damen und Herren

Wie üblich zu Beginn des Jahres haben Sie die Steuererklärung erhalten. Die Steuern, die Sie für unsere Gemeinde zahlen, sind für den Erhalt der Gemeindetätigkeit in Trimbach von grosser Wichtigkeit. Wenn die Steuerzahler in Trimbach nicht ihren Beitrag leisten würden, hätte unsere 6226 Einwohner zählende Gemeinde stark darunter zu leiden. Mit Ihren Steuern tragen Sie dazu bei, dass Trimbach als Gemeinde für die Einwohner attraktiv bleibt.

Im Gegensatz zu anderen Ländern haben die Bürger in der Schweiz die Möglichkeit, am Gesetzgebungsprozess aktiv mitzuwirken. Dieser Vorzug zeigt sich auch in der Steuergesetzgebung, welche das Ausfüllen der Selbstdeklaration durch den Einwohner vorsieht. Das in der Schweiz geschaffene System geht von verantwortungsbewussten Bürgern aus, die bereit sind, das Funktionieren der Gemeinde, des Kantons und des Bundes aufrechtzuerhalten. Mit Ihrer gewissenhaften Steuerdeklaration leisten Sie einen wertvollen Beitrag zum Erhalt dieser demokratisch und freiheitlich geprägten Struktur.

Haben Sie Unsicherheiten oder Schwierigkeiten beim Ausfüllen der Steuererklärung, beachten Sie unser grünes Mitteilungsblatt bei der Steuererklärung.

Mit freundlichen Grüssen
Ihr Finanzverwalter

Adolf Müller

Einwohnergemeinde Trimbach, Baslerstrasse 122, 4632 Trimbach

Translation

Dear Madam, dear Sir

As at the beginning of every year, you have just received the tax form. The taxes you pay are vital for maintaining the municipal tasks in Trimbach. If the taxpayers did not contribute their share, our commune with its 6226 inhabitants would suffer greatly. With your taxes, you help keep Trimbach attractive for its inhabitants.

In Switzerland, contrary to other countries, the citizens have the opportunity to actively participate in the legislative procedure. This advantage is also reflected in the tax legislation, which stipulates self-declaration by the taxpayers. This Swiss system presupposes that citizens have a sense of responsibility and are ready to maintain the functioning of municipalities, cantons and the state. With your conscientious tax declaration, you contribute to preserving this democratic and liberal structure.

If you encounter any difficulties or doubts when filling in your tax declaration, please refer to the green sheet enclosed with the form.

Yours sincerely,

Your tax administrator

Figure A8.1   The sample letter

NOTES

1. This data has been collected by the Institute for Empirical Research in Economics of the University of Zurich, using a survey. Thanks are due to Alois Stutzer for giving me this information.
2. The time-varying control variables were not available for the years 1999 and 2000. Using more than one year would have allowed better testing of a possible treatment effect, controlling for other independent variables.
3. TP: three-point scale from 0 to 2.
4. It is possible that a non-filer is a timely payer. Thus, one can pay without filling out the tax form, as all taxpayers are recorded by the tax administration. Non-filers receive a bill based on estimations done by the tax administration.
5. It should be noted that the coefficient is statistically significant only in Equation 2. It seems that the positive correlation is washed out by excluding non-filers in Equations 3 and 4, as non-filers have, on average, a lower payment compliance than other taxpayers.

REFERENCES

Andreoni, J., B. Erard and J. Feinstein (1998), 'Tax compliance', *Journal of Economic Literature*, **36**, 818–60.

Baumol, W.J. and W.E. Oates (1979), *Economics, Environmental Policy, and the Quality of Life*, Englewood Cliffs: Prentice-Hall.

Becker, G.S. (1996), *Accounting for Tastes*, Cambridge, MA: Harvard University Press.

Blumenthal, M., C. Christian and J. Slemrod (2001), 'Do normative appeals affect tax compliance? Evidence from a controlled experiment in Minnesota', *National Tax Journal*, **54**, 125–38.

Bosco, L. and L. Mittone (1997), 'Tax evasion and moral constraints: some experimental evidence', *KYKLOS*, **50**, 297–324.

Bowles, S. (1998), 'Endogenous preferences: the cultural consequences of markets and other economic institutions', *Journal of Economic Literature*, **46**, 75–111.

Breton, A. and R. Wintrobe (1978), 'A theory of "moral suasion"', *Canadian Journal of Economics*, **11**, 210–19.

Burtless, G. (1995), 'The case for randomized field trials in economic and policy research', *Journal of Economic Perspective*, **9**, 63–84.

Clotfelter, C.T. (1983), 'Tax evasion and tax rate: an analysis of individual return', *The Review of Economics and Statistics*, **65**, 363–73.

De Alessi, L. (1975), 'Toward an analysis of postdisaster cooperation', *American Economic Review*, **65**, 127–38.

Erard, B. and J.S. Feinstein (1994), 'The role of moral sentiments and audit perceptions in tax compliance', *Public Finance*, **49**, 70–89.

Erard, B. and C.C. Ho (2001), 'Searching for ghosts: who are the nonfilers and how much tax do they owe?' *Journal of Public Economics*, **81**, 25–50.

Feinstein, J.S. (1991), 'An econometric analysis of income tax evasion and its detection', *RAND Journal of Economics*, **22**, 14–35.

Feld, L.P. and B.S. Frey (2002a), 'Trust breeds trust: how taxpayers are treated', *Economics of Governance*, **3**, 87–99.

Feld, L.P. and B.S. Frey (2002b), 'The tax authority and the taxpayer. An exploratory analysis', paper presented at the 2002 Annual Meeting of the European Public Choice Society, Belgirate.

Frey, B.S. (1997), *Not Just for Money. An Economic Theory of Personal Motivation*, Cheltenham, UK and Lyme, USA: Edward Elgar.

Frey, B.S. and G. Kirchgässner (1994), *Demokratische Wirtschaftspolitik: Theorie und Anwendung*, München: Vahlen.

Hasseldine, J. (2000), 'Using persuasive communications to increase tax compliance: what experimental research has (and has not) told us', *Australian Tax Forum*, **15**, 227–24.

McGraw, K. and J.T. Scholz (1991), 'Appeals to civic virtue versus attention to self-interest: effects on tax compliance', *Law and Society Review*, **25**, 471–98.

Roth, J.A., J.T. Scholz and A.D. Witte (eds) (1989), *Taxpayer Compliance*, Vols 1 and 2, Philadelphia: University of Pennsylvania Press.

Schwartz, R. and S. Orleans (1967), 'On legal sanctions', *University of Chicago Law Review*, **34**, 282–300.

Slemrod, J., M. Blumenthal and C. Christian (2001), 'Taxpayer response to an increase probability of audit: evidence from a controlled experiment in Minnesota', *Journal of Public Economics*, **79**, 455–83.

Taylor, M. (1996), 'When rationality fails', in J. Friedman (ed.), *The Rational Choice Controversy*, New Haven: Yale University Press, pp. 223–3.

Tittle, C. (1980), *Sanctions and Social Deviance: The Question of Deterrence*, New York: Praeger.

Torgler, B. (2001), 'What do we know about tax morale and tax compliance?', *International Review of Economics and Business (RISEC)*, **48**, 395–419.

Torgler, B. (2002a), 'Speaking to theorists and searching for facts: tax morale and tax compliance in experiments', *Journal of Economic Surveys*, **16**, 656–83.

Torgler, B. (2002b), 'The economic analysis of creative compliance', WWZ-Discussion Paper 02/05, Basel: WWZ.

Torgler, B., C.A. Schaltegger and M. Schaffner (2003), 'Is forgiveness divine? A cross-culture comparison of tax amnesties', *Swiss Journal of Economics and Statistics*, **139**, 375–96.

Yitzhaki, S. (1974), 'A note on income tax evasion: a theoretical analysis', *Journal of Public Economics*, **3**, 201–2.

9. Tax amnesties and political participation
Written with Christoph A. Schaltegger

INTRODUCTION

Tax amnesties are increasingly used by governments around the world. For example, in November 2001, Italian finance minister Giulio Tremonti declared a six-month tax amnesty, the 'scudo fiscale'. During the amnesty, some €56 billion of exiled money was returned to the fold, and generated €1.4 billion additional tax revenues (about 0.4 per cent of the total tax revenue). Similarly, the Polish government enacted a tax amnesty between September 2002 and April 2003. In summer 2002, the German chancellor Gerhard Schröder brought up a tax amnesty for discussion, with the intention of inducing a major inflow of German capital lying in tax havens abroad. In the United States, most states have introduced tax amnesties. Since 1982, more than 60 amnesty programmes have been conducted in US states, indicating strong variation of the repatriated revenues among the states.[1] Similarly, over the past 30 years national amnesty programmes have taken place virtually all over the world (see Table 9.1).

Such a huge political interest in tax amnesty programmes might suggest that tax amnesties are a major financial success for governments, at least in the short run. However, the degree of financial success among the countries is very diverse, and amnesty revenues are seldom more than a small percentage of the total tax revenues. Similarly, in a comprehensive overview of 43 tax amnesties in 35 US states between 1982 and 1997, Hasseldine (1998) showed that the highest amount of money collected through a tax amnesty did not exceed 2.6 per cent of the total tax revenues, while the lowest collection rate accounted for only 0.008 percent.

It is debated whether in the long run tax amnesties undermine tax compliance. Honest taxpayers may feel upset by an amnesty. If most taxpayers voluntarily comply with tax laws, the option of an amnesty given to a small group of tax evaders can be understood by a majority of taxpayers as a violation of equity. The issue has also a moral dimension, since it touches the sentiments of taxpayers. Thus, it is also possible that an amnesty will end up by resulting in a lower *ex-post* level of tax compliance.

When deciding whether or not to conduct an amnesty, it is crucial to take taxpayers' attitudes towards an amnesty into account. However, in hardly any country has an amnesty been subject to approval.[2] The aim of this chapter is to evaluate the impact of voter participation on tax amnesties by conducting laboratory experiments in several countries. Voters might interpret the remission given by the government as a signal that tax evasion must be high and that other taxpayers' 'tax morale', defined as the 'intrinsic motivation for individuals to pay taxes' (see previous chapters), is very low. Thus, voters may not want to reward tax evaders with an amnesty. Nevertheless, the results of our experiments show that the mere possibility for taxpayers to decide on a tax amnesty increases future tax compliance. Our results are consistent with the argument that the voting procedure, namely public discussion prior to voting, brings about a sense of civic duty, as taxpayers become aware of the importance of contributing to public goods. In addition, tax compliance may increase after the voting given the possibility of an increasing likelihood of stricter enforcement efforts.

THEORETICAL CONSIDERATIONS AND HYPOTHESES

Tax amnesties are controversial. On the one hand, a tax amnesty can generate an immediate increase in tax revenues and reduce administrative costs such as the backlog of paperwork and arrears (Alm, 1998). Furthermore, it might get evaders 'back to the route of honesty'. This is particularly important when correct declaration is difficult due to a complex tax system. Leonard and Zeckhauser (1986) point out that some people become tax delinquents only by mistake.[3] When they are not confronted with punishment mechanisms such as prosecution and penalties, such individuals might be willing to correct their behaviour and to become honest citizens. Thus, future compliance might be increased by integrating former tax delinquents into the taxation procedures.

On the other hand, there are also disadvantages of tax amnesties. Honest taxpayers get informed about the existence of tax evasion, because of the probability that other taxpayers are less compliant (Alm and Beck, 1993). Thus, previously honest taxpayers often view an amnesty as unfair, and feel less motivated to comply in the future. They interpret the amnesty as a signal that tax evasion is a forgivable and insignificant 'peccadillo' (Leonard and Zeckhauser, 1986). This might increase their feeling that they have paid too much in the past compared to other taxpayers. Therefore, the psychological

Table 9.1 Tax amnesties around the world

Country	Amnesty year	Form/main taxes covered	Collection ($ million)	Percentage of tax revenues
Argentina	1987	Previously unreported income for investment purposes	Virtually no revenue	
Argentina	1995	General tax amnesty	3900	
Australia	Twice during the 1980s	Participants in specific avoidance scheme, persons not lodging returns		
Austria	1982	All tax claims prior to 1979	Poor results	
Austria	1993	Special programme to encourage repatriation of untaxed assets	Increase of the tax base (around 58%)	
Belgium	1984–1985	Income exempted from tax if invested (e.g. government bonds)	Poor results	
Belgium	2004	Scheme to repatriate untaxed foreign assets to Belgian accounts	496	
Colombia	1987	Report previously unreported assets or over-reported liabilities	100	0.3% of gross domestic product
Finland	1982–1984	Surplus Interest Affairs		
France	1982	General tax amnesty	19 (only 2786 participants)	0.007
France	1986	Second special amnesty for assets held abroad	22 (only 276 participants)	0.008
India	1981	Government bonds designed for untaxed income		

India	1997	General tax amnesty	2500	8.5
Ireland	1988	General tax amnesty	700–750	4.5
Ireland	1993	General tax amnesty	Significantly lower than 1988	
Italy	1982	General tax amnesty	100	15
Italy	1984	Entrepreneurs and self-employed	5000	
Italy	2001–2002	Special programme to encourage repatriation of untaxed assets	1750	0.4
Netherlands	1934, 1940, 1945, 1955	1955, exemption from penalties and interest	Very good	
New Zealand	1988	General tax amnesty	18 (good response)	
Portugal	1981, 1982, 1986, 1988	Limited to income taxation	40% of the forecast amount	
Russia	1993	Enterprises, organizations, private entrepreneurs not liable for any sanctions on unpaid liabilities		
Russia	1996, 1997	Enterprises and organizations were allowed to defer payments on the arrears	1996 (1997) negative (positive) but insignificant effect on revenues	
Spain	1977	Exemption from penalty for tax liabilities settled prior to 1976		
South Africa	2003–2004	General tax amnesty	8000	

Sources: Alm (1998), Alm et al. (2001), Cassone and Marchese (1995), Marchese and Privileggi (1997), Feld (2003), Hasseldine (1998), OECD (1990), US Joint Committee on Taxation 1998 (JCS-2-98), Torgler and Schaltegger (2005) and Uchitelle (1989).

costs of not complying are reduced when observing others' opportunistic behaviour, which results in a crowding-out of the intrinsic motivation to comply. Furthermore, an amnesty may induce anticipatory behaviour of taxpayers. After an amnesty, previously honest taxpayers may anticipate further amnesties by reducing their tax honesty (Leonard and Zeckhauser, 1986). All in all, the success of an amnesty depends both on its short-run revenue effects and also on the long-term effects on tax compliance.

Fisher et al. (1989) point out that those individuals who have been most involved in tax evasion are less likely to participate in amnesties. Compared to other taxpayers, they face higher marginal participation costs. Furthermore, participants may fear that the government will use the new information for deterrence activities after the amnesty. The successful Italian tax amnesty in 1982 paid attention to this problem, and integrated the 'condono tombale', with the goal of preventing the tax authority from acquiring information about the evaded tax base (Cassone and Marchese, 1995). However, for taxpayers who found themselves in such a position by accident, the marginal cost of participation is low, and an amnesty offers a new start on an honest life.

Empirical evidence on these theoretical effects of a tax amnesty is rare. It is difficult to measure the real effects of tax amnesties, because data from official investigations are often not available. Most empirical results are reported from the United States, since the database is relatively well developed and because US state amnesties are more comparable than amnesties between countries with very different backgrounds.

In their empirical work with field data, Alm and Beck (1993) analysed the long-run effects of the Colorado tax amnesty for the period from January 1980 to December 1989. Their time-series analysis indicates that the amnesty in Colorado had virtually no long-run effect on the level and the trend of tax collection, despite the fact that the Colorado Department of Revenue increased the post-amnesty enforcement efforts. In a cross-sectional analysis including 28 US states, Alm and Beck (1991) empirically analysed the effects of tax amnesties on the total amnesty revenues and on the total per capita amnesty revenues divided by the state population. Their results indicate that the participation of known delinquents and a reduction of interest payments on back taxes increase the amnesty revenues significantly.[4] Furthermore, stricter post-amnesty penalties and enforcement mechanisms also increase amnesty revenues. Alm and Beck (1991) additionally stress the fact that a government can implement all of these strategies without cost, with the obvious exception of the enforcement mechanism.

As field data on tax amnesties are rare, the possibilities for investigations are rather limited. Alm et al. (1990) point out that, in particular, there is no data on the post-amnesty impact of taxpayers' expectations about future amnesties. Field data also pose the problem that it is difficult to separate different structural effects, such as enforcement efforts, and other changes based on the tax amnesty (Alm and Beck, 1993). Experiments offer the possibility of generating data under controlled circumstances, in order to check specific circumstances that are difficult to control in field studies (for a survey, see Torgler, 2002). Tax amnesty experiments help to control this problem, since they allow analysis of the effects of different tax amnesty structures.

Currently, there are only a few tax amnesty experiments. A notable exception is the work of Alm et al. (1990). They found that the average level of compliance falls after an amnesty. However, taxpayers who revealed a high compliance before an amnesty continued to be compliant afterwards. In contrast, subjects with a moderate tax compliance rate reduced their compliance in the post-amnesty phase. They also found that a successful strategy to increase tax compliance after an amnesty is to intensify enforcement efforts. Enhancing the enforcement mechanism increases the cost of evasion and thus reduces the cost of participating in an amnesty. In this context, the immediate amnesty revenues may support the transition to a new tax system (Graetz, 1999). The amnesty might be seen as a fair warning, especially for those taxpayers who were honest before the tax amnesty, and it aims at convincing tax delinquents that the probability of getting caught increases, thus signalling that tax evasion is morally wrong (Fisher et al., 1989). Alm et al. (1990) also found that the anticipation of a further amnesty increases if individuals get the opportunity to participate in an amnesty even though the subjects had been told that no further amnesty would take place. The 'government' loses credibility from the amnesty, and makes evasion seemingly forgivable. Taxpayers also get the incentive to wait for further grace periods.

In our experiment, we check for these effects. According to Alm (1999), experiments should be administered in a uniform and consistent manner to allow replicability. This allows for testing of the robustness of the design and prevents erroneous conclusions.

However, our main focus in this chapter is a different one. In contrast to other experiments, we analyse whether the possibility for subjects to vote for or against an amnesty affects tax compliance. Previous approaches have not analysed whether the ability of individuals to vote on an amnesty influences compliance. As discussed below, our experimental evidence will show that voting on issues such as a tax amnesty will have a positive effect on tax compliance.[5] Similar tendencies can be observed with field data. Pommerehne and Weck-Hannemann (1996) find in a cross-sectional/time-series regression with Swiss data that tax evasion is lower in cantons with a higher degree of direct political control. Torgler (2005) provides evidence, using Swiss survey data, that the stronger direct democracy is in a jurisdiction, the stronger is tax morale. Furthermore, Alm and Torgler (2006) analyse tax morale in the United States and in Europe. The results, based on a multivariate analysis indicate that, compared to other countries, tax morale in the United States and in Switzerland – two countries with strong direct democratic traditions – is higher than in other countries. Feld and Frey (2002) conclude that differences in the treatment of taxpayers by the tax authority are decisive, based on their empirical results using data from Switzerland.

We predict that the possibility of voting will have a positive effect on tax compliance. The voting procedure, and especially public discussions prior to voting, creates a sense of civic duty, as taxpayers become aware of the importance of contributing to public goods. The voting possibility also provides utility in itself. Citizens value the right to participate, because it produces a kind of procedural utility as the opportunity set increases. This leads to an outcome (acceptance of the amnesty or not) that is more favourable compared to a situation in which no such voting possibility exists. From an institutional perspective, the relationship between tax morale and tax compliance can be understood as a 'psychological contract'. If taxpayers can vote on the way taxes will be spent, they may feel more inclined to pay their taxes. The more taxpayers are able to participate in the political decision-making process by popular rights, the more this contract is based on trust, and trust in turn will foster tax morale. A lack of participation may lead to a lower level of satisfaction with the system and a feeling of powerlessness, which may lower tax compliance (Alm et al., 1993). Rules attained through an active involvement of people enhance rule obedience and the willingness to co-operate and act in line with the determined rules. The more people are involved in establishing rules, the stronger is their sense of obligation (Lempert, 1972; McEwen and Maiman, 1986; Cialdini, 1989; Kidder and McEwen, 1989). Tyler's research (1990a,b, 1997) also provides support for the importance of legitimacy and allegiance to authority in compliance decisions. The way people are treated by the authorities affects their evaluations of authorities and their willingness to co-operate (see, e.g., Tyler et al., 1989). Tyler (1997) argues that understanding what people want in a legal procedure helps to explain public dissatisfaction with the law and points towards directions for building public support for the law in the future. Alm et al. (1993) analyse the effects of fiscal institutions on compliance by varying the process by which tax collection becomes a public good (voting versus imposition). Donations given to a campus organization were taken as a public good. Therefore, the public good was not distributed directly to the subjects, but sent to a specific organization. The experimental results provide evidence that tax compliance is higher when individuals can vote on the use of their taxes than when there is no voting over alternatives. Individuals are more likely to comply with their taxes when they themselves are able to select the public-sector expenditure programme. On the other hand, tax compliance is lower when subjects cannot control the use of their tax payments. Feld and Tyran (2002) found in an experiment that tax compliance was higher in an endogenous fine treatment in which subjects had the possibility of approving or rejecting a fine proposal, compared to a situation in which the fine was exogenously fixed. Similarly, Tyran and Feld (2006) analysed under what circumstances the enactment of mild law induced law-abiding behaviour. For this, they compared exogenously imposed law (enacted by the experimenter) and endogenously chosen law (participants could vote in a referendum). The results show that mild law imposed by an exogenous authority does not induce widespread law-abiding behaviour. But mild law induces voluntary compliance if it is accepted in a referendum. The authors state that voting for mild law can be interpreted as a signal for co-operation and so induces expectations of co-operation, which increases co-operation. Furthermore, if mild law is accepted endogenously, individuals expect others to be committed not to free-ride.

On the basis of these considerations, the following hypothesis can be developed:

Hypothesis 1: The possibility of voting on a tax amnesty will increase tax morale and will foster tax compliance.

A key determinant in the voting procedure is discussion. Discussion allows for an exchange of arguments and enhances group identification. Others' preferences become visible, while the moral costs of free-riding increase, which has a positive effect on tax compliance. If discussion is possible prior to voting, citizens are confronted with arguments from both sides – those favouring and those opposing a certain outcome – and this increases the overall level of information. Additionally, citizens become involved, and feel responsible for the result. The voting and discussion procedure creates a sense of civic duty, as taxpayers become aware of the importance of contributing to public goods. Their interaction in a face-to-face situation gives citizens the opportunity to identify others' preferences, which may also enhance people's willingness to accept the final voting decision (Bohnet and Frey, 1994). Alm et al. (1999) argue that there is a social norm of tax compliance that affects individual reporting decisions. Their findings indicate that communication combined with the vote influences tax compliance, so that paying taxes becomes the accepted mode of behaviour. Discussion provides an opportunity to clarify the benefits and costs of a topic and thus increases co-operation among group members. In general, Alm (1996) argues, after surveying experimental findings that 'I believe that the cheap talk in combination with vote allows individuals to change the social norms, in this case to demonstrate that evasion will not be accepted' (p. 123).

Based on these considerations, we deconstruct the voting parameter into voting without discussion and voting with discussion. Thus, the following additional hypothesis can be developed:

Hypothesis 2: Discussion prior to the vote more strongly fosters tax compliance as compared to a voting procedure without discussion.

The next section discusses the experimental design that tests these hypotheses.

THE DESIGN OF THE EXPERIMENTS

The General Structure of the Experiment

We have conducted experiments in Switzerland and Costa Rica. In total, 122 subjects have participated in the experiment, 68 in Switzerland and 54 in Costa Rica. The experiment in Switzerland was done at the University of Basel; those in Costa Rica were done at the University INCAE in Alajuela and at the University Fidélitas in San José. A natural question that occurs in this context is: why have Switzerland and Costa Rica been chosen as the sites for the experiments? Is there something unique about them that makes it especially appropriate to examine these two countries (and to compare them with one another)? Both countries can be considered as small and open economies, which are highly influenced by the policy decisions of neighbouring governments. In both countries, tax amnesties were on the political agenda as a result of experiences in neighbouring countries at the time the experiments were conducted. In Switzerland, the minister of finance presented a model for a general tax amnesty in 2000. However, the proposal was not accepted in the cabinet. At the time when the experiments were being conducted, the Swiss federal parliament was discussing a model for a tax amnesty that only applied to inherited money, which had not been declared before. Similarly, Costa Rica was planning a tax reform incorporating a tax amnesty programme granting taxpayers a tax amnesty over a two-month period, cancelling the fine rate for taxes managed by the tax authorities (income tax, sales tax, selective consumption tax, property tax on vehicles, transfer tax for property and vehicles, education and culture stamp tax, tax on offshore companies, taxes on gambling houses, specific tax on alcoholic beverage and so on; see Arroyo, 2002). Hence, it could be expected that participants in both countries were aware of the topic. For them, a tax amnesty was not an artificial situation. However, despite the fact that the legal system in both countries is based on a civil law system, only Switzerland makes extended use of forms of direct democracy. This means that the Swiss constituency has to approve the implementation of a tax amnesty by popular vote. Thus, the design of the experiment was expected to be a very familiar situation for Swiss participants. In contrast, participants from Costa Rica differ in their real-world experience of political participation. Consequently, using data from both countries would allow us to test whether there were significant differences of the impact of voting in two different institutional settings. Costa Rica also has the advantage of being one of the most stable countries in Latin America and also has a high level of education, which allows the experiment to be conducted in line with the one in Switzerland in English. Both aspects help to reduce possible 'noises and biases' in cross-cultural comparisons. In addition, these two countries were chosen because of the lack of comparative research on tax compliance between Europe and Latin America, and the fact that evidence on tax compliance in countries outside the United States is rare (Andreoni et al., 1998).

Almost all of the subjects were participating in an experiment for the first time.[6] The experiment lasted about an hour and participants earned between $7 and $20 in Switzerland and between $5 and $15 in Costa Rica, depending on the individual performance.[7] Each session consisted of 25 rounds. Subjects did not know in advance when the experiment would end. Communication was not allowed, except in the situation where discussion was explicitly promoted by the experimenters (Session 5). The laboratory currency was 'lab dollars'. The income distribution was exogenous, as all subjects received the same income in every period (200 lab dollars), thus, the obtained income per round did not change during the 25 rounds.[8] The experiment also implemented a public good structure. The taxes on the declared income were doubled, and then redistributed in equal shares to the members of the group. After a round, each subjects' net income could thus be calculated as income less taxes plus the share of the group tax fund. The tax rate was held constant at 20 per cent. Figure A9.1 in the Appendix shows the 'Income Declaration' monitor screen. Subjects were told that all the accumulated earnings during the experiment would be redeemed for cash at the end of the experiment at a fixed conversion rate.

With the exception of a short instruction sheet at the beginning, the complete experiment was conducted on computers and was programmed using z-Tree, on the *Zurich Toolbox for Readymade Economic Experiments* (Fischbacher, 1998), an interactive experimental software program. Each subject was informed in each round about the audit probability, the penalty rate, the accumulated income (fortune) and the individual tax redistribution. The use of a computer allows for minimal experimenter–subject interaction during experimental sessions, which reduces possible framing effects. Furthermore, a computer system facilitates the accounting process (income distribution, tax redistribution and the accumulation of the income).

Before playing 25 rounds in every session, three practice rounds took place to make sure that everyone understood the design. Subjects were informed that their performance in the practice periods did not affect their payments. Subjects were confronted with an explicit tax-context language. We used tax terms such as 'income to declare', 'tax rate', 'audit probability' and 'fine rate', in order to integrate contextual factors that are important in determining tax reporting behaviour, and this procedure also helps subjects to perceive the experiment as something more complex than a mere gamble. However, tax terms may bias subject choices (Alm et al., 1992; Alm and McKee, 2004). For example, subjects' responses may be biased because of certain values that they associate with words such as taxes, audits or fines. Most tax compliance experiments use neutral terminology, although Alm et al. (1992) concluded that there is no difference in behaviour between experiments that use neutral terminology and those that use a tax-specific language, as long as subjects receive full information. Subjects also completed a post-experimental questionnaire, which helped us to control for gender differences in our econometric estimations.

We assumed that the tax agencies use information from the 'returns' to determine whom to audit. Such an experimental design parallels reality, since many countries select returns for audit based on previous tax return information (Roth et al., 1989; Alm et al., 1993). Thus, our experimental design has an endogenous audit selection rule. If a subject is audited and found to have evaded taxes in the current round, then the previous four periods are also audited. With an audit, the unpaid taxes, including a penalty on unpaid taxes of the same amount, must be paid, so that the fine rate equals 2. If the audited subject has reported all income in the current round, the previous periods are not examined. Thus, the tax agency goes back in time to previous periods' declarations. Furthermore, for a subject found to be non-compliant, the audit probability increases from 5 per cent to 10 per cent, in order to capture the consideration that the tax administration may react strongly to observed differences between two declarations.[9] In such an experimental design, the probability of audit is endogenous, depending on the behaviour of taxpayers throughout the experiment.

Several other design features should be noted, in order to reduce problems that arise in conducting a cross-cultural experiment (Roth, 1995). The main experimenters were the same in Costa Rica and Switzerland, to eliminate possible variations arising from uncontrolled procedural differences or uncontrolled personal differences between the experimenters. All instructions were presented in the same language (English) in both countries, to avoid systematic differences between countries that might arise due to the way in which the instructions were translated. Furthermore, as already mentioned, payments given to the subjects were adjusted to the income levels in the country, so that differences in compliance were not caused by differences related to the experimental payments.

Experimental Sessions

Six sessions with different sets of individuals were conducted (see Table 9.2). The design of the sessions was in line with government policy strategies. In session 1, the control case, no amnesty was granted. In session 2 an amnesty was introduced after round 13; at this point, the subjects were given further instructions on the monitor (see the screen in Figure A9.2 in the Appendix), and they did not have any information about the possibility of a tax amnesty. In session 3, the probability of audit and penalty was doubled from the baseline session 1 for non-compliant taxpayers. A tax amnesty indicates that the system has failed to enforce the law and an increase in the enforcement regime indicates that the state is willing to find solutions to the tax evasion problem. In sessions 2 and 3, subjects were also told that the amnesty would be a one-time opportunity to pay back unpaid taxes. In sessions 4 and 5, subjects had the possibility of deciding whether or not they wanted an amnesty after round 13. Subjects did not have any information about the possibility of voting before round 14. In session 5, subjects were given the possibility of having five-minute discussions with each other, before giving their vote. The decision as to whether or not they wanted an amnesty in sessions 4 and 5 was based on a simple majority vote (see the screen for session 5 in Table A9.3). Session 6 analysed the effects of taxpayers' expectations of future amnesties.

Table 9.2 The parameters of the experimental design

Sessions	Amnesty	Voting	Discussion	Audit probability	Fine rate	Tax rate
S1	No	No	No	5%	2	20%
S2	Yes	No	No	5%	2	20%
S3	Yes	No	No	10%[a]	4	20%
S4	No	Yes	No	5%	2	20%
S5	No	Yes	Yes	5%	2	20%
S6	Yes	No	No	5%	2	20%

Note: [a] Only for noncompliant taxpayers.

The first amnesty was declared without previous warning after round 10. Subjects were then informed that no further amnesties would take place. However, contrary to this announcement, subjects were again confronted with an amnesty after round 18. The parameters of the experimental design are summarized in Table 9.2.

Individuals' pay-off

In this subsection we determine the optimal one-period strategy for a subject. We assume that the individual's goal is to maximize the expected value and that an individual takes the actions of others as given. We can then define the expected value from the choice of how much income to report, in line with Alm et al. (1999), as follows:

$$EV = Y - tY^D + ms(G + tY^D) - pf(t(Y - Y^D)) \qquad (9.1)$$

where Y is income before taxation, Y^D is the declared income, t is the tax rate, m is the surplus multiplier, s is the individual's share of the group tax fund, G are taxes paid by all other group members, p is the probability of detection and f is the fine rate on unpaid taxes. If we maximize equation (9.1) by the declared income Y^D, individuals will report all income if

$$pf + ms \geq 1 \qquad (9.2)$$

However, two limitations should be considered. First, the endogenous audit selection rule is not integrated into the model; doing so would make compliance more likeable. Furthermore, the model does not integrate the aspect that the game covers more than one period. Effects of previous experiences or wealth changes are ignored. Subjects may learn during the experiment. Generally, the literature on voluntary contribution mechanisms and social dilemmas shows that public good contributions decline with each repetition (Andreoni, 1988; Dawes and Thaler, 1988; Isaac and Walker, 1988).

The opportunity to vote and the chance of an amnesty may affect individuals' social norm of tax compliance. This makes it relevant to introduce the role of social norms in equation (9.1). In line with Alm et al. (1999), the following extension can be carried out:

$$EV = Y - tY^D + ms(G + tY^D) - pf(t(Y - Y^D)) - \alpha t(Y - Y^D) \qquad (9.3)$$

The value α can be viewed as a 'tax morale' coefficient. The higher the non-compliance $(Y - Y^D)$ and thus the lower the paid taxes t, the higher the psychological costs and thus the psychological loss in the expected income.

In other words, α measures how much an individual would pay to avoid the psychological costs or the loss associated with each dollar of unreported taxes. Condition (9.2) now has the following structure:

$$pf + ms + \alpha \geq 1 \qquad (9.4)$$

The voting procedure increases the psychological costs of evading taxes. The value α thus increases and thus condition (9.4) is more easily satisfied than condition (9.2). However, clear predictions cannot be derived, as we have no information about the magnitude of α.

Amnesties may also change tax morale. For those taxpayers who can get back to the 'route of honesty', and especially for those who became delinquents by mistake, the possibility of an amnesty may increase tax morale. However, the tax morale of honest taxpayers may be undermined if they feel upset about an amnesty (decrease of α). An increase in tax enforcement after an amnesty may send the signal that the tax administration is trying to improve compliance and this action may in turn help restore honest taxpayers' tax morale. Offering more than one tax amnesty, even though subjects are told that only one amnesty will take place, undermines tax morale. A government's credibility is harmed by signalling that tax evasion is a harmless 'peccadillo', so that the anticipation of further tax amnesties will emerge.

Table 9.3 presents the results of applying condition (9.2) to the different groups according to the values in Table 9.2. For example, we receive values of 0.322 (Experiment 1) and 0.282 (Experiment 2) for the control groups, which are below 1, suggesting that the optimal strategy for each individual is to evade paying tax on the whole income. In all the pre-voting and pre-amnesty rounds the optimal strategy is to evade the whole income. However, Table 9.3 indicates that compliance rates vary between 67 and 86 per cent. Thus, in line with other tax compliance experiments, individuals behave more compliantly than the traditional theoretical framework would suggest. Only the implication of a social norm/tax morale coefficient α alters this prediction, leading to a higher level of compliance. But, it should be noted that a high level of α is required to predict a higher level of tax compliance.

EXPERIMENTAL RESULTS

Descriptive Findings

The main variable of interest is the individual's compliance rate (CR) in a given round, specified as the ratio of the reported income (RI) to the true income (TI) in a specific round; that is, $CR = RI/TI$. We present in Table

Table 9.3 The average compliance rate pre- and post-amnesty period and conditions for being honest

Sessions	Compliance rate, rounds 1–13 (pre-amnesty)	Conditions: if value < 1, optimal strategy = evade all the income; else, declare the whole income	Compliance rate, rounds 14–25 (post-amnesty)	Conditions	Required α to ensure that full compliance is the optimal strategy	Subjects
Total						
SESSION (S) 1 EXP 1 & 2	0.714		0.710			
SESSION (S) 2 EXP 1 & 2	0.804		0.828			
SESSION (S) 3 EXP 1 & 2	0.713		0.750			
SESSION (S) 4 EXP 1 & 2	0.700		0.691			
SESSION (S) 5 EXP 1 & 2	0.805		0.840			
SESSION (S) 6 EXP 1 & 2	*Rounds 1–10 (pre-amnesty)*		*Rounds 11–18 (post-amnesty 1)*			
	0.673		0.728			
			Rounds 19–25 (post-amnesty 2)			
			0.750			
Costa Rica						
SESSION (S) 1 EXP 1	0.709	0.322	0.810	0.322	0.613	9
SESSION (S) 2 EXP 1	0.855	0.387	0.890	$0.387 + \alpha_2$	0.314	7
SESSION (S) 3 EXP 1	0.719	0.686	0.742	$0.686 + \alpha_3$	0.718	7
SESSION (S) 4 EXP 1	0.802	0.282	0.829	$0.282 + \alpha_4$	0.718	11
SESSION (S) 5 EXP 1	0.858	0.282	0.906	$0.282 + \alpha_5$		11
SESSION (S) 6 EXP 1	*Rounds 1–10 (pre-amnesty)*		*Rounds 11–18 (post-amnesty 1)*	*Rounds 11–18*	0.700	10
	0.667	0.300	0.751	$0.300 + \alpha_6$		
			Rounds 19–25 (post-amnesty 2)		0.700	
			0.736	$0.300 + \alpha_7$		

Switzerland

Session	Rounds 1–10 (pre-amnesty)		Rounds 11–18 (post-amnesty 1)		Rounds 19–25 (post-amnesty 2)		n
SESSION (S) 1 EXP 2	0.718	0.282	0.628	0.282		0.650	11
SESSION (S) 2 EXP 2	0.760	0.350	0.774	$0.350 + \alpha_2$		0.434	8
SESSION (S) 3 EXP 2	0.653	0.566	0.725	$0.566 + \alpha_3$		0.678 and 0.5^a	12
SESSION (S) 4 EXP 2	0.619	0.322 and 0.500^a	0.583	0.322 and $0.5^a + \alpha_4$		0.746	9 and 5^a
SESSION (S) 5 EXP 2	0.760	0.254	0.785	$0.254 + \alpha_5$			13
SESSION (S) 6 EXP 2	0.677	0.254	0.712	$0.254 + \alpha_6$	0.761	$0.254 + \alpha_7$	13
						0.746	7

Note: ^{a} Run twice.

9.3 the average compliance rate across all sessions, differentiating between the pre-amnesty and the post-amnesty periods. Taking both country experiments together, we observe that for the reference group (session 1) the average compliance rate is virtually tied over all rounds in the session. On the other hand, the compliance rate of the other sessions increases in the post-amnesty period (except for session 4). We observe differences between Experiments 1 (CR, Costa Rica) and 2 (CH, Switzerland). In Experiment 1, the compliance rate is in general higher and in session 4, contrary to Experiment 2, we observe an increase in the compliance rate in the post-amnesty period.

In Figures 9.1–9.3 we also present average compliance rates across rounds in a given session. In general, we observe a high compliance rate over time. Individuals are clearly more compliant than our expected value calculations predicted. In fact, the average compliance rate in any particular round never falls below 40 per cent.

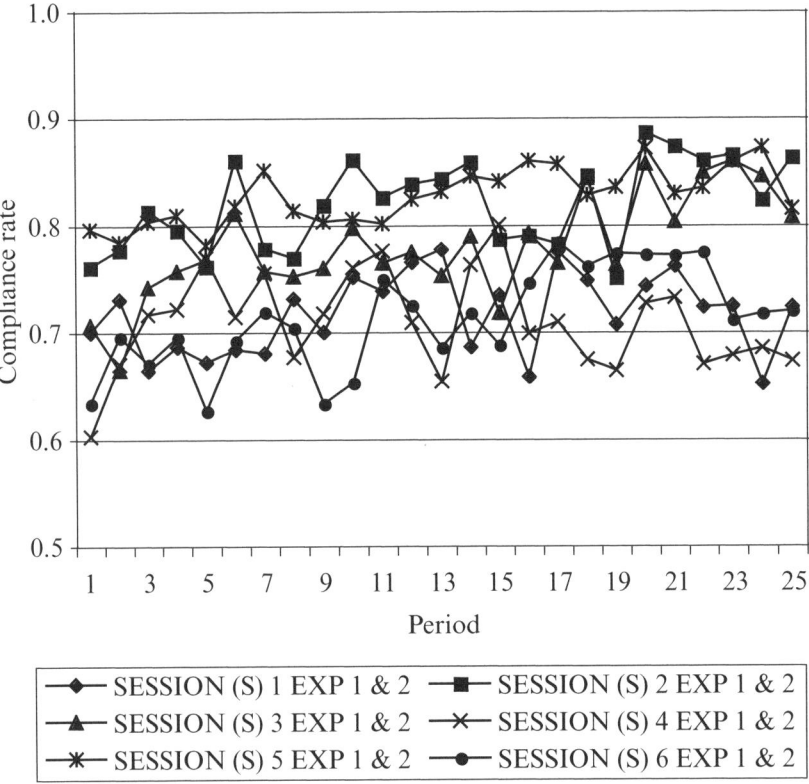

Figure 9.1   The compliance rate in Experiments 1 and 2

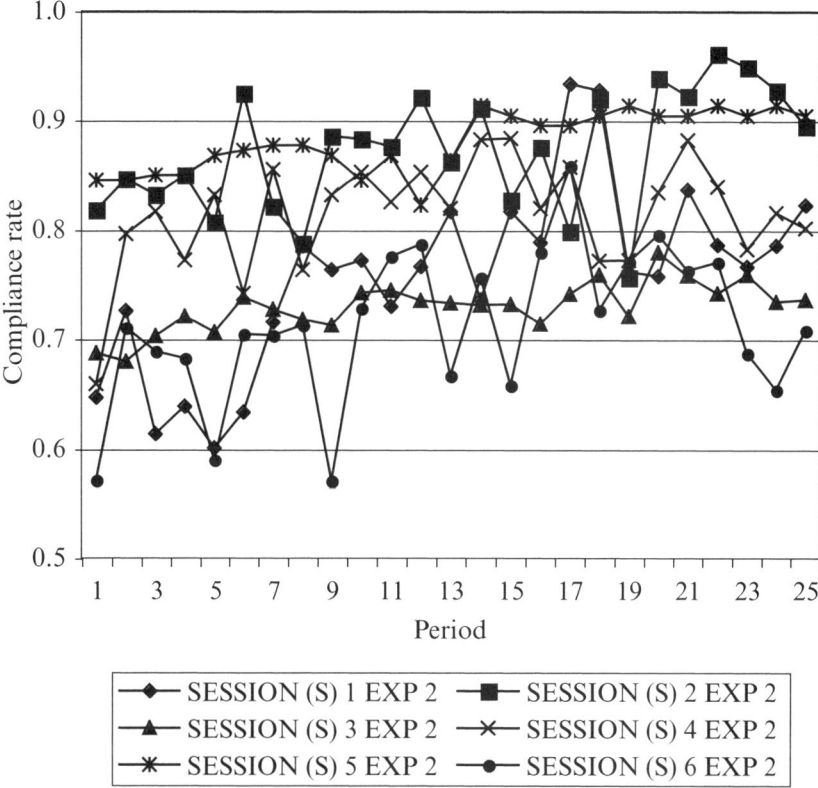

Figure 9.2   The compliance rate of Experiment 2

Surprisingly, in most of the sessions the compliance rate does not tend to decline over time. This result is not in line with many studies on voluntary contribution mechanisms and social dilemmas, which show that public good contributions decline with each repetition (see Andreoni, 1988; Dawes and Thaler, 1988; Isaac and Walker, 1988), and this is probably due to the presence of an enforcement mechanism.

Multivariate Analysis

We also conducted a multivariate regression analysis better to investigate the causes and effects of the different treatments. The variables are described in Table 9.4. We used different models to check the robustness of the obtained findings. First, we present Tobit maximum likelihood estimations, as the compliance rate CR varies between 0 and 1 and there are many observations

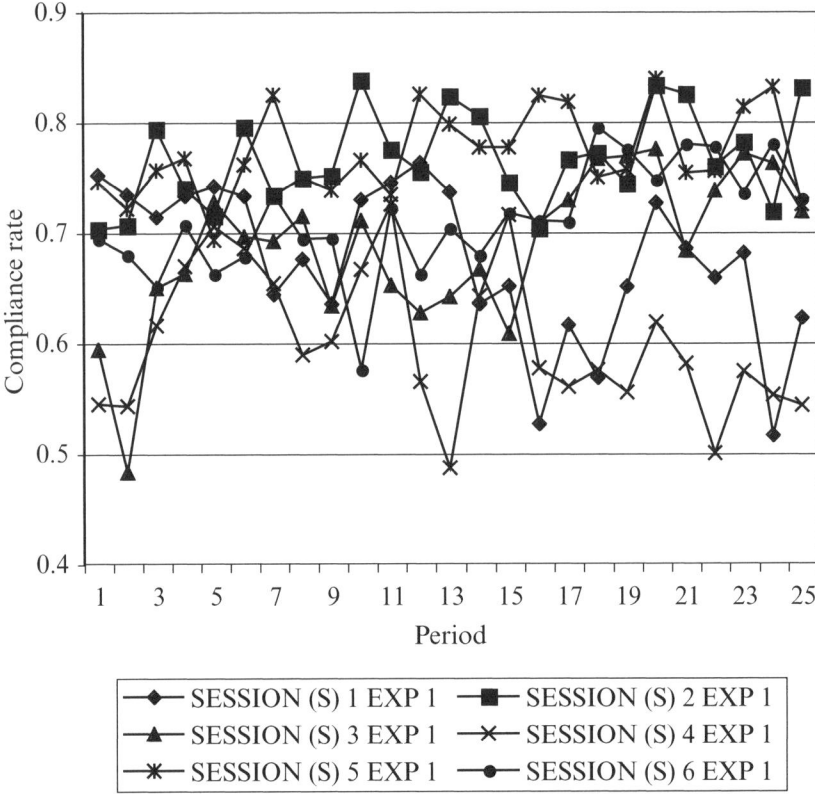

Figure 9.3   The compliance rate of Experiment 1

with the values 0 and 1.[10] To include the panel structure of the data, we additionally include a random-effects estimation in order to control for time-specific effects. The random-effects model is appropriate if we assume that the individual specific constant terms are randomly distributed across cross-sectional units. Because of the presence of the public good, which means that one subject's pay-off depends upon the behaviour of all other subjects in a group, it seems reasonable to add pooled least-squares estimations with clustering over groups.[11] Our estimation equation reads as follows:

$$TCR_{it} = \beta_0 + \beta_1 \cdot CTRL_{it} + \beta_2 \cdot AM1_{it} + \beta_3 \cdot AM2_{it} + \beta_4 \cdot VOTE_{it} + \beta_5 \cdot GENDER_i + \varepsilon_{it} \qquad (9.5)$$

where TCR_{it} denotes the tax compliance rate. $CTRL_{it}$ is a panel of control variables, which includes a dummy variable equal to 1 if the individual was audited in the previous round and 0 otherwise, the nominal fine for tax evasion, and the transfer payment obtained in each period. $AM1_{it}$ is a dummy variable that compares the pre-amnesty period with the post-amnesty period (value = 1) whereas $AM2_{it}$ considers the case for a second amnesty. $VOTE_{it}$ is the dummy that differentiates between the pre-voting and the post-voting period. Furthermore, with the dummy variable $GENDER_i$ we differentiate between women and men. To analyse whether there is a difference in tax compliance when the voting procedure is accompanied by public discussions prior to the ballots, in contrast to when this option is not allowed, we deconstruct the dummy variable 'voting' into the dummy variables VOTING WITH DISCUSSION and VOTING WITHOUT DISCUSSION. We also differentiate between whether or not enforcement increases in the post-amnesty period (TAX AMNESTY WITH ENFORCEMENT and TAX AMNESTY WITHOUT ENFORCEMENT). Alm et al. (1990) found in their tax amnesty experimental study that revenues from an amnesty are greater if post-amnesty enforcement increases.

Table 9.4 A description of the variables

Variables	Description
Compliance rate	Ratio of the reported income to the true income.
Audit	Dummy equal to 1 if the individual was audited in the previous round and 0 otherwise.
Penalty	Total penalty amount after detection.
Transfers	The amount an individual obtains from the group fund at the end of the previous round.
Voting without discussion	Dummy variable equal to 1 in the post-voting period and 0 in the pre-voting period.
Voting with discussion	Dummy variable equal to 1 in the post-voting period with discussion; otherwise 0.
Amnesty without enforcement	Dummy variable equal to 1 in the post-amnesty period (enforcement variables remain constant) and 0 in the pre-amnesty period.
Amnesty with enforcement	Dummy variable equal to 1 in the post-amnesty period (enforcement variables multiplied by a factor 2) and 0 in the pre-amnesty period.
Second amnesty	Dummy variable equal to 1 in the post-second amnesty period after the enforcement parameters have been doubled, and 0 in the pre-second amnesty period.
Woman	Gender dummy variable, woman = 1; man in the reference group.

Table 9.5 presents the results. We report the pooled estimations (Experiments 1 and 2 together) and the findings at each experiment independently. Presenting experimental evidence from two different nations allows for a robustness check of our main hypotheses. As we can see, most results remain robust throughout different estimation methods. In the TOTAL regressions we include a dummy variable without reporting it in Table 9.5, differentiating between Experiments 1 and 2. It can be argued that the audit variable is endogenous. However, a Hausman Chi-square test rejects the hypothesis that the variable is endogenous.[12]

The coefficient of the variable VOTING WITH DISCUSSION is significant, whereas this does not hold for the variable VOTING WITHOUT DISCUSSION. The coefficient VOTING WITHOUT DISCUSSION is only statistically significant with a positive sign in Experiment 1. In Experiment 2 and the pooled estimation in models 1a and 1b, we even observe a negative sign. Thus, the key message is this: fostering public communication before casting votes for a tax amnesty favours tax compliance; that is, communication and identification seem to be key elements in enforcing co-operation.[13] Our results are in line with experimental evidence demonstrating that communication supports co-operation (Sally, 1995). Discussion may clarify the benefits and costs of an amnesty, and may also increase the concern about other group members' welfare. Thus, 'institutionalized communication opportunities enable individuals to privatize a decision' (Bohnet and Frey, 1994).

In general, in both experiments compliance behaviour in the post-vote period is clearly different from the pre-vote behaviour under the same fiscal regime. This result is very much in line with the experimental findings of Alm et al. (1999), indicating that voting in combination with discussion has a positive impact on tax compliance. All groups in Experiment 2 rejected the choice of an amnesty, while all groups in Experiment 1 decided for an amnesty. This suggests that a rejection of an amnesty has a negative impact on tax compliance if voting is not accompanied by cheap talk.

Looking at specifications 1a and 1b, we observe that a tax amnesty has a positive impact on tax compliance. Contrary to the findings of Alm et al. (1990), an amnesty with increased post-enforcement does not generate higher levels of compliance compared to an amnesty in which post-amnesty enforcement remains constant. In general, the positive impact is driven by the results in Experiment 2. Furthermore, the use of a least-squares estimation clustering over groups reduces the statistical significance of an amnesty. It should be noticed that the second amnesty did not increase compliance significantly in the post-amnesty period. In most cases the coefficient is even negative, but is not statistically significant. These findings support the view that amnesties should not be conducted in short intervals, since individuals anticipate future tax amnesties and this eventually crowds out tax compliance. These results are in line with the findings of Alm et al. (1990), indicating that amnesty expectations and a reduction of the state's credibility lower the positive effect of a tax amnesty.

The economics-of-crime approach would predict that the extent of tax evasion depends negatively on the probability of being caught and the severity of the punishment in the case of being caught. Some empirical findings indicate that a higher probability of being caught discourages evasion (Witte and Woodbury, 1985; Crane and Nourzad, 1987; Dubin and Wilde, 1988; Joulfaian and Rider, 1996). In experiments, there is also a tendency for a higher audit rate to lead to more compliance (Friedland et al., 1978; Beck et al., 1991; Alm et al., 1992a,b; Alm et al., 1993). However, the pooled cross-sectional time-series estimation for Swiss cantons over the years 1970, 1978, 1985, 1990 and 1995 done by Frey and Feld (2002), using tax evasion as the dependent variable, indicates that the probability of detection has a theoretically unexpected positive sign that is not statistically significant, while the size of the fine is statistically significant at the 5 per cent level. Beron et al. (1992) found, using tax return data from 1969, a weak deterrent effect from audits on tax compliance. Pommerehne and Weck-Hannemann (1996) found that the coefficients of the probability of detection and the penalty tax rate have a negative sign, but that none of them was statistically significant. Slemrod et al. (2001) used a controlled field experiment in Minnesota to analyse taxpayers response to an increased probability of audit. While low- and middle-income taxpayers increased their reported tax between 1993 and 1994 relative to the control group, the reported income of high-income taxpayers fell sharply in relation to the control group. Torgler (2005) found, in an empirical study with Swiss data, that the effects of deterrence parameters on tax morale are not positive. In our experiment, the audit probability does not have a statistically significant impact, and the penalty rate even has a negative impact on tax compliance.

Not surprisingly, a higher group transfer leads to significantly higher tax compliance.[14] Higher transfers give subjects a signal that the group on average behaves honestly. The moral costs of being opportunistic increase. Furthermore, the results show a significantly higher tax compliance in Experiment 1 (Costa Rica) than in Experiment 2 (Switzerland). Finally, women reveal significantly higher tax compliance than men.

CONCLUSIONS

Although many tax amnesties have been conducted all around the world, evidence on their long-term effects is largely lacking. This chapter has analysed

Table 9.5 The determinants of tax compliance (tobit)

	Random-effects Tobit regressions						Least squares, clustering over groups					
	Total		Exp. 1		Exp. 2		Total		Exp. 1		Exp. 2	
Variables	Coeff. Equation 1a	z-Stat.	Coeff. Equation 2a	z-Stat.	Coeff. Equation 3a	z-Stat.	Coeff. Equation 1b	t-Stat.	Coeff. Equation 2b	t-Stat.	Coeff. Equation 3b	t-Stat.
(a) Deterrence												
Audit	−0.009	−0.20	−0.132	−1.25	0.018	0.35	0.016	0.55	0.014	0.24	0.017	0.73
Penalty	−0.003***	−7.92	−0.002***	−4.52	−0.003***	−5.45	−0.002***	−4.56	−0.002***	−5.25	−0.001***	−4.19
(b) Group transfer												
Transfers	0.001***	2.64	0.002**	2.50	0.001*	1.81	0.001***	2.79	0.001**	2.19	0.001**	2.58
(c) Political participation												
Voting with discussion	0.206***	4.60	0.532***	5.64	0.130**	2.31	0.082***	5.34	0.114***	4.98	0.092***	3.31
Voting without discussion	−0.117***	−2.89	0.210**	2.51	−0.209***	−3.98	−0.059***	−4.27	0.063**	2.06	−0.127***	−3.59
(d) Tax amnesty												
Amnesty without enforc. incr.	0.135***	3.99	−0.082	−1.34	0.122**	2.30	0.058**	2.02	0.001	0.03	0.052	1.69
Amnesty with enforc. incr.	0.094*	1.92	−0.046	−0.61	0.147**	2.25	0.014	0.52	−0.025	−0.67	0.032	1.06
Second amnesty	−0.081	−1.20	−0.003	−0.03	0.025	0.27	−0.026	−1.14	−0.031	−1.02	0.016	0.71
(e) Gender												
Woman	0.220***	8.86	0.256***	6.05	0.239***	7.42	0.128***	2.95	0.120***	3.01	0.152**	2.49

(f) Experiment

	Experiment 1 Dummy (CR)				
	0.277***	10.77		0.100***	3.31
Log-likelihood	−2465.023		−944.199		−1503.794
Probability > χ2	0.000		0.000		0.000
Number of observations	3050		1350		1700
R-squared					
	3050		1350		1700
	0.11		0.12		0.09

Notes: Dependent variable: tax compliance rate as the ratio of reported income to true income. In the reference group is MAN, EXPERIMENT 2. Significance levels: * $0.05 < p < 0.10$; ** $0.01 < p < 0.05$; *** $p < 0.01$.

the impact of voter participation on tax amnesties using experiments. The novel framework in our analysis was to combine a tax amnesty experiment with voting. Furthermore, by conducting two experiments, each in a different country with a different cultural and historical background, we could check whether similar cross-country tendencies were observable. Our results provide strong evidence that individuals are more compliant when they have the opportunity to vote coupled with communication among group members prior to the vote. Voting without discussion produces mixed findings. Thus, discussion before voting is an essential feature in increasing group co-operation: it enhances the moral costs of free-riding and thus increases the social norm of compliances, generating a higher tax compliance. This result is in line with a previous study carried out by Alm et al. (1999).

Furthermore, in line with Alm et al. (1990), amnesties tend to increase tax compliance in our experiments. However, contrary to the findings of Alm et al. (1990), an amnesty with an increase in the post-amnesty enforcement parameters does not outperform an amnesty without changes in the enforcement factors. The results also indicate that the effect of a second amnesty does not improve tax compliance. The coefficient is mostly negative, but not statistically significant. Amnesty expectations reduce the positive effects of an amnesty. When the government does not keep its promise, tax compliance decreases. Such a result has a strong policy implication. If a government has the intention of increasing the long-term effects of a tax amnesty, its commitment should be reliable, and only one amnesty should be conducted.

Generally, our results indicate that there are limitations to the economics-of-crime approach. The results show the importance of incorporating the role of societal institutions and social norms into tax compliance models better to understand why so many individuals comply.

APPENDIX

Year ⎯⎯⎯⎯⎯⎯⎯⎯⎯⎯
            [1   ]

INCOME TAX DECLARATION

Tax Policy Information:

    Tax rate 20%
    Probability of audit 5%
(increases with an increasing difference between this year's declared income and last year's declared income, max. 10%)
If you were selected for an audit, the actual and the declared income for the previous 4 rounds are compared. If you did not fully comply, any back taxes are collected, and a fine equal to the unpaid taxes is also imposed.
    Fine rate: 2.0 (200% of the unpaid taxes)

Personal Information:

    taxable income: 200 lab$
    Accumulated income (fortune): 0 lab$
    therefrom: 0 lab$ state's transfer from last year
    Taxes: 0 lab$ from last year

Declaration:

    Herewith I declare an assigned income of

                                lab$: [0]

Furthermore, you should know that the whole tax revenue from your group is multiplied with the factor 2 and redistributed in equal shares among the participants. Revenue from penalty tax and after taxes is not redistributed. If the whole amount of taxes (i.e., the sum of all single payments of all members of a group of 10 persons) is 100 $, every participant receives transfer payment of 20 $.

                                                                    (OK)

Figure A9.1   Income declaration

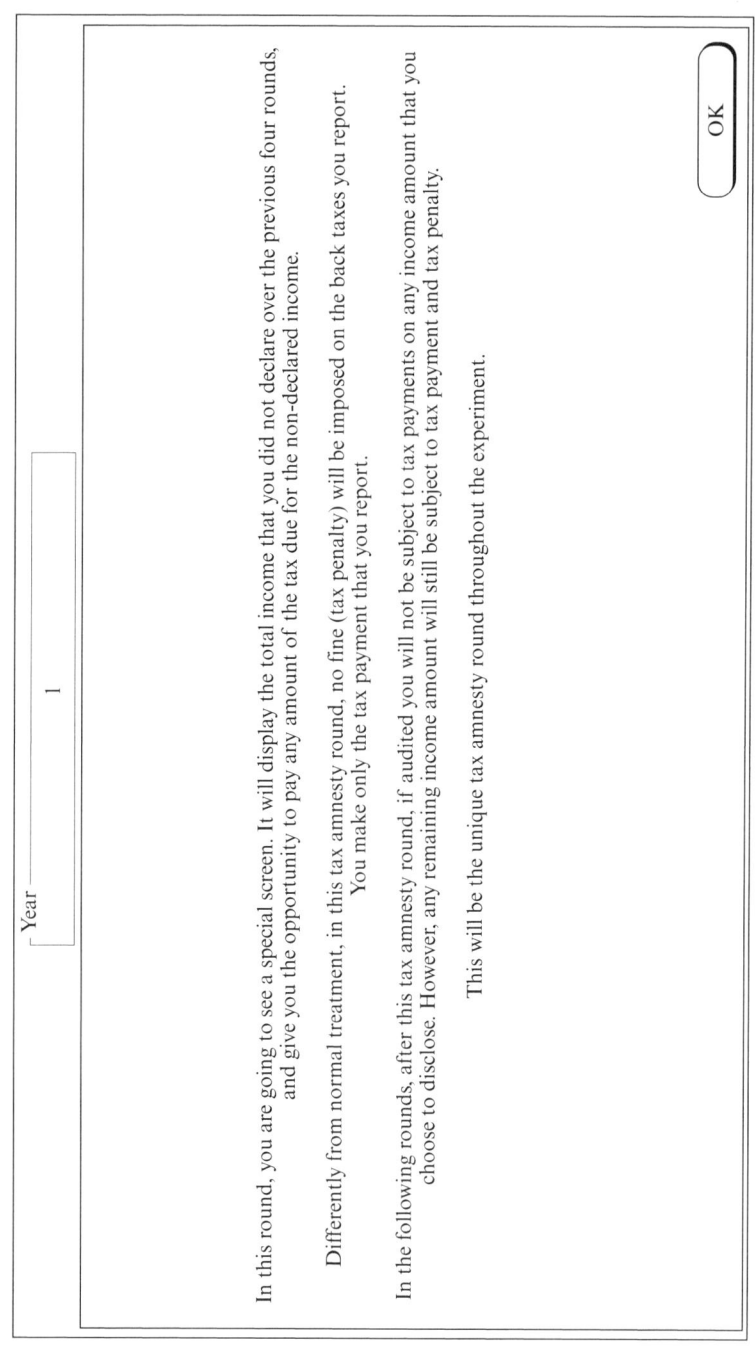

Figure A9.2   The tax amnesty (session 2)

Notes: The screen for session 3 additionally points out 'Furthermore, the audit probability will be increased from 5% to 10% and the fine rate from 2 to 4'.

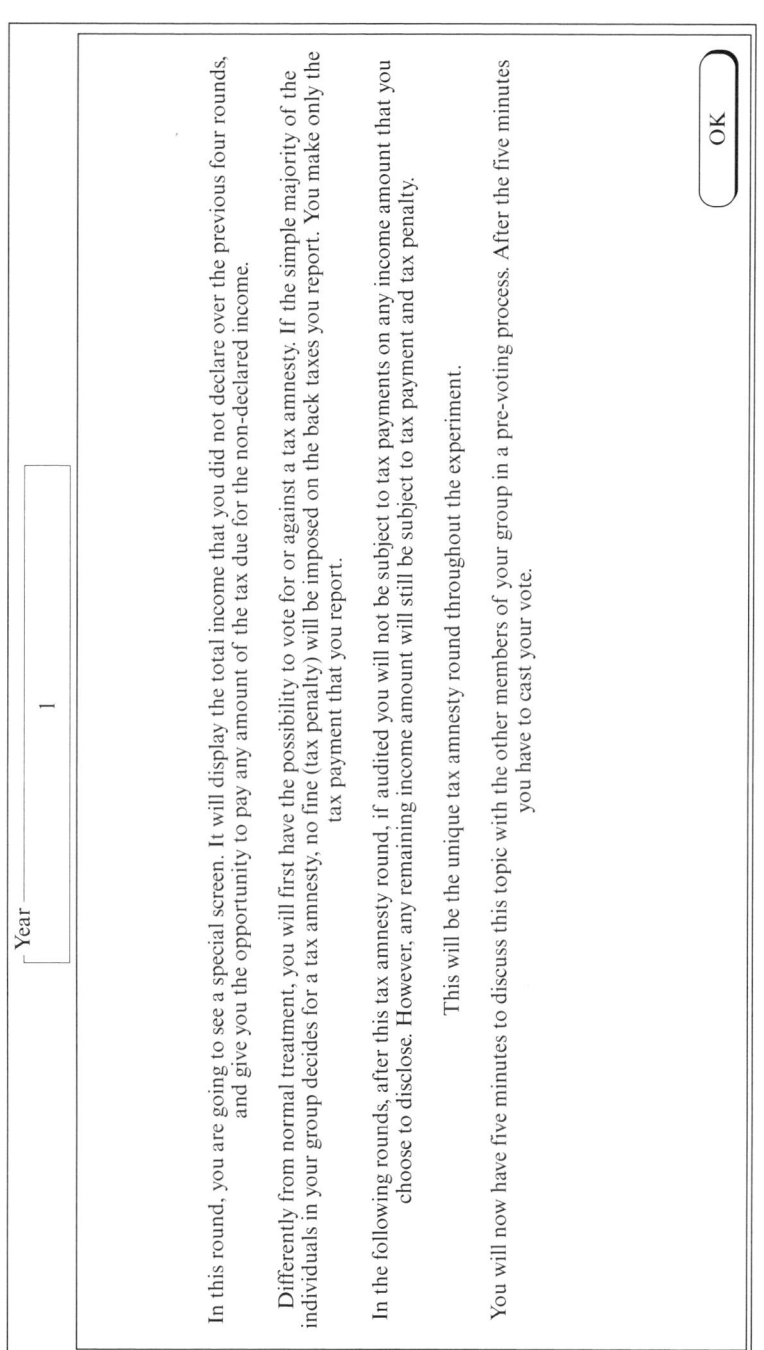

Figure A9.3 Voting (session 5, with discussion)

NOTES

1. See, for example, http://www.taxadmin.org/fta/rate/amnesty1.html and Hasseldine (1998, p. 307).
2. An important exception is Switzerland, where the latest tax amnesty in 1969 only passed a popular referendum after a major revision of the original law, which had been refused in 1964.
3. Joulfaian and Rider (1996) report from an empirical analysis with 'Earned Income Tax Credits' that taxpayers' mistakes in their income declarations are quantitatively quite important. This is not only true for under-reporting, but also for over-reporting income.
4. Alm and Beck (1991) use a dummy variable 'DELINQUENT' to measure a reduction in the amnesty tax rate, as criminal penalties are forgiven for delinquents who participate in an amnesty.
5. However, for previous experimental evidence on voting, see Alm et al. (1999) and Feld and Tyran (2002).
6. We administered a survey questionnaire after the experiment and asked whether a subject had prior experience with experiments in general (e.g. whether a subject had experimental experience). In Switzerland, 4 out 68 had prior experience, but in all cases, the experiments were never related to ours. In Costa Rica, nobody had previously taken part in an experiment.
7. The differences in the payment amounts between Switzerland and Costa Rica are deduced from price comparisons of homogenous goods among different cultures (e.g. a Coca Cola, a Big Mac and the price of a cinema ticket).
8. Certainly, one can argue that distributing the same income throughout the 25 rounds might be boring for the subjects. However, a change in income might produce biases, which we wanted to avoid since treatment changes occurred within a session.
9. Comparisons between the years may help a tax administration to make a pre-selection before choosing the tax forms to be analysed more closely. Thus, the audit rate does not only increase for the subject audited. It is a linear increase from 5 per cent to 10 per cent. For example, a subject who does not evade taxes between two rounds will be controlled with a probability of 5 per cent. On the other hand, a subject who was honest at first and then evades tax on all of the income will be controlled with a probability of 10 per cent.
10. The Tobit model assumes that the disturbance term has a normal distribution. However, the criteria of unbiasedness and efficiency do not depend on this assumption. Furthermore, if the sample is moderately large as in our estimations (3050 observations), normality of the disturbance term is not required in order to guarantee that the confidence intervals and p values are accurate. The 'Central Limit Theorem' indicates that the confidence intervals and the p values are good approximations even when the disturbance term is not normally distributed if an estimation has any more than 200 cases. See Allison (1999).
11. Clustering helps us to deal with the fact that the number of subjects varies in each session.
12. We used the number of times a subject has been controlled (adjusted after every audit) as an instrument for our AUDIT variable. The Hausman test allows us to test whether there is a sufficient difference between the coefficients of the instrumental variables regression and those of the regression used. The Prob>chi2 value of 0.1301 (specification 1b – in the table Equation 1b) clearly indicates that our used regression is a consistent estimator for this equation. Similar values have been obtained for the other estimations.
13. Frey and Bohnet (2001) also point out that discourse between citizens is an important element of a lawful state and allows a consensus to be reached.
14. In each round, the group transfer sum of the previous round was shown on the screen. Subjects could see on the monitor in each round their group transfer sum from the previous round.

REFERENCES

Allison, P.D. (1999), *Multiple Regression: a Primer*, California: Pine Forge Press.
Alm, J. (1996), 'Explaining tax compliance', in S. Pozo (ed.), *Exploring the Underground Economy*, Kalamazoo: W.E. Upjohn Institute for Employment Research, pp. 103–28.
Alm, J. (1998), 'Tax policy analysis: the introduction of a Russian tax amnesty', Working Paper 98–6, International Studies Program, Georgia State University.
Alm, J. (1999), 'Tax compliance and administration', in H. Bartley and J.A. Richardson (eds), *Handbook on Taxation*, New York: Marcel Dekker, pp. 741–68.
Alm, J. and W. Beck (1991), 'Wiping the slate clean: individual response to state amnesties', *Southern Economic Journal*, **57**, 1043–53.
Alm, J. and W. Beck (1993), 'Tax amnesties and compliance in the long run: a time series analysis', *National Tax Journal*, **46**, 53–60.
Alm, J. and M. McKee (2004), 'Tax compliance as a coordination game', *Journal of Economic Behavior and Organization*, **54**, 297–312.
Alm, J. and B. Torgler (2006), 'Culture differences and tax morale in the United States and Europe', *Journal of Economic Psychology*, **27**, 224–46.
Alm, J., M.B. Cronshaw and M. McKee (1993), 'Tax compliance with endogenous audit selection rules', *KYKLOS*, **1**, 27–45.
Alm, J., B. Jackson and M. McKee (1992a), 'Deterrence and beyond: toward a kinder, gentler IRS', in J. Slemrod (ed.), *Why People Pay Taxes*, Ann Arbor: University of Michigan Press, pp. 311–29.
Alm, J., B.R. Jackson and M. McKee (1992b), 'Estimating the determinants of taxpayer compliance with experimental data', *National Tax Journal*, **45**, 107–15.
Alm, J., B.R. Jackson and M. McKee (1993), 'Fiscal exchange, collective decision institutions, and tax compliance', *Journal of Economic Behavior and Organization*, **22**, 285–303.
Alm J., J. Martinez-Vazquez and S. Wallace (2001), 'Tax amnesties and tax collections in the Russian Federation', Working Paper 01–4, International Studies Program, Georgia State University.
Alm, J., G.H. McClelland and W.D. Schulze (1992), 'Why do people pay taxes?', *Journal of Public Economics*, **48**, 21–48.
Alm, J., G.H. McClelland and W. D. Schulze (1999), 'Changing the social norm of tax compliance by voting', *KYKLOS* **52**, 141–71.
Alm, J., G.H. McKee and W. Beck (1990), 'Amazing grace: tax amnesties and tax compliance', *National Tax Journal*, **43**: 23–37.
Andreoni, J. (1988), 'Why free ride? Strategies and learning in public goods experiments', *Journal of Public Economics*, **37**, 291–304.
Andreoni, J., B. Erard and J. Feinstein (1998), 'Tax compliance', *Journal of Economic Literature*, **36**, 818–60.
Arroyo, A. (2002), 'Proyecto ley de contingencia fiscal', *Tax&Legal news*, 24 October.
Beck, P.J., J.S. Davis and W.-O. Jung (1991), 'Experimental evidence on taxpayer reporting behavior', *The Accounting Review*, **66**, 535–58.
Beron, K. J., H.V. Tauchen and A.D. Witte (1992), 'The effect of audits and socioeconomic variables on compliance', in J. Slemrod (ed.), *Why People Pay Taxes. Tax Compliance and Enforcement*, Ann Arbor: The University of Michigan Press, pp. 67–89.

Bohnet, I. and B.S. Frey (1994), 'Direct-democratic rules: the role of discussion', *KYKLOS*, **47**, 341–54.
Cassone, A. and C. Marchese (1995), 'Tax amnesties as special sales offers: the Italian experience', *Public Finance*, **50**, 51–66.
Cialdini, R. B. (1989), 'Social motivations to comply: norms, values and principles', in J.A. Roth and J.T. Scholz (eds), *Taxpayer Compliance*, Vol. 2, Philadelphia: University of Pennsylvania Press, pp. 200–27.
Crane, S.E. and F. Nourzad (1987), 'On the treatment of income tax rates in empirical analysis of tax evasion', *KYKLOS*, **40**, 338–48.
Dawes, R.M. and R.H. Thaler (1988), 'Anomalies: cooperation', *Journal of Economic Perspectives*, **2**, 187–97.
Dubin, J.A. and L.L. Wilde (1988), 'An empirical analysis of federal income tax auditing and compliance', *National Tax Journal*, **41**, 61–74.
Feld, L.P. (2003), 'Rückführung von Fluchtkapital als Voraussetzung für den fiskalischen Erfolg einer Abgeltungssteuer?', in G. Schick (ed.), Veranlagung – Abgeltung – Steuerfreiheit: Besteuerung von Kapitalerträgen im Rechtsstaat, Berlin: Stiftung Marktwirtschaft/Frankfurter Institut, pp. 43–53.
Feld, L.P. and B.S. Frey (2002), 'Trust breeds trust: how taxpayers are treated', *Economics of Governance*, **3**, 87–99.
Feld, L.P. and J.-R. Tyran (2002), 'Tax evasion and voting: an experimental analysis', *KYKLOS*, **55**, 197–222.
Fischbacher, U. (1998), *Zurich Toolbox for Readymade Economic Experiments, Experimenter's Manual*, Zurich: University of Zurich.
Fisher, R.C., J.H. Goddeeris and J.C. Young (1989), 'Participation in amnesties: the individual income tax', *National Tax Journal*, **42**, 15–27.
Frey, B.S. and I. Bohnet (2001), 'Identification in democratic society', in B.S. Frey (ed.), *Inspiring Economics. Human Motivation in Political Economy*, Cheltenham, UK and Northampton, MA, USA: Edward Elgar, pp. 103–17.
Frey, B.S. and L.P. Feld (2002), 'Deterrence and morale in taxation: an empirical analysis', CESifo Working Paper No. 760, August 2002.
Friedland, N., S. Maital and A. Rutenberg (1978), 'A simulation study of income tax evasion', *Journal of Public Economics*, **10**, 107–16.
Graetz, M.J. (1999), *The U.S. Income Tax. What It Is, How It Got That Way, And Where We Go From Here*, New York: W.W. Norton.
Hasseldine, J. (1998), 'Tax amnesties: an international review', *Bulletin for International Fiscal Documentation*, **52**, 303–10.
Isaac, R.M. and J.M. Walker (1988), 'Group size effects in public goods provision: the voluntary contributions mechanism', *Quarterly Journal of Economics*, **53**, 179–200.
Joulfaian, D. and M. Rider (1996), 'Tax evasion in the presence of negative income tax rates', *National Tax Journal*, **49**, 553–70.
Kidder, R. and C. McEwen (1989), 'Taxpaying behavior in social context: a tentative typology of tax compliance and noncompliance', in J.A. Roth and J.T. Scholz (eds), *Taxpayer Compliance*, Vol. 2. Philadelphia: University of Pennsylvania Press, pp. 46–75.
Lempert, R.O. (1972), 'Norm-making in social exchange: a contract law model', *Law and Society Review*, **1**, 1–32.
Leonard, H.B. and R.J. Zeckhauser (1986), 'Amnesty, enforcement and tax policy', NBER Working Paper Series, No. 2096, National Bureau of Economic Research, Cambridge, MA.

Marchese, C. and F. Priviléggi (1997), 'Taxpayer's attitudes toward risk and amnesty participation: economic analysis and evidence for the Italian case', *Public Finance*, **52**, 394–410.

McEwen, C.A. and R.J. Maiman (1986), 'In search of legitimacy: toward an empirical response analysis', *Law & Policy*, **8**, 257–73.

OECD (1990), *Taxpayer Rights and Obligations. A Survey of the Legal Situation in OECD Countries*, Paris: OECD.

Pommerehne, W.W. and H. Weck-Hannemann (1996), 'Tax rates, tax administration and income tax evasion in Switzerland', *Public Choice* **88**, 161–70.

Roth, A.E. (1995), 'Introduction to experimental economics', in J.H. Kagel and A.E. Roth (eds), *The Handbook of Experimental Economics*, Princeton: Princeton University Press, pp. 1–98.

Roth, J.A., J.T. Scholz and A.D. Witte (eds) (1989), *Taxpayer Compliance*, Vols. 1 and 2, Philadelphia: University of Pennsylvania Press.

Sally, D. (1995), 'Conversation and cooperation in social dilemmas. A meta-analysis of experiments from 1958 to 1992', *Rationality and Society*, **7**, 58–92.

Slemrod, J., M. Blumenthal and C. Christian (2001), 'Taxpayer response to an increased probability of audit: evidence from a controlled experiment in Minnesota', *Journal of Public Economics*, **79**, 455–83.

Torgler, B. (2002), 'Speaking to theorists and searching for facts: tax morale and tax compliance in experiments', *Journal of Economic Surveys*, **16**, 657–84.

Torgler, B. (2005), 'Tax morale and direct democracy', *European Journal of Political Economy*, **21**, 525–31.

Torgler, B. and C.A. Schaltegger (2005), 'Tax amnesties in Switzerland and around the world', *Tax Notes International*, 27 June, 1193–203.

Tyler, T.R. (1990a), 'Justice, self-interest, and the legitimacy of legal and political authority', in J.J. Mansbridge (ed.), *Beyond Self-Interest*, Chicago: University of Chicago Press, pp. 171–9.

Tyler, T.R. (1990b), *Why People Obey the Law*, New Haven: Yale University Press.

Tyler, T.R. (1997), 'Procedural fairness and compliance with the law', *Swiss Journal of Economics and Statistics*, **133**, 219–40.

Tyler, T.R., J.D. Casper and B. Fisher (1989), 'Maintaining allegiance toward political authorities: the role of prior attitudes and the use of fair procedures', *American Journal of Political Science*, **33**, 629–52.

Tyran, J.-R. and L.P. Feld (2006), 'Achieving compliance when legal sanctions are non-deterrent', *Scandinavian Journal of Economics*, **101**, 135–56.

Uchitelle, E. (1989), 'The effectiveness of tax amnesty programs in selected countries', *Federal Reserve Bank of New York Quarterly Review*, **14**, 48–53.

US Joint Committee on Taxation (1998), *Tax Amnesty* (JCS-2-98).

Witte, A.D. and D.F. Woodbury (1985), 'The effect of tax laws and tax administration on tax compliance', *National Tax Journal*, **38**, 1–14.

Index

Adams, C. 3, 195
Adams, J.S. 72, 95
'Afrobarometro' 53
age, impact of 30, 119–20, 121, 157
   German study 25, 224, 225, 232
   Latin American study 201, 205
   moral suasion experiment 251, 253
   religiosity study 125
   risk aversion 123
Agha, A. 57–8
Aitken, S. 68, 117, 119, 120
Ajzen, I. 191
Akerlof, G.A. 73
Alexandrin, G. 125
Allingham, M.G. 4, 64, 88
Alm, J.
   audit selection rules 87, 88
   compliance, US v Spain 93
   expected utility model 4, 89, 90–91, 105
   experiments, importance of 85
   experiments, structure of 12, 19, 85, 101, 102, 269, 274
   higher audit rate 285
   'honest'/intentional errors 7
   language in experiments 101, 274
   misallocations in resource use 189
   overestimate probability of unlikely events/audits 68, 89
   public goods/use of tax revenues 72, 75, 97–100
   rewards 94
   social norm, compliance 17, 66, 67, 271–2
   students as participants 12
   tax amnesties 103, 265, 268–9, 274, 276, 284–5, 288
   tax morale in US and Switzerland 270
   uncertainty, fiscal 97, 98
   voting and pre-election discussion 20, 99, 153, 270–72, 284, 288

altruistic approach 67
amnesties, tax 3, 264–5, 284–5, 288
   anticipation of further 29, 268, 269, 284–5, 288
   complex tax systems 265, 268, 292
   discussed in Germany 264
   experiment on 103, 269, 274, 276, 284–5, 288
   honesty and 28, 264, 265–8
   India 242, 259, 266, 267
   Italy 264, 267, 268
   list of 266–7
   Poland 264
   post-amnesty enforcement 29, 268, 269, 283, 284, 288
   Rosetta Stone 3
   selection bias in data 208
   Switzerland 259, 292
   unfair 264, 265
   United States 264, 268
amnesty with voting, experiment on tax 28–9, 265, 284–5, 288
   anticipation of further amnesties 29, 268, 269, 284–5, 288
   audit selection rule 274
   compliance rates 277–81
   experimental sessions 275–6
   individuals' pay-off 276–7
   multivariate analysis 281–5
   post-amnesty enforcement 29, 268, 269, 283, 284, 288
   signal of honesty in group 285
   structure of 272–5
   tax-specific language 14, 274
   voting on amnesty 28, 265, 269–72, 284, 288
   voting without discussion 28, 284, 288
Anderhub, V. 101
Anderson, G.M. 114, 115
Andreoni, J. 5, 7, 64, 85, 120, 273
   public good games 98, 276, 281
   tax rate and income level 157, 252

297

Argentina 195, 205, 266
Aronson, E. 86
Arroyo, A. 272
audit courts 56
audits 19, 89, 104, 156
　fines and 69, 86–7
　overestimation of probability of 55, 68–9, 89
　probability of 22, 86–7, 156, 158, 159, 285
　selection bias in data 208
　selection rules 87–8
　subsequent to 50
　uncertainty experiment 96–7
Australia 50–52, 266
Austria, tax amnesties in 266
authoritarian systems 9, 194, 230
avoidance distinguished from evasion, tax 8–9, 199, 200–201, 210
Axelrod, R. 74

Bahl, R. 154, 190
Baldry, J.C. 12, 89, 101, 119, 120
banks 239–40
basic tax evasion model *see* expected utility model
Baumol, W.J. 27, 71, 240, 241, 242
Beck, P.J. 285
Becker, G.S. 64, 70, 71, 114, 240
Becker, W. 98, 101
Bejakovi, P. 190
Belgium, tax amnesties in 266
Beron, K.J. 156, 285
Binmore, K.G. 71–2
Bird, R. 23–4
'blue-collar' workers 123
Blumenthal, M. 27, 239, 242, 243, 244, 245, 258, 259
Bohnet, I. 91, 104, 271, 284
Bordignon, M. 72
Bosco, L. 12, 92, 102, 239
Botswana 92
Bowles, S. 78, 240–41
Breton, A. 239–40
British Social Attitudes Survey 5, 53, 196
Brown-Kruse, J. 120
Buchanan, J.M. 71
Buddhists 124, 125
Burgess, R. 190, 201

Burtless, G. 15, 16, 258
business start-ups 191, 192–3
business tax 57–8

Cabezas, R.M. 190
Caribbean area 24, 210
Casanegra de Jantscher, M. 189
Cassone, A. 268
Catholics 124, 138
causality 11, 15, 186, 258
Central America 24, 200, 210
　World Values Survey 201, 205
Central/Eastern European countries (CEE) 220–21
　see also transition countries
Chile 194, 195, 205
Chung, P. 67
Cialdini, R.B. 74, 231, 270
Clotfelter, C.T. 7, 120, 121, 122, 252
Coleman, J.S. 71
'Cologne school of tax psychology' 4
Colombia, tax amnesty in 266
communication, group 91–2
　pre-election 96, 265, 269–72, 284, 288
communist countries, post- 124
　see also transition countries
communist systems 216–17, 230
complexity of tax system 56–7
　tax amnesties 265, 268, 292
'compliers' 65
Confucius 116
contract, psychological/relational 74, 159, 194, 208, 244
　maintenance of 35, 41, 153, 194, 210, 244
　renegotiate 22, 153
　voting 270
corruption 3, 79
　Latin America 24, 193, 194–5, 208
　measurement of 20–21, 113
　religiosity study 113, 125, 138
Costa Rica *see* amnesty with voting, experiment on tax
Cowell, F.A. 64, 72, 73, 85, 101, 103
Crane, S.E. 285
crime and religiosity 20, 116, 205
Cross, J. 12
cross-cultural
　comparisons, caution with 9

culture, definition of 25, 216
  element in field experiment in Switzerland 251–2, 253
  experiment in Costa Rica and Switzerland *see* amnesty with voting, experiment on tax
  experiment on social norms 92–3
  experiments, design of 15
  future research 56, 94
  study of Germany *see* Germany, study of former East and West
  study of Swiss institutions 172
crowding-out effects 18, 70, 79
  aware of tax evasion 199
  corruption 125, 138
  deterrence factors 156, 158, 159
  European Union 35
  future research 103
  Latin America 193, 199
  rewards 94
  tax amnesties 268, 285
  taxes poorly spent 193
Cuba 192
culture *see* cross-cultural
Cummings, R.G. 52, 53, 92
customer service approach 50–52

Das-Gupta, A. 190
data sources 6, 7–9
Dawes, R.M. 98, 276, 281
De Alessi, L. 27, 241
De Juan, A. 67
de Soto, H. 189, 193
decentralization *see* local autonomy
definition of tax morale 4
democracy
  direct *see* direct democracy
  direct v representative 75–6, 77
  Latin American study 24, 41, 205, 210, 211
  transition countries 41
detection, probability of *see* audits
deterrence factors 4, 50, 156, 285
  audits *see* audits
  fines *see* fines
  institutions, study of 157–9, 176
  Latin American study 196, 200, 201
deterrence model *see* expected utility model

developing countries *see individual countries*; Latin America; Latin American study
dictator games 90, 120
direct democracy 21–3, 175–6
  causality issue 186
  local autonomy and 23, 172–5
  referenda 21, 22, 153, 163, 172, 186, 269–72, 292
  rights in Swiss cantons 152, 159, 177–8
  rule setters via initiative 21, 22, 153, 163, 186
  tax authorities 77, 258, 270
  tax morale and 41, 76, 152–3, 159, 162, 175–6, 269–70
  trust in government 162
  see also amnesty with voting, experiment on tax
Dominican Republic 192, 196, 205
Dubin, J.A. 7, 285
duty and fear 69, 79

Eckel, C.C. 120
econometric estimation models 9–10, 13, 16–17
  amnesty experiment 276–7, 281–4
  German study 221, 232–4
  institutions, study of Swiss 155–6, 179–81
  Latin American study 199–200
  moral suasion experiment 27–8, 246, 248–53
  religiosity study 118–23
economic class, impact of 122
  Latin American study 205
  religiosity study 122, 125, 141
economics-of-crime approach 4
  insufficient 90–91, 156, 157–9, 285, 288
Ecuador 194, 195
education, impact of 31, 121–2, 157
  German study 224, 228, 234
  institutions, study of 158
  Latin America study 205
Egypt, Ancient 3, 195
El Salvador 194, 195
Elffers, H. 4, 5, 65
Elster, J. 17, 66, 71
emergency situations 27, 241

employees *see* occupational status, impact of
endogeneity, preference 240–41
equity theory 18, 95–6
  see also fairness
Erard, B. 5, 68, 69, 240, 245–6
Eriksen, K. 121
Europe
  shadow economy and tax morale 191
  tax morale and tax evasion 199
European Union 35, 41
European Values Surveys (EVS) 7
evasion distinguished from avoidance, tax 8–9, 199, 200–201, 210
expected utility model 4, 22, 88–9, 157–9
  predicts too much tax evasion 4, 19, 88, 104, 105, 175, 240
  social custom utility and 73
expected utility-maximization approach 4, 156, 159, 175
experiments 10–15, 19, 78, 85, 269
  audit selection rule 14–15, 87–8
  categories 86, 103–4
  causality 11
  cross-cultural 15, 92–4
  dynamic 92
  on economic and deterrence variables 86–9, 104
  on equity 95–6
  future research 54–5, 100–104
  institutional variables 96–100, 104
  lab and field 92–3
  number of participants 87
  objective for participants 12, 87
  post-experiment questionnaire 13–14
  pre-experiment discussions 88
  on public goods 97–100
  realism of 11–13, 85–6
  on rewards 94
  on social factors 90–96, 104
  students as participants 12, 101
  on tax amnesties 103, 269, 274, 276, 284–5, 288
  tax reporting institutions controlled 85, 105
  tax-context language 14, 101, 274
  on uncertainty 96–7, 98
  z-tree software 14, 273
  see also amnesty with voting, experiment on tax
experiments, field 15–17, 258
  causality 15, 258
  future research 55
  increased probability of audit 88, 156
  lab and 92–3
  moral suasion in Minnesota 242, 258, 259
  see also moral suasion, field experiment in Switzerland on

fairness 17, 18, 71–3
  equity theory 18, 95–6
  Latin America 193–4, 208–10
  procedural 74, 75
  tax amnesties seen as unfair 264, 265
Falkinger, J. 72, 73, 94
fear and duty 69, 79
federalism *see* local autonomy
Fehr, E. 11, 12, 13, 14, 71
  reciprocity 74, 78
  social norms 66, 90
Feinstein, J.S. 121, 122, 252
Feld, L.P. 111
  deterrence factors 4, 176
  direct democracy 76, 77, 156, 258, 270
  local autonomy 175
  psychological/relational tax contract 194, 210, 244
  questionnaire data 179, 181
  referenda restrict governments 163
  respectful treatment of taxpayers 77, 154, 258, 270
  rewards 94
  voting 153, 271
Festinger, L. 123
field experiments *see* experiments, field
financial dis/satisfaction, impact of 123
  institutions, study of 162, 180
  Latin American study 24, 208, 211
  religiosity study 125, 141
fines
  audits and 69, 86–7
  size of 22, 86–7, 158, 159, 285
  Swiss cantons 156
Finland, tax amnesty in 266

Fischbacher, U. 14, 273
Fisher, R.C. 268, 269
formal economy, start-up costs/
    obstacles 191, 192–3
Forsythe, R. 90
Forte, F. 56
France 57, 266
Freud, S. 114
Frey, B.S.
    authoritarian political system 230
    behaviour of other taxpayers 199
    'citizens' basic goodwill' 196
    deterrence factors 50, 156, 159, 285
    direct democracy 153, 155, 162, 172, 175
    econometric estimation models 10, 200
    European Union 35, 41
    fairness 71
    group communication 92
    happiness 6
    Homo Oeconomicus Maturus (HOM) 18, 77
    intrinsic motivation and crowding-out effects 18, 26, 70, 159, 241–2
    ipsative theory 71
    Italy, civic virtue in 56
    limits of traditional economic model 4, 17, 18, 50, 70–71, 77, 241
    local autonomy 22, 154, 172, 175
    'over'/'under' government 193
    progression of tax schedule 157
    questionnaire data 179, 181
    reciprocity 74
    Swiss political elite and taxpayers 163, 172
    two kinds of tax systems 76
Frey, L.R. 4
Friedland, N. 12, 86–7, 95, 119, 122, 285
Friedman, E. 125
Frijters, P. 228
Furnham, A. 124
future research
    experiments 54–5, 100–104
    methodology 52–3
    surveys 53–4
    topics 55–8

Gambetta, D. 66
Geeroms, H. 121

gender, impact of 30–31, 120, 157
    amnesty experiment 285
    German study 224
    institutions, study of 158
    Latin American study 205
    religiosity study 125
    risk aversion 123
German institute Forschungsstelle für empirische Sozialökonomik 25, 217
German Socio-Economic Panel (GSOEP) 228
Germany, tax amnesty discussed 264
Germany, study of former East and West 24–6, 215, 231–2
    age 25, 224, 225, 232
    bias, possible 26, 231, 232
    class variable 224, 233
    cultural differences 215–17, 228, 232
    education 224, 228, 234
    FSU and CEE countries 220–21
    gender 224
    income variable 224, 228, 233
    life satisfaction 228
    marital status 224
    measurement of tax morale 218, 232
    model 221
    occupational status 224
    tax morale development over time 25–6, 225, 228–32
    tax morale differences 25–6, 218–19, 224–5, 232
    variables 221, 232–4
Gërxhani, K. 12
Giese, S. 101
Gordon, J.P.F. 73
Gouldner, A.W. 74
government by tax evasion, disagree with 193
government expenditure 72, 74, 75, 76, 97–100, 193, 208–10
government and legal system, trust in 18, 23, 35, 41, 152, 153–4, 159–62
    customer service approach 50–52
    Latin America 193–6, 200, 201, 210
    measurement of trust 154
    minor violations 79
    respectful treatment of taxpayers 3, 5, 50–52, 74–7, 78, 154, 258, 270

governments, taxing power and subnational 154–5
Graetz, M.J. 4, 65, 269
Graham, C. 8
Grasmick, H.G. 119, 120, 122
  guilt and shame 68, 116, 117
  informal sanctions 20, 116
  religiosity 20, 113, 118, 162
Groenland, E.A.G. 119, 122
group communication 91–2
  pre-election 96, 265, 269–72, 284, 288
Guatemala 194
guilt and shame 68–9, 116–17
Güth, W. 90, 98

happiness 24, 208, 211
Hardin, R. 66, 115, 153
Harris, L. and Associates, Inc. 68
Hartog, J. 123
Hasseldine, J. 27, 242, 264
Hays, S. 121
Heiner, R.A. 116
Henrich, J. 18, 25, 94, 172, 216
Hessing, D.J. 103
heuristic, duty 69, 79
Higgs, R. 115, 117–18
Hindriks, J. 195
Hindus 124
Hirschi, T. 20, 116, 205
Hirschman, A.O. 22, 70, 155, 230
Hirshleifer, J. 70
Homans, G.C. 72, 95
Homo economicus 18
Homo Oeconomicus Maturus (HOM) 18, 77
Homo Reciprocan 78
house owners 253
Hull, B.B. 20, 116, 205
Hume, D. 78
Hunt, J. 228, 231

Iannaccone, L.R. 114, 117, 139
'identifiers' 65
immoral state activities *see* moral duty to evade taxes
income level, impact of 19, 35, 89, 104, 122
  increased probability of audit 88, 156, 285
institutions, study of 158
  Latin American study, proxies in 201, 211
  moral suasion experiment 252, 253
  risk aversion 123
India 195
  Hindus 124
  tax amnesties 242, 259, 266, 267
informal economy *see* shadow economy
Inglehart, R. 8, 118
institutions 18
  direct democracy *see* direct democracy
  government *see* government and legal system, trust in
  just 78
  local autonomy *see* local autonomy
institutions, study of Swiss 21–3, 175–6
  cultural differences 172
  derivation of variables 179–81
  deterrence factors 157–9, 176
  direct democracy 21–3, 152–3, 159, 162–3, 172–5, 186
  financial dis/satisfaction 162, 180
  initiatives 163
  local autonomy 22, 23, 152, 154–5, 172–5
  measurement of tax morale 179, 181
  model 155–7
  referenda 163, 172
  religiosity 162, 179, 181
  trust in government/legal system 153–4, 159–62, 179, 181
'internalizers' 65
International Social Survey Programme (ISSP) 6, 53
  institutions, study of 21, 152
  RELIGION II 9, 21, 152
ipsative theory 70–71
Ireland, tax amnesties in 267
Isaac, R.M. 98, 276, 281
Italy
  future research 56
  tax amnesties 264, 267, 268
  VAT 57

Jackson, B.R. 6, 35, 120, 122
Jain, A.K. 138, 195
Japan 50

Jenkins, G.P. 190
Jews 124
Joulfaian, D. 285

Kahneman, D. 68, 71, 123
'Kantian' morality approach 67–8
Kantona, G. 65
Kaplan, S.E. 119
Karsten, S.G. 230
Kaspar, W. 216, 231
Kelman, H. 65
Kennedy, P. 119
Kidder, R. 99, 270
Kim, C.K. 99
Kirchler, E. 100
Knack, S. 8, 56, 66, 118
Knight, J. 66
knowledge, economic theory of 115
Kucher, M. 154

Ladner, A. 156
Laffont, J.J. 67
Latin America 23–4, 189
 civic conscience and honesty 195–6, 208, 210
 corruption and discretionary power 193, 195
 corruption in tax administration 194–5
 fairness of tax system 193–4, 208–10
 tax morale and shadow economy 191–3, 208
 tax system and administration in 190
Latin American study 24, 196–8, 208–10
 age 201, 205
 corruption 24, 195, 208
 democratic government 24, 41, 205, 210, 211
 economic class 205
 education 205
 fairness 193–4, 208–10
 financial dis/satisfaction 24, 208, 211
 gender 205
 happiness 24, 208, 211
 income level proxies 201, 211
 marital status 201, 205
 measurement of tax morale 191, 196–8
 Mexico as special case 23, 198

 multivariate analysis with Latinobarómetro 198–201
 multivariate analysis with WVS 201, 205–8
 national pride 24, 208, 211
 occupational status 201
 perceived probability of being caught 200, 201, 211
 religiosity 205, 211
 satisfaction with life 24, 208, 211
 satisfaction with officials 205, 210
 shadow economy 208
 tax avoidance 199, 200–201, 210
 taxes ill-spent 193
 trust in authorities 194, 200, 201, 210, 211
 trust in president 200, 201, 210, 211
 trust that others obey law 200, 201, 210, 211
 variables, main 199–200
Latinobarómetro 6, 8, 23, 189, 191–2, 196, 198–9, 208
law abidance 5, 99, 271
Leijonhufvud, A. 5
Leitzel, J. 54
Lempert, R.O. 270
Leonard, H.B. 265, 268
Levi, M. 153, 237
Lewis, A. 4, 67, 123, 191, 199
 education level 31, 121, 157
Lewis, H.B. 68, 117
Lind, E.A. 74, 193
Lipford, J. 20, 116, 205
local autonomy 22, 23, 41, 152, 154–5, 172, 175
 direct democracy and 23, 172–5
 moral suasion and 243
Long, S. 5

McCloskey, D.N. 10
McEwen, C.A. 270
McGee, R.W. 124–5, 230
McGraw, K. 240
Maciejovsky, B. 100
Mackscheidt, K. 97
McLure, C. Jr. 190
Margolis, H. 116
marital status, impact of 31, 120–21, 157
 German study 224

institutions, study of 158
  Latin American study 201, 205
  moral suasion experiment 252, 253
  religiosity study 125
marketing campaigns 241, 242, 259
Martinez-Vazquez, J. 23, 190
Mason, R. 120, 122
measurement of tax morale 6–7, 8, 9
  institutions, study of 179, 181
  Latin American study 191, 196–8
  religiosity study 119, 140
Mendis, P. 125
methodology 5–6
  experiments 10–15
  field experiments 15–17
  surveys 6–10
Mexico 23, 24, 193, 195, 198, 200, 205, 210, 211
  democracy 205
Minor, W. 120
Mittone, L. 92
moral appeals *see* moral suasion
moral duty to evade taxes 9, 125, 230
moral rules and sentiments 5, 17, 65–6, 104, 240
  duty and fear 69, 79
  guilt and shame 68–9, 116–17
  intrinsic and extrinsic motivation 70, 241–2
  ipsative theory 70–71
  religion as constraint on behaviour 114–17
  social norms *see* social norms
  tax amnesties 28, 264–5
moral suasion 102, 239–42, 258
  competitive pressure 241
  emergency situations 27, 241
  field experiment in Minnesota 242, 258, 259
  local v central level 243
moral suasion, field experiment in Switzerland on 27–8, 239, 258
  age 251, 253
  compliance variables 243, 245
  difference-in-difference analysis 246–51
  economic status 252–3
  foreigners 251–2, 253
  future research 258–9
  house owners 253

income levels 252, 253
letter to taxpayers 243–5, 260–61
marital status 252, 253
multivariate analysis 251–7
non-filers 245–6, 253, 261
selection of town 242–3
tax rate 252, 253
timely filling out (*TF*) (2001) 246, 247
timely paying (*TP*) (2001) 246, 247
Mueller, D.S. 114–15
Mummert, A. 25, 217
Murphy, K. 50
Muslims 124–5
Myles, G.D. 73

national pride 24, 41, 208, 211
Naylor, R.A. 73
Netherlands 57, 267
New Zealand, tax amnesty in 267
non-filing of returns 246, 253, 261
norms *see* social norms
North, D.C. 114
Nowell, C. 120
Nuttin, J. 94

occupational status, impact of 31–5, 123
  German study 224
  institutions, study of 158
  Latin American study 201
  religiosity study 125
  self-employed 4, 31, 123, 157, 193, 201, 224, 242, 246
  taxation at source 157
Ochs, J. 90
Ockenfels, A. 25, 94, 216
OECD countries, tax revenues in 190
Opp, K.-D. 71
opportunity to evade 5, 123, 157, 242
Orthodox religion 124, 138
Orviska, M. 5, 53, 196

Paldam, M. 91, 230
Pardo, S.R. 190
penalties *see* fines
Peru 195
  reforms in 194, 210
Poland 264
Polinsky, M.A. 67, 217

political systems
  authoritarian 9, 194, 230
  communist 216–17, 230
  democratic *see* democracy
  socialistic 216–17
Pommerehne, W.W. 4, 64, 157, 285
  direct democracy 75–6, 269
  government and taxpayer 75–7
Portugal, tax amnesty in 267
positive inducements 19, 94
Posner, E.A. 217
Posner, R.A. 78–9
post-communist countries 124
  see also transition countries
preference endogeneity 240–41
pride, national 24, 41, 208, 211
Prinz, A. 153
procedural fairness 74, 75
  see also fairness
property rights 192
prospect theory 105, 123
Protestants 124, 138
psychological/relational contract *see* contract
psychology, Cologne school of tax 4
public good contributions 276, 281
public good games 98, 120
public goods 72, 74, 75, 76, 97–100
  Latin America 193, 208–10
Puerto Rico 192, 196
punishment, perverse effect 71
  see also fines
Putnam, R. 56, 66
Pyle, D.J. 4, 7, 189

Rabin, M. 71
Radano, A.H.J. 190
rate of tax 19, 22, 86–7, 89, 104, 156–7, 252
  dual incomes 121, 157, 252
  duty and fear 69
  institutions, study of 158
  moral suasion experiment 252, 253
  tax schedule 157
Rawls, J. 71, 78
reciprocity 18, 74, 75, 78
  German study 231
referenda *see* direct democracy
Regan, D.T. 74

relational/psychological, contract *see* contract
religiosity 20, 35
  as constraint on behaviour 114–17, 205
  institutions, study of 162, 179, 181
  Latin American study 205, 211
religiosity study 20–21, 113, 139
  age 119, 125
  'behavioural' and 'belief' variables 138
  corruption levels 113, 125, 138
  economic classes 122, 125, 141
  education 121, 140
  financial dis/satisfaction 123, 125, 141
  gender 125
  marital status 120, 125
  measurement of religiosity 113, 117–18, 140
  measurement of tax morale 119, 140
  occupational status 123, 125
  results 124–5
  risk aversion 123, 125, 141
  sensitivity analysis 125, 138–9
  trustworthiness 113, 138–9, 141
'representativeness', theory of 68–9
rewards 19, 94
risk aversion 4, 123, 157
  equity and 73
  religiosity study 123, 125, 141
Robben, H.S.J. 54
Rose-Ackermann, S. 138, 195
Rosetta Stone 3
Roth, A.E. 10, 86, 90, 103
  cross-cultural experiments 15, 93, 274
Roth, J.A. 4, 240, 274
Rubinstein, A. 87, 102
Russia, tax amnesties in 267
  see also Soviet Union, Former

Sally, D. 284
satisfaction with life 24, 208, 211
  German study 228
Schaltegger, C.A. 66
Schelker, M. 56
Schlicht, E. 71
Schmölders, G. 4, 65
Schneider, F. 191

Scholz, J.T. 69
Schröder, Gerhard 264
Schwartz, R. 4, 102, 240
self-declaration of income 76, 210
  Switzerland 242
self-defence, tax evasion as 68
self-employed 4, 31, 157
  former East Germany 31, 224
  Latin America 193, 201
  moral suasion 242
  non-filing of returns 246
  Sweden 123
Sen, A.K. 70, 71, 114
shadow economy 5, 9
  former East and West Germany 217
  Latin America 24, 190, 191–3, 208
  Mexico 23
  tax morale and 191–3, 208
shame and guilt 68–9, 116–17
Silvani, C.A. 190
Slemrod, J. 8, 26, 111, 118
  increased probability of audit 88, 156, 285
  social capital 66, 154
Smith, A. 114
Smith, I. 115, 118
Smith, K.W. 74, 75, 208
social capital 66, 154, 210
social cohesion 67
social norms 17, 66–8, 90–94
  former East Germany 25, 216–17, 225, 232
  incentives for obeying 78–9
  local areas 243
socialistic systems 216–17
Song, Y. 72, 95, 120, 122
South Africa 92, 267
South America 24, 200, 210
Soviet Union (FSU), Former 220–21
  see also Russia
Spain 93, 267
Spicer, M.W. 72, 75, 95, 120, 122, 157
  artificiality of lab setting 85
  level of information and heuristics 96–7
  social norms 67, 196
'spirit of trust' 210
standard model of tax evasion see expected utility model
Stark, R. 114

Starmer, C. 5–6, 12, 13
Streim, H. 56
Strümpel, B. 4–5
Stutzer, A. 22, 155, 159
Sugden, R. 67
surveys 6–10
  combined with experiments 13–14
  future research 53–4
Sweden, self-employed 123
Switzerland
  causality issue 186
  deterrence factors, impact of 157–9, 176
  direct democracy, effects of 41, 76–7, 159, 172–6, 258, 269–70
  direct democratic rights in 152, 159, 177–8
  dual incomes 157, 252
  local autonomy 41, 172–5
  political elite and taxpayers 163, 172
  risk aversion 4
  tax amnesty 259, 292
  tax authority treatment of taxpayers 77, 154, 258, 270
  see also amnesty with voting, experiment on tax; institutions, study of Swiss

Taiwan 195
Tanzi, V. 190, 191, 194
tax rate see rate of tax
Taxpayer Compliance Measurement Program (TCMP) 7, 30
Taxpayer Opinion Survey 57, 191, 196
taxpayers
  respectful treatment of 3, 5, 50–52, 74–7, 78, 154, 258, 270
  three types 103
taxpayers, interaction among 50, 89, 99, 199, 200–201, 210
  signal of honesty in group 285
  tax evaders as friends 67, 199
Taylor, M. 243
Thaler, R.H. 71
Tittle, C. 30, 31, 119, 120–21, 157
  religiosity 20, 113, 117, 162
Torgler, B. 4, 18, 239, 240, 269
  audit courts 56
  complexity of tax system 57
  cultural studies 56

deterrence factors 156, 159, 285
direct democracy and tax morale 269–70
equity theory 193
moral rules and sentiments 65
psychological contract 153
religiosity 162
respect for authority and tax morale 196
shadow economy and tax morale 191
tax amnesty 259
tax evasion and tax morale 191
tax strategies in Australia and Japan 50
willingness to go to war 58
World Values Survey 8, 118
transition countries
East Germany *see* Germany, study of former East and West
shadow economy and tax morale 191
tax morale in 41, 220–21
Tremonti, Giulio 264
trustworthiness 21, 113
future research 54
religiosity study 113, 138–9, 141
see also government and legal system, trust in
Tversky, A. 123
Tyler, T.R. 74, 95, 193, 270
Tyran, J.-R. 99, 271

ultimatum bargaining games 90
uncertainty, experiments involving 96–7
United States
audit and penalty levels 78
direct democracy 41, 270
dual incomes 121
increased probability of audit 88, 156, 285
Internal Revenue Service (IRS) 75
local autonomy 41
moral suasion field experiment 242, 258, 259
non-filing of returns 246
risk aversion 4
Spain and 93
tax amnesties 264, 268

tax morale and tax evasion 191
Taxpayer Compliance Measurement Program (TCMP) 7
unofficial economy *see* shadow economy

van Staveren, I. 114
VAT 57–8
Verhorn, C.L. 52
violent crime and religiosity 20, 116, 205
Vogel, J. 65, 67, 119, 120, 121, 157
self-employed 123
voluntarism 242
voting 19–20, 153
measurement of trust 154
pre-election discussion 91–2, 96, 265, 269–72, 284, 288
rejection of stricter sanctions 91
Swiss referenda and initiatives 21, 22, 153, 163, 172, 186, 292
on tax spending 99–100

Walster, E. 72
war, willingness to go to 58
Wartick, M.L. 101
Webley, P. 12, 72, 75, 95–6
experimental design 54, 100, 101, 102
Weck, H. 5, 191
Westat, Inc. 119, 122, 123
'white-collar' taxpayers 123
Wilde, L. 11
Wintrobe, R. 230
Witte, A.D. 7, 121, 122, 285
World Values Survey (WVS) 6, 7–8, 53, 54
German study 24, 216, 221
institutions, study of 21, 152, 186
Latin American study 23, 189, 196, 198, 201, 205–8
religiosity study 113, 118
transition countries 220

Yankelovich, Skelly and White, Inc. 67, 75, 120, 122
Yitzhaki, S. 88, 252

z-Tree software 14, 273